Software Sizing, Estimation, and Risk Management

Software Sizing, Estimation, and Risk Management

When Performance is Measured
Performance Improves

Daniel D. Galorath • Michael W. Evans

Forewords by Dr. Barry Boehm & Donald Reifer

Auerbach Publications
Taylor & Francis Group
Boca Raton   New York

Published in 2006 by
Auerbach Publications
Taylor & Francis Group
6000 Broken Sound Parkway NW, Suite 300
Boca Raton, FL 33487-2742

International Standard Book Number-10: 0-8493-3593-0 (Hardcover)
International Standard Book Number-13: 978-0-8493-3593-8 (Hardcover)
Library of Congress Card Number 2005058144

Library of Congress Cataloging-in-Publication Data

Galorath, Daniel D.
    Software sizing, estimation, and risk management : when performance is measured performance improves / Daniel D. Galorath, Michael W. Evans.
        p. cm.
    Includes bibliographical references and index.
    ISBN 0-8493-3593-0 (alk. paper)
    1. Computer software--Development. 2. Risk management. I. Evans, Michael W. II. Title.

QA76.76.D47G347 2006
005.1--dc22

2005058144

Dedication

Dan Galorath dedicates this book to my wife

Judy Galorath

who is an inspiration in all areas of my life and without whom this book may have never gotten finished.

Mike Evans dedicates this book to the memory of

Elliot Needleman

"A Friend, a Mentor and a Heck of a Good Guy"

Contents

Foreword: Under the Tip of the Estimation Iceberg

Many people who acquire a software estimation model assume that its use involves furnishing it with a few project parameters, taking the resulting outputs, and plugging them into proposals, project plans, work breakdown structures, budgets, and schedules.

However, people experienced in software estimation have learned that running the model is just the small tip of a very large iceberg of activities essential to successful estimates, projects, and enterprises. Those activities include:

- **Identifying what is being estimated and why.** One early cost model's answer to questions asking whether the model estimates included costs of management or quality assurance was, "What would you like the estimates to include?" This is not a strong confidence builder.
- **Defining the project's requirements and design as well as possible.** If you don't know whether a product function will be fulfilled by new, modified, or commercial software, your estimates can be way off.
- **Using several perspectives to estimate software size, cost, and schedule.** Otherwise, there is no way to tell whether your estimates are reasonably accurate or not.
- **Identifying ranges of uncertainty in the project parameters.** This enables techniques such as Monte Carlo analysis to determine the likelihood of finishing within a given budget or schedule. Just using a "most likely" point estimate will overrun roughly half of the time.

- **Performing a business case relating estimated costs to estimated benefits and return on investment.** Otherwise, scarce resources are likely to be spent on low-payoff capabilities.
- **Negotiation of trade-offs among cost, schedule, quality, performance, and functionality.** Optimizing on one of these parameters at the expense of the others has been the source of many failed projects.
- **Matching desired capabilities to available budgets, schedules, and skilled personnel.** Neglecting this activity has been the source of many project overruns.
- **Tracking not only cost and progress with respect to original cost and schedule estimates, but also changes in cost driver parameters.** Tracking to obsolete estimates has been the source of many painful surprises.

The authors of this book, Daniel Galorath and Michael Evans, are both highly experienced estimators and project managers. Much of this book is devoted to their helping you understand and apply these "under the tip of the iceberg" activities. Their ten-step approach to software estimation provides a logical progression of estimation activities that help you avoid these sources of project overruns and failures.

The book naturally focuses on the use of Galorath Incorporated's SEER-SEM software cost model to address software estimation activities. But it does so in the context of advice to use multiple perspectives in size, cost, and schedule estimation. And it provides a lot of valuable information about the SEER-SEM cost and size drivers that are often not available for proprietary cost models. It also shows how to use your estimation and project tracking data to improve your estimation accuracy and to identify the best investments for improving your software productivity and cycle time. Investing in acquiring this book and following its advice is highly likely to provide you with a robust return on your investment.

Barry Boehm
Another veteran of the consequences
of neglecting the bottom of the iceberg

Foreword

In order to survive the pressures of today's fast-paced software development projects, all software professionals need to develop estimates. The project manager needs estimates to develop schedules and budgets. The engineers working on the project need estimates to set realistic expectations and pace their work. Customers need estimates to determine whether the project's value is worth the forecasted cost. However, like most forecasts involving time and money, numbers generated are both used and abused for a variety of reasons. Numbers are frightful when you think about it because those in control put such relevance on them.

In my experience, nobody likes to prepare an estimate. Why? Simply, because most of the time it is wrong. Worse yet, your bosses will remind you that you were wrong just when you do not want to hear it. Why are you wrong? There are many reasons for poor estimates. Probably the biggest cause is the lack of knowledge. To estimate well, you need to understand how to estimate and have details about what you are estimating. That is why this book should be helpful. It starts by providing you with a ten-step estimation process. As it takes you through the process, it then highlights the information you have to gather in order to estimate the job more accurately.

This book is also about estimating software effort and duration using the SEER-SEM model. While I do not endorse any one model, I do endorse their use for estimating. Cost models like SEER-SEM are valuable tools because they capture a communal knowledge base of experience that their users can employ to generate more accurate estimates of the resources that they will need to deliver software products and services. Such tools also provide their users with insight into the many trade-offs that occur as they plan and execute their projects.

The book addresses estimating in the context of both current and future topics in software engineering. It focuses on using estimates for planning and control. It talks to the strengths and weaknesses that exist in source lines of code and function points as measures of software size. It provides guidance on how to estimate resources for projects that employ both conventional and object-oriented techniques, systematic reuse concepts, and commercial off-the-shelf (COTS) packages. It touches on use cases as a future measure of size and discusses Web Objects. Most important, the book focuses on how to use the estimate to control risk, and manage and monitor performance. I have often said when people have told me that they have an estimate, "So what, how are you going to use it once your schedules and budgets have been established?"

I have known both authors for more years than I would like to report. Both have grown up in the trenches. I have worked with them and seen them grow. Both have held many positions and been through the wars. I have seen them under pressure and relaxed. Both are practitioners whose advice is useful and actionable. Be sensitive to the pointers that they sprinkle throughout the pages. These are what I got from this book. Look for and use the "golden gems" within this book. You will be glad that you did.

Donald J. Reifer
Author, practitioner, and friend

Preface

This book is the blend of a software project cost/schedule expert (Dan Galorath) with a software risk expert's (Mike Evans) work. This book comes from years of experience in software project management, and building and applying tools to understand and manage software cost, schedule, and risk. Galorath's disciplines of project planning and control fit like a glove with the risk management and project assessment approaches of Evans.

How This Book Came about from a Galorath Viewpoint

From a Galorath viewpoint, this book is a product of a commitment to better software project planning and control. Many years ago a project was never developed because of my realistic, but politically incorrect estimate. I wondered if I had done the right thing, which was try to provide an achievable project plan and a realistic estimate, even though that estimate was longer than the company desired. This experience made me wonder if I had failed as a manager. However, some years later I tried to reproduce the estimate using SEER-SEM and discovered that I had significantly underestimated the project. SEER-SEM enabled me to understand that I had not failed and that my refusal to give in to the division head's pressure had been the best thing for that company.

This experience was the beginning of my mission to understand how long software development should take and how many people are needed. A few years later Don Reifer and I were tasked with developing a concept for software estimation within NASA JPL. The results of the study prompted the development of the JPL Softcost software estimation model.*

---

* Tausworth, R. *Softcost*. Pasadena: Jet Propulsion Laboratory, 1981.

In 1981, when Dr. Barry Boehm's classic book, *Software Engineering Economics*, was published, I was operating a consulting business that remedied failing projects. I still used the early Softcost model which was automated, and performed risk and trade-off analysis. In 1984 I began consulting for Computer Economics, Inc., where I met Dr. Randall Jensen and was introduced to the "Jensen model." This model had been implemented as the JS-2. I recognized its strengths, which were its ability to conduct uncertainty estimation and minimum time estimation, but from a product viewpoint it had challenges. After redesign, it was released as the CEI System-3, which was relatively successful in helping people answer the difficult questions surrounding software development.

In 1988 Galorath Incorporated began developing SEER-SEM, deciding to implement it under Microsoft Windows version 2 (version 2.03 to be exact). The initial product, which was approximately 22,000 lines of code, relied heavily on the mathematics that served as the foundation of Jensen's public domain model. We shipped a run-time version of Windows on 13, 5.25 in. floppies. DOS was pervasive at this time, and some people complained about being required to use Microsoft Windows, but this decision was critical to SEER-SEM's early success. At one time there were Macintosh and Sun Solaris versions of SEER-SEM as well, but both were based on the Windows code baseline.

As the state of software development progressed, and as user demand grew more sophisticated, SEER-SEM continually required more robust and advanced mathematics and refined knowledge bases to handle the situations our users found themselves confronting. Users wanted to know the answers to questions such as: "How do I plan with my real-world staffing constraints?"; "How do I estimate my COTS software?"; "Do risk and uncertainty affect schedule independently of effort?"; "How can I calibrate for special situations or to my particular environment?"; and a host of other situations. SEER-SEM has also evolved from using lines of code as the only size input to function points, developing its own function-based sizing and the ability to accommodate objects, Web pages, use cases, classes, and a host of other sizing methods.

Most software estimation models have common ancestors, and SEER-SEM is no different. SEER-SEM, which was based on the Jensen model developed at Hughes Aircraft Company, diverged significantly in the early 1990s. Earlier work by Doty Associates introduced the idea of factoring in development environment influences via parameters. Barry Boehm's COCOMO work contributed to the original Jensen model technology parameters and has been a valuable cross-check to the SEER work. Research with Don Reifer that stimulated work on the NASA Softcost model also influenced SEER-SEM, as did Halstead's software science metrics and McCabe's complexity metrics. Today, through the process of Galorath Incorporated's "continuous product improvement," the SEER-SEM suite has grown to nearly 200,000 lines of code. Using this process, Galorath engineers analyze and begin to address software industry trends even before the trends become visible in the mainstream. The SEER models continue to evolve with data collection, application, research and development being conducted continuously.

At a high level, software sizing and estimation risks are the root of numerous project failures: unachievable commitments made by projects based on incorrect projections of cost, schedule, and resources. Thus Mike Evans entered the picture.

This book explores the various software sizing techniques, how these size projections are used to project cost and schedule, how projects can manage against these constraints and what risks result from constraints that are unrealistic or not achievable. This book describes how the risks can be managed and how tools, models, and other automated facilities can be used to enable better estimation and lower project risk.

In the chapters that follow, software sizing metrics and other software estimation factors are discussed. This book also covers the software estimation state of the practice, and leading trends and practices in software sizing technology.

While software size has the biggest impact on estimation, other factors such as technology, environment, complexity factors, staffing, scheduling, risk, and probability are also key. This book focuses on the techniques of the SEER family of cost, schedule risk, reliability models from Galorath Incorporated, as well as a brief look at the software project management life cycle and how software estimation makes a perfect management tool. The book is unique in that it doesn't stop at describing the sizing and estimation process but goes further in describing the core risks that result from the estimation process and commonly cause programs to not perform in accordance with the initial estimates. The specific methods for managing these risks, mitigating them, and getting the program completed successfully are provided.

Audience

This book is written for people who manage, engineer and assure software, stakeholders who need to understand software estimation techniques and metrics, and, finally, how to identify, manage, and mitigate estimate risks and their project impacts. The book is important to individual readers as follows:

- **Senior Management** —— Provides insight into the estimation process; the effects that management and corporate decisions, attitudes, and culture have on the integrity of estimates; and the risks that result from these estimates, which place systems and software intensive projects in jeopardy.
- **Customers and Users** —— Provides customers and users essential insight into how estimates are developed; and cultural factors and management attitudes, which could impact integrity of the estimate and the resulting risks.
- **Stakeholders** —— Provides insights into the processes and risks associated with software estimates and methods that can be used to monitor project progress and determine the risk of receiving a product that will meet the needs and expectations of the user developed within the cost and schedule constraints.
- **Engineering Management** —— Provides engineering management insight into the estimation process and how engineering decisions, shortcuts, trade studies and trade-offs, and other engineering factors affect the integrity of the estimate and the resultant risk to the project.
- **Project Management** —— Provides specific factors which can be used to understand how estimates are developed and the essential relationship that exists between the initial estimates and the need to perform at a productivity rate consistent with the estimate.
- **System Engineers** —— Provides specific factors to consider when establishing the essential system relationships and operational specifications that impact the estimate and increase the risk of meeting plans.
- **Software Engineers** —— Provides comprehensive information that software engineers can use to develop more accurate estimates, project resource requirements and schedule, and determine potential threats to software integrity, quality, and system effectiveness.
- **Quality Assurance** —— Provides specific information concerning the cost of adding various quality factors to the product, and the added costs of assuring the quality of the product or the effectiveness of the processes used.
- **Test Personnel** —— Identifies cost factors which should be considered when planning, implementing, or evaluating the results of a test program, and the estimation of defects insertion and removal.
- **Risk Management Personnel** —— Identifies specific risks related to estimates and describes risk management strategies that can be used to identify and control their impacts.
- **Students** —— Helps students understand how estimation and risk management are important to the complete understanding of the costs associated with management, engineering, assurance, and monitoring of software products and systems.

Structure of the Book

This book is divided into four major parts, which describe the estimation issues, the various estimation steps, the various metrics and special estimation cases, and the use of the SEER family of tools to assist in developing more accurate estimates faster.

> ***Part I: Estimation Issues.*** Chapter 1 discusses specific issues that impact the validity of estimates and the difficulty of the process.
>
> ***Part II: Estimation Process.*** Chapters 2, 3, and 4 discuss the various steps involved in developing and validating estimates.
>
> ***Part III: Metrics and Special Estimation Cases.*** Chapters 5 through 9 discuss the various size measures and special estimation cases.
>
> ***Part IV: Risk Management and Estimation Tools and Techniques.*** Chapters 10 through 12 discuss the risk management process and how the SEER family of tools can be used to expedite the estimation process and generate more accurate estimates.

What Can You Expect from the Book?

Before discussing what can be expected from the book it is important that it is clear what it is not. It is not an academic text describing estimation theories or concepts. It is a practical, hands-on discussion of critical factors and considerations that impact estimates, how to select and apply the appropriate measures to project and document size, and how to identify and manage risks. The authors, Mike Evans and Dan Galorath, are recognized experts in estimation, process engineering, and risk management. The book captures much of their unique experience providing practical solutions to many of the difficult problems that make estimates invalid or high risk. The information is presented in a way that will help readers identify and deal with project actions and attitudes that can result in an invalid estimate or high risk projects because of inadequate estimates. The content of the book will provide insight not readily available through other sources, which will help organizations recognize and avoid downstream impacts that can be caused by poor estimates.

Without a map (or GPS) there is no way to determine which way to go or how long it will take to get there. This book provides a map for successful software project planning and control — helping developers *plan* which way to go, how long it will take to get there, and minimize the side trips, detours, and flat tires. While writing this book, the motto for the text became: "Preparation precedes performance. When performance is measured performance improves."

Acknowledgments

Many people helped and supported us in the development of this book.

First, we'd like to thank Mike's wife, Charlotte, for again supporting him in the painful process of developing a manuscript, bringing him sandwiches, putting up with his moods, and acting as a sounding board when he got stuck. This support is much appreciated. Carl Blitz's thorough review of early drafts and honest comments made us rethink where we were headed. The results of this early soul searching made this a better book. Special thanks to Dan's wife, Judy Galorath, who should have been listed as coauthor thanks to her diligent work in reading, writing, and editing for many months, including an entire week on vacation in Jamaica. Many of the ideas in all sections are Judy's. Ian Brown's review of functional sizing was invaluable in ensuring the book covers both today and the future. Karen McRitchie's support throughout the process and diligent review were invaluable. Special thanks to Evin Stump who was brutal in his review of certain chapters, and Chris Hutchings and Corinne Segura for their diligent reviews of the risk component. Brian Glauser's reading of the manuscript also found several items that, when corrected, made this a better book. Thanks to Don Reifer for his suggesting this book be written and for his review comments. Thanks go as well to Dr. Ricardo Valerdi who poured over pages of drafts and provided many comments and suggestions. Ricardo did all this while working on his Ph.D. thesis, his wedding, and his move cross-country. Special thanks to Lee Fischman for his work and editing of functional and object size chapters, some even twice. Thanks to Cheryl Kung who prepared the figures and did many other production tasks.

Finally, we would like to thank all those whose work and publications provided a strong basis for the book. Barry Boehm, Fredrick Brooks, Tom DeMarco, Lee Fishman, David Garmus, Randy Jensen, Capers Jones, Tim

Lister, Karen McRitchie, Bob Park, Larry Putnam, Don Reifer, Richard Stutzke, Mike Ross, and a host of others established a rich body of knowledge, which is the basis for much of the book's content.

The Authors

Daniel D. Galorath has over 35 years of experience in the software industry where he has solved a variety of management, costing, systems, and software problems, and performed all aspects of software development and management. Mr. Galorath is founder and president of Galorath Incorporated, maker of the SEER suite of estimation tools.

Galorath Incorporated has developed tools, methods, and training for software cost, schedule, risk analysis, and management decision support. Mr. Galorath is one of the principal developers of the SEER-SEM™ Software Estimation Model and has been involved in the concepts and evolution of the SEER suite of models. He has participated in numerous software sizing and costing studies, both using his company's tools and performing such studies manually.

One of Mr. Galorath's strengths has been reorganizing troubled software projects, assessing their progress, applying methodology and plans for completion, and managing them to completion. In this role, he applied the earned value, cost and schedule management, and defect tracking techniques discussed in this book. He has created and implemented software management policies, and reorganized (as well as designed and managed) development projects.

Mr. Galorath's teaching experience includes development and presentation of courses in software cost, schedule, and risk analysis; software management; software engineering; systems architecture; and others. He has lectured internationally and is the author of many papers about software project management and software cost, schedule, and risk analysis. Among these published works are papers encompassing software cost modeling, testing theory, software life cycle error prediction and reduction, and software and systems requirements definition.

Mr. Galorath completed his undergraduate work and MBA from California State Universities. He is a member of the International Society of

Parametric Analysis (ISPA), Society of Cost Estimation and Analysis (SCEA), IEEE, the International Function Point Users Group (IFPUG), and the Association of Computing Machinery (ACM). He was honored with the Freiman Award, recognizing his long-term contributions to the field of parametric analysis.

Michael W. Evans is an executive vice president of American Systems Corporation, responsible for software and software risk management programs. He founded and served as president of Integrated Computer Engineering, Inc. (ICE), where he worked on software risk management approaches, software technical, management, and risk project assessments. His IT and software experience extends back to 1963 when he worked on the development and modification of compilers for the U.S. Army and then for Univac. During the ensuing years, he worked with IBM, Litton Industries, Ford Aerospace, and other companies in development, documentation, and application of standards, processes, and process improvement. As an adjunct to this effort, he developed and implemented a quantitative and objective assessment process.

Mr. Evans founded Expertware Inc. and, among other activities, worked with NASA, supporting the Software Management and Productivity Council for over four years. In this capacity he developed Versions 3 and 4 of the NASA software standard applied as an agencywide requirement. In the late 1980s, he founded CANDCA Associates, which later became ICE.

He was a founding member of the Software Program Managers Network (SPMN). He is a member of the Airlie Council, a group of industry leaders who advised the U.S. Department of Defense on practices and other areas that focused on project improvement and improvement in the bottom line metrics of cost schedule, quality, and user satisfaction. SPMN has over 10,000 members and at its peak was involved with more than 250 large-scale software programs across the DoD.

Mr. Evans is experienced in providing direct technical services and support in software engineering methods and processes, software standards, quality assurance, and configuration management, and testing. He is the author of over 250 papers along with *Principles of Productive Software Management, Productive Test Management, Software Quality Assurance and Management*, and *The Software Factory* published by John Wiley & Sons.

Chapter 1

The Problem

I have not seen any problem, however complicated, which, when you looked at it in the right way, did not become still more complicated.

Paul Anderson

Introduction

In 1976, early in my career, I became interested in effort and schedule estimation as a result of a confrontation with a vice president at a company for which I worked. Unknown to me, the organization had an unstated effort and schedule in mind. I was a software project manager while working on my MBA. There were no software estimation models available to me at the time. I was told to prepare an estimate for a four-terminal cluster system. Using the techniques learned through my MBA and my knowledge and experience as a software developer and project manager, I developed the estimate manually. It included a range of effort accompanied with estimates for risk and uncertainty.

When presenting the estimate to the VP, I was told, "This estimate is too high, go cut it by a third." When I said "I can't," the VP then said, "You have assumed people would work only eight hours per day. Go away and assume they will work twelve hours." I said something to the effect of, "I did assume eight hours per day. I assumed the other four hours would cover the things that go wrong that I haven't thought of."

The VP provided several more ideas on how to cut the schedule and effort estimates, all of which I stated were impractical. The VP was insistent that the estimate be cut by a third. Whether I was naive or a hero has never been determined. I stood by the estimate and the project was cancelled. Some years later, I reestimated the project by using a parametric cost model and determined that my original estimate was significantly low. There simply wasn't enough time and money projected and, if the project had gone forward, it would have failed miserably.[1]

"Far too many ... software projects have become unaffordable and unable to deliver needed quality, reliability, and capability within the required time frame. Their outputs are not predictable. Their processes are little more than chaotic and do not effectively utilize the kinds of disciplines necessary to achieve success."[2] "Unaffordable and unable to deliver," "not predictable," and "chaotic." These are words that no one wants to have associated with his or her software project. But the reality is that these situations are manifested in far too many projects.

Several years ago a commercial company hired consultants to assess a large software project that would significantly affect the organization's business processes. The discovery was soon made that the project had been plagued with problems from the beginning. Initially the organization had difficulty defining a set of requirements on which all stakeholders could agree. In order to hold to critical schedules, the project leaders were forced to delay functionality to later releases. Additionally, they built significant concurrency into the project to try to recover the schedule. Unfortunately, by developing different aspects of the project concurrently, the project team never seemed to have the resources to support all the activities required to meet the schedule.

To understand the project's dynamics, the consultants first interviewed the project management team, who admitted that the project was slow to begin but asserted they now had a good handle on their problems. The project management team said they were taking steps to address the troublesome but manageable schedule problems and they projected that they would turn the corner sometime in the third quarter.

Staff members were interviewed next. They presented a far different story. An obviously overworked engineer told of having to work 12 to 16 hours a day for seven days a week for months on end under unreasonable pressure. As soon as they could find jobs, he and many of his associates were planning to leave. Obviously the consultants were interested in why this had happened and asked the engineer if he thought the situation would change. He explained:

> We started on a bad foot with an initial estimate that was unreasonable. Management knew the amount that had been

budgeted for the system and had committed to build it for 60 percent of that number with a 40 percent reserve. A team of consultants brought in by management estimated the project would cost three times what was finally presented to the customer, based on a size projection that was two times what had been previously estimated. In addition to the discrepancy in the size projection, the consultants felt that the productivity projections used by management were not based on the historical performance of the organization and had not included many tasks essential for the project to succeed. These independent estimates were dismissed by management as being done by an organization who were not team players and who didn't understand the dramatic productivity benefits modern software engineering would provide.

Despite the rocky start the project was funded and the team was hired, although staffing took four months longer than projected and project experience was minimal. As the schedules started to erode, management took a "hands on" role in resolving the problems. Critical functions such as risk management, inspections, trade-off studies and independent QA were gutted or not done at all in the name of schedule and cost reduction. The result is the situation we are now in; too much work that is expanding at a rapid pace due to unanticipated rework and too many defects, not enough money or time to do even the basic things necessary to get the project back on schedule and keep it on track. Management's attempts at restructuring the project by moving tasks in parallel have compounded the problem by further compressing the schedule. It's so bad now we seem to lose a half day every day we work because of new tasks we identify or defects we uncover. I can't see this problem getting any better soon.[3]

This engineer had a far more realistic view of what goes on in real-world projects than many managers or experts in the field. He understood that estimates are only as good as the size projections that they are based on. He also understood that projections of productivity must consider all the costs and tasks associated with a project — not only those related to production.

As Tom DeMarco[4] pointed out, "Are overruns and busted budgets happening too frequently? When performance doesn't meet the estimate, there are two possible causes: poor performance or poor estimates. In the software world, we have ample evidence that our estimates stink, but virtually no evidence that people in general don't work hard enough or intelligently enough."

In the situation noted above, the management team lost sight of the fundamental elements of successful project management: that estimates for project cost and schedule should be based on reality, and there is a minimum time required for any software development. Successful project management also requires an estimate that corresponds to and is driven by (a) how the process is to be managed, monitored, and controlled, and (b) how risks are to be identified, managed, and mitigated.

> Managers and project staff often recognize the potential for impending productivity shortfalls but assume that things will work out even though the available evidence points to the contrary. Managers often flock to unproven or unrealistic "silver bullets" rather than addressing the true nature of a problem. "If we can only get the tool installed by Friday we'll be OK." "If Joe doesn't quit...." "If we can squeeze 86 hours from the staff next week...." "Changing our method will give us the productivity we need." "They probably won't catch that defect." These are typical comments in projects falling into this behavior.[5]

Focus of the Book

The focus of this book is how to make software projects more successful by properly estimating and planning costs, schedules, risks, and resources. The examples cited of unreasonable software project estimation expose some of the fundamental problems: not planning up front; failure to use viable estimates as the basis of an achievable project plan, not updating the plan and estimates when a project changes, and failing to consider the uncertainties inherent in estimates. Most estimates are prepared early on in the life cycle of a project, when there are typically a large number of undefined areas related to the project. The steps presented in this book provide a method for developing realistic estimates and plans, as well as managing the risk associated with estimates.

Why Software Projects Fail

A recent search of the World Wide Web identified over 2100 sites that describe over 5000 reasons that software projects fail, ranging from the poor use of technology to lack of communication to management inattention. While certainly these factors can contribute to the failure of a project, the most pertinent reasons include (1) a lack of understanding of the requirements of a project, (2) insufficient time or discipline to plan the project properly from the first day, and (3) a loss of focus when the project is under way.

In his book *Winning with Software*,[6] Watts Humphrey identifies several causes for software project failure, including unrealistic schedules, inappropriate staffing, changing requirements, poor quality work, and believing in magic. It is interesting to note that in both references cited, technology issues are not factors and that Humphrey lists management and sociological issues as primary causes of dysfunctional projects. Many software managers focus on the "technology of the software process" and fail to acknowledge or even recognize the sociological factors that make projects work.[7] These factors include the need to:

1. Adequately project the resources and time required to deliver a quality product that meets the commitments of the project and the expectations of the users.
2. Be sensitive and responsive to the needs, frustrations, and concerns of the staff and foster a project environment based on the project team.
3. Adequately and effectively plan and provide sufficient time and resources to accomplish the project and recognize that technology-based "silver bullets" cannot substitute for adequate planning.
4. Understand that risk is an inherent part of any worthwhile endeavor; that risk can be identified and managed before the project is affected; and that addressing risk is a responsible management function and does not reflect badly on the state of the project or its potential for success.
5. Deny additional customer requests to prevent disruptions to the project's process or unspecified changes to the product.
6. Treat product quality and project commitments as absolute commitments.
7. Collect meaningful, objective status data concerning progress, quality, productivity, and risk.
8. Define the expectations and true requirements of the user.
9. Address issues that threaten the project with effective and timely solutions.

"A maxim of project management is that projects don't fail in implementation; they fail in the planning stage."[8] If this is true, why then do competent managers agree to budgets, schedules, and technical commitments that they have no idea how to meet? Why do seasoned, rational executives pursue irrational solutions to project issues when the engineers offer no evidence that the solutions can meet those commitments? As Humphrey notes, "Where software is concerned, many otherwise hard-headed executives willingly accept vague promises and incomplete plans. Management's undisciplined approach to schedule commitments contributes to every one of the ... most common causes of project failure."[9]

Almost all software-intensive projects start with the potential for some degree of failure. The first risk of any software project is rooted in the initial estimate used to forecast needed resources. The basic equation traditionally used to estimate the project effort is:

$$\text{Effort} = \frac{(\text{Size} \times \text{Complexity})}{\text{Productivity}}$$

At the beginning of any project the three variables in the equation are unknown. A baseline set of validated requirements is lacking so what needs to be built cannot be accurately defined; the trade-off analyses and architecture are not complete, so complexity is still unknown; and the team has not been formed or, if it has, the team members have not yet gone through the "forming, storming, norming, and performing"[10] steps that are essential for team success. All these unknown factors mean productivity projections are little better than educated guesses.

The question then arising is where does that leave the project manager? Is the project doomed to success or failure based on the whims of fate or the clairvoyance of an estimator? No. Over the years, estimation methods and tools that significantly lower the initial estimation risks have been developed. However, failure to realize the potential imprecise natures of initial estimates and effectively manage and control the risks associated with them certainly is a major contributor to downstream problems, including project failure.

Although software development organizations range from the completely ad hoc to the fully process-driven, most of them use some manner of software estimates at the beginning of a project. Ad hoc organizations may use off-the-cuff, back-of-the-napkin methods, while others may proceed in a very well thought out fashion, defining the risks and uncertainties up front. Sometimes the customer for a project is an internal organization, while other projects must be bid and awarded; alternatively they may be outsourced to organizations that respond to formal requests for proposals (RFPs). This book addresses projects for both internal and external customers. Some of the case studies and examples cited come from the outside contractor's world and others are based on in-house projects.

Why Software Projects Fail: Problems with Estimation

Accurately projecting and tracking software costs is difficult, and cost overruns often occur. It is very important, therefore, to understand software estimating processes and methods. According to the *Parametric Estimating Handbook* of the International Society of Parametric Analysis (ISPA),[11] software estimating problems often occur because of the:

- Inability to accurately size a software project
- Inability to accurately specify an appropriate software development and support environment
- Improper assessment of staffing levels and skills
- Lack of well-defined requirements for the software activity estimated

Problems resulting from poor software estimation are some of the most difficult problems a software development team will face. Many people think that it is impossible to accurately project the time required to develop or update a product, the size of an application, or productivity, and that the best that can be done is to establish targets. Some experts feel that software estimation is not precise enough to ever satisfy business expectations.[12] Often, engineers who are not software specialists will prepare estimates while attempting to satisfy ulterior agendas that are unconcerned with determining the true cost of development. Estimates are frequently overly optimistic, attempting to achieve a number that will satisfy a budget constraint. Sometimes they are unrealistic in an effort to "take the heat off" a manager who must defend them, or they may be trimmed to provide stretch goals to help motivate staff. In the words of Capers Jones, "Most software projects still tend to run late because of arbitrary estimate overruling by customers and senior executives, creeping requirements, and inadequate early quality control."[13]

If used properly, estimates can provide basic constraints that potentially limit the options available when planning a project. The estimates also identify the resource limitations that must be considered when scheduling a project, which in turn may dictate the selection of methods and tools. Budget and resource constraints affect a project's schedule, the phasing of activities, the logical relationships of the work activities, and the structuring and packaging of the products. In addition, the estimate determines the options available to increase the quality of the products, either precluding or enabling the use of practices such as structured inspections or enhanced testing.

Software estimation methods have been applied with varying degrees of success, to small and large projects. Table 1.1 summarizes popular estimation methods.

Table 1.1   Estimation Methods[14]

Estimation Method	Objective	Advantages	Limitations
Analogy	Compare project with past similar projects	Estimates are based on actual experience	Truly similar projects must exist
Expert judgment	Consult with one or more experts	Little or no historical data is needed; good for new or unique projects	Experts tend to be biased; knowledge level is sometimes questionable; may not be consistent
Top-down estimation	A hierarchical decomposition of the system into progressively smaller components is used to estimate the size of a software component	Provides an estimate linked to requirements and allows common libraries to size lower-level components	Need valid requirements; difficult to track architecture; engineering bias may lead to underestimation
Bottom-up estimation	Individuals assess each component; estimates are summed to calculate the total estimate	Accurate estimates are possible because of detailed basis of estimate (BOE); promotes individual responsibility	Methods are time-consuming; detailed data may not be available, especially early in a program; integration costs are sometimes disregarded; engineering bias often leads to underestimation
Design to cost	Uses expert judgment to determine how much functionality can be provided for given budget	Easy to get under customer number	Need reasonable assessment of cost of defined functionality; may have little engineering basis

Table 1.1 (continued)   Estimation Methods[14]

Estimation Method	Objective	Advantages	Limitations
Parametric models	Perform overall estimate using design parameters and mathematical algorithms	Models are usually fast and easy to use, and useful early in a program; they are also objective and repeatable	Models can be inaccurate if not properly applied; underestimation of size will underestimate scope; excessive optimism in parameters may lead to underestimation

Why Software Projects Fail: Size Estimates

As shown earlier, one of the main inputs to software development effort is software size. If size is estimated correctly, the effort estimate will be realistic and will translate to a realistic cost estimate. This is illustrated by the following example.

Before asking, "How many people over what period of time should it take to move this pile of dirt from my front yard to my back yard?" one should answer, "How big is the pile?" While other questions may have related to the capabilities of the people doing the work, the availabilities of various tools, access to the back yard, and other factors, intuition suggests that the size of the pile is probably the key element in this problem.

Relating this physical example to software development, the likely first question should be, "How much software are we going to develop?" Unfortunately, we have no pile of software to measure at the beginning of the project; we have only an idea about what is desired. We therefore need ways to predict software size given whatever knowledge we have about that software. Since this evolving knowledge manifests itself in one or more evolving abstractions, we need to count elements of these abstractions and somehow relate them to work.[15]

In the physical world, size is a measure of volume or mass. In the software world, size is a measure of functionality. Various expressions of size include measures such as lines of code, number of features, or functions, function points and their derivatives, SEER function-based sizing, use cases, and objects. Additionally, the amount of rework of existing systems is a key size measure for modifications. Software size is the main driver of software development effort, cost and schedule via parametric models, and base productivity measures.[16]

Sizing measures that enable valid comparisons across (or within) systems based on the relative sizes of each system are the yardsticks used to project how big a product will be and the amount of effort necessary to produce it. It is not easy to project productivity without a consistent and current sizing measure of the software to be developed. Despite the importance of these measures, neither a generally accepted unit of measure nor a common definition of how one should be computed currently exists.

What effect does a lack of standards have on the software sizing and estimation process? To begin with, definitions for a unit of measure are inconsistent for numerous size definitions such as function points, feature points, and lines of code. Individual approaches such as expert opinion, analogy, parametric modeling, and others can be applied without consistent guidance. Sizing estimates are accepted without consistent guidance as to what constitutes quality. Without guidance, the acceptance and management of the sizing metrics are left to each project to determine. In short, the lack of realistic, accepted software sizing standards precludes, or at least makes difficult, consistency of the estimation process.

Two software sizing measures are widely used today: source lines of code (SLOC or LOC) and function points (FP). While both are sizing measures, they actually measure different things and have very different characteristics.

> In the past, most parametric models determined software costs based on an estimated number of source lines of code. Many of these experienced an extremely high error rate (up to 400 percent) associated with estimating software costs using source lines of code-based parametric software models early in the lifecycle. The problem lies not with the accuracy of the algorithms in the models, but with the inaccuracy of the size measurements fed into the models.[17]

Source lines of code — SLOC is a software metric used to measure the amount of code in a program. SLOC is typically used to estimate the amount of effort that will be required to develop a program as well as to quantify productivity or effort once the software is produced.

One of the problems with using SLOC has been the lack of a standardized definition. Physical SLOC measures (counting physical line endings like lines on a page) are sensitive to the formatting and style conventions of the language used to develop the code. Logical SLOC measures the number of "statements." Logical SLOC definitions are tied to particular computer languages. Logical SLOC is less sensitive to formatting and style conventions, but is sensitive to programming language and technology. SLOC measures are often stated without a definition, which constitutes a problem because the SLOC represents a count of unknown units. Additionally, SLOC that are hand-generated should be separately identified from autogenerated SLOC, and new SLOC must be separated from reused SLOC. Despite these problems, SLOC counts have been and will continue to be successfully used by many companies, organizations, and projects as units of software size.

Function points — Function points measure delivered functionality in a way that is independent of the technology used to develop the system. function points compute size by counting functional components (inputs, outputs, external interfaces, files, and inquiries). As illustrated in Figure 1.1, function points project what will be provided by the system rather than how big the end product will be. This approach is analogous to projecting the cost of a car by anticipating what capabilities it will have rather than by its size. Table 1.2 illustrates some advantages and disadvantages of SLOC counts and function points.

When the size of a proposed software product is projected from requirements, the project has taken the first essential step toward estimating the cost and time that will be needed for its development. "The problem of project management, like that of most management, [is] to find an acceptable balance among time, cost, and performance."[20] "When a project moves out of balance a risk results. Often schedule performance becomes most important due to customer pressures, so cost and product performance lose emphasis. Often the product takes center stage due to a customer review so cost and schedule performance focus drifts out of the shadows. What was once well controlled now becomes less well managed, resulting in risk."[21] The means by which software projects

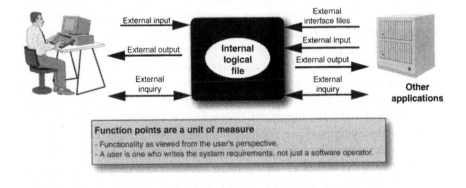

Figure 1.1 Function points — a user's perspective.[18]

Table 1.2   Advantages and Disadvantages of SLOC and Function Point Counts[19]

	Advantages	*Disadvantages*
Lines of Code	Easy to compute	No incentive to optimize code
	Intuitive	Multiple definitions for what constitutes a line of code; autogenerated code may artificially inflate a SLOC count
	Granular	Varies dramatically based on technology used
	Natural by-product of process	Difficult to relate to requirements early in the project
		Some languages difficult to count automatically
Function Points	Measures system from user perspective	User perspective must be available for detailed count
	Better defined counting rules	Not all information available early in project
	Relatively independent of technology	Not intuitive to managers
	Maintains link to functionality	Counters must be trained

establish such balance is through the size projections used to estimate the work, develop the schedule, and monitor the changing size projections, which alter the balance point. If these projections are flawed, either through poor application of process, incorrect use of historical information, or management malpractice,[22] this essential balance cannot be reached.

Incorrect size projections are often the culprits when bad or unachievable estimates are made. Projecting size, whether you use SLOC, function points, or another measure, is probably the most difficult step in the estimation process and, because of this, is often ignored, performed in a hurry to deal with management pressure, or completed superficially to ensure the resultant estimate is below a target cost. (It is NOT uncommon for a developer to use either the schedule or budget and the expected productivity to compute a size!) There is often insufficient information available, estimators are often under intense pressure to "get under a number" and the easiest way is to do this is to manipulate the size projection. However, if you don't know what you have to develop you really don't have a good base from which to predict how big the project will be or a solid basis to evaluate the estimate once it's completed.

Why Estimates Fail

Capers Jones's definition of software estimation,[23] "Predicting the future outcome of a project in terms of various factors, including sizes, schedules, effort, costs, value, and risk," highlights the difficulty of the software sizing and estimation process. Many components are critical to the accuracy and usefulness of an estimate, but very few are common, accurate, and available when an estimate is made. The problems associated with generating consistent, reliable, and repeatable estimates are compounded by the inconsistency of the process; by differences in what the basic elements in the estimate are and how they should be represented; and by differences in the motivations, experience, training, and biases that individual estimators bring to the process.

It is often difficult to achieve acceptance of a realistic estimate by management and customers. Everyone wants things cheaper, but for any project there is a real cost that will allow that project to include the required functionality and produce a quality output. Project managers have to determine what you can do for a particular price and educate all stakeholders about what is and what is not possible. This opens up the greatest threat to realistic sizing projections: management denial.

Software estimation techniques used in various combinations have varying degrees of success. One study conducted in England of thousands of software products revealed that 66 percent overran time schedules, 55 percent were over budget, and 58 percent experienced unexpected major problems. Another study showed that between 30 and 70 percent of estimates were incorrect.[24]

Estimates can be set up for failure if a point estimate is used. Estimates might be treated as a range of possible outcomes by saying, for example, that a project will take five to seven months instead of stating it will be complete on June 15. Many experienced estimators express uncertainty as an accompanying probability value by qualifying the estimate, for example, as an 80 percent probability that a project will complete on or before June 15. As Karl Wiegers stated,

> Most software professionals must provide estimates for their work, but few of us are skillful estimators. Many of us haven't been trained in estimation techniques. We're too optimistic, with short memories that mask the painful overruns from previous

projects. We don't incorporate contingency buffers to accommodate unexpected events or risks that materialize. And we often overlook necessary aspects of an activity, so that when we eventually confront those tasks, we either perform them — thereby exceeding our estimates — or skip them, perhaps compromising quality in the process.[25]

It often is difficult for management to understand or accept these probabilities in basic estimates, especially if one of the numbers happens to match management's preconceived number or the budget of a known customer or stakeholder. Management will often disregard estimates that are inconsistent with immediate needs while embracing those that are immediately useful in gaining the work and initiating the effort.

Due to the number of variables in the estimation process, an estimation range should be used. This range, which can be designated as *optimistic*, *most likely*, and *pessimistic*, allows projects to link the initial estimates to the performance monitoring and risk management processes from the outset. It provides a prenegotiated set of targets that reflects realistic project scenarios and it provides management some flexibility should progress not proceed exactly as planned. Providing and working toward a single point estimate provides none of these advantages. As shown in Figure 1.2, software estimates are generally inaccurate at inception, although this inaccuracy can be minimized through the use of reputable sizing and cost models. Unfortunately, the need for rapid estimates has bred an estimation process that is prone to error. In addition to the size and other issues discussed above, several of the major reasons for estimation failure include:

■ Lack of or misuse of historical data
■ Overoptimistic leadership or management (failure to build the estimate on a solid foundation)
■ Failure to use the estimate
■ Failure to keep the estimate current

Historical Data

Many organizations fail to collect and evaluate historical information on the true cost, schedule, quality, and risk performance of development, which is often perceived as threatening individual managers rather than serving as an essential element of an effective process to lower risk. The use of historical information provides estimators a quantitative way to establish what has been done in the past so they can project future performance with some accuracy. It is essential that organizations that

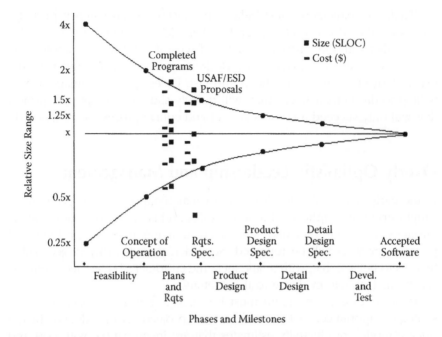

Figure 1.2 Estimate convergence graph.[26]

want to lower project risk related to cost and schedule projections establish some fundamental project metrics that can be collected for every project and used to predict the size of future applications and expected team performance.

Although not a universal practice, some organizations do keep historical records of how much projects of various types cost and how long they took. Fewer organizations, on the other hand, keep useful records of what went wrong on a project, what productivity impacts were experienced, what risks were addressed and which risks weren't, what unanticipated problems affected the project, and how large the effects were. While cost and schedule information is useful, it does not explain the reasons for the reported cost performance and why a project ended up costing so much or so little; such information is therefore of marginal use when developing an estimate for a new project. To paraphrase Tim Lister, each project is unique. Each has its own quirky clients, its own unique staff, and its own expectations of success. Could it be that adaptation of process is 90 percent of the problem and the common processes are marginal?[27] Productivity and project performance are keyed to the processes applied to each project, and even in the world of common process each implementation is unique. While cost and schedule histories are important, these factors must be tempered with the unique circumstances of each project.

Finally, management must believe the history, even when it provides an answer they don't want to hear. Past histories can often provide insights that conflict with the customer's views of what it will take to complete the project, with senior management's desire to win the work, and with the user's desire for something cheap and fast. Unless project management is willing to dig in their heels, they will quickly slide into a high risk project that will only succeed if corners are cut and critical processes are ignored.

Overly Optimistic Leadership and Management

In the early stages of a development or maintenance project, everyone is caught up in the euphoria of a new project and is optimistic that the same mistakes won't be repeated, effectively denying that the problems of previous projects will be repeated. Such denial leads many project stakeholders to believe that, with a little luck, the customer's budget requirements can be met despite evidence to the contrary.

In some cases, a program must be managed at a loss because of its strategic importance. Details such as size projections that do not fit the pricing model, productivity estimates that are incompatible with cost and schedule constraints, and risk scenarios that fail to match the early optimism are rejected as painting a doomsday scenario, leading managers to agree to impossible commitments in the interest of being team players. Only when the harsh reality of the project execution becomes evident are these commitments questioned and the optimism tempered. Only then are size projections believed, early dissenting views given credence, and previously ignored risks addressed. Too many times this awareness of reality is too late, and a project is headed for rough times.

Failure to Use Estimate

As Judy Galorath explains, "Contractors and developers sometimes don't do a realistic estimate — they build an estimate to give the results that match the budget or schedule that has been dictated to them. The models really aren't that far off. It is the misuse of the models that creates the huge variance."[28]

The best estimate is only as good as the project leadership's commitment to manage, control, and track the process, the work, and the quality of the product and the staff productivity. Even a well-planned software project will encounter many unexpected events, unanticipated issues and problems, and planned or unplanned delays that can negatively affect productivity, divert the project from its planned course, or sink it altogether. Unstable requirements, personnel issues, and changing technology can delay progress and force a project into alternative strategies such as increased schedule concurrency. Factors beyond anyone's control can create insurmountable obstacles for a project and preclude successful satisfaction of basic commitments. When planning has been rushed or is less than adequate, the effects of problems are amplified.

To steer a software project successfully to completion, a project manager needs a way to constantly monitor variances from the original project plan, project the potential impacts, and institute preplanned mitigation strategies that will minimize the effects. If variances are not addressed in a timely fashion, a project can quickly spin out of control and lead straight to disaster. A successful project manager should carefully plan and apply effective processes, support them as required, and trust them. Effective processes include measurement, risk management, frequent project reviews, and independent assessments. Project measurement should be issue-based,[29] focusing on schedule and budget progress, product quality and performance, compliance to established and agreed to commitments, and productivity against projections. While the measures are collected at a specific frequency, it is essential that decisions are based on trend information that enables the project manager to track individual data points against threshold values.

Project managers require a method or process for maintaining schedule, budget, and productivity performance in the face of uncontrolled external circumstances to maintain control. The most commonly applied process for controlling projects is commonly referred to as *earned value*. Earned value requires a good baseline estimate. As described by the Software Project Managers Network:

> Earned value project management uses project performance measurements and charts to plan work, assign a value to planned work, track progress as work is completed, and predict the future performance of the project. To guide a project to completion, the project manager is concerned primarily with three factors: cost, schedule, and completed work.[30]

As Hayes and Over explained:

> A particular task's earned value is based on the percentage of the total planned project effort that the task will take. As tasks are completed, the task's planned value becomes earned value for the project. The project's earned value then becomes an indicator of the percentage of completed work. When tracked week by week, the project's earned value can be compared to its planned value to determine status, to estimate rate of progress, and to project the completion date for the project.[31]

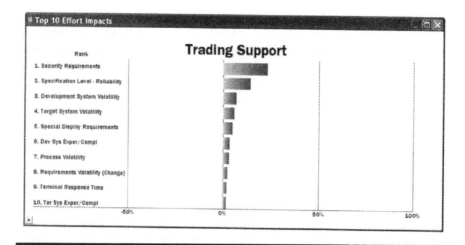

Figure 1.3 Critical considerations for estimating software application development.[32]

Earned value can serve as an important "early warning" that enables managers to identify and control problems before they become insurmountable. This topic is covered in detail in Chapter 9.

Failure to Keep Estimate Current

As illustrated in Figure 1.3, many project factors are critical considerations for estimating software application development or maintenance. Over time, the relative importance of these factors changes and their impact on an estimate may become either more or less critical to the accuracy of the estimate, depending on the characteristics of the factor and its role in the estimation process. While some of the factors are sensitive to the specific time phase of the estimate, others span the entire software project. In fact, some are not finalized until the project is completed and delivered to the customer.

Role of Risk Management in Estimating

All software projects, when they are initially conceived, structured, and planned, include the potential for failure, regardless of the quality of the requirements, the maturity of the organization, the detail of the plan, or the repeatability of key processes used. Many projects share an initial sizing and cost estimate that in actuality is a projection based on incomplete information that often has not been validated.

A project that succeeds often seems to have more than its share of luck or benefits from a management team experienced at anticipating and responding to problems as they occur. Such management teams know the vulnerabilities of the project should growth occur in software size and they understand the threat to the validity of the software estimates and the need to reestimate if growth occurs. They put processes in place to monitor specific conditions and take action sufficiently early to minimize the impact, or they put measures in place that provide early warning as to performance problems that could invalidate the software estimate. These steps constitute risk management, and a culturally integrated risk management process is what distinguishes a successful project.

In order to adequately address the true nature of the threats affecting software projects resulting from the initial sizing, resource, and cost estimates, a robust and consistent risk management process should be in place from the very beginning of a project. Budhram noted that:

> Risk surrounds all aspects of life …. One must therefore confront it, analyze it, quantify it, and determine whether to avoid it, pass it on, or minimize it. Use of a risk management model, including risk identification, quantification, response development and response control, is vitally important to a project's success.[33]

Many project managers find themselves unable to adequately identify and manage risks and take mitigation steps when the results of the mitigation will have the most effect. Budhram again:

> The program managers (PMs) who were unaccustomed to dealing with risks were unable to effectively quantify and manage them. They tended to handle risks as 'new crises' and consequently scrambled to look after them. This type of risk management can be classified as the 'fire fighter approach.' Instead of anticipating potential risks and preparing contingency plans, the PMs dealt with the consequences of each problem as they developed. This reactive form of management — crisis management — can be both inefficient and ineffective, potentially leading to project failure. As a result of this crisis management mentality, risks may not be fully understood within project management.[34]

Risk resolution cost is usually manageable if the risk is identified early, the mitigation is planned, and effective action is taken early enough to minimize or avoid the impacts associated with the risk. The impact of the risk increases dramatically as the project progresses. Despite the importance of the process, most software projects only give lip service to risk management. The absence of a comprehensive risk management program is a leading indicator of incipient project failure. Effective risk management requires acceptance and decriminalization of risk as a major consideration for software program management; commitment of program resources; and use of formal methods for identifying, monitoring, and managing risk. Chapter 10 discusses the risk management process in detail.

Instead of asking why software costs so much, we need to begin asking what we have done to make it possible for today's software to cost so little.[35] Several important studies of software development have concluded that most problems are management problems — not technical problems. The risks associated with these problems are particularly insidious because they are difficult to monitor until the problems associated with the risk become visible. The same individual who caused the risks, often the manager, is also the one who must identify, monitor, and respond to them.

Because risk management is so important to the health and well-being of a project, it is difficult to understand why projects do not embrace it as a core project discipline. The answer lies in the nature of the risk management process. The process focuses on what can go wrong in a project instead of highlighting the potential for success. Glass stated:

> Our cultures guide us to think only of success, to concentrate on winning, not losing. The plan-for-success mentality sounds great, but it makes risk management almost impossible. And risk management is your most effective tool in a risk-intensive world. To do real risk management, you have to develop a deep understanding of the factors that have undone those who have gone before you, understand how these factors acted, and what measures proved insufficient to contain them. If such factors proved fatal to your predecessors, they may prove equally fatal to you.[36]

It is often said that failure is not an option, and this is true, as no one would ever choose to fail. But failure certainly is a possibility and it is best to be prepared to deal with those factors that could lead to it.

The Solution: Software Estimation — Ten-Step Process

An effective software estimate provides the information needed to design a workable software development plan. This book provides a ten-step process to aid in the management of software estimation risk. The ten steps are covered in Chapters 2 through 4:

Chapter 2:

> Step One: Establish the software estimate scope and purpose
> Step Two: Establish technical baseline, ground rules, and assumptions
> Step Three: Collect data

Chapter 3:

> Step Four: Software sizing
> Step Five: Prepare baseline estimate
> Step Six: Quantify risks and risk analysis

Chapter 4:

> Step Seven: Review, verify, and validate estimate
> Step Eight: Generate a project plan
> Step Nine: Document the estimate and lessons learned
> Step Ten: Track project throughout development

Summary

This chapter has discussed the major contributors to software development project and estimation failure. Evidence shows that more projects fail due to poor planning than technological issues.[37] The message of the remainder of this book is that software development can be successful. This book will address the processes and critical information that will help make size and cost estimates more accurate, relevant in relation to the specific project environment, and consistent in relation to the real experience of the organization performing the work.

Endnotes

1. Galorath, Dan. Personal experience.
2. Software Program Managers Network. *The Program Manager's Guide to Software Acquisition Best Practices.* Ver. 2.1. Arlington: Computers and Concepts Associates, April 1998. Preface.
3. Evans, Michael. Personal experience.
4. DeMarco, Tom. *Why Does Software Cost So Much?* New York: Dorsett House Publishing, 1995. 144.
5. Evans Michael, Alex Abela, and Tom Beltz. "Seven Characteristics of Dysfunctional Software Projects." *CrossTalk: The Journal of Defense Software Engineering*, April 2002.

6. Humphrey, Watts. *Winning with Software: An Executive Strategy*. Boston: Addison-Wesley, 2002.

7. DeMarco, Tom. *Why Does Software Cost So Much?* New York: Dorsett House Publishing, 1995. 141.

8. Wells, George. "Why Projects Fail." *Management Science Journal*, March 22, 2003.

9. Humphrey, Watts. *Winning With Software: An Executive Strategy*. Boston: Addison-Wesley, 2002.

10. Streibel, Barbara, Brian L. Joiner, and Peter R. Scholtes. *The Team Handbook*. 2nd ed. Madison: Joiner/Oriel Inc., 1996.

11. International Society of Parametric Analysts. *Parametric Estimating Handbook*. 3rd ed. Sponsored by the U.S. Department of Defense. Chandler: ISPA, 2003. Chap 6. <http://www.ispa-cost.org/PEIWeb/newbook.htm>

12. Lewis, J.P. "Large Limits to Software Estimation." *ACM Software Engineering Notes*. 26.4, 2001. 54-59.

13. Jones, Capers. "Software Cost Estimation in 2002." *CrossTalk: The Journal of Defense Software Engineering*, June 2002. 4.

14. International Society of Parametric Analysts. *Parametric Estimating Handbook*. 3rd ed. Sponsored by the U.S. Department of Defense. Chandler: ISPA, 2003. Chap. 6. <http://www.ispa-cost.org/PEIWeb/newbook.htm>

15. Ross, Michael. "Software Project Management Process Estimation." El Segundo: Galorath Incorporated, 2004.

16. Galorath, Daniel D. and Daniel V. Ferens. "A Software Model Based on Architecture," *SCEA National Conference*, Scottsdale, 2002.

17. Nelson, Mike, James Clark, and Martha Ann Spurlock. "Curing the Software Requirements and Cost Estimating Blues: The Fix is Easier Than You Might Think." *Program Manager Magazine*, December 1999.

18. International Function Point Users Group (IFPUG). "Introduction to the International Function Point Users Group." IFPUG Introductory Briefing, 1999.

19. Mosaic Inc. "Software Sizing Measures." *Sizing Using Testable Requirements: Overview of Testable Requirements Concepts. 2001–2004*, 9 Sept. 2005. <http://www.testablerequirements.com/testablerequirements/soft_size_meas.htm>.

20. Norden, P.V., and B.V. Dean, Eds. *Useful Tools For Project Management, Operations Research in Research and Development*. New York: John Wiley & Sons, 1963.

21. Evans Michael, Alex Abela, and Tom Beltz. "Seven Characteristics of Dysfunctional Software Projects." *CrossTalk: The Journal of Defense Software Engineering*, April 2002.

22. Jones, T. Capers. *Software Assessments, Benchmarks, and Best Practices*. Boston: Addison Wesley, 2000.

23. Jones, T. Capers. *Assessment and Control of Software Risks*. Indianapolis: Yourdon Press Computing Series, Prentice Hall, 1994.

24. Cost As An Independent Variable. Course for Software Acquisition, Naval Postgraduate School. 9 Sept. 2005. <http://www.nps.navy.mil/wings/acq_topics/caiv.htm>

25. Weigers, Karl E. "Stop Promising Miracles." *Process Impact Publications: Software Management.* 9 Sept. 2005. <http://www.processimpact.com/articles/delphi.html>
26. Weber, Christopher R. "The Software Estimation Story." *DSW Group: Resources.* 9 Sept. 2005. <http://www.thedswgroup.com/HTML/reference/SoftwareEst.html>
27. Lister, Tim. "Software Management For Adults," *Software Technology Conference.* Salt Lake City, 1996.
28. Galorath, Judy. Personal interview, July 2000.
29. Practical Software and System Measurement (PSM). "Practical Software and Systems Measurement: A Foundation for Objective Project Management." October 2000, Ver. 4.0b. Sponsored by the U.S. Department of Defense and the U.S. Army. 10 Oct. 2000. <www.psmsc.com>
30. Software Program Managers Network. *Practice Area Development: Earned Value Metrics.* Arlington: Computers and Concepts Associates, 1998.
31. Hayes, W. and J. W. Over. *The Personal Software Process: An Empirical Study of the Impact of PSP on Individual Engineers.* Pittsburgh: Carnegie Mellon Software Engineering Institute, 1997.
32. Galorath Incorporated. *SEER-SEM v 7.1.30.* El Segundo, 2005.
33. Budhram, Stanley C. and J. Edward Kunz. "Risk Management and the Photogrammetric Project Manager." *Earth Observation Magazine,* December 2000. Reprinted courtesy of *Professional Surveyor Magazine* (www.profsurv.com).
34. Budhram, Stanley C. and J. Edward Kunz. "Risk Management and the Photogrammetric Project Manager." *Earth Observation Magazine,* December 2000. Reprinted courtesy of *Professional Surveyor Magazine* (www.profsurv.com).
35. DeMarco, Tom. *Why Does Software Cost So Much?* New York: Dorsett House Publishing, 1995.
36. Glass, Robert L. *ComputingFailure.com: War Stories from the Electronic Revolution.* Upper Saddle River: Prentice Hall, 2001.
37. United States. Office of the Under Secretary of Defense, Acquisition and Technology, Defense Science Board. Report of Defense Science Board Task Force on Defense Software, November 2001.

Chapter 2

Introduction to Software Estimation Techniques and Estimate Planning

We do not what we ought,
What we ought not, we do,
And lean upon the thought
That Chance will bring us through.

Matthew Arnold

Introduction and Chapter Goals

An effective software estimate provides the information needed to design a workable software development plan. "Good estimates are key to project (and product) success. Estimates provide information to make decisions, define feasible performance, objectives and plans ... bad estimates affect everyone associated with the project ..."[1] This chapter addresses the need for project metrics and the fundamental software estimation concepts and discusses the first three steps in the software estimation process.

Need for Efficient Software Project Management Metrics

When some managers insist that "you can't manage what you can't measure,"[2] they are focusing on the ideal and ignoring the real. The fact is we manage things we can't measure all the time. Pure research, product design, and manuscript development are managed without metrics or by using metrics that at best are inadequate and at worst are misleading. In reality, metrics used to manage intellectual and creative processes often do not provide the insights managers would like to have. They do not answer questions such as: How good are the processes we are using? What quality can we expect? When can we finish this effort? How much will it cost? As a result, managers tend to measure intellectual processes, including software engineering, qualitatively rather than quantitatively.

Alternate strategies to quantitatively measure the progress of intellectual and creative activities do exist, although they are best suited for measuring specific issues such as defect rates rather than broader issues such as quality. Indeed, monitoring intellectual activities such as software development by using metrics to evaluate broad issues such as project progress is often counterproductive. However, measuring specific progress against an identified quantitative constraint to determine the likelihood of meeting that constraint is a realistic goal. For example, quantitative measures can be used to monitor specific issues such as defect rates, the sufficiency of assigned resources, and whether enough money or time is left to complete the project based on the task completion rate.

Many organizations employ this type of issue-based measurement, which is a tested and mature process, and resources are available to help determine effective metrics. For example, *Practical Software and Systems Measurement*,[3] a guide describing a useful process with supporting measures, and *Sixteen Critical Software Practices*, a program manager's guide,[4] provide issue-based metrics linked to specific project practices. The practical software measurement (PSM) process can be applied to all stages of a software project: planning, requirements analysis, design, implementation, and integration of hardware and software. It provides a means to collect and analyze project data — includes estimates, plans, changes to plans, and counts of actual activities, products, and expenditures — at a sufficient level of detail to identify and isolate problems.

These resources provide measurement structures that address the needs of software managers. They rely on reasonable projections of targets and they evaluate narrow project factors or attributes against established project goals and issues. Issue-based measurement helps you make statements such as, "Based on your current milestone completion rate you will (or will not) meet the September 7 deadline." This measurement process provides objective and quantitative information required to make informed decisions that affect project cost, schedule, and technical performance objectives.

Metrics should be set and decided on as part of a software development plan before development begins. By measuring specific project factors, project teams can gain the information needed to monitor key issues related to progress and quality and performance against the plan. With current objective information, managers can also answer critical questions and take corrective actions early enough to avoid or minimize problems before they get out of hand.

Crucial to the measurement process is the ability to distinguish a metric, a measure, and an indicator. A metric is a parameter that provides a quantitative standard of measurement of the degree to which a system, component, or process possesses a given attribute. Software lines of code (SLOC) is a metric used throughout this book. A measure is quantitative evidence of the extent, amount, dimensions, capacity, or size of a specific attribute (metric) of a product or process. For example, we would show the measure of software size (software size is the metric) by saying it is comprised of 150,000 source lines of code (the measure of the metric). An indicator is a metric or combination of metrics that provides qualitative information describing the state of a process, a project, or the product itself, for example, number of defects per SLOC might be an indicator of project testing or quality. A software project benefits from an effective measurement process by acquiring the information needed to:

- **Enable effective communication** — Keeping information current enables effective communication among stakeholders throughout all levels of an organization, reduces ambiguity, and enables supplier and acquirer organizations to accurately communicate status.
- **Make timely trade-offs** — With accurate information, software managers can objectively assess the effects of their decisions, which enables them to evaluate viable trade-offs that will better support project objectives.
- **Monitor progress toward meeting specific project objectives** — Quantitative information enables managers to answer questions such as: Will the project meet its schedule if we continue with the same productivity? Can we anticipate excessive rework if our productivity continues at the current level? Will we deliver a product with too many defects to meet user expectations? The answers to such questions allow managers to track progress toward project and organizational objectives.
- **Identify and correct problems and address risk early** — Measurement provides the information software managers and project

staff need to effectively identify and manage potential problems before they become intractable.

■ **Manage, control, and contain risk** — Measurement processes are integral components of risk management, which is a core best practice of any software project (see Chapter 10). Many software project measurements are leading indicators, the analysis of which enables managers to forecast project conditions. (Trailing indicators, on the other hand, provide information about past performance.) By analyzing leading indicators based on quantitative information, managers can identify risks while it is possible to mitigate them effectively and will have the information required to analyze a specific risk's likelihood of occurrence and likely impact. In addition, the objective information that results from effective measurement enables managers to consistently monitor potential risks by setting realistic thresholds against which they can evaluate risks and monitor project performance against established metrics.

■ **Defend and justify decisions** — By measuring specific project factors, managers are provided the objective information regarding performance (i.e., current, historical, and trend) they need to make effective decisions regarding schedule, cost, product (or code) growth, quality, developer capability and process maturity, technology, and user satisfaction. Such information enables project management, stakeholders and staff to accurately determine whether a project is meeting its goals and requirements.

As important as measurement is, it should be noted that not all indicators of a project's success are measurable. Many indicators are subjective or result from qualitative factors. For example, no quantifiable metric exists to objectively measure morale. Managers can get a feel for the state of staff morale, but any objective measure would for all practical purposes be meaningless. The effects of poor morale, however, can potentially be identified by tracking project performance through earned value, which measures output against effort. (For a detailed discussion on earned value see Chapter 9.)

Core Metrics Categories

Ideally, the following attributes of a software project would be measured:

1. Cost
   a. Staff effort
   b. Phase effort
   c. Total effort

2. Defects
   a. Found or corrected
   b. Effort required
   c. Defect source and class
   d. Defect density
3. Process characteristics
   a. Development language
   b. Process model
   c. Technology
4. Project dynamics
   a. Changes or growth in requirements or code
   b. Schedule and schedule compression[5]
5. Project progress (earned value; see Chapter 9)
   a. Development dates
   b. Project size
   c. Total effort
   d. Budget performance
   e. Schedule performance
   f. Cost performance index (CPI)[6]
   g. Schedule performance index (SPI)[7]
   h. To-complete performance index (TCPI)[8]
6. Software structure
   a. Size
   b. Complexity

Project managers, stakeholders, and staff members can use software metrics to more accurately estimate progress toward project milestones, especially when historical (trailing) indicators or trend data are available. Measurement enables project participants to plot weekly or monthly changes that can reveal trends, and in turn this information can enable prediction of problem areas such that action can be taken.

These metrics and others have their basis in the size projections, cost estimates, and schedules and work plans that are based on them. Size and cost estimates serve as basis for many project measures. They are the basic criteria used to evaluate project performance, progress against plans, product quality based on defect density, and other measures that are needed to accurately monitor schedule, cost, product (or code) growth, quality, and other key factors.

Size and cost estimates are not the same as targets, although estimates may be used as targets. In principle, estimates should be used to assess the feasibility of targets (i.e., budget or schedule constraints) and to confirm that the current status of a project indicates that final project targets are feasible.

Software Project Estimates: Foundations of Software Project Management

Many elements are involved in determining the structure of a project, including requirements, architecture, quality provisions, and staffing mix. Perhaps the most important element in the success or failure of a project is the initial estimate of its scope, in terms of both the time and cost that will be required. The initial estimate drives every aspect of the project, constrains the actions that can be taken in the development or upgrade of a product, and limits available options. Although many people think they can estimate project scope based on their engineering or management experience, most off-the-cuff estimates are incorrect and are most often based on simple assumptions and over-optimism, or worse, are made to accord with what others want to hear. Needless to say, such estimates often lead to disaster. The variability in these estimates was previously shown in an estimate convergence graph (Figure 1.2 in Chapter 1).

A software project estimate is the most knowledgeable statement that can be made at a particular point in time regarding effort, cost, schedule, and risk. A complete estimate covers definitions, uncertainties, ground rules, and assumptions. Too often an analyst is requested to prepare an estimate on short notice and with limited information. Upon investigation of the estimate requirement, he finds that (1) the proposal schedule requires that the estimate be available in less than a week, (2) few if any software requirements documents describe the product, (3) no decisions have been made regarding architecture, (4) the company maintains inadequate documentation of similar jobs, and (5) both management and the customer have preconceived ideas on what estimate (dollars and/or schedule) is required to win the work. Given these constraints, the analyst still must quickly build a team to develop the estimate which, at best, can be considered a rough order of magnitude.

Unfortunately the rough order of magnitude is often the best case scenario. If so inclined, the analyst will merely make an off-the-cuff estimate based on the best recollection of the last project in which he was involved. Nevertheless, the estimate will be highly imprecise, although more often than not the proposal team will be faced with a projected cost that is larger than the available customer budget. If the analyst is thorough, the estimate will include a description of the ground rules used and assumptions made as well as a range of risk and uncertainty. Without these details, the proposal team will be working with a number with very little contextual meaning.

Too often hapless analysts are berated for not understanding what it takes to win a job, and if they argue that any lower number will result in an unacceptable risk that the project will be unable to perform, their arguments will be considered unrealistic. Faced with discomfiting initial estimates, management too often hopes for luck, assumes the customer will be willing to cooperate, and tells the estimating team to sharpen their pencils and try again.

When the estimate is finally scrubbed to a number management can live with, it is integrated into an overall project estimate that is then compared against the known or suspected customer budget. If the aggregate number is too high, the software estimate is cut again. After the proposal is submitted to the customer, estimates are often cut again to meet a "competitive range" and finally to present a "best and final offer" based on a fairy tale, at least as far as the software component of the job is concerned. Even if winning the job means bidding a number below what the software development will actually take, managing to a fairy tale will generally yield disastrous results. After all of these "gyrations," one can be left with an estimate that is unrelated to the software development effort. The moral of the story is to prepare and keep viable project estimates even if bidding something else.

Now let us investigate how an estimate should be conducted. Recently we were involved in preparing an estimate for a fixed-price enhancement project using the SEER-SEM cost model. In addition to providing a product for the contracting agency, this work had strategic value to the developer because the resulting product enhancements could be made available to all users of the product and would open up a new vertical market. Because it was a fixed-price situation, the developer's team assumed an 80 percent probability of achieving the projected cost and prepared a most-likely schedule. The developer team used its sizing database and the SEER-AccuScope tool to determine the range of size for the new functionality, which gave the project leads meaningful insight into what to expect. Because the existing product infrastructure would need to be changed and its baseline retested, the developer team recognized the bid would be higher than expected, so the developer consciously decided to "cost share," that is, they agreed among themselves that the developer would ask the customer to pay for the new custom work and the developer would absorb the cost of integrating the new work into the existing product baseline and conducting the necessary tests.

Unfortunately, the customer still had sticker shock, but because of the work's strategic value, the developer's team agreed to take on more of the risk, reestimating the project using 50 percent as a most likely probability and presenting the reduction to the customer as an additional developer cost share. Everyone inside the development organization understood the additional risk, and management agreed to take it on.

Because the development team estimated the most likely schedule to be several months longer than the customer's requirement, it structured an incremental delivery plan that provided the most sought-after features first.

The incremental delivery had a negative impact on the overall project schedule and cost. The point is that by using this rigorous methodology, uncertainty was defined up front and all parties understood the realm of possibilities before the project started. Knowledge is power — the project was completed close to the estimates (before the cuts and cost share options) and won an award as "Product of the Year."

Steve McConnell, in "Ten Deadly Sins of Software Estimation,"[9] defined the ten common mistakes people make in estimating the scope of a software project. In the first scenario described above, the project team committed almost all the "sins" cited in his article. In the second, the project team was nearly flawless. The sins are:

1. **Confusing estimates with targets** — Targets such as trade shows and sales are set without any analysis. Target setting is a very important step in software estimation. Best treated as an iterative process that brings target and estimate into alignment.

2. **Saying yes when really meaning no** — Vigorous, job-defending estimation based on insufficient data or quantities. Problems in schedule negotiation between young, junior, introvert software engineer and sales person who is more experienced, senior, and extrovert.

3. **Committing too early with lots of uncertainties** — Based on the "cone of uncertainty," uncertainties decrease as the project comes near to the end. Early in the software development life cycle, the tendency is to underestimate.

4. **Assuming underestimation has no impact on project result** — Overestimation shows linear impact on project according to Parkinson's law (work expands to fill the time available), whereas underestimation brings higher, nonlinear impact.

5. **Estimating in the "impossible zone"** — Estimations are probability statements, not single points. Schedule compression increases the total cost or effort for the project. The impossible zone is a compressed schedule with a zero chance of success.

6. **Overestimating savings from new tools or methods** — Payoff is less than expected. Assume the productivity loss from initial use of new tools or methods, considering learning curve and error proneness.

7. **Using only one estimation technique** — Estimate via different ways and different views. Multiple approaches contribute to

Brooks' "vigorous defense" (difficult to defend without supporting data).

8. **Not using estimation software** — Use of software can bring more credibility. The science of estimation is supported by the tools.

9. **Not including risk impact** — New technology does not meet expectations at times. Team members can get sick or have family emergencies. Government regulations can change. Risk exposure is where "risk buffer planning" starts.

10. **Providing off-the-cuff estimates** — Treat estimation as a mini-project. Simple arithmetic is better than guessing or intuition. Define a standardized estimation procedure (multiple approaches, description of imprecision, reestimate schedule, point of estimate becoming commitment). Decompose big estimates into smaller ones (system modules).

The problems inherent in accurately estimating the resources required to develop software have been understood and have received significant attention for the past 20 years, and many tools and methods have been developed to address them. As a result, many people have high expectations that the software delivery process has been improved such that these problems have been removed altogether. But the tools are not used widely enough, and overzealous managers still attempt to misuse them to justify unreasonable plans that result in insufficient resources to develop a quality product on time and within budget. As Lorin May stated:

> This problem occurs any time someone 'makes up a number and won't listen to anyone about how long other projects took.' According to DeMarco, projects are often intentionally underbid 'because of the attitude that putting a development team under sufficient pressure can get them to deliver almost anything.'

> The opposite is what usually happens. For example, if a program should realistically take five programmers one year to complete, but instead you are given four programmers and eight months, you will have to skimp on design time and on quality checks to reach project milestones.

> 'Cutting a corner that undermines the entire foundation of the project is not cutting the corner,' states Robert Gezelter, a software consultant in Flushing, New York. 'There will be heavily disproportionate costs downstream.' Skimping leads to

weak designs, dramatically higher defect densities, much more rework, and virtually endless testing. In the end, the project will cost more, take longer, and have worse quality than would have been possible if a realistic schedule and budget had been followed.[10]

As this section has demonstrated, a sound and reliable estimate is the linchpin of a realistic software project plan. The assumptions, requirements, and projections on which the estimate is based allow you to plan a project or define a product with a realistic understanding of the limits that constrain what can actually be done. If the estimate is unrealistically low, the project will be understaffed from its outset and, worse still, the resulting excessive overtime or staff burnout will cause attrition and compound the problems facing the project. If the estimate of the required quality assurance effort is too low, the project may produce low quality deliverables that necessitate excessive, unanticipated rework. Poorly developed estimates may result in schedules that are too short, demoralizing the staff and resulting in loss of credibility as key milestones are missed. "Not knowing what you don't know" causes project staff and management to think they can accomplish what they can't.[11]

Overestimation is not the answer. Simply inflating the estimate to lower risk without sufficient scope controls leads to other problems, such as Parkinson's law (work expands so as to fill the time available for its completion). Indeed, overestimating a project can have the same effects as any other inaccurate estimate. The customer will have unrealistic expectations about project performance and product quality, and the project will likely cost more than it should, take longer to deliver, and delay the use of resources on the next project. As we have learned, sound estimates are based on a viable approach, accurate size projections, meaningful productivity projections, and requirements that reflect agreements with customers and users.

Software Estimation Concepts

Many project managers and project management offices have unrealistic expectations about estimates. The definition of the verb *estimate* is to produce a statement of the approximate value of some quantity. Estimates are based upon incomplete, imperfect knowledge and assumptions about the future. For these reasons, many estimates of software costs tend to be too low due to omissions of important product functions and project activities. Most importantly, however, all estimates have uncertainty. There is no such thing as a precise, single-value estimate. Managers should always ask how large the uncertainty of an estimate is! A manager can use the size of this uncertainty in conjunction with other factors such as perceived risks, funding constraints, and business objectives to make decisions about a project.[12]

How can projects address the uncertainty of poor estimates? How can the risks associated with initial estimates be identified, managed, and controlled? The answer is straightforward: by defining, establishing, planning, and applying a consistent, repeatable, and effective estimation process.

A software estimation process that is integrated with the software development process can help projects establish realistic and credible plans to implement the project requirements and satisfy commitments. It also can support other management activities by providing accurate and timely planning information.

Any software project that wants to be successful requires realistic, credible plans that describe how the project will meet specified objectives, and credible plans must be based on accurate estimates of the required effort, duration, and cost of the project. Realistic plans will also describe how the resources that are required to undertake the initiative in accordance with the schedule will be secured. The planning process, as critical as it is, is difficult and takes time to perform correctly.

Managers often truncate the planning process by using "easily available" information that is often inadequate; by employing whoever has the time, even if those individuals are not qualified to perform the estimate; and by using only one estimation method to save time.

Successful software engineering requires the application of engineering principles guided by informed management. The principles must themselves be rooted in sound theory. While it is tempting to search for miracles and panaceas, it is unlikely that they will appear. The best course of action is to stick to age-old engineering principles. There simply are no silver bullets.[13]

Cost estimates are projections of required effort, time, and staffing levels. Because all estimates, particularly those made at the beginning of a project, are based on assumptions, they should be considered probabilistic. Cost estimates in particular should provide a range with an indication of accuracy, i.e., least, probable, and most, with the least and most values representing the upper and lower bounds of the projected cost.

Project Estimation Process

Ideally an estimate should be produced using the ten-step process described in Figure 2.1. This chapter focuses on the first three steps. Subsequent chapters address the remaining steps.

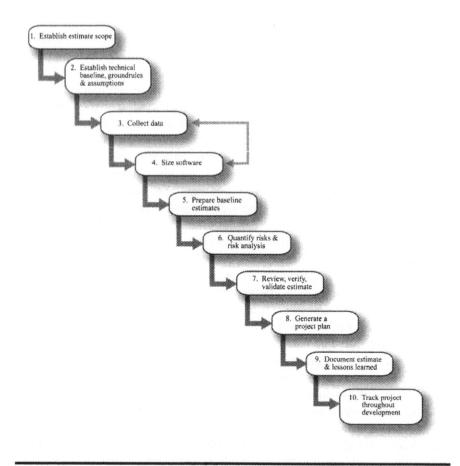

Figure 2.1 Ten-step project estimation process.

Step One: Establish Estimate Scope and Purpose

Any project will benefit if the participants establish and understand the scope and purpose of the project estimates. Ideally, stakeholders will define what is required and agree to written specifications before an estimate is completed. However, this is often not the case and estimates must be performed with incomplete information. By explicitly defining and documenting expectations, the project will be provided a baseline against which the effect of future changes on existing plans and estimates can be assessed. In addition, if expectations are defined beforehand, the following risks can be exposed and discussed, thus reducing the chance that they will occur during the course of the project:

- Misunderstandings about what is expected
- Contradictory assumptions
- Business, technical, or practical details that could prevent risk exposure

By documenting and agreeing to specifications, the project will gain valuable input for estimating the resources required to develop an application. Specifications usually provide insight into the global (business) context of a project and provide information regarding what will be needed to develop, deploy, and certify the product before it is placed into operational use. Specifications identify how products may be used within or across discrete business areas and can identify interface or external dependencies that must be explicitly addressed. Such dependencies could have a bearing on relative priorities, resource allocation, the sequence of events, and timing. By exposing them, the project will have a basis for establishing realistic development or assurance costs and the cost of transitioning the product into operational configurations.

Any specification, from a statement of intent to a business requirement specification or project definition, is of benefit to the estimation process. Of course, the amount and quality of the detail that is provided have a direct bearing on the quality of the estimates produced and dramatically affect the ability to identify and control the overall risks to the project. The more detailed the specification, the better the estimate.

Any information used to produce an estimate should be considered as dynamic and thus should be subject to change control. Because subsequent estimates, management monitoring, and progress tracking, as well as the technical and assurance aspects of the project, are all based on this information, if it changes, the changes must be documented and accounted for in the estimates. Otherwise, the integrity of the initial estimates can quickly erode and a project can rapidly descend into chaos.

Although this book focuses on the estimation of software development costs, it is important to understand that many other factors influence the estimate of overall project costs, including the costs associated with hardware and software purchases or rentals, travel for meeting or testing purposes, telecommunications (e.g., long distance phone calls, videoconferences, dedicated lines for testing, etc.), training courses, and required office space, among other expenses.

The estimation process is extremely sensitive to how an organization allocates or tracks costs. Some costs may be treated by adding an overhead value to labor rates (dollars per hour) and are not tracked within individual projects. Many managers estimate only labor costs and identify any additional project costs as organizational overhead. It is very important that cost considerations be understood from the outset of a project because this information is necessary to produce a complete and accurate estimate. By understanding what is needed, estimators will be able to determine whether the required information is available from historical databases or whether an external resources such as program controls or finance offices should be involved.

Step Two: Establish Technical Baseline, Ground Rules, and Assumptions

Establishing a technical baseline — In the most basic terms, a technical baseline is a complete definition of the functionality that must be estimated. In order for the estimate to be used properly in the generation of a software development plan, all functionality included in the estimate must be clearly defined. To establish an accurate baseline, the estimator must understand the constraints associated with the application and the project. Because the cost of building functionality versus buying functionality can be great, the analyst must understand what must be developed and what can be met by using commercial off-the-shelf (COTS) software or reusing existing software. For example, by using a standard graphics library instead of building all the graphics software, the cost of project software development can be significantly reduced. Of course, if such decisions have not yet been made, the uncertainty can be factored into the estimate range.

Establishing ground rules and assumptions — Ground rules are concise statements that describe the basis from which the estimate is made. "This estimate includes functions a, b, and c only; no costs associated with travel are included" is an example of a ground rule. Assumptions are suppositions that describe unknown variables that will affect an estimate. "This estimate assumes the software developer will use development system X" is an example of an assumption. As an estimate is refined as more information becomes available, many assumptions will be confirmed and will thus become ground rules.

Because the initial ground rules and assumptions serve to frame estimates, particularly at the start of a project, they have a direct bearing on the validity of the estimates. Although they are preliminary in nature and therefore encompass a range of uncertainty, they must be credible and they must be documented and reviewed as the estimate is refined. Because many factors of a project — including requirements, interfaces, resources, qualified personnel; factors that influence the complexity of a project, such as security, safety, and stringent reliability or performance constraints; and many others — can dramatically affect the estimate, ground rules and assumptions must be established and documented.

Step Three: Collect Data

Underlying Information

"You can't measure pure thought stuff," sniffed the young programmer, loosening the laces of his tennis shoes to let more blood flow to his brain. "Maybe not," grunted the old timer, "but we used to weigh the box of punch cards containing the program." "But the program was the holes," the young programmer shot back. "They don't weigh anything."[14]

The validity of an estimate is based on how detailed it is and on the range of its uncertainty. In order to establish that range, all estimate inputs should be characterized as least, likely, and most, rather than expressed as a single point. Even if the scope of the system is not well known, using ranges for inputs can bound the problem and allow the development of viable estimates for planning purposes.

In order to ensure consistency in the estimating process, certain core information is required from the outset. This core information will enable the analyst to conduct the estimate process in an efficient and effective manner and thus ensure valid outputs; it will also enable him to validate the estimates, which in turn will serve to support future estimates and thus narrow their range of uncertainty. Not all of this information may be available when an estimate is being planned or during its initial stages, but it is critical that it be provided as it is needed during the process. It should also be noted that not all this information will be available from within the team. Stakeholder organizations, external engineering organizations, and management must provide some of it, and much of it will result from extrapolations of validated historical information. Table 2.1 indicates categories of information that must be collected and used in the estimation process.* The column heads cited in the table are defined as follows:

Attribute ID provides a unique identifier for each attribute. The letter indicators describe the attribute (G = general descriptor; S = sizing; C = complexity; P = productivity).

Attribute Description identifies the attribute, including, in some cases, examples of information elements.

When Required indicates whether the attribute is required at the start of the estimate or whether it will evolve as the estimate proceeds.

Information Source provides an indication whether the information can be derived by the responsible organization or whether it must be solicited from external or stakeholder sources.

---

* Data collection forms can be obtained from www.galorath.com/estimationbook2006.

Table 2.1 Estimation Information

Attribute ID	Attribute Description	When Required		Information Source		Information Form		
		Initial Parameter	Evolving Parameter	Local	External	Descriptive	Quantitative	Indicator
1G	Purpose of estimate	X		X		X		
2G	Description of project (prose plus platform, application)	X		X		X		
3S	Size (new, reused, COTS)	X	X	X	X		X	
4S,C	Legacy percentages (as is defined, as is undefined, to be defined, to be undefined)		X	X	X		X	
5S,C	COTS and reuse percentages (redesign percentage, reimplementation percentage, retest percentage)		X	X	X	X	X	
6S	Requirements (projected functional, interface, interoperability, unique product requirement, projected volatility)	X	X	X	X	X	X	

7C	Specialized project requirements (safety, security, privacy…)	X	X	X	X	X
8C	Unique operational requirements (reliability, performance, maintainability…)	X	X	X	X	X
9C	Projected certification requirements (security, safety, interoperability, legislative…)	X	X	X	X	
10P	Team composition (established-trained, established-untrained, newly formed-trained, newly formed-untrained, unknown)	X	X	X	X	X
11C,P	Geographical team distribution	X	X	X	X	X
12C,P	Organizational team distribution	X	X	X	X	X

Table 2.1 (continued) Estimation Information

| Attribute ID | Attribute Description | When Required | | Information Source | | Information Form | | |
		Initial Parameter	Evolving Parameter	Local	External	Descriptive	Quantitative	Indicator
13P	Team expertise (level of capability of analysts working on software product, level of applications experience of project team developing software product, level of capability of programmers working on software product, level of host, target machine experience of project team developing product, level of programming language experience of project team developing product, process experience)		X	X	X	X	X	
14G	Scope of estimate (range)	X		X		X		

15C	Product attributes (number and relative frequency of data interactions required, special display requirements, security requirements, response time constraints)	X	X	X	X	X	
16C	Software product complexity (level of complexity of product to be developed)	X	X	X	X	X	X
17C	Computer attributes (execution time constraint, degree of execution constraint imposed upon software product; main storage constraint, degree of main storage constraint imposed upon software product; host and target product; turnaround time, volatility; turnaround time, level of computer response time experienced by project team developing product)	X	X	X	X	X	X

Table 2.1 (continued) Estimation Information

Attribute ID	Attribute Description	When Required		Information Source		Information Form		
		Initial Parameter	Evolving Parameter	Local	External	Descriptive	Quantitative	Indicator
18C	Project attributes (use of modern programming practices [MPPs], degree to which MPPs are used in developing software product; use of software tools, degree to which software tools are used in developing software product; schedule constraint, level of schedule constraint imposed upon project team developing software product)		X	X	X	X	X	X
19C	Projected technologies to be used (proven, new, unknown)		X	X	X			X
20P	Developer information (domain expertise, process expertise, tool expertise, available staff resources, maturity level, historical performance)		X	X	X	X	X	X

Information Form indicates the predominant form of the information (Descriptive = primarily textual describing an element; Quantitative = an individual value or series of values providing quantitative information to be used in the development, validation, or update of an estimate; Indicator = an indication of the existence of a condition or factor, the occurrence of an event, or the presence of an essential or undesired factor).

Interview with Judy Galorath

In the following interview, Judy Galorath, a principal analyst at Galorath, Incorporated, describes how this information is gathered and evaluated. She outlines the key considerations she is concerned about when preparing for and conducting an assessment. While her answers to the interview questions focus on the use of the SEER-SEM cost model, the information she provides can also support the application of manual procedures and other models.

Q: ***Is the software architecture sufficiently well defined to support a valid estimate?***

A: Even though SEER-SEM provides the ability to estimate the software as one WBS item with a parameter to tell it how many separate computer programs are included in the size, it is much better to have the software broken down by major computer program. When this information has not been provided to us, it is one of the first things that I do. This accomplishes two things: (1) it provides a more detailed and accurate estimate and (2) it gives a clear definition of the functionality that we have included in the estimate (in briefings to the customer it is easy to verify whether we have included or excluded all the expected functionality).

Q: ***Do you understand the purpose of the estimate?***

A: I like to know why they want an estimate done. If I know why they want an estimate (i.e., for a new project plan, remediation with a struggling subcontractor, impacts of trying new technology), then I know more specifically the type of information to look for.

Q: ***Do you customize a questionnaire for the assessment?***

A: Usually, I start with the SEER-SEM data collection form, and then I customize it for the job. The simplest form is to delete all the parameters that have nothing to do with the current estimate and the parameters associated with the information that can be obtained from the provided documentation. The fewer questions you need to ask the customer, the better response and cooperation you get.

*Q: **Is this a cost-to-complete, earned-value, or estimate-to-complete assessment?***

A: SEER-SEM and SEER-PPMC provide the capabilities necessary to estimate and/or track the different scenarios. The key is collecting the data from the contractor necessary to figure out what portion of each software development activity has been completed and then input that into SEER-SEM.

*Q: **Do you understand the ground rules and assumptions and is it the same list that the client understands?***

A: From the very first day I keep a constant list of all the assumptions and ground rules that impact the estimate. I don't want the person who looks at the estimate to think that the costs associated with requirements are excluded when they are actually included and vice versa.

*Q: **Besides the data that you normally collect as input to the SEER-SEM model, do you conduct basic data collection to find out what else is important to the customer?***

A: In addition to collecting the data necessary for input into SEER-SEM, I also try to collect "non-input" data that may have an impact on the development in some way, such as contract award delays, availability of software packages, personnel availability and other staffing challenges, hardware availability and dependencies.

*Q: **Do you understand or try to identify, document, and analyze risks as you are conducting an assessment?***

A: During data collection I also try to collect risk-related information. There are several choices for risk evaluation. One is SEER-SEM's probability inputs, but some customers like to see the risk items identified and quantified. This requires a little more work (and according to an independent study I did several years ago, no more accuracy), but it gives a nice detailed report to the people using the information and allows them to make decisions to mitigate the risk factors. I also ask each person from whom I collect data to identify his or her five top risk items.[15]

Table 2.2 illustrates representative data requirements for the estimate and potential sources where they may be found. If this information is unavailable, the estimate is potentially limited to estimating based on industry or customer sources not specifically tied to the project.

Table 2.2 Potential Data Sources

Data Needed for Software Estimate	Potential Data Sources		
	Developer/ Potential Developer	Acquisition Office (Program Office)	Estimation Team
Software size range (functions, lines, objects)	Best source (closest to requirements definition)		Excellent source; can use program documents to prepare estimates; provides independent evaluation
Amount of new, reused, and COTS software; work required to reuse existing software	Best source (if they are using their own existing software)	May have control over this information if it dictates software that must be reused	Best source if existing software will be provided to contractor
Software development environment: processes, methods, tools, practices	Best source because they will actually do the development	Source selection requirements	Can provide industry standards; extract historical data from contractor; or combination
Capability of development team	Best source if the development team has been selected; knows capabilities that are necessary for team	May be dictated by constraints put on program (e.g., cost, schedule, CMMI required minimum rating)	Can provide industry standards; extract historical data from contractor; or combination
Difficulty of application	Gets information from the requirements specifications	Provided in requirements specifications	Gets information from requirements specifications

Table 2.2 (continued)   Potential Data Sources

| | Potential Data Sources | | |
Data Needed for Software Estimate	Developer/ Potential Developer	Acquisition Office (Program Office)	Estimation Team
Amount and type of documentation required	Gets information from program office	Dictates required specifications	Gets information from contracting/ program office
Project staffing constraints	Best source for providing actual personnel available to work on project		Best source for estimating required personnel to meet cost and schedule constraints
Cost and schedule constraints	Budget and schedule are given by program office; contractor can show expected deviations, if any	Dictates budget and desired and/or required schedule	Can provide alternative development scenarios if desired end product cannot be completed within given constraints
Level of acceptable risk	Can identify factors at risk and show various alternatives for reducing risk	Can decide acceptable risk for cost and schedule	Can identify factors at risk and show various alternatives for reducing risk

Software Data Collection Process

Figure 2.2 illustrates a general process for collecting software data. It assumes sufficient personnel are available to participate in the required interviews and to clarify the data. The text that follows describes what each activity entails.

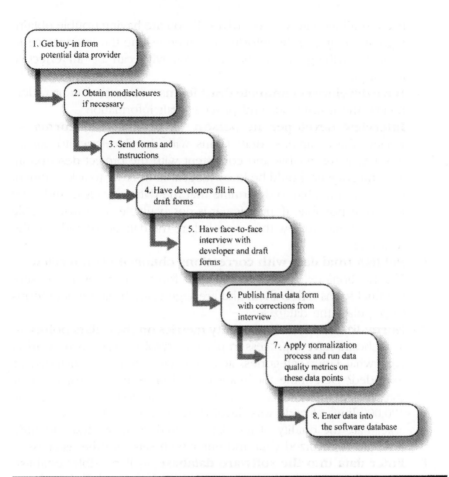

Figure 2.2 Software data collection process.

1. **Get buy-in from potential data provider** — Inform the organization that will provide the information of your needs and persuade them of the value it will bring to the process.

2. **Obtain necessary nondisclosures** — Some organizations may ask for nondisclosure agreements in order to share their data. If possible, the data can be made generic, precluding the need for an agreement. If one is required, start the process early and follow up regularly to ensure you will have access to the data you need.

3. **Send forms and instructions** — When soliciting data, provide the forms as early as possible in both hard copy and electronically to facilitate data collection. Follow up with the recipient to encourage a timely response, realizing that no action will probably be

taken until the interviewer arrives. If you are having trouble obtaining data, filling in the information, then asking the interviewee to correct anything he or she disagrees with can be an effective technique.

4. **Have developers complete draft forms** — Ensure data providers review the instructions and provide draft information.

5. **Interview developer in person to review draft forms** — Review the completed draft forms with the developer to ensure the data is reasonable and consistent with the project description. The interviewer should be knowledgeable in order to ask pertinent questions and able to determine that the data is realistic and valid insofar as possible. If interviewer is not available, a knowledgeable person should review the forms before the data is entered into the database.

6. **Publish final data with corrections obtained via interview** — If corrections or updates to the draft forms are necessary, ensure the final forms reflect them and are segregated from the draft forms to populate the database.

7. **Normalize and run data quality metrics on these data points** — You should have a process in place to resolve issues as they arise, e.g., what labor categories, activities, etc. should be included or excluded? Determine the realism of data points against a set of established metrics. For example, a data point indicating that 100,000 lines of code was developed in one month is not reasonable. Rate the quality of the data to guide your analysts. Identify raw and normalized data and enter both sets into the database.

8. **Enter data into the software database** — If possible, establish a true database in which your data can be stored and analyzed (rather than an ad hoc Excel spreadsheet). This will help to ensure the data is consistent and facilitate configuration management.

Software Data Collection Lessons Learned

Collecting software data can be frustrating for many reasons and may even cause unforeseen problems. Sometimes the data simply does not exist. Those who have the data may not want to provide it for fear of exposing a problem, while others may consider data to be proprietary and will refuse to share it. Through years of experience, we have learned many lessons about how best to collect the data needed. First and foremost, the forms you use to collect the data should be tailored to your organization's specific needs. A sample data collection form can be obtained electronically from www.galorath.com/estimationbook2006.

Clearly define the data you are soliciting — Even if you do provide clear definitions, your respondent may ignore them, but providing clear and detailed definitions will increase your chances of obtaining the data you need.

Send respondents the forms in advance of making a personal visit to interview them — This gives respondents an advanced opportunity to familiarize themselves with the format and scope of the data collection process.

People will not always read the instructions — Even if you provide clear instructions and definitions in the software data collection package, many respondents may ignore them and provide answers with little thought. Some respondents may misrepresent the data intentionally to make themselves look better or complete one form in response to a program and use it inappropriately to respond to other programs.

Respondents may cite proprietary restrictions as excuses for not providing required data — To attempt to overcome this obstacle, ensure the respondent that the data will be made generic so that the program and organization cannot be identified.

Prime contractors will not want to provide subcontractor data — To address this difficult issue, contact subcontractors directly if possible and get their commitments.

Developers can have valid concerns regarding data distribution — Some developers do not want to enable their competitors to determine their productivity and other factors or enable their customers to use certain information in negotiations. Although sanitizing the data can help, you must assure your respondents that you are collecting data to improve the process and your ability to fund programs, not to increase their exposure.

Program offices often do not have required data — Developers are the most probable sources, but be sure the program office understands that the data being collected will improve everyone's ability to estimate and substantiate the project.

Developers may use the cost of data collection as an excuse to not cooperate — If a developer complains of the costs or claims it was not paid to provide data, determine its claimed CMM or CMMI rating. If the developer is assessed at a level 3 or above, it should be collecting data for its own use. Although the developer will likely still resist, ask for the data in the developer's format and offer to complete the form. Some will not have data even though they should.

Use a known good code counter for collecting size of completed software — Although code counters are available on the Web, many have significant defects. Recommend one or two that are known to work, such as the no-cost code counters available from Galorath.com and USC (University of Southern California). The Galorath version is available in source code so it can be compiled on whatever platform is necessary (see Chapter 5 for a more detailed discussion).

Both hard copy and electronic collection forms can be useful — Some organizations prefer hard copy because it facilitates their ability to collect the data, while others prefer electronic to reduce paper use and facilitate editing. In any case, have hard copies available for the interviews.

Be sure to discriminate autogenerated code from hand-generated code — Because autogenerated code does not have the same correlation to effort as hand-generated code, make sure you know what data you are getting.

Do not let a data collection contractor lock up your database — Sometimes a contractor will execute an exclusive nondisclosure agreement with the development contractors that keeps other contractors from seeing the data at all. This situation limits the usefulness of the data.

Collect completed project actuals first — Collect information from completed projects rather than estimates from underway projects. Estimate data is good to have to determine growth and other information, but collect actual data first, if available, for use in forecasting new projects.

Qualify the data quality — Despite your best effort, some data you collect will not make sense. You can eliminate this data, which is not recommended because the data will be lost, or you can mark it with a qualifier. For example, rate it A through F to indicate to your analyst the level of associated risk.

Capture both total size and amount of reuse — Because reuse is an essential part of software size, it is necessary to collect new, reuse, and redesign reimplementation and retest for the reuse from the developers. Total size does not necessarily correlate with effort because it does not indicate the amount of reuse. Simply collecting effective size does not fully indicate size estimation of the delivered systems (the amount of new versus reuse is unknown). You can compute the effective size and add it to the database, but always collect the individual numbers for the reasons indicated.

Make it easy (but not too easy) for the developer to provide the data — You can categorize the data you request as *required, highly desirable*, or *desirable*. Do not ask for so little data that the resulting database is not useful. Make sure the data collection form used is clear and simple.

Do not rely only on past program productivity — The productivity of a completed program should not be used as the basis for a new program because it will not account for the idiosyncrasies of the new program, such as security, rehosting, complexity, entropy, etc. Use productivity to check parametrics and vice versa.

Do not eliminate data points just because of the programming language — Because size can be converted from one language to another, do not eliminate data points that are not in your language of interest.

Ensure that COTS items really are COTS — Developers will sometimes include items in their sizes that were not developed (COTS or other high quality reusable software application) by this application to make their projects look bigger. Separate such items in the database so project size is not inflated or misstated.

Nondisclosure agreements — It is much easier to have non-disclosure agreements approved when companies use their own internal templates.[16]

No-destruction clauses — When NDAs are provided, the data collector must make sure that there are no clauses that require the destruction of the data after a certain period of time or intellectual property clauses that may jeopardize the status of the model being used.[17]

Implement a process to normalize the data and store it in both raw and normalized forms — Collected data will likely describe varying phases, labor categories, size definitions, etc. Keep this raw data in the database. You should implement and rigorously follow a standard, well documented process to normalize the data to a standard set of activities, phases, etc.

Have a structure for data storage — Although you can use an Excel spreadsheet to capture data, it will become unwieldy as the database grows and your data entry personnel can easily enter data in the wrong format. Develop an open database as soon as practical.

Offer your respondents something in return as an incentive if possible for cases where a data product is being developed — You could offer them a sanitized copy of the database (if you can obtain buy-in across the domain), or at least offer a benchmark that shows how their data fits with the rest of the database.

During the collection process, project management should:

- Identify the activities necessary to accomplish the project's purpose.
- Determine dependencies among activities.

- Define a schedule for conducting the required activities.
- Define and locate the resources needed to accomplish the activities and determine how much they will cost (by resource or category).
- Monitor and control the resources in order to achieve the required result on schedule.

Prioritizing Estimation Effort

If you lack the time to complete all the activities described in the ten-step process, use the following list to help prioritize the estimation effort:

- Spend the bulk of the time available on sizing (sizing databases and tools like SEER-AccuScope can help save time in this process).
- Using an automated software cost and schedule tool like SEER-SEM can provide the analyst with time-saving tools (SEER-SEM knowledge bases save time in the data collection process).
- Use ranges (least, likely, and most) for the inputs.
- Outputs and results should be presented as most likely and as risks to bound the uncertainties associated with the estimated.

Summary

This chapter provided an overview of the ten-step project estimation process. It focused on the first three steps of the process and provided a set of lessons learned that can aid in the data collection process. The succeeding chapters address the remaining seven steps in the process and venture into other important areas of software cost, size, schedule, and risk.

Endnotes

1. Stutzke, Richard D. *Estimating Software-Intensive Systems*. Upper Saddle River: Pearson Education Inc., 2005.
2. DeMarco, Tom. *Controlling Software Projects: Management, Measurement, and Estimation*. Englewood Cliffs: Yourdon Press, 1998.
3. Florac, William A., Robert Park, and Anita D. Carleton. *Practical Software Measurement: Measuring for Process Management and Improvement*. Pittsburgh: Carnegie Mellon Software Engineering Institute, 1997.
4. Software Program Managers Network. *Sixteen Critical Software Practices: Program Manager's Guide Based on the 16-Point Plan and Related Metrics*. Ver. 1.0. Chesapeake: American Systems Corporation, 2002.

5. Schedule compression involves a reduction in the overall duration of project, without reducing the project scope.
6. CPI represents how much work was performed for each dollar spent, or "bang for the buck." When CPI has a value of 1.0, the project team is delivering a dollar of planned work for each dollar of cost. When CPI is less than 1.0, there is a possible productivity problem. For example, a CPI of .80 means that you received 80 cents' worth of planned work for each dollar you paid in cost. A CPI of less than 1.0 may indicate that the project team did not perform as well as expected or that the original budget was too aggressive for the amount of work to be performed.
7. SPI indicates performance as compared to the schedule. The CPI and SPI indices represent the standard cost and schedule performance measures for both government and industry. The closer the CPI and SPI are to a value of 1.00, the more successful a project can be considered, at least in terms of cost and schedule. These metrics help establish performance baselines against which a project can compare actual performance data.
8. TCPI must be used in conjunction with CPI. TCPI should be compared with CPI to determine how realistic the most recent estimated total cost (EAC) is for a project. Note that CPI measures the average historic productivity to date. If TCPI is greater than CPI or, stated differently, if the ratio of the two measures is less than 1, then the project team is anticipating an efficiency improvement to make it more productive.
9. McConnell, Steve. Adapted with permission from "Ten Deadly Sins of Software Estimation." in the Software Developers Conference. Wellington and Melbourne, 2002; and Steve MConnell, *Software Estimation: Demystifying the Black Art*. Redmond, WA: Microsoft Press, 2006.
10. May, Lorin J. "Major Causes of Software Project Failures." *Crosstalk: The Journal of Defense Software Engineering*, July 1998.
11. Evans Michael, Alex Abela, and Tom Beltz. "Seven Characteristics of Dysfunctional Software Projects." *CrossTalk: The Journal of Defense Software Engineering*, April 2002.
12. Stutzke, Richard D. "How To Prepare Good Software Estimates." Software Technology Conference, Salt Lake City, 2000.
13. Ghezzi, C., M. Jazayeri, and D. Mandrioli. *Fundamentals of Software Engineering*. Englewood Cliffs: Prentice Hall, 1991.
14. Putnam, Lawrence H., and Ware Meyers. *Industrial Strength Software, Effective Management Using Measurement*. Washington, D.C.: IEEE Computer Press, 1997. 55.
15. Galorath, Judy. Personal interview, July 2005.
16. Valerdi, R. "Lessons Learned From Collecting Systems Engineering Data." Second Annual Conference on Systems Engineering Research. Hoboken, 2004.
17. Valerdi, R. "Lessons Learned From Collecting Systems Engineering Data." Second Annual Conference on Systems Engineering Research. Hoboken. 2004.

Chapter 3

Executing the Estimate

Everything should be made as simple as possible, but not simpler.

Albert Einstein

Introduction and Chapter Goal

The goal of this chapter is to discuss the work required to actually generate an estimate. The steps involved include sizing the software, generating the actual software project estimate, and performing risk/uncertainty analysis.

Step Four: Software Sizing

"One of the most important steps in any software estimate is to predict the size of the deliverables that must be constructed."[1] In order for size estimates to be accurate, the analyst must possess a significant understanding of the project and the application or at least its relative size. Size is generally the most significant cost and schedule driver. However, it is important to understand that many other factors in addition to size form the basis of accurate software estimates. These include project labor rates, requirements, the required schedule, customer expectations, and costs associated with nonlabor activities among many others.

Overall scope of a software project is defined by identifying not only the amount of new software that must be developed, but also must include the amount of preexisting, COTS, and other software that will be integrated into the new system. In addition to estimating product size, you will need to estimate any rework that will be required to develop the product, which will generally be expressed as source lines of code (SLOC) or function points (FPs), although there are other possible units of measure. The size estimate should be expressed as a range, least size (smallest it could be), likely (size it is expected to be), and most (largest it could be). These ranges will help to establish the overall uncertainty. At this point in the process, you should have enough information to confirm your assumptions regarding the reuse of software, the benefits to be gained by using COTS, and enough information to bound the uncertainty of your assumptions.

Predicting Size

Whenever possible, start the process of size estimation using formal descriptions of the requirements such as the customer's requirements specification or request for proposal, a system specification, or a software requirements specification. Even if you do not have a formal document (and often you may have only a verbal description or a whiteboard outline), you must make an initial project estimate and communicate its levels of risk and uncertainty to all concerned. You should reestimate the project as soon as more scope information is determined. During later phases of the project's life cycle, you can use design documents to provide additional detail and use your initial estimate as a useful baseline upon which to base the later estimate. The most widely used methods of estimating product size are:

- **Expert opinion** — This is an estimate based on recollection of prior systems and assumptions regarding what will happen with this system, and the experts' past experience.
- **Analogy** — The analogy estimation method follows these rough guidelines:
  - Understand the system to be estimated as well as possible.
  - Obtain descriptions and accurate sizes for as many similar systems as you can. Try to match the level of detail for the target system, that is, if you know the system being estimated down to its functions, then comparisons to it are also best made at the functional level.
  - Compare each proposed component to known components, finding the closest match.
  - Most matches will be approximate. Therefore, for each closest match, make additional size adjustments as necessary. For example, if the proposed component looks slightly less complicated

than the known component, adjust the size of the proposed component downward.

A relative sizing approach such as SEER-AccuScope™ can provide viable size ranges based on comparisons to known projects. Alternatively, other characteristics may be reasonable early predictors of size. For example, in some development organizations, a software program may generally range from 20K SLOC to 60K SLOC. If the developers estimate that a particular project will amount to five software programs, it can reasonably be expected that the project will average out to about 100K SLOC to 300K SLOC.

■ **Formalized methodology** — Use of automated tools and/or pre-defined algorithms such as counting the number of subsystems or classes and converting them to function points.

■ **Statistical sizing** — This method provides a range of potential sizes that is characterized by *least*, *likely*, and *most*. In our experience with this method, it is best to initially ask a developer, "What do you think the size of the product will be?" and record that answer. Then, ask the developer, "What is the best case (if everything goes right)?" Most often the answers to these first two questions will be the same. Now, ask the developer again for the expected size of the product, then ask, "Does your estimate account for any unanticipated problems that the software will need to correct, such as fixing hardware problems or addressing anomaly conditions?" The developer will often answer, "No." You are using this methodology to bound the risk. You can continue this exercise by asking, "What if everything that can go wrong does?" If you account for this extreme condition, you can be 99 percent assured that the size of the product will not exceed this estimate. Of course, when your analyst realizes that the original estimate was nowhere near accurate, she may want to take a little revenge. She may think, "If everything goes wrong and we have to rewrite the operating system and enter it back into the computer in binary, the size will be X!" This, of course, is way beyond the 99 percent probability. We really want to know the largest size this software reasonably can be. The end result of this exercise should be:

– Least = What is the best case?
– Likely = What is the expected size?*
– Most = What is the worst case size — including things that may go wrong?

---

* Asked the second time.

One way to use the statistical sizing method works as follows. Use the following formula to determine the expected value:

$$\text{Expected value} = [\text{Least} + (4 \times \text{Likely}) + \text{Most}]/6$$

The standard deviation of the expected value shown above will be:

$$\text{Standard deviation} = \text{Most} - \text{Least}$$

With the standard deviation known, and using the normal "bell curve" probability table, you can calculate expected size at any probability level. For example, if you want to find a prospective size figure for which the actual size has a 70 percent probability of being lower than the estimated size, you would do the following:

1. Use a normal probability table (or the corresponding function in an electronic spreadsheet) to look up the value corresponding to 70 percent.
2. Multiply this value by the standard deviation.
3. Take the resulting number and add it to the expected value. The result is projected size at the 70 percent probability or confidence level.

Of the many metrics available to measure software, size metrics are most widely used; the most widely accepted software size metrics are SLOC and function points. In our experience, both can be effectively used to measure product size. Alternatively a binormal distribution will more accurately reflect the skew toward larger size estimates.

Size Estimation Approaches

Approaches to size estimation can generally be characterized as: bottom-up and top-down. Estimation by expert opinion, analogy, or cost model can employ a top-down or bottom-up approach, but decomposition is inherently a top-down (i.e., starting with the entire software program and decomposing it into smaller pieces) method. No matter which approach you choose, the two predominant sizing measures are SLOC and function points.

■ SLOC are straightforward measures of the number of lines of *programmed code* in an item of software. SLOC was among the first, and remains the most common, sizing measure because lines can be very easily and precisely — even automatically — counted. The SLOC method provides a firm indication of the volume of software developed, which is a critical first step in making comparisons and predictions. SLOC estimates are most accurate at the end of a project when lines of code can be counted. At project start, when few accurate project descriptors exist, the SLOC may have a wide range in its least, likely, and most values.

■ Function Points — SLOC has been criticized as being too indiscriminate, in that it is simply a measure of size and does not specifically indicate how much functionality an item of software contains. Furthermore, it is not easy to estimate the number of lines of code before they have been written. Function points provide a logical (functional) unit of measure (size) for the software functions of a system as seen by the user. They provide the essential value of what the software is and what it does with data from a user's point of view. It includes internal logical files, external interface files, external inputs, external outputs, and external inquires. Its power comes from the emphasis on the external point of view. Function points alone do not capture the impacts of requirements volatility and scope creep (additional requirements).

You can also use estimation methods, such as the SEER function-based sizing method, to approximate functions without requiring function point training. Additionally, for algorithmic intense systems, SEER function-based sizing captures the functionality not included in traditional function points. (See Chapter 6 for a detailed discussion of SEER function-based sizing.)

Deciding on a Metric

Both SLOC and function points metrics are uniquely powerful, are useful, and can be used individually or in combination. Each has its own strengths and weaknesses. Table 3.1 provides an overview of both metrics.

You can use Table 3.1 to compare the characteristics of each metric and as a guide to decide which to use. It should be noted that in order to count function points you must have resources in house that are trained in function point analysis or hire knowledgeable consultants. It generally takes one to two weeks to learn basic function point counting skills, and a trainee must count a few thousand function points to become adept with this method.

To date, no reliable automatic function point counter has been developed that can accurately count function points of development artifacts; counts must either be compiled by hand or estimated using a sizing model such as SEER-AccuScope. New product SEER enhancements automatically extract artifacts from use case models in order to arrive at an estimate early in the development process that expresses a range of software size.[2] This capability will augment other sizing methods, serve as a sanity check of other sizing methods, and provide an entry in the size methodology table.

Table 3.1 Estimation Measures

Issue	Source Lines of Code	Function Points
Nature of metric	Quantitative: simply a count of existing lines	Quantitative and qualitative: takes the software's final functionality into account
Consistency of independent estimates	Consistent if SLOC counting standards are followed Potentially inconsistent if poor or undocumented definitions are used	Potentially inconsistent; two counters may estimate the same project differently
Dependence on development implementation methods	Dependent: must be adjusted for factors such as language and approach	Independent; tied to basic specifications
Adjustments for implementation complexity	Unadjusted; unless represented with other complexity measures, significance of any given size is not clearly represented	Adjusted (for adjusted function point counts only); complexity adjustments are built in; however, these adjustments may be too arbitrary
Work-up speed	Fast: can be done automatically for existing systems	Slow: requires training and experience; there are approximation methods which can be used quickly
Comprehension	Easy: analogous to a basic measure of volume	Harder: function point definition not well understood by managers
Usefulness	Basic measure of productivity	A more elaborate measure of productivity
Estimation accuracy	Accurate: final counts have been shown to be highly accurate; this simple size metric does not miss anything as long as hand-generated lines are segregated from autogenerated lines and new lines are distinguished from reuse lines	Generally accurate; may be as accurate; however, standard function points do not address some highly algorithmic functionality

Table 3.1 (continued) Estimation Measures

Issue	Source Lines of Code	Function Points
Postmortem use	Useful; easy to compare before-and-after results	Useful: easy to compare before-and-after results; easy to see exactly where variation occurred
Expense of estimate	Low: rapid and very inexpensive	Moderate to high; slower and potentially expensive
Ability to estimate with automated tools	High: tools such as SEER-AccuScope can estimate lines with relative ease	High; tools such as SEER-AccuScope can estimate function points with relative ease

When to Use SLOC

SLOC has been the dominant method for sizing complicated, real time or embedded systems and works well for hand-generated systems in general. Use lines of code when SLOC-based historical data exists, when the development organization is comfortable with SLOC estimates, when add-ons to existing systems allow counting of actual SLOC in a system, and as a relatively easy check on other methods.

The great strength of SLOC is that it is easy to obtain. All other factors aside, it remains a fairly accurate predictor of development effort. By comparing code counts from past projects against a "rough order of magnitude" estimate for a proposed project, you can gain your first real understanding of project scope. By pairing SLOC estimates with other development factors, you will generally have enough information to develop a reliable estimate.

SLOC counts provide a firm indication of the volume of software generated, which is a first critical step for making comparisons and predictions. Despite the dominance of SLOC measures, some confusion exists regarding *which types* of lines to count, which has led to difficulty in comparing methods of counting SLOC. However, within the past several years, code counting methods have become more standardized. See Chapter 5 for a detailed discussion of lines of code.

When to Use Function Points

It is best to develop estimates based on function points when your project is largely comprised of information technology and the system's functions are adequately specified. Alternatively, you can estimate a function point count using other means such as SEER-AccuScope to estimate size. In addition, you should use function points when sizing by SLOC could be misleading. For example, code generators can automatically generate many lines of code, which makes the number of lines generated an unreliable predictor of the amount of effort required. The great strength of function point counts is that they are developed directly from specifications, independent of implementation, which means estimates of project scope are more comparable across projects.

Counting function points is a sophisticated method that cannot be done automatically. There are few shortcuts; you must ensure that it will be done properly by assigning adequately trained and experienced personnel. If you have counts from previous similar projects, be sure to study those counts carefully to ensure that the work performed on your current project is consistent with the method used on those projects. Although experienced counters can accomplish this method fairly quickly and efficiently, it is very important that the counts be performed correctly and consistently.

The function point counting process should be put in perspective. An experienced function point counter is usually able to count project specifications amounting to about 600 function points per day. As a typical MIS database project of this size might take a bit more than a year to develop and consume a bit more than a hundred person-months of effort, using function points does not necessarily involve a big investment in upfront planning. Many large organizations therefore keep a function point counter on staff or hire outside consultants when necessary. By using the SEER function-based sizing method, function points can be estimated without conducting detailed counts. Finally, it is important to understand that a combination of SLOC and function-based sizing can be the most appropriate way of estimating the size of an existing system to which functional enhancements are being made.

Steps to Estimating Software Size

Managers of software development projects are responsible for ascertaining progress, risk, productivity, and a host of other factors that are critical to success of their projects. Two important factors are the size of the product and the subsequent effort that will be required to develop it. If you want to contain the risk of unexpected cost growth for your project, it is essential that you use a software sizing method that is consistent and repeatable.

In order to usefully apply the general concepts and techniques of managing risk to your software engineering project, it is also essential that you regularly reestimate the size of the product and the associated cost of the project as project conditions change or product specifications are modified. Unless the size estimates reflect the true state of the product (or at least the range), you cannot assume that your estimates are accurate and thus the analyses that flow from them will be suspect. The techniques used to estimate effort and schedule also provide the foundation for effective software management and many of the measures managers need to carry out their responsibilities.

By applying the sizing steps described below, you can make consistent and relevant size projections and use them to derive cost estimates.

Sizing Step 1: Baseline Definition of the Size Metric You Will Use

There are numerous idiosyncrasies in using any size metric (i.e., Function Points Version 3, Mark II Function Points, Function Points Version 4, Feature Points). Identify the definition that will be used for the current project and a normalization process that will be used if size information is provided in a format different from the definition chosen.

Sizing Step 2: Define Sizing Objectives

Accurate size estimates are needed to support the software project estimate for cost and schedule at any point during the software development lifecycle. Examples of the major objectives are:

■ **Product/portfolio planning** — A rough-order-of-magnitude (ROM) can be completed using the limited documentation and time available.
■ **Project budgeting** — A more detailed size estimate that describes individual computer programs. A more detailed statement of objectives for the software should be available for use at this point.
■ **Major milestone project planning** — Increased detail in the size estimate. Software can be broken into detailed components including the use of COTS and preexisting software to be reused. At least a strawman software architecture should exist at this point to assist in the size estimation process.
■ **Detailed project planning** — Increased detail and decomposition of size for day-to-day management of a project. A detailed definition of the project, including work packages or something similar, should be available for use in the size estimation exercise.
■ **Project tracking and replanning** — Adjusting the size estimates based on project dynamics, e.g., requirements growth increases the software size estimates.

If all of the functions the software must perform are analyzed in detail up front, it is less likely that you will fail to size the less notable components.

It is imperative that you understand the job at hand, the basic tendency to underestimate software size, and that you apply this understanding as you conduct the necessary software sizing activities.

Sizing Step 3: Plan Data and Resource Requirements

If you treat the software sizing activity as a small project, then you will generate an estimation plan early in the process. The plan need be nothing more than a set of preliminary notes covering the who, what, why, where, when, and how much of the sizing activity.

Sizing Step 4: Identify and Evaluate Software Requirements

It is helpful to have a set of software specifications that are as unambiguous as possible (which of course are subject to qualifications with respect to the estimating objectives). This documentation can help provide a definition of the scope of the software to be sized. In lieu of this documentation, at least a statement of concept or objectives is needed.

Sizing Step 5: Use Several Independent Techniques and Sources

Kathleen Peters noted that:

> None of the different techniques for software sizing is better than the others from all aspects, their strengths and weaknesses are complementary. It is important to use a combination of techniques in order to avoid the weakness of any single method and to capitalize on their joint strengths. Just as different techniques provide better results, attacking estimator differences through use of Delphi techniques will address bias and other differences between estimators. Use several different people to estimate and use several different estimation techniques (using an estimation tool should be considered as one of the techniques), and compare the results. Look at the convergence or spread among the estimates. Convergence tells you that you've probably got a good estimate. Spread means that there are probably things that have been overlooked and that you need to understand better. The Delphi approach or Wideband Delphi can be used to gather and discuss estimates using a group of people, the intention being to produce an accurate, unbiased estimate.[3]

Figure 3.1 depicts the Galorath sizing methodology. Size estimates and data are collected in as many different ways as possible. The results from

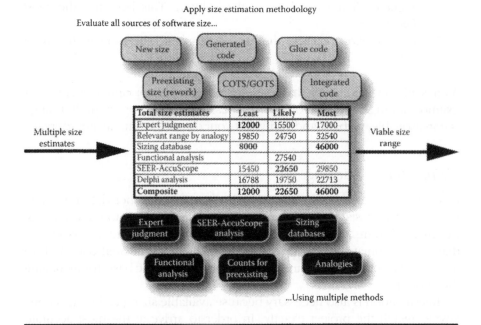

Apply size estimation methodology

Evaluate all sources of software size...

Total size estimates	Least	Likely	Most
Expert judgment	12000	15500	17000
Relevant range by analogy	19850	24750	32540
Sizing database	8000		46000
Functional analysis		27540	
SEER-AccuScope	15450	22650	29850
Delphi analysis	16788	19750	22713
Composite	12000	22650	46000

Multiple size estimates →

Viable size range →

...Using multiple methods

Figure 3.1   Galorath size methodology estimation measures.

each of these sources is entered into a table. With all of the data points in one place, you are ready to convert all of these data points into a size estimate.

1. Collect size estimates from as many different sources as possible, such as:
   - Expert judgment
   - Analogy/sizing database
   - Functional analysis
   - Delphi analysis
   - Sizing tools
2. Rank the data sources for each data point in order of reliability.
3. The smallest size in the *least* column is deleted from the group. This is done because history has shown that size is rarely underestimated.
4. If the *most* column contains a number that is extremely out of range from the other numbers in that column, it is deleted also. (This rarely happens, and if the source of the data point is the most reliable source, the data point would not be thrown out.)
5. Choose the remaining smallest number in the least column for the *least* size.
6. Choose from the *likely* column the number from your most reliable source or, alternatively, depending on the reliability of the source,

average all the numbers in the column. This becomes the *most likely* size.

7. For the *most*, choose the largest number remaining in the *most* column.

As a sanity check, verify that the size ranges are not unreasonable (for example a range of 2,000 to 500,000 lines) for a single program. If a range is unreasonable, go back and verify that your data selections are appropriate.

Sizing Step 6: Tracking

Once a software project is started, it is essential to gather data regarding its actual size, costs, and progress, and compare this data to the estimates. Because software sizing is based on imperfect information, it is critical that you reestimate the product size periodically with actual data both to improve the sizing models and to obtain a more realistic basis for managing the project.

Reestimation is also necessary because available sizing techniques don't always match the project exactly. In order to arrive at the most accurate estimates as the project progresses, you will need feedback. Software projects tend to be volatile (components are added, split up, re-scoped, or combined in unforeseeable ways as the project progresses); the project manager must identify these changes and realistically update the projected product size.

Sizing Databases

Sizing databases for both defense and commercial projects exist and may be useful for understanding the basic size ranges for the type of project you are estimating. Because analogy estimates rely on good historical data, sizing databases are good tools for comparing the actual code counts of past projects to the software that you must estimate. However, because the detailed specifications for these projects are not provided, it is not possible to conduct detailed comparison-based sizing.

Proprietary in-house sizing databases can include much more relevant information about past projects. If your organization does not already have such a database, you should consider establishing one. Not only can internal sizing databases have very specific and revealing contents, but they describe work that *your organization* has done — such databases are clearly appropriate for future internal estimates and should contain, for instance:

- Project name
- Description of program
- Detailed description of each module
- Description of key features, such as the number of inputs, outputs, screens, and files
- Rating categories that are commonly found in software estimating models
- A quantitative appraisal of each module's features using, for example, function points
- Actual size of completed program and/or modules

The payoff for time spent establishing an internal software sizing database that includes both size estimates and summary specifications for completed projects comes with the very first estimate. As you refine the database, you can increase its granularity and add entries that describe not only whole programs but lower level modules as well, which will enable you to make more accurate comparisons. A well developed sizing database will also enable you to produce detailed bottom-up estimates significantly more quickly than if you had to develop such estimates from scratch.

Legacy Software Rework

The maxim for software is that not all code is created *at once*. In fact, use of preexisting or legacy code that has a definite cost associated with it and the rework required are substantial issues in many development projects. Rework encompasses the effort required to understand the legacy code, modify it to a new project, and retest it once it is incorporated. Rework is composed of three basic activities that are typically expressed in terms of percentage:

- Redesign
- Reimplementation
- Retest

Applying rework percentages to preexisting software measures results in an *effective volume* measure that describes rework effort in terms of what effort would be required to develop new lines of code. See Chapter 8, "Software Reuse and Commercial Off-the-Shelf Software," for a detailed discussion of software reuse.

Table 3.2 Lessons Learned from Software Sizing Efforts

Size Mistake	Consequence
Failure to spend sufficient time on software sizing	Size estimates do not reflect the program; programs overrun cost and schedule estimates
Failure to use clear definitions of size	Size measures are unreliable for cost and schedule estimates
Failure to consider size growth in estimates or reducing size estimates to achieve desired costs	Optimistic schedules and costs; programs overrun
Ignoring historical estimates as basis for analogy due to differences in languages and methodology	Lost opportunity to forecast future better from the past

Sizing Number of Functions to Be Learned, Used and Integrated for COTS

When your project is integrating a COTS product, your software estimate should only include that portion of the COTS product your project will actually use. For example, if your project is using a small set of a COTS product's large library of function calls or visual tools, in estimating the size of your product you would only count the set your product actually uses. You should also count only those portions of the overall architecture that your product will use. Some COTS packages may be intended as developer's tools, for example, as debuggers and editors, but not for installment in final deliverables. Of course, you would not count these in estimating the size of your product. For a full treatment of COTS sizing issues, see Chapter 8.

There are other considerations regarding the use of COTS or reused components in making size estimates. Often the developer does not have the source code, so using measures such as SLOC is not feasible. Of course, function points can be counted for COTS systems, but in estimating the required size and effort, remember the developer needs only to understand, integrate, and test that portion of a component's interfaces and functionality that is actually used. Table 3.2 identifies sizing mistakes and their consequences.

Step Five: Prepare Baseline Estimate

Capers Jones noted that good cost estimators generally estimate the cost of a project within 20 percent of the actual cost at delivery. According to

Jones, a good schedule estimate should be within 5 percent of actual schedule at least 95 percent of the time and should not underestimate the actual schedule by more than 12 percent.[4] SEER-SEM users have documented accuracy within ±5 percent.[5]

An estimate must be adequate to the task at hand, consistent, repeatable, and accurately describe what it will actually take to accomplish a project. If the estimate does not have all of these characteristics, the resulting budgets and schedules will be based on bad information and you most likely will find it impossible to perform within these constraints. Given the importance of the estimation task, developers who want to improve their software estimation skills should understand and embrace some basic practices. First, trained, experienced, and skilled people should be assigned to size the software and prepare the estimates. Second, it is critically important that they be given the proper technology and tools. And third, the project manager must define and implement a mature, documented, and repeatable estimation process, which is at least as important as the quality of the people assigned and the technology they use.

To prepare the baseline estimate there are various approaches that can be used, including guessing, using existing productivity data exclusively, the bottom-up approach, expert judgment, and cost models. Table 1.1 in Chapter 1 summarized the advantages and disadvantages of these approaches.

Guessing — This may be the most common approach. However, guesses are almost always incorrect. Pure guessing should be avoided.

Estimating exclusively from productivity data — To obtain a cost estimate, some analysts will divide the estimated size of their application by some nominal productivity data that has been established from completed projects. This approach assumes that the organization's productivity is constant and ignores entropy (the bigger the program is, the lower the productivity will be). This approach can work if the domain is very stable and the applications are of similar size and use similar technology, and if the same or similar people and tools are used to develop the new application. However, if any of these factors do not pertain to your new project, this approach is bound to be highly inaccurate. Alternatively, the analysts can make adjustments based on the differences between past projects and the one being estimated. For example, they could increase the estimate by 10 percent if new tools are being used, decrease it by 15 percent if seasoned personnel have been assigned, etc. This technique leads to a kind of home-grown parametric model, but one that lacks the robustness of a commercially available model.

To ensure the validity of the projections, all three elements: people, technology, and process, must be incorporated into the effort. It is not enough that skilled people be assigned if they are given improper tools or use a poorly defined process.

Brad Clark, in "Quantifying the Effect of Process Improvement," has a startling message for more process-oriented readers:

> A one-CMM level improvement by itself accounts for only an 11 percent increase in productivity. In comparing medium-size projects (100,000 lines of code), the one with the worst process will require 1.43 times as much effort as the one with the best process, all other things being equal. In other words, the maximum influence of process maturity on a project's productivity is 1.43.[6]

Software Productivity Laws

The following list describes the laws of software productivity. These laws help explain the dynamics of an engineering development project. These are used in models such as SEER-SEM to estimate schedule and cost. These laws illustrate some of the reasons that just using productivity to estimate is inadequate.[7] Figure 3.2 illustrates a staffing profile for use in conjunction with the software productivity laws.

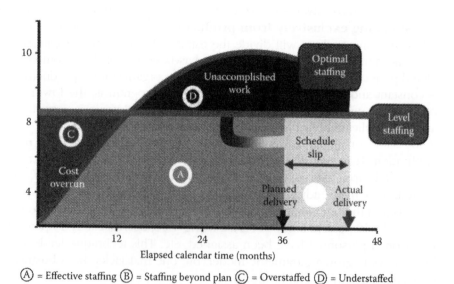

(A) = Effective staffing (B) = Staffing beyond plan (C) = Overstaffed (D) = Understaffed

Figure 3.2 Staffing profile. (© Galorath Incorporated, 2003. Reprinted with permission.)

Law 1 — Smaller teams are more efficient. The smaller the team, the higher the productivity of each individual person. Theoretically the most efficient team from an effort viewpoint is two people working closely together. Of course, schedules could not be met for most systems with such a small team.

Law 2 — Some schedule compression can be bought. Adding people to a project, to a point, decreases the time and increases the cost as larger teams work together.

Law 3 — Every project has a minimum time. There is an incremental person who consumes more energy than he or she produces. Team size beyond this point decreases productivity and increases time. (Law 3 is also known as Brooks' law.)

Law 4 — Productivity is scalable. Projects of larger software size can use larger teams without violating Law 3.

Law 5 — Complexity limits staffing. As complexity increases, the number of people that can effectively work on the project and the rate at which they can be added decreases.

Law 6 — Staffing can be optimized. There exists an optimal staffing function (shape) that is generally modeled by the Rayleigh function. Flat (level of effort) staffing is rarely optimal.

Law 7 — Projects that get behind, stay behind. It is extremely difficult to bring a project that is behind schedule back on plan.

Law 8 — Work expands to fill the available volume. It is possible to allow too much time to complete a project. (Law 8 is also known as Parkinson's law.)

Law 9 —Better technology yields higher productivity. More capable teams, better tools, and advanced, stable processes yield higher productivity.

Law 10 — There are no silver bullets. There is no methodology, tool, or process improvement strategy available that yields revolutionary improvements in project efficiency.

In order to determine the effort that will be required to complete your project, you will need information that describes the personnel who are available — in terms of their qualifications and the optimal composition of the team — and you will need to develop an initial estimate of how long it will take them to fulfill the project requirements. Productivity is a measure of the effectiveness of an organization in producing *units of measure* (that are based on the units used to size the product) over a given period. In the most basic terms, productivity is simply a measure of software production expressed as SLOC or function points one person can produce in an hour, a week, or a month. There is a base productivity figure that reflects what individual team members could perform if their only job was to produce software.

Table 3.3 summarizes the relative impact that SEER-SEM technology and environment parameters have on a developer's potential for productivity on the specific program being evaluated. This table is effective in isolating the effects of different cost drivers on the overall estimate. These numbers illustrate the full impact of each parameter on effective technology. Impacts on cost are somewhat larger but similar in scope. For example, the impact of programmer capabilities from worst to best is 67 percent.

Table 3.4 provides a second view of the effects of cost drivers extracted from the COCOMO II model. When these are input into the estimation process or into the cost model, they modify the productivity projections the model provides to reflect the specifics of the project.

As can be seen from these two examples changing the way that a project is planned and modifying certain product assumptions can have a dramatic effect on both the projected productivity and the projected cost. Adapting the process productivity projections to the realities of the application and organization is critical if your projections of required effort are to be realistic.

In projecting staff productivity, you must also consider the effect that certain factors related to the dynamics of your team and the environment in which they will be performing the product development will have on the productivity of your staff. Much useful work has been done on the effect of team dynamics on the productivities of individuals who comprise the team. Landmark works such as the *Team Handbook*,[10] *Peopleware: Productive Projects and Teams*,[11] and others have pointed out that the formation, performance, and enlightened management of "jelled teams" can lead to significant productivity benefits. As Grady Booch wrote:

> Staffing a project with the right people who have the right skills is important, but that alone does not explain the differences in productivity one sees among such teams. In this context, DeMarco and Lister speak of a 'jelled team,' which they define as 'a group of people so strongly knit that the whole is greater than the sum of the parts. The productivity of such a team is greater than that of the same people working in unjelled form. Once a team begins to jell, the probability of success goes up dramatically.' Essential to the formation of jelled teams is this precondition: a project must honor and respect the role of every one of its developers. This means that each project must recognize that its developers are not interchangeable parts, and that each brings to the table unique skills and idiosyncrasies that must be matched to the needs at hand and calibrated within the organization's development culture. This is one of the five

Table 3.3   Approximate Effective Technology Offsets in SEER-SEM[8]

Parameter	Relative Contribution (Percent)	Parameter	Relative Contribution (Percent)
Security requirements	347	Resource dedication	25
Rehost from development to target	93	Process volatility	24
Analyst capabilities	71	Specification level; reliability	22
Programmer capabilities	67	Logon through hardcopy turnaround	22
Time constraints	60	Real time code	21
Practices and methods experience/ process improvement	47	Test level	21
Requirements volatility	47	Host system volatility	19
Product reusability	44	Target system volatility	16
Analyst's application experience/ application class complexity	40	Host development system experience/ complexity	15
Automated tool use	35	Multiple site development	24
Memory constraints	33	Terminal response time	13
Modern development practices	31	Special display requirements	11
Programmer's language experience/ language complexity	30	Target system experience/ complexity	7
Resource and support location	28	QA level	6

Table 3.4   Example COCOMO II Cost Drivers[9]

Attribute	Rating					
	VL	*LO*	*NM*	*HI*	*VH*	*XH*
Required reliability (RELY)	0.82	0.92	1.00	1.10	1.26	
Database size (DATA)		0.90	1.00	1.14	1.28	
Product complexity (CPLX)	0.73	0.87	1.00	1.17	1.34	1.74
Required reusability (RUSE)		0.95	1.00	1.07	1.15	1.24
Documentation required (DOCU)	0.81	0.91	1.00	1.11	1.23	
Execution time constraints (TIME)			1.00	1.11	1.29	1.63
Main storage constraint (STOR)			1.00	1.05	1.17	1.46
Platform volatility (PVOL)		0.87	1.00	1.15	1.30	
Analyst capability (ACAP)	1.42	1.19	1.00	0.85	0.71	
Applications experience (APEX)	1.22	1.10	1.00	0.88	0.81	
Programmer capability (PCAP)	1.34	1.15	1.00	0.88	0.76	
Personnel continuity (PCON)	1.29	1.12	1.00	0.90	0.81	
Platform experience (PLEX)	1.19	1.09	1.00	0.91	0.85	
Language and tools experience (LTEX)	1.20	1.09	1.00	0.91	0.84	
Use of software tools (TOOL)	1.17	1.09	1.00	0.90	0.78	
Multiple site development (SITE)	1.22	1.09	1.00	0.93	0.86	0.80
Required development schedule (SCED)	1.43	1.14	1.00	1.00	1.00	

VL = very low; productivity effects minimal or negative.
LO = low; productivity impact negligible, little or no offset.
NM = normal; productivity scaled to cost driver.
HI = high; nominal impacts to productivity.
VH = very high; significant productivity impacts.
XH = extra high; high productivity impact.

basic principles of software staffing that Boehm describes: 'fit the tasks to the skills and motivation of the people available.'[12]

Productivity can improve dramatically if you do have a team that jells and continues to produce at a high level, and you will see other benefits as well. Staff attrition will be minimal and your team will be absolutely focused on its goals, such as the established quality targets. However, a jelled team in and of itself will not necessarily lead to improved productivity. If it is not managed effectively, you can also see dramatic negative effects on productivity. If there is no effective organizational framework that honors and respects the role of every one of its developers, chaos can result. For example, attrition may be high for your best people, those who can find other work.

If you are forced to compress your schedule because you assumed a level of productivity that did not occur, excessive overtime and further attrition will result and morale will become a joke. The point is that you cannot foresee early in a project how your team dynamics will play out as the project proceeds. Although management often likes to flatter itself and its customers on the ability to form a smoothly functioning team and assumes a high level of productivity in an initial estimate, simple prudence dictates that you should estimate normal productivity factors based on historical performance. If you do indeed achieve higher productivity, then significant benefits will accrue to your project and your reputation as a manager.

Table 3.5 summarizes some of the team and environmental factors you should consider when addressing team productivity. These factors, which are included in the cost models, provide realistic examples of cost factors that can be safely applied.

Table 3.5 Team and Environmental Productivity Factors

Attribute	Description
Application domain	Knowledge of the application domain is essential for effective software development; engineers who already understand a domain are likely to be the most productive; the use of less knowledgeable developers reduces productivity until they become more familiar with the application domain
Process quality	The development process used can have a significant effect on productivity
Project size	If your project is very large, you will need to spend significant time communicating with your team and thus less time will be available for development; individual productivity will be reduced as a result
Technology support	Good support technology such as advanced tools and configuration management systems can improve productivity
Working environment	A quiet working environment with private work areas contributes to improved productivity

Bottom-Up Estimating

Bottom-up estimating, which is also referred to as "grassroots" or "engineering" estimating, entails decomposing the software to its lowest levels by function or task and then summing the resulting data into work elements. This approach can be very effective for estimating the costs of smaller systems. It breaks down the required effort into traceable components that can be effectively sized, estimated, and tracked; the component estimates can then be rolled up to provide a traceable estimate that is comprised of individual components that are more easily managed. You thus end up with a detailed basis for your overall estimate. However, if certain conditions are not understood and controlled, this approach can lead to problems:

1. The project team must have a clear vision of the project's scope in order to ensure it is decomposed into all of its constituent elements. Some experts are of the opinion that the bottom-up approach cannot be effective until the detailed design is complete, which is much too late for project planning purposes.[13]
2. Optimism about the resources required to complete individual tasks must be kept in check.
3. Because this approach does not automatically capture the costs associated with integrating units to form higher level components and major programs, estimates can easily omit the work required to integrate the lowest level units. Integration costs must be separately estimated.
4. This approach can be very time consuming for larger systems, making it inappropriate when sufficient time or adequate personnel are not available.
5. Excessive decomposition can lead to justification of unnecessary functionality.[14]

Software Cost Models

Capers Jones noted in a 2002 article that:

> Software cost estimation is simple in concept, but difficult and complex in reality. The difficulty and complexity required for successful estimates exceed the capabilities of most software project managers. As a result, manual estimates are not sufficient for large applications above roughly 1,000 function points in size.[15]

Different cost models have different information requirements. However, any cost model will require the user to provide at least a few — and sometimes many — project attributes or parameters. This information serves to describe the project, its characteristics, the team's experience and training levels, and various other attributes the model requires to be effective, such as the processes, methods, and tools that will be used. However, the process of gathering this information can benefit the project in and of itself. Rick Grehan has said, "I suspect that SEER-SEM's greatest benefit is largely hidden. As you fill in the blanks, you are forced to dig up information about the project that cannot help but lead you to a greater understanding of it. The journey becomes its own reward."[16] By collecting detailed, accurate information as early in the project as possible, you will significantly improve the quality of your estimate, produce a better project plan, and have a greater understanding of just what your project will entail.

Parametric cost models offer significant advantages to a project in that they provide a means for applying a consistent method for subjecting uncertain situations to rigorous mathematical and statistical analysis. Thus they are more comprehensive than other estimating techniques and help to reduce the amount of bias that goes into estimating software projects. They also provide a means for organizing the information that serves to describe the project, which facilitates the identification and analysis of risk. Despite their proven benefits, they can have certain disadvantages. For example, they allow unscrupulous estimators to enter inaccurate information to justify an unachievable plan and can give a false sense of security when poor size ranges have been entered.

A cost model uses various algorithms to project the schedule and cost of a product from specific inputs. Those who attempt to merely estimate size and divide it by a productivity factor are sorely missing the mark. The people, the products, and the process are all key components of a successful software project. Cost models typically use a historical database calibrated to the organization to derive the estimates, or, if this information is unavailable, they use typical information that is derived from industry or vendor sources. Cost models range from simple, single formula models to complex models that involve hundreds or even thousands of calculations. Numerous well known models exist to estimate software cost and effort, including: Boehm's COCOMO suite of models, Putnam's SLIM model, and Galorath's family of SEER models. Generally speaking, these models estimate effort by making effort a (predefined) function of one or more variables, e.g., size of product, complexity, available staff.

Software estimation models fall into two broad categories: cost models and constraint models. Cost models provide direct estimates of effort or duration from one main input (some measure of product size) and several adjustment factors (cost drivers). These factors typically influence productivity and have a significant effect on the project effort.

Constraint models, on the other hand, derive their estimates from the relationship over time between two or more cost parameters, e.g., effort, duration, and staffing level. The Rayleigh curve model developed by Norden[17] and refined by Putnam, Jensen, and Galorath Incorporated's McRitchie, is a typical example of a constraint model.

Most current models allow calibration to reflect the actual experience of the organization. The organization must collect data related to its own projects and must develop cost estimation procedures that evolve when data on more projects becomes available. SEER-SEM provides knowledge bases that include the range of inputs and calibrations, so users generally must change only the input parameters to perform their calibrations if desired. The best estimates are produced by the project manager and trained users of automated models. When the project manager takes ownership of the model he becomes committed to the estimate and it becomes part of the software development plan.

Organizations that want to use more than one technique to arrive at a comparative estimate should develop and embed cost estimation processes. If your organization uses cost models as its primary method of estimating effort and duration, using two different models, a single model with built-in cross checks, or multiple sizing techniques[18] can give better results than a single estimate. Whether an estimate is arrived at manually, via application of a cost model, or with one or more techniques, the process is still dependent on the information available when the estimate is done. Table 3.6 describes the majority of commercial models available today.

When selecting a cost model, it is important that you clearly understand the model's maturity, compatibility with the requirements of the estimation, ability of the staff to use the model, its accuracy in the specific domain of the estimate, its consistency across estimates, and the objectivity of the parameters used to derive the projection. The following criteria are helpful in evaluating the utility of a software cost model for practical estimation purposes.[19]

- **Definition** — Has the model clearly defined the costs it is estimating and the costs it is excluding?
- **Fidelity** — Are the estimates close to the actual costs expended on the projects?
- **Objectivity** — Does the model avoid allocating most of the software cost variance to poorly calibrated subjective factors (such as complexity)?

Table 3.6 Commercial Model Overview

Description	Platform	Web Site
COCOMO II		
COCOMO II is the second generation COCOMO model developed by Dr. Barry Boehm's team at the University of Southern California with industry sponsorship. COCOMO II is really three different models: (1) the Application Composition Model is suitable for projects built with modern GUI-builder tools and for addressing COTS and other software issues; (2) the Early Design Model provides rough estimates of cost and duration before the design's entire architecture has been determined, using a small set of cost drivers and using function points or SLOC; (3) the Post-Architecture Model is the most detailed and is intended to be used after the project architecture is developed. Several commercial products also implement the COCOMO II model.	Windows	http://sunset.usc.edu/research/COCOMOII/
CONSTRUX		
Construx Estimate leverages a blend of the COCOMO and Putnam estimation models and Monte Carlo analysis to predict effort, budget, and schedule based on size estimates. Estimate comes calibrated with industry data and may be calibrated with organization-specific data. Construx supports function point and SLOC to create detailed effort and schedule estimates and enables estimation of multiple modules. Users may enter constraints on cost, schedule, peak staff, and maximum effort allowed. This tool is now offered by Borland.	Windows	http://www.borland.com/

Table 3.6 (continued) Commercial Model Overview

Description	Platform	Web Site
COST XPERT		
Cost Xpert is a COCOMO compliant cost estimation model that integrates multiple software sizing methods and generates a WBS that can be used as a starting point for a project plan. Cost Xpert allows incorporation of historical information into the estimate, allowing benchmarking.	Windows	http://www.costxpert.com/
COSTAR		
A user-friendly version of COCOMO, Costar is an implementation of the original COCOMO, COCOMO II, and other COCOMO derivatives.	Windows	http://www.softstarsystems.com
PRICE S		
Developed by Price Systems, PRICE S is based on cost estimation relationships (CERs) that make use of product characteristics to generate estimates. A major input to PRICE S is SLOC. Software size may be input directly or automatically calculated from quantitative descriptions (function point sizing). Other inputs include software function, operating environment, software reuse, complexity factors, productivity factors, and risk analysis factors. Successful use of PRICE S depends on the ability of the user to define inputs correctly. It can be customized and calibrated to the needs of the user.	Windows	http://www.pricesystems.com/

SAGE Developed by Dr. Randal Jensen, Sage implements the original Jensen model and incorporates qualitative measures of personal, management, and environment effectiveness, process technology, and product characteristics. Sage estimates target worst-case cost and schedule predictions, cost and schedule risk estimates including optional growth.	Windows	www.seisage.com
SEER-ACCUSCOPE Developed by Galorath, Incorporated, SEER-AccuScope produces software size estimates in SLOC, function points, and any other metric. It also provides its own historical database in producing the size estimate. SEER-AccuScope works with the SEER-SEM software estimating tool or on a stand-alone basis.	Windows	www.galorath.com
SEER-SEM Developed by Galorath, Incorporated, SEER-SEM provides software estimates with knowledge bases developed from many years of completed projects. The knowledge base allows estimates with only minimal high level inputs or users may drill down in detail. A user need only to select the platform (i.e., ground, unmanned space, etc.), application (i.e., command and control, diagnostic), development method (i.e., prototype, incremental), and development standards. SEER-SEM is applicable to all types of software projects and considers all phases of software development. SEER-SEM also estimates total life-cycle costs, tracks development throughout the life cycle, and tracks and estimates defects.	Windows	www.galorath.com

Table 3.6 (continued) Commercial Model Overview

Description	Platform	Web Site
SEER-SSM		
Developed by Dr. George Bozoki, SEER-SSM produces size estimates in SLOC or function points and adjusts sizes based on language. SEER-SSM allows expert judgment to be applied to the problem of software sizing and generates a size range of *least, likely,* and *most.*	Windows	www.galorath.com
SLIM		
The Software Life Cycle Model (SLIM) is marketed by Quantitative Software Management (QSM). SLIM can be customized for the user's development environment. Success in using SLIM depends on the user's ability to customize the tool to fit the software development environment and to estimate both a Productivity Index (a measure of the software developer's efficiency) and a Manpower Buildup Index (a measure of the software developer's staffing capability). SLIM also provides a life cycle option which extrapolates development costs into the maintenance phase. QSM also provides performance measurement and metrics.	Windows	www.qsm.com

- **Constructiveness** — Can a user tell why the model gives the estimates it does? Does it help the user understand the software job to be done?
- **Detail** — Does the model easily accommodate the estimation of a software system consisting of a number of subsystems and units? Does it give (accurate) phase and activity breakdowns?
- **Stability** — Do small differences in inputs produce small differences in output cost estimates?
- **Scope** — Does the model cover the class of software projects whose costs you need to estimate?
- **Ease of use** — Are the model inputs, outputs and options easy to understand and specify?
- **Prospectiveness** — Does the model avoid the use of information that will not be well known until the project is complete?[20]

When you evaluate a model, keep in mind that the required functional capabilities are based on the needs and desired capabilities specific to the project and will differ from project to project. Match the available tools with the overall needs of the project. In general, estimation tools should:

- Allow easy adaptation to an organization's development environment. You must be able to customize the tool to fit your development environment, which will enable you to continuously improve its estimation capability since the software estimate generated will include your organization's historical data and current project data.
- Be relatively easy to learn and use. The tool, including the methods and equations it uses, should be well documented at an easily understandable level. It should include help menus and examples that are sufficient to train the support staff and answer their questions. It should require minimal formal training to use, required inputs should be well defined, and visibility into internal equations and theories should be provided.
- Provide early estimates. The tool should be capable of generating estimates early and quickly in the life-cycle process when requirements and development environments are not fully defined. It should also allow task detail to be added incrementally as functions, activities, and other information become more completely defined. Since many unknowns exist early in the estimating process, the tool should reflect degrees of uncertainty based on the level of detail input (risk analysis). In general, the tool should provide sufficient information to allow initial project resource planning as well as reasonably early go or no-go decisions.

■ Be based on software life-cycle phases and activities. The tool should be capable of providing estimates for all phases and activities of the most commonly used software life-cycle models. It should allow the organization to decompose and map software development tasks into those phases and activities, as well as support a program WBS. In addition, it should allow for what-if situations and include factors for design trade-off studies.

■ Understand language and application impacts. It should allow for variations in application languages and application function. It is very important that the tool provide estimates specific to the application of the software project, since the associated cost driver settings, and life-cycle phases could be unique to each application.

■ Provide accurate size estimates. The size of a software development project is a major cost driver in most estimating tools, yet size is one of the most difficult input parameters to estimate accurately. The tool should include the capability to help estimate the size of the software development project or at least help define a method for estimating the size.

■ Provide accurate schedule estimates. Schedule overruns are common and can be extremely costly. The software estimating tool should be able to provide accurate schedule estimates. The purpose of scheduling is not only to predict task completion given task sequence and available resources, but also to establish starting and ending dates for the associated work packages and life-cycle phases.

■ Provide maintenance estimates separately. The software estimating tool should be able to provide software maintenance estimates as a separate item. Software maintenance includes such activities as correcting errors, modifying the software to accommodate changes in requirements, and extending and enhancing software performance.[21]

Organizing the Estimating Process

While a rigorous, repeatable estimation process will most likely result in an accurate range projection of the size and cost of an application, estimator inexperience or bias and the different experience levels of different estimators can undermine the potential for achieving a valid and accurate estimate. To overcome this basic fact of life, you must use a documented and standardized estimation process and apply standardized templates to collect and itemize tasks. Doing so will help ensure the information you gather is complete and that the subsequent analysis follows a proven process. It will also help you document, for historical purposes, the processes and assumptions you have used to develop the estimate and to record the results of each estimation activity. See the Postestimation Process Evaluation Questionnaire (in Chapter 4) for assessment checklists.

Delphi and Wideband Delphi

Following a rigorous process is essential to arriving at a useful estimate that is relatively free of the bias that results from estimators who have predetermined opinions or agendas, who are inexperienced, or who have divergent objectives or hidden agendas. You can further offset the effects of these factors that lead to biased estimates by implementing the Delphi estimation method as an integral part of the estimation process. With this method, several expert teams or individuals, each with an equal voice and an understanding up front that there are no correct answers, start with the same description of the task at hand and generate estimates anonymously, repeating the process until consensus is reached. Creating multiple estimates serves to eliminate any biases and hidden agendas.

Barry Boehm developed an alternative to the standard Delphi approach, known as Wideband Delphi.[22] Wideband Delphi facilitates interactions of estimation teams and helps them to draw on their actual experience to build a complete task list or detailed work breakdown structure for major activities, which is necessary to estimate the size of the project, conduct bottom-up estimates of the required effort, and develop and time-phase the activity network. It is an effective technique for addressing many problems in the estimation process, such as determining how large subsystems will be, how complex the components will need to be to implement a specific subsystem, what productivity can be expected, and what effect reaching Level 3 in the CMMI will have on productivity projections.

A Wideband Delphi session is initiated by presenting to the participants a specification of the problem or a high-level task list or project schedule. Starting with this information, each participant produces a detailed project task list; a list of associated quality, process, and overhead tasks; a description of estimation assumptions; and a set of estimates describing the tasks and the overall project. Figure 3.3 illustrates the seven steps that comprise the Wideband Delphi method.

The planning step entails defining the problem to be estimated, selecting the participants, and briefing them on the requirements at a kickoff meeting. At the meeting, project management focuses the attention of the participants on the estimation problem, identifies expectations and requirements, recommends an estimation method, technique, or tool, and identifies the exit criteria that, when met, will end the process. Each participant

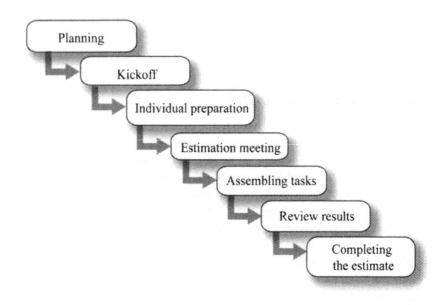

Figure 3.3 Wideband Delphi method.

then applies the recommended method, etc., to the core assumptions and prepares initial task lists and estimates. The participants then convene for the estimation meeting, during which a moderator presents the independent estimates without identifying their authors. Step 3 (individual preparation) may be repeated several times in order to produce a more comprehensive task list and to refine the estimates toward the exit criteria. In Step 5 (assembling tasks), the moderator or project manager consolidates the individual estimates, after which the entire team reviews the results. If the exit criteria have been satisfied, the process is concluded. The final result is a range of estimates that represent a more realistic projection of tasks, size, cost, or schedule than could result from a single estimate.

The process of estimation in general leads to an imprecise, albeit educated, projection of a project's size, cost, schedule, and required tasks as well as an initial identification of the risks that could occur during the acquisition, development, or update of the software product. If the estimates were completely accurate and could be verified as such, they would be predictions, not estimates. The major benefit of the Wideband Delphi technique is that it elicits the perspectives of multiple experts to arrive at a range of estimates that can then be normalized to filter out the initial extreme values that may result from differences in estimator experience, their biases, and their agendas, and reach a realistic projection. You may be wondering at this point if this seemingly major effort is worth the money and time it requires. If you consider the dramatic effects inaccurate estimates have on a project and the significant risks that result, you may well consider this method to be relatively inexpensive insurance.

Activity-Based Estimates

Another way to estimate the various elements of a software project is to begin with the requirements of the project and the size of the application, and then, based on this information, define the required tasks, which will serve to identify the overall effort that will be required. Table 3.7 provides a summary of the numerous ancillary tasks a successful project must consider in addition to those that must be conducted to actually develop the software product.

As Table 3.7 demonstrates, the major cost drivers on a typical project are focused on the non-coding tasks that must be adequately considered, planned for, and included in any estimate of required effort. Of course, not every project will require all of these tasks, and you should tailor the list to the specific requirements of your project, adding and deleting tasks as necessary and modifying task descriptions if required, and then build a task hierarchy — that usually takes the form of a WBS — that represents how the work will be organized and performed.

The resulting work breakdown structure is the backbone of the project plan and provides a means to identify the tasks to be implemented on a specific project. It is not a to-do list of every possible activity required for the project; it does provide a structure of tasks that, when completed, will result in satisfaction of all project commitments. With this approach, the development of the WBS is especially critical for deriving an accurate cost projection because it identifies what work has to be performed and the overall relationships of the tasks that comprise the work.

The WBS is an important element of the estimation process for three reasons. First, it enables the estimator, early in the process, to perform a bottom-up estimate based on projected work activities that are scaled to the size of the project and the projected tasks that must be performed. Second, with a detailed WBS, project management can develop an optimum projection of the tasks to be performed versus effort to be expended by trading off the tasks defined in the WBS against the available funding. Third the WBS is critical to estimating a project, because not understanding the full range of tasks required to support a project can create a host of problems such as incorrect staffing levels (overstaffing or understaffing), assigning the wrong personnel mix, overselling, overworking, the need to condense activities, etc., that will ultimately lead to missed delivery dates, poor deliverable quality, the disenchantment and poor morale of the project team. and the disappointment of the stakeholders.

Table 3.7   Sample Project Task Summary

Task Area	Task Description
Management and Project Support	Investment. Plan and implement the procedures and tools required to achieve and initially sustain full operational capability (FOC) [and the operational and economic return on investment estimated in the project's benefit analysis ROI and economic analysis]. Activities are conducted from the time of program initiation through the complete fielding, implementation, and testing required to meet FOC requirements. This activity includes elements from the beginning of the program through purchases of operational systems, upgrades to the system to satisfy approved requirements, and other initial items (e.g., initial training, spares, supplies, etc.). Also included are the elements to implement the system, such as implementation and acceptance team testing, facility construction, and site activation, upgrades, and disposal or reuse.
	Project management. These tasks provide project planning, administrative services, project control, and support and will establish the environment essential for controlling the project. The tasks define the business and administrative planning, organization, direction, coordination, control, and approval actions designated to accomplish overall program objectives. Examples of the activities are cost, schedule, performance measurement management, warranty administration, contract management, data management, vendor liaison, subcontract management, etc.
	Contracting and contract monitoring. These tasks plan and execute the requirements for contracting and contract monitoring and the acceptance of deliverables.
	Customer and user support. Planning, execution, and support of a customer and user program to ensure these parties are adequately involved during the project.
	Documentation. These tasks will develop, document, conduct, and support the contractual training requirement.
	Metrics and measures. These tasks will plan, identify, collect, evaluate and report issue based metrics to monitor quality, project status and health, progress, and risk.

Table 3.7 (continued)   Sample Project Task Summary

Task Area	Task Description
Management and Project Support	Risk management. All technical effort required to identify program risks of all types; assess and quantify their likelihood of occurrence and potential adverse impact; develop risk mitigation strategies and plans; and monitor measures to indicate the need to implement mitigation plans.
	Data management. All management activities required to identify required data items; select and tailor project data requirements; prepare contracting requirements and delivery structure; monitor delivery, review, and acceptance of data deliveries; and archive and distribute data items.
	Budget, schedule, and financial management. All management activities required to identify required documentation structure, and content; prepare and execute the contract; monitor delivery, review, and acceptance of data deliveries; and archive and distribute data items.
	Process and product standards, method and tool selection, documentation, implementation, and monitoring. This area includes all tasks needed to establish the standards for the project and to develop the standards required for all major processes and underlying methods as well as standards for products, artifacts, and documentation that are consistent with the methods used. Also included are criteria that can be used to evaluate compliance with the standards and the acceptability of the products developed or acquired.
Technical	Concept exploration. This task includes all activities associated with the study, analysis, design development, and testing involved in investigating alternative methods of delivering prototype(s) or end item(s) to fulfill a requirement.
	System engineering. This task area involves the technical and management efforts of directing and controlling a totally integrated engineering effort of a system or program. It encompasses the systems engineering effort to define system alternatives and associated integrated planning and control of the technical program efforts of design engineering, specialty engineering, production engineering, and

Table 3.7 (continued) Sample Project Task Summary

Task Area	Task Description
Technical	integrated test planning. It also includes the systems engineering efforts required to transform an operational need or new requirement into a description of system requirements and a preferred system configuration; and the technical planning and control effort required to plan, monitor, measure, evaluate, and direct the management of the technical program.
	Database standards, definition, and development. This is the effort required to plan, implement, and execute in an integrated fashion the activities associated with the development of database definition standards and a single database dictionary to support multiple applications, functional disciplines, and the operational (service) units that will be supported.
	Requirements specification and validation. This is the effort required to plan, define, specify, and validate the basic requirements for the system. These requirements will provide the basis for the functional capabilities to be supported by the software configuration.
	Requirements translation. The effort required to translate requirements into a functional set of requirements to be allocated to the software organization for implementation.
	Trade-off analysis. Conduct whatever trade-off analyses are required to validate system assumptions or select a design approach for either the total system or for the software component alone. Where required, the software development organization will support the conduct of these trade-off analyses.
	Design synthesis. Defining and documenting the top-level design of the system and specifying to the subsystem level the functional requirements for each of the three software subsystems and the database. In addition, the systems engineering organization will define the top-level requirements for the database and specify the technical requirements for accessing the database for each of the remote sites as well as the centralized facility.

Table 3.7 (continued) Sample Project Task Summary

Task Area	Task Description
Technical	Systems design. These tasks will define the basic requirements of the application and translate these into subsystem architecture for implementation by the development organizations.
	Subsystem design. These tasks will translate the system design into subsystem architecture for implementation by the development organizations.
	Software architecture definition. Defining and documenting a high-level architecture from the functional specifications and system design provided by the systems engineering organization.
	Software development. This task encompasses the effort required to plan, implement and execute all activities required to develop the software deliverable. It may include the lease, purchase, or modification of products that assist in the planning, design, testing, debugging, validation, and documentation of the application software necessary to automate a specific function or operation and integrate that function into the overall system. In the case of legacy software development, these activities should reflect the amount of code to be transferred without modification, transferred with minor modification, bridged, redesigned, and eliminated. For contractor-developed software, include architecture and unit definition, coding, and unit test completed prior to integration testing and other contractor-related activities.
	Database development. This task captures the activities associated with a variety of data types and includes all design of the logical data model to support the applications: DBMS requirements analysis; file design; data standardization and configuration management; data transitioning, conversion and migration; and data validation. Include all activities associated with the requirements for conforming with data standards or participation in activity for the data element dictionary development. Included are the COTS DBMS licenses to support the application development.

Table 3.7 (continued)   Sample Project Task Summary

Task Area	Task Description
Assurance	Quality assurance. The activity required to plan, implement, execute, and analyze the quality assurance process to evaluate products and processes against project requirements, contracts, and standards.
	Support analyses. Planning and conduct of any analyses required to verify the system design project, evaluate the expected performance, or investigate the technical integrity of the system. These analyses can be requested by any organization within the project and may require support from the software organization or other project organizations such as logistics.
	Structured inspections. These tasks plan, execute, evaluate, and monitor the structured inspection process required to identify and remove defects and track against rework projections.
	Hardware–software integration. If the system software will be assembled and integrated in a series of progressive *builds*, all of the technical effort required to verify that the build of the software product will load and operate on the operationally configured hardware suite.
	System architecture validation. These tasks encompass the activity necessary to plan, develop, chair, and conduct all project reviews. Those conducting these tasks will be technically responsible for all project documentation submitted to the customer and for any updates or notifications released; will also chair all program technical boards or committees and serve as program office technical representative at the customer review meetings.
	Development testing. These tasks include the test and evaluation conducted to: (a) demonstrate that the engineering design and development process is complete; (b) demonstrate that the design risks have been minimized; (c) demonstrate that the system will meet specifications; (d) estimate the system's utility when introduced; (e) determine whether the

Table 3.7 (continued)   Sample Project Task Summary

Task Area	Task Description
Assurance	engineering design is supportable for operational use; (f) provide test data with which to examine and evaluate trade-offs against specification requirements, life-cycle cost, and schedule; and (g) perform the logistics testing efforts to evaluate the achievement of supportability goals and the adequacy of the support package for the system (e.g., deliverable maintenance tools, test equipment, technical publications, maintenance instructions, and personnel skills and training requirements, etc.). Development test and evaluation includes all contractor and in-house effort and is planned, conducted, and monitored by the customer.
	Technical monitoring. This task encompasses the activity required to plan, define criteria for, execute, and analyze the technical integrity of all data developed or used by the project. Through a series of project reviews and audits, the technical monitoring organization will assess the status of the program.
	Independent verification and validation (IV&V). Planning, implementation, and execution of all activities associated with the independent study, analysis, modeling, and testing involved in the independent evaluation of products against their requirements and the integrity of technical baselines to fulfill a requirement. This element encompasses the systems engineering effort required to analyze the technical program efforts of design engineering, specialty engineering, production engineering, and integrated test planning. It also includes the project efforts to transform an operational need or statement of deficiency into a description of system requirements and a preferred system configuration; and the technical planning and control effort for planning, monitoring, measuring, evaluating, directing, and executing the technical program. It specifically excludes the actual design engineering and the production engineering tasks performed by the project.

Table 3.7 (continued)   Sample Project Task Summary

Task Area	Task Description
Assurance	Operational testing. These tasks include support of tests conducted by organizations other than the developer to assess the prospective system's utility, operational effectiveness, operational suitability, logistics supportability, cost of ownership, and needs for modifications. These tasks encompass such tests as system demonstration, qualification, operational test and evaluation, etc., and support of testing that demonstrates the operational capability of the delivered system. They include developer support provided during this phase of the testing and also performing the logistics testing efforts required to evaluate the achievement of supportability goals and the adequacy of the support for the system.
	System test and evaluation. These tasks will plan, develop, execute, and support the functional and system testing.
	Software integration and testing. These tasks involve testing and integrating all software in accordance with project requirements and releasing integrated builds to the test and evaluation organization for functional testing.
	Specialized testing. These tasks will plan, implement, execute and analyze tests specifically required to demonstrate product or process compliance to external requirements such as safety, security, operational factors.
	Certification. These tasks support all activities required to certify the product prior to operational use, including security certification, privacy certification, safety certification, interoperability certification, operational certification, etc., that are unique to each project.
Documentation	User documentation. Includes the preparation of all technical publications required to use, operate, and maintain the system hardware and software.
	System operating manuals. All efforts to prepare manuals that explain how the user will interact with the systems application software to perform day-to-day operational functions.
	System administration manuals. All efforts to prepare manuals for use by system administrators and system

Table 3.7 (continued) Sample Project Task Summary

Task Area	Task Description
Documentation	operators that describe the procedures for registering, changing, and deleting users; entering their individual access privileges; updating system databases; starting up and rebooting the system; archiving and restoring data, etc.
	System operator manuals. All work to prepare the manuals system operators and maintainers require to troubleshoot system problems, make necessary minor repairs or component replacements, and restore the system or subsystem to operational use.
	Training plan. This activity includes all work required to prepare an overall plan for accomplishing system training, including the identification of overall training objectives, audience skill and knowledge levels, course types and content, delivery and instructional methods, unique training resource requirements, etc.
	Training curricula development. All effort required to prepare detailed course curricula, including course objectives, training module flow and content, unique course material requirements, performance measurement techniques, etc.
	Training course development. All work required to prepare unique course materials, which typically include instructor guides, student workbooks, presentations, student exercises, instructional videos, computer-based training software, etc.
	Technical documentation. Activities associated with the preparation, revision, and reproduction of drawings, technical documents, plans, procedures, manuals, and other system documentation required by the contract or requested by the customer.
Delivery and Support	System maintenance. Includes providing maintenance and repair for the system regardless of who has *ownership*. These activities include problem identification and analysis, defect correction, system update, programmed maintenance, component repair, minor facilities modifications and upkeep, support equipment acquisition and support, tool calibration, support data, and administrative support required for maintenance operations.

Table 3.7 (continued)   Sample Project Task Summary

Task Area	Task Description
Delivery and Support	Site surveys. All the effort required to characterize the site environment, locate the proposed equipment, design the equipment installation, identify needed communications and facility upgrades, and acquire other site unique information required to successfully field the system.
	Site preparation. All work needed to prepare the site for system installation. Typical tasks include providing additional ventilation, cooling, and electrical power; upgrading or adding LAN connections; minor facility construction; etc.
	Site assembly and installation. All the efforts and minor materials required to assemble the system hardware and software components, install them at their site locations, and check the operation of the integrated system prior to formal system testing.
	System operations and support. Include all activities required to operate and sustain the system after installation at all sites prior to system turnover. They include the activities required to manage and maintain the hardware and software, whether centrally or at each unit, to sustain operations throughout the lifecycle along with all activities associated with the operations of the system and conducting operator familiarization at user sites.
	Site testing and acceptance. These tasks include activities for system-related production test activities associated with the integration and evaluation of the system at a user site, including the test equipment, hardware, and/or software required to obtain or validate data. This activity also includes the planning, execution, support, data reduction, and reports from such testing and test items consumed in the conduct of such operations, and any contracts, as well as the design and production of models, specimens, fixtures, and instrumentation in support of the test program. It also includes the system operational test activities to ensure proper system installation and operation and all efforts associated with the design and production of models, fixtures, and the instrumentation in support of the test program.

Step Six: Quantify Risks and Risk Analysis

Cost Estimation Risks

"What distinguishes the best organizations and best managers is not just how well they do in their successful efforts, but how well they contain their failures."[23] The best managers of software projects seem to have an uncanny ability to anticipate what can happen to their projects and devise just-in-time mitigation approaches to avoid the full impacts of the problems. In reality, this ability is not magic nor is there anything uncanny about it. It is simply the skillful application of well known risk management techniques to the well known problems of software management. Unfortunately, too many software managers are skilled in seeing potential risks and then ignoring them outright.

"The problem of project management, like that of most management [is] to find an acceptable balance among time, cost and performance."[24] What was once well controlled now becomes less well managed, resulting in risk. "An effective risk-management program is dynamic and ongoing throughout the development process and requires the participation of everyone involved."[25]

Before we explore the risk management process and how to apply it to the risks associated with sizing and estimation, it is important to understand what a risk is and that a risk, in itself, does not necessarily pose a threat to a software project if it is recognized and addressed before it becomes a problem. Many events occur during software development. As Pfleeger explained:

> We distinguish risks from other project events by looking for three things:
>
> 1. A loss associated with the event. The event must create a situation where something negative happens to the project: loss of time, quality, money, control, understanding, and so on. For example, if requirements change dramatically after the design is done, then the project can suffer from loss of control and understanding if the new requirements are for functions or features with which the design team is unfamiliar. A radical change in requirements is likely to lead to losses of time and money if the design is not flexible enough to be changed quickly and easily. The loss associated with a risk is called the risk impact.
> 2. The likelihood that the event will occur. We must have some idea of the probability that the event will occur. For example, suppose a project is being developed on one machine and will be ported to another when the system is fully tested. If the second machine

is a new model to be delivered by the vendor, we must estimate the likelihood that it will not be ready on time. The likelihood of the risk, measured from 0 (impossible) to 1 (certainty) is called the risk probability. When the risk probability is 1, then the risk is called a problem, since it is certain to happen.

3. The degree to which we can change the outcome. For each risk, we must determine what we can do to minimize or avoid the impact of the event. Risk control involves a set of actions taken to reduce or eliminate a risk. For example, if the requirements may change after design, we can minimize the impact of the change by creating a flexible design. If the second machine is not ready when the software is tested, we may be able to identify other models or brands that have the same functionality and performance and can run our new software until the new model is delivered."[26]

Risk management enables you to identify and address potential threats to a project, whether they result from internal issues or conditions or from external factors that you may not be able to control. As we have discussed, problems associated with sizing and estimating software potentially can have dramatic negative effects. The key word here is *potentially*, which means that if problems can be foreseen and their causes acted upon in time, effects can be mitigated. The risk management process is the means of doing so.

The risk management process is straightforward and, from a process standpoint, one of the easier disciplines to plan and implement. You should be able to complete a fully functional risk management process — that is, devise a policy, plan, and procedures, perform essential training, implement a tool loaded with an initial set of risks, and conduct an initial risk identification session — within 30 days of identifying your requirement. That is the easy part. Ideally, an organization's management will recognize that the risk management process is an essential management tool and thus value, support, and effectively use it. However, in reality, the bias against risk management is often so strong that it may take years to achieve cultural acceptance and integration of the process if they can be achieved at all. This peculiar bias has three primary causes:

■ Risk management is the antithesis of the can-do attitude. Risks highlight the potential for failure and remind management of factors which, should they occur, will affect the expected success of a plan or endeavor.

■ Upper management often buys into the stereotype that risk management is merely an attempt to establish excuses to justify future failures, and thus will not pursue or encourage the discipline.

- An organization often possesses an arrogance that leads to a corporate culture in which the lone hero slays the dragons one at a time, which is characterized by the attitude: "There is nothing I can't overcome with hard work, just bring it on." Risk management removes the hero from the process because problems are anticipated and addressed as a normal course of business.

Many managers incorrectly perceive that if they identify risks that subsequently become problems they will be held responsible for the problems. In fact, the opposite is true. By using risk management techniques to anticipate potential risks, the manager is protected against liability because if the problem does occur, it can be demonstrated that the cause was beyond what any prudent manager could have foreseen. As Capers Jones states:

> There is a major cultural barrier to accurate estimation [and schedules] which must be highlighted .... If an early estimate [or schedule] predicts higher cost, longer schedules or lower quality than client or manager expectations, there is a strong tendency to challenge the validity of the estimate. What often occurs in this situation is that the project manager is directed to recast the estimate so that it falls within preset and arbitrary boundary conditions."[27]

This situation is what leads to the bias against risk management, because, as the Bible saying goes, "A prophet is not without honor, except in his own country." Managers do not necessarily want to be told that an estimate is considered high risk, especially before the estimate is used to establish a firm project commitment, when they are challenged by a customer to "come in under a number" or "deliver by a given date."

In order for risk management to become a cultural imperative, that is, a discipline that is essential to the health of their enterprise, senior management must be convinced that it will maximize the organization's potential by maximizing the time and resources available to successfully address risks before they become problems and damage the organization as a whole. Indeed, risk management will become an imperative if senior management understands that having a method in place to anticipate risks and prepare mitigation plans will eliminate the need for crisis management that requires the application of any and all resources to address a problem, at considerable expense to other long-term activities and commitments.

Although cost, schedule, and product performance risks are interrelated, they can also be analyzed independently. Various methods are used to quantify risks associated with these elements of a project, including table methods, analytical methods, knowledge-based techniques, and questionnaire-based methods. In practice, risks must be identified as specific instances in order to be manageable. Chapter 10 titled "Risk Management Process" discusses risk and risk handling in detail.

Summary

This chapter covered Steps 4 through 6 of the ten-step estimation process: software sizing, preparing the baseline estimate, and quantifying risk and risk analysis. Completing these steps forms the foundation for the rest of the estimation, planning, and successful execution process.

Endnotes

1. Jones, Capers. "Software Cost Estimation in 2002." *CrossTalk: The Journal of Defense Software Engineering*, June 2002. 4.
2. Ferens, Daniel, L. Fischman, T. Fitzpatrick, D. Galorath, and D. Tarbet. "Automated Software Project Size Estimation via Use Case Points." Report to the U.S. Government, January 2002.
3. Peters, Kathleen. "Software Estimation." Software Productivity Centre: Resources: Estimation. 1999. 9 Sept. 2005. <http://www.spc.ca/downloads/resources/estimate/estbasics.pdf>
4. Jones, Capers. *Estimating Software Costs.* New York: McGraw-Hill, 1998.
5. Porter, Ralph, and Joseph Lees. "Improve Software Cost Estimating." Case Studies: General Dynamics Electronic Systems. 2002. 3 Jan. 2003. <http://www.galorath.com/customer_case-dynamics.html>
6. Clark, Brad. "Quantifying the Effect of Process Improvement." *IEEE Software*, 17. no. 6, November–December 2000. © IEEE 2000.
7. Galorath, Dan. "Software Productivity Laws." Arthur Anderson Symposium, 1997.
8. Galorath Incorporated. *SEER-SEM Internal Mathematical Specification.* El Segundo, 2004.
9. International Society of Parametric Analysis. *Parametric Estimating Handbook*, 2nd ed. Sponsored by the U.S. Department of Defense. Chandler, 2002. <http://www.ispa-cost.org/PEIWeb/newbook.htm>
10. Streibel, Barbara, Brian L. Joiner, and Peter R. Scholtes. *The Team Handbook*, 2nd ed., Madison: Joiner/Oriel Inc., 1996.
11. DeMarco, Tom and Tim Lister. *Peopleware; Productive Projects and Teams*, 2nd ed. New York: Dorsett House, 1999.
12. Booch, Grady. *The Software Development Team Whitepaper.* Cupertino: Rational Software Corporation, 1999.
13. Federal Aviation Administration Acquisition System Toolset. *FAA Government Pricing Handbook.* Sponsored by Federal Aviation Administration, March 1999. <http://fast.faa.gov/pricing/>
14. Webber, Blaine. Personal interview, 2004.

15. Jones, Capers. "Software Cost Estimation in 2002." *CrossTalk: The Journal of Defense Software Engineering*, June 2002. 4.

16. Grehan, Rick. "SEER-SEM Offers Realistic Forecasting for Programmers." *Byte Magazine*, September 1994. <http://www.byte.com/art/9409/sec4/art6.htm>

17. Norden, P.V. and B.V. Dean, Eds., *Useful Tools for Project Management, Operations Research in Research and Development.* New York: John Wiley & Sons, 1963.

18. Galorath, Dan, Lee Fischman, and Dan Ferens. "Critical Mass: Advancing the Software Sizing State of the Art, Progress and Lessons Learned." International ISPA Conference, Frascati, Italy, 2004.

19. Boehm, B.W., C. Abts, A.W. Brown, S. Chulani, B. Clark, E. Horowitz, R. Madachy, D. Reifer, and B. Steece. *Software Cost Estimation with COCOMO II.* Upper Saddle River: Prentice Hall, 2000.

20. Globaltester.com. "Software Cost Estimation," 2004. <www.globaltester.com>

21. International Society of Parametric Analysts. *Parametric Estimating Handbook*, 2nd ed. Sponsored by the U.S. Department of Defense. Chandler, 2002. <http://www.ispa-cost.org/PEIWeb/newbook.htm>

22. Boehm, Barry. *Software Engineering Economics.* Upper Saddle River: Prentice Hall, 1981.

23. DeMarco, Tom. *Why Does Software Cost So Much?* New York: Dorsett House, 1995. 62.

24. Norden, P.V. and B.V. Dean, Eds., *Useful Tools for Project Management, Operations Research in Research and Development.* New York: John Wiley & Sons, 1963.

25. Molt, George. "Risk Management Fundamentals in Software Development." *CrossTalk: The Journal of Defense Software Engineering*, August 2000.

26. Pfleeger, Shari Lawrence. *Software Engineering: Theory and Practice*, 2nd ed. Englewood Cliffs: Prentice Hall, February 2001.

27. Jones, Capers T. *Assessment and Control of Software Risks.* Englewood Cliffs: Prentice Hall, February 1994. 158.

Chapter 4

Planning and Controlling the Project via the Estimate

> For which one of you, when he wants to build a tower, does not first sit down and count the cost, to see if he has enough to complete it? Otherwise, when he has laid a foundation, and is not able to finish, all who observe it begin to ridicule him, saying, "This man began to build and was not able to finish."
>
> **Luke 14:28**
> "The Interlinear NASB-NIV"

Introduction

In the previous chapters we focused on how to build a viable project estimate. This chapter encompasses validation of the estimate, obtaining lessons learned, and use of the estimate throughout the project.

Step Seven: Estimate Validation and Review

Once you have accomplished the first six of the ten steps, you should have a reasonably good estimate, but *should have* does not mean *do have*.

In order to make certain that the estimate is viable, it should be validated, verified, and reviewed. Projects that fail to validate their estimates because of tight schedules, fear of exposure, unavailability of resources, or any other reason run the risk of providing an erroneous basis for the entire project, the cost of which would far exceed any expenditures needed to validate the estimates.

Estimate validation simply means reviewing and confirming the integrity of the estimate, ensuring the estimate was performed properly, and that the correct functionality was estimated. While the validation process is in itself straightforward, its application can involve some complexity. There are many ways to validate an estimate:

- Evaluate both the process used to derive an estimate and the estimate that resulted.
- If possible, an independent and objective individual who was not involved in preparing the estimate should conduct the validation.
- Use a separately derived set of inputs or use a method or tool different from that used to derive the original estimate.
- Thresholds should be established in advance describing what actions might be taken based on differences between the estimate and the validation results (e.g., below 10 percent, use management discretion; 10 to 30 percent, meet to resolve differences; 30 to 70 percent, analyze both estimates to identify the causes of the difference; 70 to 100 percent, reestimate).

A validation will also affirm the process used to develop the estimate and the currency of the information used, and it will serve to expose analyst bias and isolate errors or erroneous assumptions. In conducting the validation, a standard checklist can be useful, such as that created by Robert Park[1] who proposed seven questions to ask when assessing your willingness to rely on a cost and schedule estimate:

1. Are the objectives of the estimate clear and correct?
2. Has the task been appropriately sized?
3. Are the estimated cost and schedule consistent with demonstrated accomplishments on other projects?
4. Have the factors that affect the estimate been identified and explained?
5. Have steps been taken to ensure the integrity of the estimating process?
6. Is the organization's historical evidence capable of supporting a reliable estimate?
7. Has the situation changed since the estimate was prepared?

You may be asking at this point why an estimate must be validated at all if a mature process has been followed and abundant information was available upon which to base the estimate. The reason is that the estimation process is most often conducted under considerable pressures, such as those that result from having limited time and taking shortcuts, from having to rely on participants who do not have the time to adequately support the effort, and from basing the estimate on information that is not as reliable as it was assumed to be at first blush.

In addition, a project will often include numerous stakeholders with different agendas who are heavily invested in the success of the project. This adds to the pressures on the estimation team and affects the team's ability to present a truly unbiased estimate of project size, cost, and schedule. Validation is also important because so many risks can result from even a reasonable estimate, let alone an inaccurate estimate. Validation will allow you to objectively evaluate the estimation process used and the accuracy of the projections — which represents a clear path toward understanding what your project will actually require to succeed.

A formal validation process, which is not without a cost in time and effort, is planned and scheduled, and its execution adheres to a rigorous process intended to maximize the potential to identify errors, inconsistencies, breakdowns in process, and shortcuts and trade-offs that may have degraded the validity of the estimate. It will identify the issues and problems associated with the estimate and lead to their resolution or, at least, to a greater understanding of them. Despite the effort required, it is worthwhile considering the potential savings in time and money down the line and the fact that validation will preserve the integrity of the project.

Estimate Review Process

The review process can provide the information you need to identify any problems with the estimate. Then you can work to contain or mitigate the associated risks so as to reduce the likelihood that they will occur or, if they do, to mitigate their effects. If the risks you identify are not mitigated and do become problems, you will be forced to make trade-offs to attempt to recover lost schedule and resources. If you base your project on incorrect estimates, you likely will find yourself without the resources to achieve your project goals. This will most likely lead to uncontrolled restructuring and then to an unrealistic compression of the schedule and all of the problems concomitant to that action. If this scenario becomes reality, your goals will be severely compromised or your project will fail altogether.

The easiest way to avoid this scenario is to identify and correct any problems in the estimate before it is used to establish budgets or constraints on your project process or product engineering. You do so by conducting a rigorous, structured, and formal validation of the estimate using objective criteria to isolate problems with the estimate at their source. As we have discussed, ideally you would assign an independent third party to ensure an objective evaluation of the estimate, but in the real world this option is usually off the table because of schedule constraints or because trained resources that possess the required familiarity with the goals, requirements, and expectations of the estimate are simply not available.

Estimate Review Activities

The following discussion focuses on alternative activities available when you are reviewing an estimate.

Meta-analysis — This is the technique of using different project estimating methods in conjunction with one another for validation purposes. Analytic models are invaluable for quickly gaining insight into the validity of an estimate.

High risk development concerns —Always assess the development assumptions used to arrive at the estimate you are validating in order to ensure they are accurate and can be sustained throughout the development process. The following items should be considered high risk assumptions regarding software development.

> **Below-the-line (BTL) costs** — Costs for items such as compilers and COTS tools, are considered "below the line" because, although they are not directly associated with the development effort, they are necessary to support it and frequently represent a sizable proportion of project cost. In validating estimates, keep in mind that effort estimates capture direct labor costs but not BTL costs. Therefore, be sure to account for BTL costs by obtaining a detailed accounting of all line items or take care to document the limited scope in the ground rules and assumptions that went into the estimate you are validating.
>
> **Extraordinary requirements** — Work that explores new territory carries more risk. Independently check to see how much of the software that will be developed is routine and how much is exotic (new technology).
>
> **"Not invented here" syndrome** — Check to see that the development staff is planning to maximize its use of outside resources. If not, then time will be spent reinventing software wheels, which are often the hardest things to reinvent! Here are some items to look for:

- The extent of the commercial basis of the overall development environment included in the estimate. Are developers planning to use a vendor-provided development environment and a robust coding language?
- The extent to which code libraries will be used. Are the developers planning to purchase libraries or use those provided with the development environment or language to accomplish certain tasks such as user and device interfacing or graphics? Is the vendor viable?
- The extent to which the operating environment will be customized. Are the developers planning to "twiddle the bits" on OS level routines and, if so, is it absolutely necessary that they do so?

Requirements creep — Does the project have open-ended functionality commitments or even a too-cozy relationship with end-users that influenced the estimate? Has the project manager shown iron-willed determination to freeze requirements and save changes for future builds? Are there any *to-be-determined* (TBD) items in the requirements documentation? If so, has a risk assessment been done to define the potential risk of each TBD? Requirements creep affects the size and architectural baseline; it has been repeatedly identified as a major source of uncertainty in estimates of schedule and effort.

Overstated productivity — This is a common assumption in software estimates. Compare industry average estimates for productivity against the developer's own assessment. If the numbers disagree by 10 to 15 percent or more, you should try to reconcile them. Table 4.1 indicates productivity per effort-month for industry averages and serves as a rule-of-thumb sanity check.

Cost per Unit of Code Developed

Cost per unit of code can be a useful metric for validation when you know exactly what is and is not included. The key issue when using cost per unit of code is consistency. What is included in the cost? What comprises a line of code or function point?

Magic Bullets (Otherwise Known as Technical Leaps)

Some projects hinge upon a key technology or assumption. Magic bullets can actually work or they can operate as blunt instruments that developers

Table 4.1 Typical SLOC Productivity per Person-Month

Application Type	Least Lines per Month	Likely Lines per Month	Most Lines per Month
Business mission critical	130	193	236
Business application	154	213	272
Command and control	118	173	224
Avionics flight	64	98	136
Manned space	29	57	86

Derived from simple SEER-SEM analysis based on 50,000 lines new, 20, 50, and 80 percent probabilities; includes effort from requirements analysis through system integration and testing and the following labor categories: direct labor software management, requirements analysis design, code, test, configuration management, quality assurance, data preparation.

have inadequate experience with. Identify each magic bullet, its chance of failure, and what the impact of a failure will be. A PERT network is useful for assessing a misfired magic bullet's likely effect on a schedule.

Unrealistic Schedules

Unrealistic development schedules will lead to schedule overruns even if the staff works overtime, partly because overworked developers are not as efficient. One possibility for improvement is evaluating a schedule for parallelizing development tasks, but be careful because this has often been a failed silver bullet. Check with relevant software engineers to see how separable development tasks are. Generally the best solution is to build less software within the schedule or replan with an achievable schedule.

Inaccurate Sizing

Because sizing directly drives the magnitude of an estimate, the uncertainty and risk in software size translate directly into estimate risk and uncertainty. The best way to attack this issue is to use several different methods of sizing, including rough-order-of-magnitude, Delphi, bottom-up versus top-down, and analogy to validate the sizing estimate. The Galorath size methodology described in Figure 3.1 is extremely useful in clarifying size ranges.

Source Lines of Code (SLOC) Definition

SLOC is a common metric in use today; unfortunately, SLOC has no universal definition. If you receive an estimate of SLOC, the first thing to do is ask what the definition is. If the definition is not consistent with your standard, request a new count or ask for a sample of the code that will reveal what percentage of lines is accounted for by items left in or out. You can then adjust the SLOC estimate as appropriate. (See Chapter 5 for a detailed discussion on counting SLOC.)

Code Growth

Make sure that estimates for size include growth. Size estimates completed early in a life cycle must have growth added to account for the unknowns at the time of the estimate. (See Chapter 5 for code growth guidelines.)

Skepticism about Reported Size (Particularly with SLOC)

Developers who provide SLOC estimates often use quite rudimentary means. Ask exactly how SLOC estimates were determined and try to find secondary size estimates to serve as sanity checks. Also be certain that all functionality in the specifications has been accounted for in the size estimate. Refer to Chapter 5 for information on how to do so. If necessary, help the developer construct a proper size estimate.

Counting Code

Some organizations count all delivered code, including reused or modified code. Be certain of what is being delivered, and whether it is new, reused, or modified.

Examining Range

An even-sized range distribution may mean range analysis was not applied and instead a simple plus–minus percentage was applied to a single point estimate. Ideally, three independent values are estimated for *least*, *likely*, and *most*.

Complexity versus Risk

More complex modules mean higher risk. Obtain a comparative risk assessment for the different modules being developed. Use the risk assessment to further understand the stability of estimates for high risk modules versus lower risk modules. If necessary, vary the size range used in each module. This can be done by replacing the estimate for the *least* size with the *likely* size value. Or use different probability levels for estimates of different major computer programs to capture unusual risk, but document this choice carefully. It is not normally done.

Careful Evaluation of Preexisting and COTS Software

Evaluate preexisting and COTS software very carefully. In validating estimates, answer the following questions. What proportion of code will be reused? Will reuse eliminate security concerns or solve the most complex parts of the project? Is the additional code in fact COTS or will it require substantial rework?

Off-the-Shelf Integration

When validating estimates associated with integration efforts, ask the set of questions presented in Table 4.2.

Table 4.2   Integration Questions

COTS Characteristic	Cost Estimation Impact on COTS Integration
Does the developer's organization already have experience with this COTS software?	Yes reduces cost.
Is the COTS software vendor an established company or a garage-shop operation?	Use of an established firm will reduce risk.
Is source code available?	Yes reduces risk if the vendor is shaky.
Is the developer planning on using modified COTS?	Yes means higher costs associated with rework.
Were COTS cognition estimates based on product evaluations or guesses?	Product evaluations offer greater confidence.
Were round numbers used for size estimates without backup?	Yes means the developer may have guessed rather than analyzed.

Function Point Counting Checklist

When presented with a function point count, carefully consider the following information.

Sanity Counts

Function point counts vary with counters. It is therefore useful to have a second counter double check (conduct a sanity count) of some part of a count before the entire count has been completed. By doing this, counting methodology questions can be resolved early. Alternately, using a sizing model can approximate the count quickly.

Lack of Convergence

Unless a counter is very experienced, a function point count should be conducted over several iterations. The more experience a counter has, the better he or she will understand the technique and be able to converge on a reliable number.

Double Counting

Keep careful track of requirements and the resulting function point counts to make sure that counts have not been replicated. The following are some typical sources of double counting:

- Referencing a File More than Once
  Files should be counted in relation to the boundary of the entire application. For example, an external interface file is created completely outside the application boundary. On the other hand, an internal logical file is created completely within the application boundary. It should be clear that external and internal logical files are counted only once in a particular application, regardless of how often they are used.
- Confusing Designer's and User's Perspectives
  Counting occurs from the user's perspective, which means that certain architectural details may remain hidden from the count and will legitimately not be counted. Another source of perspective-related confusion is the difference between physical and logical files. Sometimes, what the user sees as one logical file may actually reside in several physical files, while the opposite may also be

true. In either case, conduct the count as the user would see the components.

Sample and Statistical Concerns

When validating estimates based on project histories, be sure to assess the samples and statistics used and their associated risks.

Probability Level

The acquisition type of the project can determine the probability level of the estimate. When comparing contractor estimates with your own, be aware that a contractor's acceptable risk varies with the type of contract. A contractor may choose an estimate other than at the 50 percent probability. (Internal developments may also have the same issues with the use of probability.)

On *cost plus* jobs, a developer's overriding interest is in winning the contract, and so he may offer a more daring estimate. An estimate probability of 40 percent and even 30 percent may be chosen and could lead to a 60 or 70 percent chance of a cost overrun.

On a *fixed price* award, a developer bears the expense of a cost overrun and so is more fearful of bidding lower than practical. For such projects, an estimate probability of 60 percent or even 80 percent might be chosen.

Compare your estimate range and the actual bid. If the bid lies at the probability level in your estimate range that would be predicted by the type of contract, then the estimates probably agree. You can sometimes directly ask a contractor what probability level was chosen, but this information may or may not be available to you.

Falsely Bounded Risk

A risk analysis may be populated with engineers' and estimators' assumptions that may not admit the full range of possible outcomes. One useful countermeasure is comparing assumptions from different people and program components (such as separate computer programs) so that you can reconcile inconsistencies.

Bias

You must be careful to obtain a balanced sample, one that is not biased in any way, and particularly by factors that are unrelated to the project you are analyzing. Sample bias is a particular problem with small samples.

Try to obtain a sample with characteristics that are consistent with the project you are estimating.

Outliers

When assembling a sample to help you validate the estimate of a current project, some values can lie well outside the common range; these are called outliers. Outliers must be separately examined. An outlier may be an unrepresentative event that should be ignored or it may offer special lessons. An outlier that is valuable should not necessarily be included in the main sample and in the sample statistics. It may instead be used to offer instructive lessons outside the conventional statistical analysis.

Costs

Are Staff Costs Fully Burdened?

Ask the developer what its staff costs are, and make certain that the monthly staff rate has been agreed to. Understand whether costs are fully burdened or whether additional charges will be incurred; if so, ensure that these costs are included in the complete cost estimate.

How Many Hours Are in a Staff Month?

A common United States standard is 152 hours per staff month. If a developer's hours per month vary from what the estimate uses, you must normalize the results to make a viable comparison. Multiply all effort-month figures by the developer's hours per month and then divide this number by the hours per month that you are using. (Automated cost models like SEER-SEM do this automatically.)

Staff and Effort Accounting

Does Overtime Count?

If the development staff is planning to use unreported overtime, this will cause variation from the estimate.

What Level of Management Participates?

Account for labor directly applied to this project only. Confirm that the developer has not included upper level (executive) management.

How Efficiently Is Staff Allocated?

Estimates most often assume an optimal staff profile. However, this optimal profile is often not possible and you should check with the developer to learn the true staffing plan.

Are Experience Levels Honestly Rated?

Developers often overstate the abilities of their people. Ensure that staff ratings are determined on the basis of time-based experience rather than more subjective evaluations. Also confirm that the staff being rated will regularly be on this job; otherwise adjust the staff ratings.

Schedules

What Is the Proportion of Daily Billable Work Done?

Development staff do not always devote all their time to projects, particularly during the concept and early requirements phases. This circumstance may cause the schedule to be lengthened beyond the estimate, which often does not accept fractional staff amounts. Remember too that holidays matter on a small project.

Will Development Have Lags?

When a development project is lagged, schedule estimates need to be likewise adjusted. However, under certain circumstances an elongated schedule may increase efficiency and save money. A sophisticated estimating method will reflect this. Also consider a situation where you may have to pay for a standing army while you wait for test facilities, other projects work products, etc.

If Several Software Elements Are Developed, How Are They Scheduled?

Undertaking the development of several software elements means that the schedules for all of them must be coordinated, as shown in Figure 4.1

Developing all software elements at once may require too many staff members; developing them serially conserves staff but may take too long. Ask the development team for its phasing plan. Some elements may be dependent on other elements (for example, element B cannot start until element A is complete). These dependencies must be accounted for in the detailed development schedule.

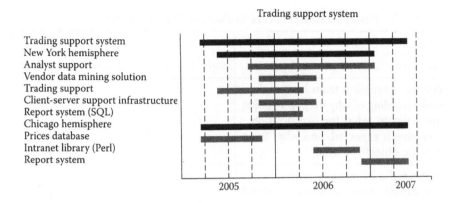

Figure 4.1   Sample schedule correlation.

Is It More Important to Save Time or Staff Cost?

Analytic models often determine an optimal solution based either on time or effort. You must specify which to use and therefore must understand what the developer's goals are.

Sanity Check

When using a model like SEER-SEM the entire estimate can be compared against an industry range. This can help identify areas of the estimate that may have been overlooked or misunderstood. Also, check the top cost drivers and ensure they are correct for this project. For example, if the top driver is multiple site development make sure that is correct and evaluate possibilities of performing a single site development.

Estimate Process Questionnaire

Table 4.3 is a sample checklist based on the SEI estimation checklist.[28] It has several fields including:

- **Primary factor** — The principal estimation factor that has a major impact on the accuracy and relevancy of the estimate.
- **Secondary factors** — Contributing factors that enable the primary factor and influence its accuracy, relevance, and consistency with the requirements of the estimation requirement.
- **Rating field** — Allows rating of factors as high, medium, or low to be assigned by the individual or team leader based on recent

Table 4.3 Postestimation Process Evaluation Questionnaire

Primary Factor (in bold)	Rating			Reason for	
Secondary Factors (with bullets)	High	Medium	Low	Low Score	Effect
Did the estimation team have a clear understanding of why they were doing the estimate, what the organization receiving it expected, and what their specific objectives were?					
■ Were the objectives of the estimate stated in writing and did the organization receiving it agree with them?					
■ Does the organization requesting the assessment have a documented life cycle to which the estimate applies and was it defined at the time the estimate was developed?					
■ Did the estimation team identify and document the tasks and activities included in (and excluded from) the estimate?					
■ Did the estimators ensure that the tasks and activities included in the estimate were consistent with the objectives of the estimate and were consistent with the capabilities of the organization to implement within the estimate's constraints?					
Did the estimation team follow a rigorous, documented sizing process and validate the result through a second size projection?					
■ Did the estimators follow a structured process to estimate and describe the size of the software product, and was the team trained and experienced in the process used?					

Table 4.3 (continued)   Postestimation Process Evaluation Questionnaire

Primary Factor (in bold)	Rating			Reason for Low Score	Effect
Secondary Factors (with bullets)	High	Medium	Low		
■ Did the rigorous process used by the estimation team estimate and describe the extent of reuse and factor it into the estimate using historical experience and parameters?					
■ Were the processes used for estimating size and reuse documented and applied consistently with the documented process?					
■ Did the size and reuse descriptions identify what was included in (and excluded from) the size and reuse measures used, and did the estimators consistently use the factors when developing the estimate?					
■ Did the reuse measures distinguish between modified code and code that will be integrated as-is into the system?					
■ Was size growth potential documented and applied consistently with the documented processes?					
■ Did the estimators use definitions, measures, and rules to describe size and reuse that were documented and consistent with the requirements (and calibrations) of the models used to estimate cost and schedule?					
Did the estimation team follow a rigorous documented estimation process?					

Table 4.3 (continued)   Postestimation Process Evaluation Questionnaire

Primary Factor (in bold)	Rating			Reason for Low Score	Effect
Secondary Factors (with bullets)	High	Medium	Low		
■ Did the estimators have training and experience in the documented, structured organizational process that they used to relate estimates to actual costs and schedules of completed work?					
■ Were the cost and schedule models used calibrated to relevant historical data and was the calibration current with the planned process and characteristics of the product?					
■ Did the cost and schedule models quantify demonstrated organizational performance in ways that normalize for differences among software products and projects and for the specific specialized requirements (safety, security, operational factors) of the product being estimated?					
■ Was the basis for the estimate the requirements and needs of the application rather than only an un-normalized source line projection?					
■ Were the cost and schedule model parameters used for the estimate validated when compared to values that fit the models well to past projects?					
■ Did the estimate address activities such as interface design, modification, integration, testing, and documentation associated with the project for newly developed software and reuse components?					

Table 4.3 (continued)   Postestimation Process Evaluation Questionnaire

Primary Factor (in bold)	Rating			Reason for	
Secondary Factors (with bullets)	High	Medium	Low	Low Score	Effect
■ Did the estimation team consider data from projects that implemented applications similar to the one being projected, and when required, were adjustments made to reflect the specific implementation characteristics of the estimate being performed?					
■ Were all assumptions made in support of the estimate identified, documented, and explained?					
■ While preparing the estimate, was a structured process used that included such tools as templates or checklists to ensure that key factors were not overlooked, and was the process validated during and after the estimate was completed?					
■ For this assessment, were any uncertainties in parameter values identified, quantified, and used to establish an initial set of risks for the organization?					
■ For the risks identified, was a risk analysis performed and were the risks that affect costs and schedules identified and documented?					
■ Were issues such as probability of occurrence, effects on parameter values, cost impacts, schedule impacts, and interactions with other organizations identified and used to characterize the risk?					
■ Did management review and agree to values for all descriptive parameters?					

Table 4.3 (continued)   Postestimation Process Evaluation Questionnaire

Primary Factor (in bold)	Rating			Reason for Low Score	Effect
Secondary Factors (with bullets)	High	Medium	Low		
■ Were any adjustments to parameter values to meet a desired cost or schedule documented, and were the reasons for the adjustments reviewed, approved, and agreed to by stakeholders and the team who must do the work?					
■ Was the size estimate confirmed by relating it to measured sizes of other software products or components, and was it validated by comparing it against a second, independently derived projection using a different method or tool?					
■ Was the size estimating *process* confirmed by testing its predictive capabilities against measured sizes of completed products, and was the last evaluation reasonably current and done against a similar type application?					
Was the process used to estimate cost and schedule proven consistent with demonstrated accomplishments on other projects similar in size, scope, and type to this one?					
■ Did the organization follow a rigorous, documented process for relating estimates to actual costs and schedules of completed work, and was the process applied to this estimate and was it followed?					
■ Were the cost and schedule models used calibrated to relevant historical data for this type application and for the planned process to be followed?					

Table 4.3 (continued)   Postestimation Process Evaluation Questionnaire

Primary Factor (in bold)	*Rating*			*Reason for Low Score*	*Effect*
Secondary Factors (with bullets)	*High*	*Medium*	*Low*		
▪ Were the cost and schedule models normalized for differences among software products and projects to quantify and normalize demonstrated organizational performance such that simple, un-normalized, lines of code per staff-month extrapolation did not become the basis for the estimate?					
▪ Has the consistency achieved when fitting the cost and schedule models to historical data been measured and reported?					
▪ Did the values used for cost and schedule model parameters appear valid when compared to values that fit the models well in past projects, and was this process completed before the estimate was completed?					
▪ Was the calibration of cost and schedule models done with the same versions of the models used to prepare the estimate, and was this calibration performed before the estimate was completed using data similar to the product and process being estimated?					
▪ Did the methods used to account for reuse account for activities such as interface design, modification, integration, testing, and documentation associated with effective reuse?					

Table 4.3 (continued)   Postestimation Process Evaluation Questionnaire

Primary Factor (in bold)	Rating			Reason for Low Score	Effect
Secondary Factors (with bullets)	High	Medium	Low		
■ Were extrapolations from past projects used to account for differences in application technology, and was data from projects that implemented different technical solutions from those being proposed adjusted to provide a valid basis for estimating, or was it confirmed that the cost models provide these capabilities?					
Were all critical factors that affect the estimate identified and explained and where an explanation was not satisfactory was a risk identified and documented?					
■ Were extrapolations from past projects used to account for observed, long-term trends in software technology improvement, and was the cost model used and calibrated to reflect historical organizational performance?					
■ Did the estimate consider the CMII rating of the organization planning to perform the task, and were the factors used to project productivity based on real values calibrated to the organization and the type of product to be developed?					
■ Were extrapolations from past projects used to account for the effects of introducing new software technology or processes required for the project, and did the estimate consider training and productivity impacts and rework normally associated with the introduction of new technologies?					

Table 4.3 (continued)   Postestimation Process Evaluation Questionnaire

Primary Factor (in bold)	Rating			Reason for Low Score	Effect
Secondary Factors (with bullets)	High	Medium	Low		
■ Was an analysis conducted to evaluate the proposed workflow against past projects to determine how this project is similar to (and how it differs from) projects used to characterize the organization's past performance?					
Did the estimate follow a process to ensure the integrity of the estimating process, and were discrepancies identified, resolved, and used to identify risks?					
■ Did a written summary of parameter values and their rationales accompany the estimate produced, and was it validated prior to the assessment?					
■ Were all assumptions made in support of the estimate identified, documented, and explained?					
■ While conducting the estimate, was a structured process including such tools as templates or checklists used to ensure that key factors were not overlooked, and was the process used validated during the estimate and after it was completed?					
■ Was a dictated schedule imposed, and, if so, was the estimate accompanied by an estimate of the normal schedule and the additional expenditures required to meet the dictated schedule?					

Table 4.3 (continued)   Postestimation Process Evaluation Questionnaire

Primary Factor (in bold)	Rating			Reason for Low Score	Effect
Secondary Factors (with bullets)	High	Medium	Low		
■ Were any uncertainties in parameter values identified and quantified before the estimate was completed, and, if they were unresolved, was a risk identified, analyzed, and entered into the risk management system for tracking?					
■ Were adjustments made to parameter values to meet a desired cost or schedule, and were they accompanied by management action that makes the values realistic, or were they just used in the estimate without analysis?					
■ For the risks identified, was a risk analysis performed, and were the risks that affect cost or schedule identified and documented?					
■ Were issues such as probability of occurrence, effects on parameter values, cost impacts, schedule impacts, and interactions with other organizations identified and used to characterize the risk?					
Did the organizations take steps to ensure the integrity of the estimating process, and did these steps involve using independent objective analysts familiar with the process and the models used?					
■ Did the groups that will do the work accept the estimate as an achievable target, and were any discrepancies or disagreements documented and entered as risks?					

Table 4.3 (continued)   Postestimation Process Evaluation Questionnaire

Primary Factor (in bold)	*Rating*			*Reason for Low Score*	*Effect*
Secondary Factors (with bullets)	*High*	*Medium*	*Low*		
■ Were memoranda of agreement completed and signed with the other organizations whose contributions affect cost or schedule, and did these stakeholders review the final estimates?					
■ Was a dictated schedule imposed, and, if so, was the estimate accompanied by an estimate of the normal schedule and the additional expenditures required to meet the dictated schedule?					
■ Were adjustments made to parameter values to meet a desired cost or schedule, and were they accompanied by management action that makes the values realistic, or were they only used in the estimate without analysis?					
■ Was more than one cost model or estimating approach used to validate the estimate, and were the differences in results analyzed and explained?					
■ Were individuals from related but different projects or disciplines involved in preparing the estimate, and were they used in its validation?					
■ Was at least one member of the estimating team an experienced estimator trained in the cost models used, familiar with the process followed and the technical characteristics and requirements of the product to be produced?					

Table 4.3 (continued)   Postestimation Process Evaluation Questionnaire

Primary Factor (in bold)	Rating			Reason for Low Score	Effect
Secondary Factors (with bullets)	High	Medium	Low		
■ Did experienced, trained estimators independent of the performing organization concur with the reasonableness of the parameter values and estimating methodology, and was their concurrence documented and based on a thorough analysis of the estimation process?					
■ Did the groups that will do the work accept the estimate as an achievable target, and were any discrepancies or disagreements documented and entered as risks?					

assessment experiences. A high rating means that the factor was a significant concern of the estimation team. A medium rating indicates that the factor was a concern but did not warrant special effort. A low rating means that the factor was not adequately addressed by the estimation team. For all medium and low scores, identify the trade-offs or decisions that led to the lack of emphasis and focus on the relevant factors.

The questionnaire is model- and method-independent. Therefore it can be used with not only commercial models, but internally developed models, and with other manual methods of estimating. The questionnaire is intended to be specific to each organization and assessment. You must refine or adapt the primary and secondary factors to the specific goals, needs, and requirement of the estimate and the specific characteristics of the project.

Step Eight: Generate Project Plan

The process of generating a project plan includes taking the estimate and allocating the cost and schedule to a function and task-oriented work breakdown structure. Models such as SEER Client for Microsoft perform this function automatically. The eight major software development phases are: (1) concept, (2) acquisition, (3) requirements, (4) design, (5) code and unit test, (6) integration, (7) acceptance, and (8) postdeployment.[2] As illustrated in Tables 4.4 through Table 4.11, the Software Engineering Process Organization at SPAWAR (a U.S. Navy program) has linked risks to specific project activities.[3]

Action Items by Project Phase

Table 4.4 Concept Phase

Action	Product	Risk If Action Not Taken
1. Define preliminary system functional requirements	Prioritized list of potential functions	Future requirements traceability problems
2. Establish method to estimate resources	Plan of action	No specific course of action on how project resources will be estimated
3. Identify similar functions from completed projects	List of functions with historical data	Lack of understanding of complexity and scope of project
4. Develop size estimates for functions with historical data	Size estimates for familiar functions	Increased uncertainty in scope and cost of project
5. Develop size estimates for new functions	Preliminary size estimate for total software product	Lack of basic parameters for cost and schedule estimate
6. Develop least, likely, and most cost and schedule estimates	Preliminary budget and schedule requirements	Lack of control in forecasting and justifying budget requirements
7. Identify potential cost, size, schedule risk areas	Definition of areas of uncertainty	Unrealistic expectations
8. Review and refine with project personnel; repeat as necessary	Estimations with increasing credibility	Preliminary estimate will continue

Table 4.5   Acquisition Phase

Action	Product	Risk If Action Not Taken
1. Clearly and concisely define software requirements	Understandable software requirements	Future requirement traceability problems
2. Establish software estimate file	Preliminary format to document all future estimates	Lack of traceability for budget justifications
3. Develop preliminary WBS	Top-level functional WBS	Lack of method to track progress
4. Develop baseline software estimates	Independent cost estimate	No foundation to verify other estimates
5. Develop risk profile	Definition of risk factors, monitoring and contingency procedures	Higher probability of future cost and schedule overruns due to unforeseen problems
6. Conduct formal review or inspection of estimate	Estimate agreed to and validated by project team	Unconfirmed or inconsistent process
7. Refine and record estimates on periodic basis	Establishment of cost metrics	Lack of management indicators for monitoring cost, size, schedule trends

Table 4.6   Requirements Phase

Action	Product	Risk If Action Not Taken
1. Develop detailed WBS	WBS that breaks work down by major function	Lack of definition of finite units of work
2. Develop baseline estimates by phase	Baseline estimate for basis of project cost and schedule tracking	Incomplete project plan
3. Update and revise risk assessment	Comprehensive plan to monitor and neutralize potential risks	Unrealistic optimism and lack of visibility
4. Conduct formal review or inspection	Validated estimate agreed to by management	Unconfirmed estimate

Table 4.6 (continued) Requirements Phase

Action	Product	Risk If Action Not Taken
5. Refine and record software estimates	Final format of method to track cost and schedule	Lack of formal vehicle to monitor project cost/schedule

Table 4.7 Design Phase

Action	Product	Risk If Action Not Taken
1. Refine WBS as necessary	Detailed WBS that accurately reflects project tasks	Possible misconceptions regarding task breakdown and progress
2. Develop cost-to-complete estimates	Increased accuracy of software product size, schedule, and costs	Lack of validated estimates derived from most recent information
3. Update and revise risk assessment	Improved insight into potential problems	Reliance on outdated information
4. Conduct formal review or inspection	Validated estimate agreed to by management	Lack of formal vehicle to track cost/schedule
5. Refine and record estimates	Timely and accurate cost status	Inability to recognize potential overruns

Table 4.8 Code and Unit Test Phase

Action	Product	Risk If Action Not Taken
1. Review and Refine detailed WBS	More accurate task breakdown for final phases of project	Possible misconceptions regarding task breakdown and progress
2. Update and revise cost-to-complete estimates	Realistic estimate of cost to complete	Lack of visibility into potential cost and schedule problems
3. Update and revise risk assessment	Risk profile that reflects current stage of project	Reliance on outdated information
4. Develop preliminary estimate for software operations and maintenance (O&M)	Preliminary inputs to computer resources life cycle management plan (CRLCMP)	Lack of visibility necessary for turnover to operations group

Table 4.9 Integration Phase

Action	Product	Risk If Action Not Taken
1. Review and refine detailed WBS	Increased awareness of O&M issues	Lack of visibility into current and future issues
2. Update and revise cost-to-complete estimates	Realistic estimate of cost to complete	Lack of ability to perform cost and schedule trend analysis
3. Update and revise risk assessments	Risk plan addressing current issues	Increased probability of unexpected problems; lack of contingency plans
4. Update and revise estimates for software O&M	Revised life cycle management plan	Non-comprehensive understanding of O&M issues and needs

Table 4.10 Acceptance (Transition to Operation) Phase

Action	Product	Risk If Action Not Taken
1. Close out development metrics: final cost, schedule, WBS, etc.	Final report for project	No history to pass on to future projects
2. Update O&M estimates and WBS	Baseline estimates and WBS for O&M	Reliance on outdated information

Table 4.11 Postdeployment (Software Support Activity) Phase

Action	Product	Risk If Action Not Taken
1. Review and Refine estimates and WBS	Updated baselines	Reliance on outdated information
2. Institute O&M metrics collection program and database	Process to continually enhance estimate of future O&M resource requirements	Lack of O&M data for cost trend analysis

Determining Costs from Effort Estimates

At this point in the estimation process, you should have a reasonably accurate projection of your project's size and required effort, that is, an estimate of the number of person-hours by component and a sum of these projections, and you can now begin to price the estimate. As software estimation models generally account only for costs related directly to development, you may need to translate the required effort to a cost and finalize the estimate by adding in essential nonlabor costs. You can do so by answering the following questions:

What types of individuals do I need and when do I need them? Identify the specific personnel requirements by task area by addressing the factors listed below. Develop a strawman schedule from the work breakdown structure or a staffing plan such as the one produced by SEER-SEM. Identify what personnel in what mix are required to support each task.

Estimating Personnel Mix

The estimation process needs to define the optimum personnel mix to complete the project within the cost and schedule. A typical WBS includes the following elements:

- **Direct software management** — Direct software management, which by definition does not include executive-level activities. Project cost accounting usually excludes workers who are not involved in directly billable work.
- **Software systems engineering** — Development of software requirements and specifications.
- **Design** — Definition of software architecture, preparation of design specifications, specification of layouts of physical data structures and interfaces, and meeting other requirements with additional necessary design.
- **Programming** — Coding, unit testing, and maintaining appropriate low-level documentation.
- **Quality assurance** — Quality engineering, inspection, and audits.
- **Configuration management** — Program configuration identification, change control, status accounting, etc.
- **Data preparation** — Preparation of specifications, standards, draft manuals, etc.
- **Testing** — Preparation and execution of test cases and test outcome reporting.

Each task identified in the WBS requires some allocation of effort. Arriving at a cost estimate for the labor mix is not always a straightforward task. One reason is that labor rates vary tremendously by region, and they also differ dramatically by the segment of the industry for which the estimate is being prepared. The National Bureau of Labor Statistics publishes labor rates at www.bls.gov.

Labor Proportions

In regard to estimating effort, initial work allocations are also nominal and must be tailored to the characteristics of the application, the needs and expectations of the user, and the operational and deployment requirements that must be met. The analyst must address factors such as security, required certifications, unique testing requirements, and essential customer and user involvement, tailoring the cost model results to these factors as they apply to the project being estimated. While the WBS at this point may be reasonably complete, usually the process of planning the work is conducted in parallel with the process of estimating the work. Therefore both processes must be repeated as the project proceeds. Table 4.12 offers a general allocation of labor that may be used as a cross-check on a planned labor mix.

How experienced do they have to be? Assign specific staff levels to the task requirements and identify the level of experience required to satisfy the task.

Some of the automated cost models will identify the tasks and develop a task-based schedule, which will minimize but not eliminate all of the work required to produce the software development plan. Table 4.13 shows the typical costs included by automated cost models.

Other Costs

Travel Costs

Projects conducted in different locations will require occasional face-to-face meetings for coordination purposes. Travel costs will depend on the size of staff, the distances between their locations, the extent and sophistication of virtual collaboration tools (teleconferencing, digital white boards, etc.), and the need for collaboration.

Personnel Costs

Software projects commonly augment permanent staff with outside consultants, which is often more expensive than using in-house staff. Augmenting internal staff by outsourcing cheaper foreign labor can reduce costs to a certain extent.

Table 4.12 Percent Effort by Labor Category

Activity	Management	S/W Requirements	Design	Code	Data Preparation	Test	CM	QA
System requirements design	12	52	14	0	6	12	2	2
S/W requirements analysis	12	46	14	6	6	12	2	2
Preliminary design	11	10	41	12	8	14	2	2
Detailed design	11	10	41	12	8	14	2	2
Code and unit test	7	3	6	55	6	1	4	4
Component integration and test	8	2	4	39	8	29	5	5
Program test	8	2	4	39	8	29	5	5
System integration through OT&E	8	2	4	19	1	59	5	2
Maintenance	8	2	4	38	1	40	5	2

S/W = software. CM = configuration management. QA = quality assurance. OT&E = operational test and evaluation.

Table 4.13   Sample Cost Model Coverage

WBS Elements	Portion Included by Cost Model
Software development	Model includes all software development costs
Test software	Model includes cost to build all necessary test software
System development support	All
Software support facility (SSF) hardware	Model does not include hardware costs for SSF
Software support facility (SSF) software	Model does not include software to be purchased for SSF
Requirements engineering and analysis	All if COTS hardware; part if developmental hardware
Logistics engineering	None
Specialty engineering	None
Technical reviews and audits	All if COTS hardware; part if developmental hardware
Production engineering	None
Engineering change analysis	All if COTS hardware; part if developmental hardware
Subcontractor engineering	Part: include software portion of subcontractor engineering; for software included in estimate
Systems engineering	Software systems engineering only
Software engineering	All
Program management office	None
Product assurance	Part
Program control	None
Training plan and analysis	None
Test planning	All if COTS hardware; part if developmental hardware
Test conduct	All if COTS hardware; part if developmental hardware
Test reporting	All if COTS hardware; part if developmental hardware

Table 4.13 (continued)   Sample Cost Model Coverage

WBS Elements	Portion Included by Cost Model
Site O&M	None
OT&E support	Part
Initial operational test and evaluation	All if COTS hardware; part if developmental hardware
Development data	All if COTS hardware; part if developmental hardware
Install and check out	None
Site activation travel and living	None

Depreciation Costs

Contractors may be allowed to deduct depreciation costs for tangible capital assets.

Training Costs

Costs are often associated with training the development staff in the use of new tools and/or methodologies. Remember to include the cost of downtime while personnel are in training rather than working on the project. Training costs may also be associated with designing and delivering a training course that accompanies the software being built.

Independent Verification and Validation or Independent Quality Assurance

Often these two independent and optional activities are excluded from cost models. If they are considered parts of the development activities, they must also be included in the costs.

Inflation

Because projects may cover multiple years, analysts must also account for factors that will vary over time. Multiyear projects can be subject to substantial inflation. The higher the inflation rate and lengthier the development period, the more current-year costs will rise. In order to accurately account for this, make certain the inflation rate is taken into account as part of the estimate.

Overhead

Accurate estimates must also account for many other costs. Expenses such as 401(k) contributions, clerical support, customer support, cost of money, etc., are not projected by the models but are addressed as an overhead percentage applied to the cost and general and administrative (G&A) calculation. At this point in the process, projections of these costs must be converted into a cost estimate, including all costs necessary to complete the project.

Estimating Schedule in Calendar Months

Projecting a schedule requires development of a preliminary work plan that describes the tasks and their sequence, dependencies and constraints that will limit scheduling options, cost and schedule trade-offs that are essential in defining a viable schedule, projected delays due to non-availability of resources or other factors, and additional items such as customer-unique requirements. While the schedule need not be considered final, it should be sufficiently well structured to provide a high probability that the projected calendar months reflect how long the actual project will take. Just as with effort, the estimate should describe a range characterized as *least*, *likely*, and *most*.

Effect of Management and Process on Estimates

Management and process maturity are critical factors in the projection of productivity. They affect the personnel capability parameters or calibrations in models such as SEER-SEM. A rating based only on process maturity factors can make any estimate invalid *unless the risks are managed and controlled or unless the model is run with a higher confidence level.* Management factors determine the project environment and how focused it will be on addressing and completing project commitments. Process maturity will determine how effective the organization will be in meeting its stated productivity targets.

Impact of Software Project Management on Software Development Plan

To avoid tomorrow's catastrophes, a software manager must confront today's challenges. A good software manager must possess a broad range of technical software development experience and domain knowledge, and must be able to manage people and the unique dynamics of a team environment, recognize project and staff dysfunction, and lead so as to achieve the expected or essential result. To paraphrase Tom DeMarco, "Managers … make the craziness go away."[4]

However, too often software managers are not equipped with these necessary skills and therefore the projects they manage run into predictable problems.

Many managers of software projects were promoted from within the company and have no training other than their engineering backgrounds. One day a manager is told he is responsible for a software project that is "so complex no one will know how it works,"[5] and by the time the dust settles, the problems he caused have resulted in poor cost and schedule performance. We have observed two types of "problem managers." The first has technical and domain level experience, often excelling in these attributes, but lacks the required leadership, personnel management, and programmatic skills. In addition, this type generally will focus on his or her area of familiarity and expertise, such as writing good code, and give little attention to meeting a program's high level objectives.

The second type of problem manager is promoted from a non-software discipline (finance, QA, human resources) and possesses a limited understanding, if any, of software engineering essentials. While he or she may possess competent management skills, this type of manager tends to trade off essential engineering steps (inspections, test steps, design rigor, simulations) to save costs, improve project image, or convince someone the project can accomplish something it can't. Both types, although they may mean well, either lead a project to an unintended conclusion or, worse, drift down the road to disaster.

"Poor project management will defeat good engineering, and is the most frequent cause of project failure."[6] As for the second management type described above, too often the people charged with managing large scale software projects have never developed software or were trained in an academic environment where they were asked to code small-scale projects over the course of a single semester. Building 5,000 lines of Visual Basic or C++ software to achieve a grade hardly prepares a manager for building 3.5M lines of software intended to run a company's finances, drive a tank, or fly an airplane. The only common issue of these two types of managers is the word *software*.

While the manager you assign may possess adequate management skills and have extensive experience on non-software-intensive projects, you can expect to run into problems if the manager lacks specific experience managing large-scale software projects that employ many creative engineers who are developing many intangible products. If a project is large, the manager cannot think small. This problem increases exponentially when the task is integration of a large program.

The type-one manager (who has technical and domain level experience, but lacks the required leadership, personnel management, and programmatic skills) presents a different set of problems that can lead to the same results. Often a highly effective software engineering professional displays staggering skills and has a reputation for on-time, quality production as part of a team. As a result, the company wants to recognize his achievements and not lose him to the competition, so they promote him to a management position. Far too frequently a company provides no training in managing people and teams, does not develop required skills such as estimation and scheduling, provides no mentoring program to smooth the transition, and has no help desk to furnish assistance when his knowledge fails. The manager simply receives a slap on the back, a bigger paycheck, responsibility for $2 million of a client's money, and, by the way, is assigned to manage a staff that doesn't think much of managers. This manager does not possess the skills, the seasoning, or the basic experience to address the day-to-day crises that must be overcome to successfully manage a software project.

Software management problems have been recognized for decades as the leading causes of software project failures. In addition to the types of management choices discussed above, three other issues contribute to project failure: bad management decisions, incorrect focus, and destructive politics. Models such as SEER-SEM handle these issues by guiding you in making appropriate changes in the environment related to people, process, and products.

Bad management decisions not only affect a project's potential for success, they can eliminate that potential altogether. Software project managers have many opportunities to make bad decisions: making inappropriate trade-offs, dropping essential activities, making bad personnel decisions, and focusing on the wrong customer and product goals. Two factors may lead to poor decisions. First, many managers, mainly due to lack of experience, are not able to evaluate what effects their decisions will have over the long run, They either lack necessary information or incorrectly believe if they take the time to develop that information, the project will suffer as a result.

Second, and even sorrier, managers make decisions based on what they think higher management wants to hear. "Project reality be damned, I'm not going to buck the vice president of engineering. We'll deliver February 12."[7] This attitude is a guaranteed ticket to disaster. A good software manager will understand what a project can realistically achieve, even if it's not what higher management wants. His job is to explain the reality in language his managers can understand.

Many factors related to management can affect the validity of an estimate. Although an estimate, especially one prepared by a cost model, may assume consistency in process, predictable productivity, and a flow of work that follows the agreed to plan, an ineffective manager will push the envelope of this predictability into a range that borders on chaos. As a result, schedules will become impossibly compressed and predictability will disappear. (This is one reason SEER-SEM's minimum time estimate is so valuable.) As the schedule is compressed, the staff becomes further demoralized and productivity drops out of the acceptable range. The processes that were so carefully planned are discarded in misguided attempts to recover lost schedule, and risks that easily could have been addressed become full blown problems with no plans to mitigate them. The result? Disaster. Even replans probably can't save a project in this situation.

Effect of Software Processes on Software Development Plan

If you want to understand the effects of improving your organization's software development processes, consider the following information. "One way to project the potential of an organization to apply best practices and experience the productivity windfall is to look at their Software Engineering Institute (SEI) Capability Maturity Model (CMM or CMMI) ratings."[8] Dave Card of the Software Productivity Consortium compiled a list of potential benefits of improving processes and obtaining an SEI CMM rating.[9]

- A 4 to 11 percent increase in productivity for each increase of one level in CMM maturity.[10]
- A 20 percent annual increase in productivity due to CMM and other improvement initiatives.[11]
- Improvements by factors ranging from 2.9 to 16.8 in productivity and defect density in reaching CMM Level 5.[12] Results are broken down by CMM maturity level.
- Significant reductions in performance variances measured by the Cost Performance and Schedule Performance Indices.[13]
- Review effectiveness increased from 40 to 80 percent at CMM Level 4.[14]
- Delivered defects reduced 94 percent at CMM Level 5.[15]

We should point out that just receiving a certification is not a silver bullet to improved productivity. Careful adherence to certified processes by trained professionals is required; and not all teams will achieve such outstanding productivity even when trained.

The cost of process improvement can be significant. However, the return on this investment can also be significant. A study performed by the Air Force Materiel Command, indicates how much:

> Table 4.14 summarizes the isolated statistics in U.S. industry on the return for process improvement initiatives. Most of the information is in the form of productivity and quality results, particularly in response to the introduction of inspections into an organization. The table summarizes, by category, the statistics uncovered in the research. It was not the intent of this phase of the research to provide extensive ROI data, only to identify the sources of existing data; therefore, this data should be construed as representative of the type of data available, not of the amount of data available.[16]

Table 4.14   Process Improvement ROI

Metric Category	Measurement	Benefits Realized by Various Software Organizations[a]
Productivity	Increase in productivity	10 to 20 percent, 90 to 100 percent, 50 percent, 15 to 20 percent, 5 percent
		130 percent, 12 percent, 2.5 to 6.3 percent, 35 percent
Quality	Reduction in defects	10 percent, 80 percent, 50 to 70 percent, 50 percent
	Reduction in error rate	45 percent
	Product error rate	From 2.0 down to 0.11 per thousand SLOC
		From 0.72 down to 0.13 per thousand non-commented source statements
Cost	Ratio of project dollars saved to dollars invested	1.5 to 1, 2.0 to 1, 4 to 1, 6 to 1, 7.7 to 1, 10 to 1, 1.26 to 1, 5 to 1
	Project dollars saved	$2 million to $3.4 million
	Code problems during integration	20 percent of original value
	Decrease in cost of retesting	50 percent

Table 4.14 (continued)   Process Improvement ROI

Metric Category	Measurement	Benefits Realized by Various Software Organizations[a]
	Cost savings of metrics program	50 to 300 percent, 40 to 290 percent
Schedule	Within estimate	5 percent of estimate
	On-time deliverables	From 51 percent up to 94 percent on time
	Project completion	From 50 percent down to 1 percent late
	Savings in schedule	10 percent, 20 percent
Effort	Reduction in rework	5 to 10 percent
		From 40 percent down to 25 percent of effort
		From 41 percent down to 11 percent of project cost
	Savings in test time	10 test hours per analysis hour

Note: Isolated statistics in U.S. industry on return for process improvement initiatives.

[a] Benefits shown as range of results within a single organization; results from different organizations are separated by commas. All organizations are not represented.

Step Nine: Document Estimate and Lessons Learned

Each time you complete an estimate and again at the end of the software development, you should document the pertinent information that constitutes the estimate and record the lessons you learned. By doing so, you will have evidence that your process was valid and that you generated the estimate in good faith, and you will have actual results with which to calibrate your estimation models. Be sure to document any missing or incomplete information and the risks, issues, and problems that the process addressed and any complications that arose from using the process. Also document all the key decisions made during the conduct of the estimate and their results and the effects of the actions you took. Finally, describe and document the dynamics that occurred during the process, such as the interactions of your estimation team, the interfaces with your clients, and trade-offs you had to make to address issues identified during the process.

Also, if you had to replan the project or restart it for any reason, record the circumstances so you can avoid similar problems in the future. Cost models, which are based on the actual costs of past projects, can be calibrated and their accuracy can be demonstrated by comparing the costs of your current estimates with both past project data and the actual costs of your completed project, thereby adjusting the model input parameters to improve future accuracy.

Conducting Lessons-Learned Review

You should conduct a lessons-learned session as soon as you can after the completion of your project while the participants' memories are still fresh. Lessons-learned sessions can range from two team members meeting to reach a consensus about the various issues that went into the estimation process to highly structured meetings conducted by external facilitators who employ formal questionnaires. No matter what form it may take, it is always better to hold a lessons-learned meeting than not, even if the meeting is a burden on those involved.

Every software project should be used as an opportunity to improve the estimating process. To document the lessons learned, follow these steps.

1. Conduct a postmortem to identify the reasons for significant estimating variances.
2. Identify the major cost drivers.
3. Log each reason for project growth as well as the cost, size, schedule, and effort impact.
4. Compare actuals to those of the similar systems used for estimating.
5. Identify any differences in estimating rationale and reality.
6. Assess the difficulty and complexity of the problem, technical staff and management team characteristics, product and process characteristics, and environment and user characteristics.[17]

The most accurate lessons-learned session would encompass three reviews; one conducted after the estimate has been accepted and two conducted upon completion of the project. The post-acceptance session (cause segment) employs a questionnaire similar to the estimating process questionnaire provided in Chapter 4 to rate the estimation process against a standard set of criteria.

The purpose of this step is to capture the experiences and views of the analysts in a structured framework and to compare what actually occurred during the project with the model used. The second meeting (effects segment) uses the same questionnaire to assess the effects of the ratings: *high*, *medium*, and *low* on the accuracy of the estimate process and on the project as a whole. The third meeting (modeling improvement segment) uses a different process to collect the information needed to improve the modeling process. These sessions are important for answering questions that are critical to the organization and for providing the information needed to validate the accuracy of the cost models used.

Cause segment — What did we do and what trade-offs did we make?

Effects segment — What were the effects of the shortcuts, trade-offs, and assumptions we made and should these changes to the process be incorporated into the standard process?

Modeling improvement segment — Based on the results of the estimate, how should the cost and schedule models be applied to more accurately reflect the process followed, the results of the project, and the quantitative values of key model factors at the completion of the project?

Cause Segment

Lessons-learned sessions are intended to assess current estimation activities in order to make them more accurate or to make them more relevant to future projects. Begin the cause segment of the session by asking each participant to fill out the questionnaire (such as the one presented in Table 4.3) to record the specific tasks each performed and what occurred during the estimate. To the extent possible, the questions on the questionnaire should elicit specific answers that can be unambiguously rated for quality using high, medium, and low criteria. After each participant has completed the questionnaire, the moderator should review them with the participants without judgment to determine why any factors in the questionnaire were rated medium or low and why such factors did not receive more attention during the estimation process.

Effects Segment

The effects segment, which can be conducted during the project in multiple sessions or in one session upon project completion, is intended to determine the effects of the shortcuts, trade-offs, and assumptions made and to decide whether the process should be changed as a result. It is most beneficial to conduct this segment in multiple meetings during the project. Doing so can help identify problems and risks that arise from estimation issues early and minimize them or avoid them altogether. The estimation team as well as management and staff members of the project team must participate in the effects segment. This segment records actual project experience and determines the extent to which that experience had an effect on specific decisions or trade-offs made during the estimate. Not all project experience is traceable to specific decisions, but if you can determine the effects of your estimation decisions you will be better positioned to avoid problems on future projects.

As a software manager, part of your responsibility is to improve the performance of your staff over time. The effects segment helps you do so by identifying estimation process activities that they found helpful and thus should be repeated. It can also help isolate estimation process activities that were detrimental to their efforts and should thus be avoided in the future. This segment also helps to give your estimation and project teams insight into what could have caused problems. Also you can see how trade-offs made in the estimation process that appeared to have short-term benefits actually produced a negative effect over the long term. Such insights will enable future development teams to work more effectively despite the pressures they inevitably face during any project. To conclude this segment, participants should be asked to use the lessons they have learned and to establish goals for their next project.

Modeling Improvement Segment

Because software estimation models provide a basic framework for estimation, they should be refined or calibrated to the maximum extent possible in order to produce the best estimates possible. Model refinement is conducted to both improve the accuracy of estimates and to better suit the people, processes, and products that are typically encountered. It can also improve the estimating process by providing information necessary for preconfiguring the model, thus shortening the learning curve on any given estimate. The estimation team at the completion of the project usually conducts the modeling improvement segment.

Step Ten: Track Project throughout Development

Refining Estimates throughout Project

Estimating software size, cost, and schedule should be an ongoing process. Preliminary estimates may be required to bid a job or to initiate the development process, or you may need to conduct a cost–benefit or return-on-investment (ROI) analysis to evaluate a project's feasibility. Preliminary estimates are the hardest to develop and are the least accurate because of the incomplete nature of the information available and the other factors discussed throughout this chapter.

You can improve the accuracy of a preliminary estimate by using the sizing methodology identified in Step 4 defined in Chapter 3 or by using two different estimation techniques and having your analysts normalize the differences. There will still be a significant risk in using the preliminary estimate to structure a project or to evaluate risk in the early stages of a project life cycle.

Once a project has started, you will need to complete more detailed estimates to accurately plan the project and throughout the conduct of the project you will need to monitor the actual effort and duration of tasks and/or phases against planned values to ensure you have the project under control. Tracking is so important that multiple chapters are included to detail the topic. Chapter 9 discusses earned value and other techniques that can be used to track a project in detail. Chapter 12 discusses SEER-PPMC and how components can be automated to provide complete planning and control.

Summary

Software cost estimation is a difficult process but a necessary part of a successful software development. You can help ensure useful results by adopting a process that is standardized and repeatable. Several of the steps we have discussed, particularly those that do not result directly in the production of the estimate (Steps 1, 6, and 7) are often deferred or, worse still, not performed at all, often for what appear to be good reasons such as a lack of adequate time or resources or a reluctance to face the need to devise a plan if a problem is detected. Sometimes you simply have more work than you can handle and such steps don't seem absolutely necessary. As Capers Jones stated:

> If an early estimate predicts higher cost, longer schedules or lower quality ... there is a strong tendency to challenge the validity of the estimate. ... the project manager is directed to recast the estimate so that it falls within preset and arbitrary boundary conditions.[18]

Sometimes management is reluctant to take these steps, not because the resources are not available, but because managers do not want to really know what they may learn as a result of scoping their estimates, quantifying and analyzing risks, or validating their estimates. This can be a costly attitude, because in reality every shortcut results in dramatic increases in project risks.

Endnotes

1. Park, Robert E. *A Manager's Checklist for Validating Software Cost and Schedule Estimates.* Pittsburgh: Carnegie Mellon Software Engineering Institute, January 1995.
2. International Standards Organization. *ISO/IEC Standard 12207, Software Life Cycle Processes.* Geneva, ISO: 2004.
3. Software Engineering Process Organization. *Software Estimation Process 2.2,* August 31, 1999. 21.
4. DeMarco, Tom. *Why Does Software Cost So Much?* New York: Dorsett House, 1995. 66.
5. Lister, Tim. "Software Management for Adults." *Software Technology Conference.* Salt Lake City, 1996.
6. Humphrey, Watts. "Three Dimensions of Process Improvement. Part I: Process Improvement." *CrossTalk: The Journal of Defense Software Engineering.* February 1998.
7. Comment from a beleaguered software manager after much pressuring at an assessment.
8. Ibrahim, Linda. "Using an Integrated Capability Maturity Model: The FAA Experience." *Tenth Annual International Symposium of International Council on Systems Engineering.* Minneapolis, July 2000. 643.
9. Card, David N. *Published Sources of Benchmarking Data.* Herndon: Software Productivity Consortium, March 2002.
10. Clark, B. "The Effect of SEI-CMM Maturity on Software Effort." *IEEE Software,* November 2000.
11. Card, David N. "The SEI Software Process Improvement Approach: A Case Study." *Auerbach Software Engineering Strategies,* December 1993.
12, Diaz, M. and J. King. "How CMM Impacts Quality, Productivity, Rework, and the Bottom Line." *CrossTalk: The Journal of Defense Software Engineering,* March 2002. [Update of Diaz, M. and J. Sligo. "How Process Improvement Helped Motorola." *IEEE Software.* September 1997.]
13. Humphrey, W.S., T.R. Snyder, and R.R. Willis. "Software Process Improvement at Hughes Aircraft." *IEEE Software,* July 1991.
14. Keeni, G. "The Evolution of Quality Processes at Tata Consultancy Services." *IEEE Software,* July 2000.
15. Pitterman, B. "Telcordia Technologies: The Journey to High Maturity." *IEEE Software,* July 2000.
16. Brodman, Judith G. and Donna L. Johnson. "Return on Investment (ROI) from Software Process Improvement as Measured by U.S. Industry." *Software Process: Improvement and Practices* (pilot issue), 1995.
17. Mathis, Randy. "Metric-Based Scheduling and Management." *CrossTalk: The Journal of Defense Software Engineering,* July 1997.
18. Jones, Capers T. *Assessment and Control of Software Risks.* Englewood Cliffs: Prentice Hall, 1994. 158.

Chapter 5

Source Lines of Code

Not everything that can be counted counts and not everything that counts can be counted.

Albert Einstein

Introduction

This chapter describes how to identify source lines of code (SLOC). It addresses the many different facets of lines and gives clear direction on the proper use and definition of lines. Included in these discussions are physical and logical source lines and a checklist for source line definitions. The chapter also describes how to handle issues and risks associated with using SLOC to determine program size. It explains how the SLOC sizing approach is affected by different computer languages, describes best practices for approaching size for different languages, and explains the proper use of the size metric. Throughout this chapter information, will be provided for counting SLOC for a completed program and for a future program in which SLOC must be estimated.

Some years ago, at a trade show, a man approached me and offered me a database of sizes for 10,000 programs. Upon inquiry, the man said these were both government and commercial programs. When asked how much, the man replied "thirty-five dollars." Trying not to salivate I reached for my wallet. Before taking out the cash, I asked one final question: "What is the definition of a line?" The seller squeamishly said he didn't know. I then asked if the sizes were non-comment source lines? "Some of them," the seller replied. "How about executable lines?" "Some of them," he again responded. "How about physical lines?" "Some of them, I believe," the man responded. "But how can I tell which is which?" "You cannot," replied the seller.

The database without the definitions was not worth the advertised price.[1] This story exemplifies the problems of software sizing and software sizing data. Inconsistent counting rules, unclear definitions of exactly what was counted, and a myriad of other roadblocks can contaminate viable software sizing. When consistently counted or when estimated with consistent definitions, lines of code can serve as an excellent measure of software size. Lines of code are reliable predictors for the amount of work required to develop software — not only for the coding activities, but for the effort and schedule associated with the entire software life cycle; from requirements definition all the way through integration and testing.

When lines of code are estimated or counted without clear definitions, these poor estimates of software size can produce even poorer estimates of software cost and schedule. Additionally, when counting or estimating SLOC, the source is extremely important. Counting hand-generated SLOC is valuable because there is a direct correlation of hand-generated code, effort, and schedule. Counting the code resulting from a code generator is not very useful for eventual cost and schedule estimation or any productivity calculations. Generated code may or may not be well correlated with the effort involved in developing that code. Generated code is best estimated using a function-based sizing approach or ratios of generated lines to effective size (see Chapter 8).

The most commonly used SLOC definition is noncomment, hand-generated logical source lines. This definition provides excellent correlation with effort and schedule and is the most common input of all SLOC definitions into many software cost models such as SEER-SEM and COCOMO II. These SLOC (noncomment, hand-generated logical source lines) also work well for nearly any programming language, with a line of code representing a unit of work.

If lines are counted using different definitions and those definitions are known, line counts can be normalized to the most desirable definition by developing conversion ratios. The Software Engineering Institute (SEI) checklist included later in this chapter is intended to define alternative sizing definitions.

Terminology and Definitions

SLOC and their derivations have been referred to by several names including lines of code (LOC), executable lines of code (ELOC), and delivered source instructions (DSI), to name a few. Unfortunately, definitions may not be consistent even when common terminology is used. The following are typical definitions.

Source lines of code (SLOC) — Generally nonblank, noncomment, logical source lines. A *K* often precedes the designation to denote thousands of SLOC (e.g., 15 KSLOC).

Lines of code (LOC) — generally a synonym for SLOC.

Delivered source instructions (DSI) — Generally DSI includes noncomment, logical source lines but excludes data declarations, compiler declarations, and other lines that do not generate executable instructions. Executable instructions are items such as *while, if,* arithmetic statements, and other functions that control the program logic.

Executable lines of code (ELOC) — ELOC are generally synonymous with DSI.

Effective source lines of code (ESLOC) — ESLOC are SLOC that have been adjusted by the amount of rework required for portions of the system that were pre-existing at the start of the development. ESLOC represent the number of effort units of work that will be developed rather than the total lines of code that will be delivered upon completion. (For a detailed discussion on ESLOC and how to compute it, see Chapter 8.)

Total lines of code (total SLOC) — Generally synonymous with SLOC; represent the number of lines before any adjustments that result in ESLOC.

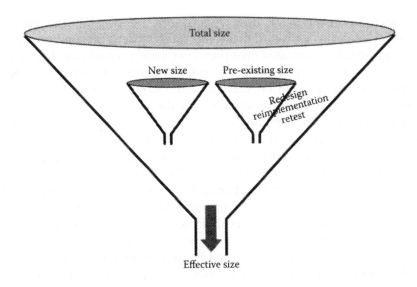

Figure 5.1   Size measures.

These definitions carry assumptions that must be verified before moving forward. This is due to the varied forms of use and, in some cases, misuse of SLOC measures over the years. For example, analysts have been asked to "back into a SLOC count" to meet a budget or customer expectation (e.g., the budget is $1M and projected cost per line of code is $200, therefore you "back into a SLOC count" of $1M/$200 independent of the system definition). Even more tragic, the optimistic biases of analysts (developers generally think of the best case) and project constraints have been used as a basis to predetermine size estimates, regardless of how many SLOC are needed to actually implement a project.

For example, a project manager could reason, "We have 10 people for 24 months and our productivity is 100 lines per person-month; therefore, the SLOC count is equal to: (10 people × 24 Months) × 100 = 24,000 SLOC." This is independent of the fact that a project may involve 50,000 SLOC over three years. Such misuse and other underlying problems can be largely overcome through proper use of sizing definitions and estimation models. Studies have indicated that as SLOC size increases,[2] more programs are cancelled, more defects are not detected, and are thus delivered. This results in substantial rework and decreased productivity. Therefore, when estimating cost and schedule, the impacts and risks of large computer programs (large SLOC counts) should be handled carefully.

SLOC Realities and Risks

"In extensive research of over 20,000 software development projects spanning 18 years, we found that more projects were doomed from poor cost and schedule estimates than they ever were from technical, political, or development team problems."[3] This is because the software project estimate, which is based on the size estimate, establishes funding constraints and a project plan that can limit the management, engineering, quality assurance, and reporting processes that can be used, the tools that can be applied, and the ability to engage in rework and risk resolution.

Unrealistic estimates caused by analyst bias, customer or management pressure, or any other factor will increase the risks to the project. Spending time in software sizing and preparing the most viable range of software sizing that serves as a foundation for the cost estimate most likely can do more to reduce risk to a project than nearly any other factor including program requirements, architecture, quality factors, and other issues that affect the integrity of the process and the timely delivery of an acceptable product within projected budgets. Figure 5.2 illustrates that size drives estimates.

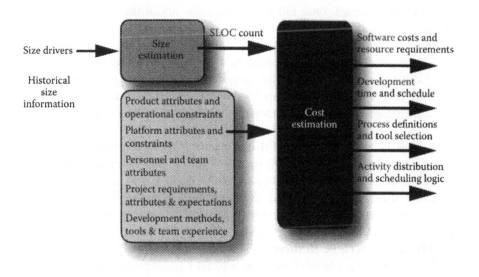

Figure 5.2   Size drives the estimate.

Using SLOC

SLOC can be used to measure either an existing program or a program yet to be built. Using SLOC to measure the size of an existing program is reasonably straightforward and involves little risk when appropriate counting rules are applied to a sound technical baseline. This straightforward process becomes more complicated if it is used to answer questions such as, "How big would the application have been if we had used a different language?" or "What savings in code would result if we modified the architecture?" Careful engineering analysis in concert with some rules provided in this chapter can help make these trade-offs possible.

Program size is the most obvious and perhaps the most fundamental measure of the amount of intellectual work needed for software development. Physical lines of code are among the easiest measurements to make; measurement simply involves counting the end-of-line markers. For example the number of SLOC in Microsoft Windows can be found by searching the Internet. However, without the definition of the SLOC, that information is nearly meaningless (unless the goal is merely to "wow" someone with big numbers). Thus, published information on software measures that depend on SLOC is difficult to interpret and compare with programs yet to be developed. Complicating the matter, many questions, such as those related to costs, schedules, progress, reuse, and productivity may be unanswered. One SEI report says this about the measurement of source code size:

> Historically, the primary problem with measures of source code size has not been in coming up with numbers — anyone can do that. Rather, it has been in identifying and communicating the attributes that describe exactly what those numbers represent.[4]

Robert E. Park, formerly of the Software Engineering Institute, developed a framework (the checklist included later in this chapter) for defining SLOC values to enable people to carefully explain and define the SLOC measure used in a project.[4] Of the numerous types of SLOC measures, three stand out as most used: physical carriage returns, physical SLOC, and logical SLOC. They are defined below.

Physical Carriage Returns — Includes a count only of physical line endings. Counting physical carriage returns has little value in estimation. Counting the comment lines does not provide significant correlation with effort. Comment lines do not involve any additional intellectual work beyond what is encompassed in the code. They simply exist for documentation purposes. Blank lines can vary by 2 or 3 to 1 based only on coding standards or personal preference on the number of blanks before and after each comment and the standard for the code preamble.

It should be noted that ratios of comments to source lines may have value from a quality viewpoint. Additionally, from a size perspective, the ratio could be used to approximate a logical line count. In converting physical carriage returns to an approximate logical SLOC count, we have seen that ranges can vary from 20 to 70 percent (i.e., physical carriage returns × 20 percent = approximate logical SLOC). You can develop these ratios for your software by doing manual counts on several samples of code.

Physical SLOC — Expresses the physical length of code, which is every single line of source code as seen by human eyes, excluding comments and blanks but counting each physical line ending of all other lines. A physical SLOC is most commonly defined as a count of non-blank, non-comment lines in a program's source code. The SEI technical report on software size measurement states that, "Counts of physical lines describe size in terms of the physical length of the code as it appears when printed for people to read."[4]

This is among the easiest measurements to make because it involves counting the end-of-line markers rather than programming language-specific syntax. You need to specify only how you will recognize the statement types that you will not count, e.g., comments and blank lines. It is relatively easy to build automated counters for physical source line measures; however, measurement results can be more subject to variations in programming style than results using other measures. Later in this chapter, Table 5.3 details differences in line counting methods.

Logical SLOC — Measures the number of logical programming "statements" that may or may not cross over more than one physical line. The ideal count examines the language syntax and counts the statement types (e.g., data declarations, math statements) explicitly. Many languages can be counted more quickly by counting terminators (e.g., C-like languages can be approximated by the number of line-terminating semicolons and closing curly braces). The rules for counting logical statements should specify how to recognize and count embedded statements for each source language to be used. Logical SLOC is less sensitive to formatting and style conventions than physical SLOC. According to the SEI technical report on software size measurement:

> The count of logical statements is an attempt to characterize size in terms of number of software instructions, irrespective of the physical format in which they appear.[4]

Logical source lines are the lines that carry programming instructions and data declarations, that is, the implementation of the software design represented by the actual instructions that convert to executable code and data. Therefore, counting logical lines is the best measure of software size. Much of the historical data that has been used to construct cost models for project estimating is based on logical measures of source code size.

Logical SLOC Counting Details

Table 5.1 contains detailed definitions for counting logical SLOC as used in cost models such as SEER-SEM.

Note that the first category of attribute on Table 5.1 is what is included or excluded. Table 5.2 states the rules that apply to this category.

Logical SLOC Detailed Definitions

Executable Statements

Executable statements are those that perform program execution and control. While every language has its unique syntax and vocabulary, generally executable statements include:

Table 5.1 Logical SLOC Definition Details

SLOC Attribute		
What is included or excluded	**Included**	**Excluded**
Executable statements	X	
Nonexecutable data declaration statements and compiler directives	X	
Comments, continuation lines, banners, blank lines, instantiated SLOC, and nonblank spacers		X
How lines are produced	**Included**	**Excluded**
Manually/hand-programmed SLOC	X	
Lines developed for use as input to a source code generator	X	
Lines generated as output from a source code generator[a]		X
Lines converted with automated code translators[b]	X	
Copied, reused, or modified lines of code[c]	X	
Deleted lines of code (rework percentages of remaining SLOC account for the work to make the program execute correctly without deleted lines)		X
Origins of lines	**Included**	**Excluded**
New lines developed from scratch	X	
Preexisting lines taken from a prior version, build, or release	X	
Invocation statements or preexisting lines requiring rework from COTS or other off-the-shelf packages; rework percentages need to be calculated	X	
Invocation statements for modified vendor-supplied or special support libraries, but not unmodified library code itself	X	
Modified vendor-supplied or special support libraries, commercial libraries, reuse libraries, or other software component libraries; rework percentages should be calculated for modifying these lines	X	

Table 5.1 (continued)   Logical SLOC Definition Details

SLOC Attribute		
Origins of lines (continued)	**Included**	**Excluded**
Lines that are part of an unmodified vendor-supplied operating system or utility or other nondeveloped code		X
End usage of each line	**Included**	**Excluded**
Lines that are in or part of primary product	X	
Lines external to or in support of primary product only if part of final or deliverable program	X	
Lines external to or in support of primary product but are not deliverable; any other nondeliverable lines		X

a   Software from a source code generator is estimated best via function point sizing, not SLOC. Some people estimate generated lines by counting the total number of generated lines and applying reuse factors to them to reduce the effective size that will be used by the cost model.

b   These lines should be considered as pre-existing lines of code and the amount of rework required on the translated code should be defined through the use of rework percentages. See Chapter 8 on software reuse.

c   These lines should be considered as pre-existing SLOC.

Table 5.2   Logical Source Line Rules

Include	Exclude
Control statements (DO WHILE, DO UNTIL, GOTO, etc.)	Comments
	Blank lines
Mathematical statements ($I = a \times b$)	BEGIN statements from begin–end pairs (count one line only for each pair)
Conditional statements (IF, THEN, ELSE)	
Deliverable job control (JCL) statements	Nondelivered programmer debugging statements
Data declarations	Continuation of formatting statements
Data typing and equivalence statements	Machine- or library-generated data statements
INPUT/OUTPUT format statements	

■ Control statements (DO WHILE, REPEAT UNTIL, CALL)
■ Mathematical statements (I = a × b/c)
■ Conditional statements (IF, THEN, ELSE)

Executable statements include procedure calls, assignment statements, conditional and unconditional branching statements, conditional statements, iterative statements, and code block identifiers. For programs written in COBOL, procedure division statements are logical statements identified by line-terminating periods.

Data Declaration Statements

Declarative statements are nonexecutable statements in a program that define data used by the program including initialization statements, declarations and definitions of constants, variables, modules, macros, and various sections of source code. For example:

■ Input/output and formatting
■ Data declarations including data typing and equivalence (i.e., int a, DIM array(16))

Types and usages of declarative statements vary by languages. The C and COBOL languages require the programmer to declare variables and constants before the executable instructions begin. These are counted as logical lines.

Compiler Directives

Compiler directives may be a compiler vendor-specific feature. For example, in the C language, #include <stdio.h> is counted as a statement.

COBOL allows a compiler directive like COPY, which may copy a library of variables into the current program. In a C program, a compiler directive like #include <[header file]> refers to a library of available functions. Compiler directives may copy an entirely new program to the current program. Each compiler directive is counted as one logical line. (Counted or not, the number of compiler directives in a computer program is generally insignificant.) However, a common mistake is to count the size of the library or other program brought in by the compiler directive. This should be counted only once, if you actually developed it, not for every instantiation.

The second and third categories contained in Table 5.1 are "how lines are produced" and "origins of lines." Figure 5.3 shows software origins (sources) and how software is produced. The software sources listed on the figure are defined below.

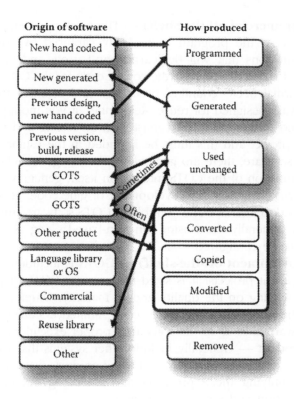

Figure 5.3 How logical lines are produced.

New, hand-coded — Estimate these SLOC using logical SLOC counting rules.

New, generated — Normally not included in code counts. The effort associated with generated SLOC can be accounted for in one of two ways: (1) use function-based sizing to describe the functionality that will be provided by the generated SLOC; or (2) collect generated SLOC and effort information and adjust the effective size value or calibration values to use the generated SLOC for effort estimates.

Previous design, new hand-coded — SLOC that will be developed new; the design documents already exist. Some reverse engineering of the design may be required. Such SLOC should be handled as reused with 100 percent reimplementation and a large amount of retesting. See Chapter 8 for information on how to handle reuse.

Previous version, build, or release — SLOC developed prior to this effort. Such SLOC should be handled as reused with appropriate percentages applied to redesign, reimplementation, and retest. See Chapter 8.

COTS (commercial off-the-shelf) — The work involved in applying COTS software to the program is generally captured by counting the number of functions that will be learned and used, and expressed in function-based sizing. If you have the source code for the COTS, you may apply the normal SLOC counting procedure and estimate this as pre-existing software designed for reuse. Remember, if you modify the COTS source, it is no longer COTS. You must plan on testing and maintaining it within the project and this must be included in the estimation. When sizing COTS software, there are generally three categories: (1) the COTS cognition, estimation of the COTS integration itself, generally using function based sizing methods; (2) development of glue code, generally new code developed to interface and control the COTS software; and (3) COTS configuration, generally sized using function-based sizing as the number of functions to be configured.

GOTS (government off-the-shelf) — GOTS is included for government development projects. It is sized the same as COTS or preexisting software, depending on the quality and/or maturity. Differences include greater likelihood of receiving source code, limited documentation, and possibly no warranties as to the software's proper execution.

Other product — Generally include other systems that will be integrated into the current system. Sizing of these products need not be done. However, identifying these products and including integration costs improves the effort and schedule estimation.

Language library or OS (operating system) — Language libraries and operating system functionality should not be included in software size. The SLOC required to set up and invoke such libraries and operating system calls must be counted as normal SLOC.

Commercial library — Same as language library.

Reuse library — Same as language library.

Other components — Same as language library.

The final category on Table 5.1 is end usage. In counting logical SLOC, count lines that are actually used in the delivered product. Exclude non-deliverable software, such as stubs, nondeliverable test software, and instrumentation. When using logical SLOC as an input to models such as SEER-SEM, the effort to build the actual product includes the effort to build this nondeliverable code.

Although different organizations have different standards for programming and in-line documentation, these variations will generally not have much impact on a logical SLOC count but can have a huge impact on physical count definitions especially when statement terminators are put on separate lines or when physical carriage returns including blanks and comments are counted.

Line Counting Example

Table 5.3 illustrates the three methods discussed in this chapter along with a comparison of logical lines with and without rules.

The example shown in Table 5.3 allows us to see size ranges from 9 lines to 36 lines, depending on the counting rules. This small example demonstrates the importance of using a consistent definition for line counting. Unfortunately, the physical carriage returns are the easiest to count and often the definition assumed by programmers. The column labeled *logical lines* assumes a line terminating parser was used. The column labeled *logical lines using language rules* uses the basic statement type counting rules shown in Table 5.2. In this small example, the variance between the two logical line counting methods is approximately 10 percent (logical lines = 9; logical lines using rules = 10). In larger programs, the variance is generally less significant.

Table 5.3   Differences in Line Counting Methods

Example C++ Program	Physical Carriage Returns	Physical Lines	Logical Lines	Logical Lines Using Language Rules
extern double MessageMonitor(double dfComplexity, double dfSuccessRate);	1	1	1	1
/**	2		comment	
* function: ExampleFunction	3		comment	
*	4		comment	
* purpose: Demonstrate counting of C code	5		comment	
*	6		comment	
* arguments: x [IN]: first argument	7		comment	
* y [IN]: second argument	8		comment	
* bar [IN]: third argument, an array of...	9		comment	
*	10		comment	
* returns: return value	11		comment	
*	12		comment	
**/	13		comment	
double ExampleFunction(double x, double y, int *bar) {	14	2	partial	2
	15		blank	
int n = (int) ((x + y) / 2);	16	3	2	3
int SuccessfulAlert = 0;	17	4	3	4
	18		Blank	
if (x < MessageMonitor (y, n))	19	5	Partial	5
	20		Blank	
/* this is a comment */	21		Comment	
	22		Blank	
SuccessfulAlert = bar[n] + 5;	23	6	4	6
	24		Blank	
else	25	7	Partial	
	26		Blank	
while (n > 0) {	27	8	Partial	7
	28		Blank	
SuccessfulAlert += (int) MessageMonitor (x, n);	29	9	5	8
	30		Blank	
n--;	31	10	6	9
	32		Blank	
}	33	11	7	
	34		Blank	
return (++x + SuccessfulAlert + bar(n));	35	12	8	10
}	36	13	9	

Estimation versus Counting SLOC

Two distinctive actions are involved when SLOC is used as a metric for project size: (1) the actual predevelopment estimation and (2) post-development code counting. When using SLOC to estimate size, an estimation model or a manual process is used to project the application's size and associated cost. After the application has been developed, its SLOC can be counted to update the historical database and compare to its original estimates. As illustrated in Figure 5.2, SLOC is a primary input to the process used to estimate the schedule and effort required to develop a program.

When using SLOC as the basic metric for measuring or projecting/estimating size, keep in mind the following points:

■ Provide consistent definitions and rules for recognizing and counting embedded statements for each source language.
■ Clearly define what constitutes an executable statement and ensure it is consistently applied. Clearly define any element you wish to count, such as declarations, comments, and compiler directives, and ensure that the definition is consistently followed.
■ For all expression-based languages such as C and C++, clearly and consistently define the rules for distinguishing between expressions and statements.

Clear definitions are equally important in estimating and in counting. Often analysts think in terms of past projects and their estimates may be based on those sizes, with whatever definitions they happen to remember.

SLOC Considerations for Sizing Databases

Databases of historical projects can be extremely useful for developing reliable SLOC estimates for new programs based on the analogy to completed programs. However, as the story about the $35 database recounted at the beginning of the chapter illustrates, a sizing database must contain more than only numbers.

■ In-house sizing databases, which are proprietary, should include significant information about past projects. Not only can internal sizing databases have very specific and revealing contents, they describe work that *your organization* has done, and therefore an internal sizing database is clearly most appropriate for making internal estimates in the future. See Chapter 3 for a detailed discussion of the contents of a sizing database. If your organization does not already have such a database, we strongly recommend establishing one.

■ Public databases, which are readily available but for which the information may have been provided "as is" may need sanity checking and pruning to ensure useful information. For example, sometimes in such databases, size and effort are included without clear definition.

A well-developed sizing database will enable you to generate detailed estimates without the considerable investment in time that such estimates normally take if prepared from scratch. (For details on estimation of size by analogy see Chapter 3.)

Language Impact on Size Conversion

When using historical size information from one language and converting to another, it is important to normalize the historical size to the new language. Over the years, general conversion factors have been developed to assist in this conversion.

The conversion factors answer questions such as, "How big would a 50,000-source line Fortran program be if written in a fourth generation language (4GL)?" The conversion factor is a percentage increase or decrease from the existing source lines of code, yielding an estimate of the lines of code in the target language. Table 5.4 shows the approximate percentage change in the number of lines of code when converting from the source language to the target language.

Table 5.4   General Language Conversion Factors

	Target Language (Percent)				
Source Language	General 3GLs[a]	4GLs	Ada	Assembly	PL-1/Pascal
General 3GLs	—	–65	22	435	19
4GL	185	—	248	1,424	238
Ada	–18	–71	—	338	–3
Assembly	–81	–93	–77	—	–78
PL-1/Pascal	–16	–70	3	351	—

How to read the table: if a program was written in Ada, then the same functionality was written in Assembly, it would take 338 percent MORE lines of code.

[a] ALGOL, BASIC, FORTRAN, JAVA, LISP, LOGO, C, C++, CMS-2, COBOL, JOVIAL, PROLOG, etc.[8]

Effective Size

As defined earlier effective SLOC (ESLOC) is a measure of how much work will be required to complete a project, factoring in new and reuse, not a measure of the total SLOC to be delivered. A software project comprising only new, build-from-scratch code may be said to have an effective size equal to the total size (number of new lines of source code equals effective lines).

When software projects economize by reusing preexisting functionality from prior projects in combination with new development, total size may be misleading because total size in this case can be used to describe value, not effort. Effort would be computed by converting the new and preexisting software into an effective (equivalent) number of size units using formulas developed from experience.

Generally speaking, reusing existing functionality requires less effort than developing equivalent new code. Typically, reuse involves three activities (redesign, reimplementation, and retest), each of which increases the effort and schedule. Redesign is necessary when the existing functionality may not be exactly suited to the new task. When this is so, the application to be reused will likely require some rework to support new functions, and it may require reverse engineering to understand its current operation.

Some design changes may be in order as well. Changing design will also result in reimplementation and coding changes. Even if redesign and reimplementation are not required, retesting is almost always needed to ensure the preexisting software operates properly in its new environment. All this is captured in effective size. (See Chapter 8 covering reuse and COTS software for a detailed discussion on computing effective size.)

Productivity Based on Effective Size

Effective size, as determined by the method described above, can be used to compute productivity, for example, SLOC produced per person-month, -hour, or -day. Effective SLOC and properly computed productivity values are valuable indicators for determining total project effort. (See Chapter 9 for a detailed discussion of productivity computations.)

Accounting for SLOC Growth

For a given set of initial requirements, an initial size estimate will usually expand over time. The reason is simple: the entire system cannot be understood or grasped at the outset of a project. It is therefore wise to build a growth factor into the estimate and to express the size estimate as a range rather than as a discrete number. However, not all analysts

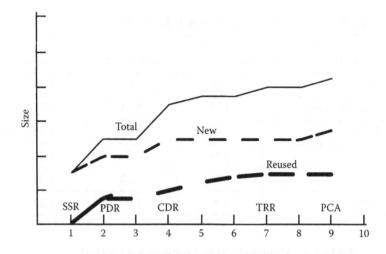

Figure 5.4   SEI Size Growth Study results.

will do so, particularly those who have not systematically compared earlier project estimates against actual outcomes.[6] Figure 5.4 shows the results of a study of size growth conducted by SEI.[7] The following conclusions were noted by SEI:

■ Projects show periods of sharp growth in lines of code, separated by periods of more moderate growth.
■ Ten percent of the code may be produced after testing starts due to requirements changes.
■ Steady size growth from approximately development midpoint through acceptance testing can occur due to response to trouble reports.
■ Changes often are driven by better understanding of the requirements.
■ These changes impact schedule and staffing, and hence cost.

The bottom line: you must understand size and factor code growth into your estimates or your effort and schedule projections probably will be low. Project growth factors may be scalar size adjustments that are applied against initial size estimates or discrete estimates of growth. For example:

■ The development team estimates that a new job will take 10K lines of code.
■ A review of the team's last few estimates reveals that they typically underestimated by an average of 35 percent.
■ As a result, a better estimate for this job would be 13.5K lines of code.

Table 5.5 Typical Software Growth Factors[8]

Project Phase When Estimate is Prepared	Least Growth	Likely Growth	Most Growth
Proposal	1.56	1.68	1.78
Requirements	1.52	1.61	1.71
Design	1.40	1.56	1.56
Code	1.18	1.20	1.24
Test	1.00	1.08	1.08
Done	1.00	1.00	1.02

Table 5.6 Humphrey Size Contingency Factors[9]

Phase at Estimate	Min. Contingency (Percent)	Max. Contingency (Percent)
Requirements	100	200
High-level design	75	150
Detailed design	50	100
Implementation	25	50
Function test	10	25
System test	0	10

Note: Treat these figures as rules of thumb. The author is careful to point out that no good published data is available to support these figures.

Galorath Incorporated developed empirical software growth factors that may be applied to SLOC or other size metrics. As shown in Table 5.5, software growth factors decrease over time as system definition converges.

In addition to the empirical data of Galorath Incorporated (Table 5.5), Watts Humphrey's rules are shown on Table 5.6.

Barry Holchin developed an empirical growth method based on system complexity and development phase as shown in Table 5.7.

Estimating Size Growth Conclusions

Galorath and others conduct ongoing research related to size growth and SEER-PPMC can be used for capturing growth during development. The current best methodology for determining size range (and therefore size

Table 5.7 Holchin Size Growth Approximations[10]

Maturity	>>>	0	10	20	30	40	50	60	70	80	90	100
Complexity				ATP		SDR		SRR		PDR	CDR	Test
Simple	0	1.15	1.14	1.12	1.11	1.09	1.08	1.06	1.05	1.03	1.02	1.00
	1	1.29	1.26	1.23	1.20	1.17	1.14	1.11	1.09	1.06	1.03	1.00
	2	1.42	1.38	1.34	1.29	1.25	1.21	1.17	1.13	1.08	1.04	1.00
	3	1.56	1.50	1.44	1.39	1.33	1.28	1.22	1.17	1.11	1.06	1.00
	4	1.69	1.62	1.55	1.48	1.41	1.35	1.28	1.21	1.14	1.07	1.00
	5	1.83	1.74	1.66	1.58	1.50	1.41	1.33	1.25	1.17	1.08	1.00
	6	1.96	1.86	1.77	1.67	1.58	1.48	1.38	1.29	1.19	1.10	1.00
	7	2.10	1.99	1.88	1.77	1.66	1.55	1.44	1.33	1.22	1.11	1.00
	8	2.23	2.11	1.98	1.86	1.74	1.62	1.49	1.37	1.25	1.12	1.00
	9	2.37	2.23	2.09	1.96	1.82	1.68	1.55	1.41	1.27	1.14	1.00
Complex	10	2.50	2.35	2.20	2.05	1.90	1.75	1.60	1.45	1.30	1.15	1.00

growth) is using relative size estimation methodologies. Relative sizing using models such as SEER-AccuScope capture likely size and growth. It has been found that when relative sizing is performed, analysts capture the growth almost automatically because past projects have already experienced growth and the range estimate includes likely and growth estimates.

Using the multiestimate size methodology described in Chapter 3, developing as many size ranges as you can, any one or all the growth factors covered here can provide rows in a size range table and provide clarity and completeness to the size estimation process. For SLOC estimates, SEER-SEM expects the analyst to provide the least, likely and most SLOC. The likely and most should include growth.

Finding Automated Code Counters for Existing Systems

There are many reasons to count existing systems. Primary reasons include obtaining scope so that rework for an incremental improvement can be estimated and new system sizes can be estimated by analogy.

A free code counter can be obtained from www.galorath.com and it can count most languages such as C, C++, and Ada that include line-terminating semicolons. It is available in both ANSI C source code (so it can be compiled on the required target computer and operating system) and as an executable within Microsoft Windows.

Table 5.7 (continued)   Holchin Size Growth Approximations[10]

System Knowledge Maturity Factor Guidelines		Complexity Factor Definition
Early System Concept phase. Few studies have been completed. Incomplete System Segment Spec. Completely new concept or minimal knowledge of systems in which similar concepts have been implemented.	0	0 = Real time not an issue. Extremely simple SW with primarily straightforward code, simple I/O, and internal storage arrays. 1 = Between 0 and 2. 2 = Background processing. Computational efficiency has some impact on development effort SAV is of low logical complexity using straightforward I/O and primarily internal data storage. 3 = Between 2 and 4. 4 = New standalone system developed on firm operating system. Minimal I/F problems exist. 5 = Typical C&C. 6 = Minor real time processing, signficant logical complexity, some changes to operating system. 7 = Between 6 and 8. 8 = Challenging response time requirements, new system with significant I/F and interaction requirements (e.g., OS and R/T with signficant logical code). 9 = Between 8 and 10. 10 = Extremely large volumes of data processing in short time, signal processing system with extremely complex I/Fs (e.g., parallel processing, microcode applications).
Early System Requirements Analysis. Often near proposal and Award of Contract Preliminary System Segment Spec. completed (SRR) and CSCIs identified. Significant knowledge of similar systems.	0.2	
SDR completed. System Functional Baseline, Operationals Concept Document, Software Development Plan completed.	0.4	
SRR completed. All CSCI requirements identified and defined (functional performance, database, testing). System Allocated Baseline complete.	0.6	
PDR	0.8	
CDR	0.9	
End of CSCI Testing	1.0	

Note: Author points out that these factors are postulated based on anecdotal information, not supported by hard data.

The Center for Software Engineering at the University of Southern California (sunset.usc.edu) also provides a free tool named CodeCount™ which counts logical and physical SLOC. Languages supported include Ada, Assembly, C and C++, COBOL, FORTRAN, Java, JOVIAL, Pascal, and PL-1.The physical SLOC definition is based on Boehm's deliverable source instruction (DSI). It is programming language syntax-independent. This enables it to collect other useful information such as comments, blank lines, and overall size, all independent of information content. The logical SLOC definitions will vary, depending on the programming language, due to language-specific syntax.

Beware: simply finding and downloading any code counter from the Internet can produce disastrous results. A code counter must be certified before the results can be trusted. The author was involved in a major program that had dramatically overestimated the number of preexisting SLOC due to the use of a code counter containing a bug.

Additional issues to consider when counting code are (1) understand what you are counting and (2) count hand-generated lines, not automatically generated lines because effort is generally related to hand-generated lines. If you have not separated automatically generated lines from code counts, cost models will likely need calibration. Generated lines may not correlate as well with effort.

The issue of counting automatically generated lines is similar to the method of counting object code used years ago. At one time, counting the number of words of executable instructions was consistent enough to be used as a size measure. As programming languages evolved and became less close to the physical computer architecture, such counts became nearly useless for estimation purposes. In one example, a FORTRAN program of about 3,000 source lines produced an executable program of about 8K words of memory. Yet when the same FORTRAN program was recompiled on a different computer, using a different compiler and architecture, the same program grew to over 220K words.

As visual development environments provide increasing amounts of generated code, similar expansions are common. The best approach is to eliminate the automatically generated lines from the counts to avoid this issue (of course, using functional measures can solve these concerns). Alternately, develop ratios of hand-generated lines to automatically generated lines and adjust your code count or calibrate the cost model.

Pros and Cons of SLOC

The primary benefits of using SLOC as a sizing metric arise from the fact that the metric has been used for years, can be well understood, and correlates well with functionality and effort. SLOC metrics are relatively easy to count using the counting standards described above. Many of the estimation models are based on SLOC measures. Furthermore, other metrics can be derived from the SLOC metric, for example, productivity (SLOC/staff-month) and quality (defects/SLOC) measurements. SLOC counts can be used to describe and compare such things as rates of defects or faults and failures. In addition, costs of documentation can be computed based on SLOC counts.

Size measurement methods have played a key role in helping to solve real-world problems of estimating, supplier and customer disputes, performance improvement, and the management of outsourced contracts.[11]

Arguments against Use of Lines of Code as Sizing Metric

Despite the benefits noted above, the use of SLOC has some drawbacks worth mentioning.

No SLOC exist at the onset of a project — During early activities such as requirements analysis or design, few or no SLOC are produced. Even when they are written, their value is minimal until they have been tested. For this reason, using *SLOC complete* as an in-process metric is not very useful. For example, during a development at Apple, lines of code developed per week served as a metric. One week, as a developer made the main algorithm for his program more efficient, he removed 2,000 lines of code and made the software run about eight times faster. When he was asked to report his productivity for that week, he wrote "minus 2,000 lines."[12] The project soon stopped collecting in-process size metrics because they proved to be ineffective.

At micro-level, SLOC can be misleading — If a superstar programmer can write a function in fewer lines than a mediocre programmer, does it make sense for the superstar to appear less productive?

Despite obvious benefits, using SLOC counts as a primary or only measure of software size presents significant risk — A range should be used to mitigate this risk. Lines of code can only be accurately counted after the product is completed. SLOC counts do not easily accommodate nonprocedural languages.

Risks Resulting from Using SLOC to Estimate

Even though SLOC counts are commonly used as sizing metrics and they are essential to the analogy estimation method, they can potentially be inaccurate, especially during the early phases of a software project before the scope is understood. Although the SLOC metric is commonly used, not least because management can understand a quantitative value, the ability to estimate a project's size quantitatively represents one of the principal risks of using SLOC. The best that can be expected of a size projection using SLOC is a range of accuracy, not a precise value, and management often attributes a degree of accuracy to the metric that is not warranted. Using sizing models, growth factors, and analogies for cross-checks can mitigate risk. Software size estimation risk generally falls into three major categories:

Overoptimism — Underestimating size can prevent scaling the development environment to reflect reality, which can lead to defining cost drivers that may be inappropriate or incorrectly estimated. It may also cause a misalignment of skills to tasks, miscalculation of schedules and level of effort required, and unrealistic estimation of project staffing requirements.

Misuse of historical SLOC data — Erroneous, incomplete, inconsistent, or irrelevant historical SLOC information can prevent accurate sizing of a software project, which can lead to low initial budget estimates and significant cost growth or even to loss of the project.

Poorly or loosely defined requirements and/or objectives — These can cause unrealistic customer expectations or unconstrained requirements growth during the software development life cycle. This can result in constant changes in size and project goals, frustration, customer dissatisfaction, cost overruns, and, ultimately, project failure.

Risk Management and Control of SLOC Estimates

One way to manage SLOC risk is to develop historical sizing information whenever a product is completed and store it in a database for use in projecting the sizes of future applications. Risks also exist in using a non-current SLOC estimate. If an estimate is not updated, it will become less valid as a project proceeds. Common results of not maintaining a current size estimate for a project can be: uncontrolled size growth, functional inconsistencies between historical size and the system being developed, and schedule and budget issues.

To control the risks associated with a SLOC estimate, the steps necessary to establish a formal estimate using SLOC and for revising and tracking the estimate throughout the life of the project need to be linked to the risk management process. See Chapter 10 for a detailed discussion of the risk management process. Because of these potential issues, extreme care should be taken to keep current SLOC estimates as a project proceeds.

Summary

Both the followers and detractors of SLOC have interesting points to make. One author went so far as to say that using lines of code for estimation constituted "professional malpractice."[13] While the use of the method is not professional malpractice, the statement emphasizes the dangers in misusing SLOC as a size metric. If defined consistently, SLOC can work well for estimating most types of systems, but using SLOC without understanding the definitions certainly can cause significant confusion. SLOC can seem confusing and inaccurate because there are so many factors to consider, such as physical versus logical lines, total size versus effective size, and hand-generated code versus total generated code.

However, the great advantage of SLOC over function-based sizing methods is that SLOC serve as actual artifacts of a developer's work and can be automatically counted when a project is completed. The count provides valuable historical data that enables you to develop an analogy base that will facilitate the development of new estimates.

In identifying the source lines, we defined both physical and logical source lines, provided a recommended definition, and include SEI's source line definition checklist below.

We also considered why different computer languages can impact SLOC counts along with the best practices for approaching size and language conversion. The risks associated with size estimation and recommended mitigation strategies were discussed. The checklist and code counting examples from various languages are included at the end of this chapter to assist readers. The next chapter focuses on function-based sizing approaches.

SEI Checklist

The SEI checklist is useful if you receive SLOC counts defined with a non-standard definition or when a definition needs to be ferreted out from developers who may not understand the definitions clearly. It is always best to get SLOC counts in logical, non-comment source statements and not have to qualify a definition using these checklists.

Different languages represent a line of code differently due to conceptual differences involved in accounting for executable statements and data declarations. The purpose of SLOC as a quantitative size measure is to provide an input to a future estimate that will determine how much effort is required to develop or modify a program. To minimize the risk of inconsistent definitions, the SEI developed a checklist for defining the physical and logical lines of code measures.[14]

SEI Definition Checklist for Source Statement Counts

One helpful tool in counting source lines of code is preparing a checklist of attributes and determining their values. Using checklists provides a detailed definition of the source line of code counting methodology so all parties involved have a clear concise definition to use. The following checklist identifies suggested attributes for size measures.

The nine attributes on the checklist describe the types of software statements for measuring the source lines of code:

1. Statement type
2. How produced
3. Origin
4. Usage
5. Delivery
6. Functionality
7. Replications
8. Development status
9. Language

These attributes take on values independently of each other. The attributes and their respective values represent statement types that are most commonly used by software development groups that seek and utilize the results of size measurement. Using SLOC as a sizing metric has its own trade-offs. It is important to identify and describe the attributes of size, without which consistency in size measurements cannot be achieved.

Statement Type	Includes	Excludes
When a line or statement contains more than one type, classify it as the type with the highest precedence.		
Executable		
Nonexecutable		
Declarations		
Compiler directives		
Comments		
On their own lines		
On lines with source code		
Banners and nonblank spacers		
Blank (empty) comments		
Blank lines		
How Produced	**Includes**	**Excludes**
Programmed		
Generated with source code generators		
Converted with automated translators		

How Produced (continued)	Includes	Excludes
Copied or reused without change		
Modified		
Removed		
Origin	**Includes**	**Excludes**
New work: no prior existence		
Prior work: taken or adapted from		
A previous version, build, or release		
Commercial, off-the-shelf software (COTS), other than libraries		
Government furnished software (GFS), other than reuse libraries		
Another product		
A vendor-supplied language support library (unmodified)		
A vendor-supplied operating system or utility (unmodified)		
A local or modified language support library or operating system		
Other commercial library		
A reuse library (software designed for reuse)		
Other software component or library		
Usage	**Includes**	**Excludes**
In or as part of primary product		
External to or in support of primary product		
Delivery	**Includes**	**Excludes**
Delivered		
Delivered as source		
Delivered in compiled or executable form, but not as source		

Delivery (continued)	Includes	Excludes
Not delivered		
Under configuration control		
Not under configuration control		
Functionality	**Includes**	**Excludes**
Operative		
Inoperative (dead, bypassed, unused, unreferenced, or unaccessed)		
Functional (intentional dead code, reactivated for special purposes)		
Nonfunctional (unintentionally present)		
Replications	**Includes**	**Excludes**
Master source statements (originals)		
Physical replications of master statements, stored in master code		
Copies inserted, instantiated, or expanded when compiling or linking		
Postproduction replicates as in distributed, redundant, or reparameterized systems		
Development Status	**Includes**	**Excludes**
Each statement has one and only one status, usually that of its parent unit.		
Estimated or planned		
Designed		
Coded		
Unit test completed		
Integrated into components		
Test readiness review completed		
Software [CSCI (computer software configuration item)] tests completed		
System tests completed		

Language	Includes	Excludes
List each source language on a separate line.		
Job control languages		
Assembly languages		
Third generation languages		
Fourth generation languages		
Microcode		
Other		

Source: SEI Report CMU/SEI-92-TR-20.

Codes for Various Programming Languages

We have included below the actual codes for a variety of languages that implement the classic "Hello World" program used to test compilers and made famous by Kerrigan and Ritchie's book, *The C Programming Language.*[15] The codes are included here to allow readers to determine the counting rules and differences among programming languages. For a more comprehensive list of languages and their codes see:

> http://www2.latech.edu/~acm/HelloWorld.shtml
> http://www.roesler-ac.de/wolfram/hello.htm
> http://en.wikipedia.org/wiki/Hello_world

Language: ABAP4

```
REPORT ZHB00001.
*Hello world in ABAP/4 *
WRITE: 'Hello world'.
```

Language: Ada

```
-- Hello World in Ada

with TEXT_IO; use TEXT_IO;
procedure Hello is
  pragma MAIN;
begin
```

```
  PUT ("Hello World!");
end Hello;
```

Language: *Assembler IBM-370*

```
ITLE 'Hello World for IBM Assembler/370 (VM/CMS)'
HELLO   START
BALR 12,0
USING *,12
*
WRTERM 'Hello World!'
*
SR   15,15
BR   14
*
END HELLO

Back to index
```

Language: *Assembler Intel*

```
; Hello World for Intel Assembler (MSDOS)

mov ax,cs
mov ds,ax
mov ah,9
mov dx, offset Hello
int 21h
xor ax,ax
int 21h

Hello:
  db "Hello World!",13,10,"$"
```

Language: *Assembler PDP11*

```
; Hello World in Assembler for the DEC PDP-11 with the
;  RSX-11M-PLUS operating system
```

```
;
    .title Hello
    .ident /V0001A/
    .mcall qiow$s, exit$s
    .psect $code,ro,i
start: qiow$s #5,#5,,,,<#str, #len, #40>
    exit$s
    .psect $data,ro,d
str:    .ascii / Hello World!/
    len=.-str
    .end start
```

Language: Basic

```
10 REM Hello World in BASIC
20 PRINT "Hello World!"
```

Language: C++

```
// Hello World in C++

#include <iostream.h>

main()
{
    cout << "Hello World!" << endl;
    return 0;
}
```

Language: C++ MFC

```
// Hello World in C++ for Microsoft Foundation Classes
// (Microsoft Visual C++).

#include <afxwin.h>

class CHello : public CFrameWnd
```

```
{
public:
  CHello()
  {
    Create(NULL,_T("Hello World!"),
    WS_OVERLAPPEDWINDOW,rectDefault);
  }
};

class CHelloApp : public CWinApp
{
public:
  virtual BOOL InitInstance();
};

BOOL CHelloApp::InitInstance()
{
  m_pMainWnd = new CHello();
  m_pMainWnd->ShowWindow(m_nCmdShow);
  m_pMainWnd->UpdateWindow();
  return TRUE;
}

CHelloApp theApp;
```

Language: C-Ansi

```c
/* Hello World in C, Ansi-style */

#include <stdio.h>
#include <stdlib.h>

int main(void)
{
  puts("Hello World!");
  return EXIT_SUCCESS;
}
```

Language: C-Sharp

```
// Hello World in Microsoft C# ("C-Sharp").

using System;

class HelloWorld
{
  public static int Main(String[] args)
  {
    Console.WriteLine("Hello, World!");
    return 0;
  }
}
```

Language: COBOL

```
      * Hello World in Cobol

*****************************
IDENTIFICATION DIVISION.
PROGRAM-ID. HELLO.
ENVIRONMENT DIVISION.
DATA DIVISION.
PROCEDURE DIVISION.
MAIN SECTION.
DISPLAY "Hello World!"
STOP RUN.
*****************************
```

Language: Forth

```
: Hello World in Forth
  ." Hello World!" cr
;
```

Back to index

Language: FORTRAN

```
C   Hello World in Fortran

PROGRAM HELLO
    WRITE (*,100)
    STOP
 100 FORMAT (' Hello World! '/)
    END
```

Back to index

Language: Fortran 77

```
C   Hello World in Fortran 77

    PROGRAM HELLO
    PRINT*, 'Hello World!'
    END
```

Back to index

Language: Fortran IV

```
    PROGRAM HELLO
c
C   Hello World in Fortran IV (supposedly for a TR440)
c
    WRITE (6,'(" Hello World!")')
    END
```

Language: HTML

```
<HTML>
<!-- Hello World in HTML -->
<HEAD>
<TITLE>Hello World!</TITLE>
</HEAD>
<BODY>
```

```
Hello World!
</BODY>
</HTML>
```

Language: Java

```
class HelloWorld {
    public static void main (String args[]) {
    for (;;) {
            System.out.print("Hello World");
            }
        }
}
```

Language: JavaScript

```
<html>
<body>
<script language="JavaScript" type="text/javas-
cript">
// Hello World in JavaScript
document.write('Hello World');
</script>
</body>
</html>
```

Job Control Language (JCL)

```
//HERIB   JOB , 'HERIBERT OTTEN',PRTY=12
//* Hello World for MVS
//HALLO   EXEC PGM=IEBGENER
//SYSPRINT DD SYSOUT=*
//SYSUT2 DD SYSOUT=T
//SYSUT1 DD *
Hello World!
/*
//
```

Language: Lisp

```
;;; Hello World in Common Lisp

(defun helloworld ()
 (print "Hello World!")
 )
```

Language: Pascal

```
{Hello World in Pascal}

program HelloWorld;
begin
 WriteLn('Hello World!');
end.
```

Language: Pascal-Windows

```
{ Hello World in Borland Pascal 7 for MS-Windows}

PROGRAM HelloWorld;

USES
 WinCRT;

BEGIN
 InitWinCRT;
 WriteLn('Hello World!');
 ReadLn;
 DoneWinCRT;
END.
```

Language: Smalltalk.simple

```
"Hello World in Smalltalk (simple version)"

Transcript show: 'Hello World!'.
Smalltalk.window
```

```
"Hello World in Smalltalk (in an own window)"
"(to be entered in a special browser)"

VisualComponent subclass: #HelloWorldView
        instanceVariableNames: "
        classVariableNames: "
        poolDictionaries: "
        category: 'test'


displayOn: aGraphicsContext

        'Hello World!' asComposedText displayOn:
        aGraphicsContext.

open

        |window|
        window := ScheduledWindow new.
        window label: 'Hello World Demo:'.
        window component: self new.
        window open.
```

Language: VisualBasic

```
REM Hello World in Visual Basic for Windows

VERSION 2.00
Begin Form Form1
   Caption      = "Form1"
   ClientHeight = 6096
   ClientLeft   = 936
   ClientTop    = 1572
   ClientWidth  = 6468
   Height       = 6540
   Left         = 876
   LinkTopic    = "Form1"
   ScaleHeight  = 6096
   ScaleWidth   = 6468
   Top          = 1188
```

```
Width        = 6588
Begin Label Label1
   Caption      = "Hello World!"
   Height       = 372
   Left         = 2760
   TabIndex     = 0
   Top          = 2880
   Width        = 972
End
End
Option Explicit
```

Endnotes

1. Galorath, Daniel. Personal experience, circa 1986.
2. Jones, Capers. *Patterns of Software Systems Failure and Success*. Stamford: Thompson, 1996. 31.
3. Roetzheim, William. *Estimating Software Costs*. Rancho San Diego: Cost Xpert Group, 2005.
4. Park, Robert E. et al. *Software Size Measurement: A Framework for Counting Source Statements: Technical Report*. Pittsburgh: Software Engineering Institute, 1992.
5. Galorath Incorporated. *SEER-SEM User Manual*. El Segundo, 2004.
6. Galorath Incorporated. *OSD Software Estimation Guidebook*. El Segundo, 1997.
7. Landis. Software Engineering Institute, 2004. <http://www.sei.cmu.edu/sema/pdf/baumert.pdf>
8. Galorath Incorporated. SEER-SEM internal information, 2005.
9. Humphrey, Watts S. *Managing the Software Process*. Boston: Addison-Wesley, 1989. Table 6.1.
10. Holchin, Barry, *Code Growth Study*. March 4, 1996. Text and table related to maturity factor revised September 17, 2003.
11. Rule, Grant. "The Importance of the Size of Software Requirements." *NASSCOM Conference*, Mumbai, India, 2001.
12. <http://www.c2.com>
13. "The use of lines of code metrics for productivity and quality studies [is] to be regarded as professional malpractice starting in 1995." Capers Jones, 1996.
14. Goethert, Wolfhart B. et al. *Software Effort and Schedule Measurement: A Framework for Counting Staff-Hours and Reporting Schedule Information*. Pittsburgh: Software Engineering Institute, 1992.
15. Kerrigan, Brian W. and Dennis Ritchie. *The C Programming Language*. Upper Saddle River: Prentice Hall, 1988.

Chapter 6

Function-Based Sizing

What we see depends mainly on what we look for.

Sir John Lubbock

Introduction

This chapter describes function-based sizing for software size definition, concentrating on the International Function Point User Group (IFPUG) counting standards. Additionally SEER-FBS (function-based sizing), which approximates function points with simple inputs for early estimation, is discussed. Uncertainties and risk related to function-based sizing are also examined. The David Consulting Group, authors of the primary book on function point counting state:

> The most important planning metrics are those having to do with scope and size of the project. One of the most frequently used sizing metrics is function points. Function points measure functionality. A key advantage of function points is that they can be counted before design and coding begin by reference to the requirements specifications, assuming that those are, as they should be, comprehensive with respect to what the software product is supposed to do.[1]

Function points constitute a logical (functional) size measure. They measure the functions of a software system as seen by the user. Of all the function-based approaches, the IFPUG method is predominant, supported by strong training, a counting practice committee, and a body of function point counting consultants.

Origins and History of Functional Metrics

In order to address some of the concerns with SLOC counting, in 1979 Allan Albrecht of IBM proposed a way to measure the size of software in terms of its *functionality* as opposed to its physical components (SLOC).[2] Albrecht and his colleagues at IBM used both function points and source lines of code (SLOC) metrics concurrently and introduced the function point metric into the public domain.

The first international publication of the function point metric appeared in Capers Jones' 1981 book titled *Programming Productivity: Issues for the Eighties*,[3] published by the IEEE Computer Society Press. In this book, Jones states: "Software organizations, looking for alternatives to the LOC metric, were drawn to the function point metric as a way to link size to the functional projections of a system."

As the use of function points among IBM's client base grew, this group formed the core of IFPUG. The work done by Albrecht and IBM in 1984 was the first major revision to the function point counting rules and the resultant method designated *function point analysis* evolved into the *IFPUG method*.[4]

By the early 1990s, the IFPUG function point metric had become a major tool for quantifying software size. The method has two components. The first measures functional size and produces *unadjusted function points*. The unadjusted function points are used by models such as SEER-SEM as a size measure and represent the work independently of people, work products, and process factors. The second component measures the contribution to overall size of 14 technical and quality factors which, when applied, yield *adjusted function points*. The adjusted function point metric is not as widely used. Several deviations from the Albrecht–IFPUG approach have been developed. The following are noteworthy:

> **Feature points** — In his 1986 paper titled "The SPR Feature Point Method," Capers Jones[5] extended the original work of Albrecht, proposing a concept known as *feature points*. They extended the metric to apply to scientific algorithms but this method was largely abandoned.

Mark II (MkII) function points — In the late 1980s in the United Kingdom, Charles Symons developed the Mark II function point method.[6] The method, used largely for management systems, is consistent with structured analysis methods, and is applicable in early stages of a life cycle. Its primary use is for application-type software. Symons enhanced Albrecht's approach by improving the way in which the internal complexity of data-rich business application software is addressed. The MkII method assumes a model of software in which all requirements or *user functionalities* are expressed in terms of logical transactions (LTs). Each LT comprises an input, some processing, and an output component. An LT is defined as triggered by an event in the real world of interest to the user or a request for information. The size of an input or output component of an LT is proportional to the number of DETs (data element types) on the component. The size of the processing component is proportional to the number of entity types referenced in the processing. The counts of input and output DETs and of entity types referenced in the processing phase are then weighted to give the MkII function point size of each LT. The size of an item of software is then the sum of the MkII FP sizes of each of its LTs.

3D function points — Scott Whitmire, while at Boeing, developed *3D function points* in the early 1990s.[7] The technique was designed to improve the Albrecht approach by (1) making counting simpler and (2) improving application to scientific and real-time systems. The 3D function point system is not widely used today.

NESMA — The Dutch Software Metrics Association (NESMA) published a variant of the IFPUG method that aimed to simplify some of the sizing rules. NESMA issued the first version of its manual titled *Definitions and Counting Guidelines for the Application of Function Point Analysis* in 1990 and subsequently updated it regularly to provide concrete, operational guidelines on complex counting issues for helping counters.[8] As a result, the counting guidelines of NESMA and IFPUG continuously became more similar. With the publication of IFPUG CPM 4.1 (January 1999), the NESMA counting guidelines became generally the same as IFPUG guidelines.

Full function points — Alain Abran's LRGL group at the University of Québec, Montréal, and others[9] published the *Full Function Point Method*, which used the IFPUG rules for business application software and added extra components for sizing real-time software. This approach addresses the measurement of software reuse from a functional perspective rather than from a technical perspective.

In 1995, Abran and Desharnais proposed the first version of functional reuse metrics based on the function point analysis (FPA) technique. They illustrated how these metrics could be used to take into account the benefits of reuse in a cost–benefit analysis. The full function point system [COSMIC-FFP (ISO 19761)] is a functional size measurement method that generalizes the measurement process to address management information systems issues as well as real-time and hybrid software projects. It provides, in particular, criteria for measuring functional size and improves upon the IFPUG function point analysis method so that the software of real-time systems can also be targeted for measurement. With COSMIC-FFP, the size of software can be determined from the functions the user requires the software to perform. The functional requirements of software are expressed as a set of functional processes, each of which is expressed in turn by an ordered set of data movements. An individual data movement is referred to as a *subprocess* within the functional process in question. The result of measurement in COSMIC-FFP is the number of data movements, i.e., the number of subprocesses, taken to represent size.

Evolved function points — In 2000, Lee Fischman of Galorath Incorporated set out to simplify the IFPUG method with relaxed terminology and counting rules.[10] This experiment was successful. It is not in use today since Galorath Incorporated determined industry would be best served by supporting the standard IFPUG approach.

SEER-FBS (function-based sizing) — In 1992, Galorath Incorporated introduced SEER-FBS. SEER-SEM's basic IFPUG mode function-based sizing is consistent with IFPUG counting rules, asks the counting questions in end user terminology, then rolls this up to an IFPUG unadjusted function point range approximation.[11] In its advanced mode, SEER-FBS adds a sixth category (internal functions) that allows users to account for highly algorithmic processes of systems such as real-time and embedded-type systems. The SEER-FBS approach can address the measurement of software reuse from a functional perspective rather than from a technical perspective. This approach is available in SEER-SEM and has been made available to the function point community at large.[12]

ISO Involvement

In 1994, Working Group 12 (WG12) of the International Organization for Standardization/International Electrotechnical Commission (ISO/IEC) Joint Technical Committee 1, deciding that no existing method was suitable for adoption as the world standard, set out to establish some basic principles of functional size measurement (FSM). This work resulted in the publication of ISO/IEC 14143/1:1997, titled *Information Technology: Software Measurement — Functional Size Measurement — Definition of Concepts.* Other standards and technical reports in the 14143 series cover subjects like conformance testing and verification of candidate FSM methods and the definitions of types of software domains for FSM.

In late 1998, some members of WG12 decided to develop a new FSM method, starting from basic established software engineering principles. They were able to draw on the experience of the past 25 years of FSM and aimed to be compliant with ISO/IEC 14143/1:2003 from the outset. They also intended that the FSM method be equally applicable to MIS and business software, to real-time and infrastructure software (e.g., operating system software), and to hybrids of these. They formed COSMIC, the Common Software Measurement International Consortium. The method, COSMIC-FFP, Version 2.0, was published in October 1999. Field trials were carried out in 2000 and 2001 (Ref. 8). COSMIC published its latest definition of the method (Version 2.2) in January 2003.

As a result of a decision of ISO/IEC to "let the market decide," international standards were published during 2002 and 2003 for the COSMIC-FFP (ISO/IEC 19761), the IFPUG — for its functional size component (ISO/IEC 20926), the MkII FPA (ISO/IEC 20968), and the NESMA (ISO/IEC 24570) methods. The IFPUG method is the most widely used today.

International Function Point User Group Counting Standards: Basic Process Definition

According to IFPUG, function point analysis is a standard method for measuring software development from the user's point of view. The process quantifies functionality of the software by providing a sizing measurement based primarily on logical design. The IFPUG function point analysis objectives[13] are to:

1. Measure the requested functionality that the user receives.
2. Independently measure software development and maintenance without considering the technology used for implementation.
3. Use a measurement that is simple enough to minimize the overhead of the measurement process.
4. Apply a consistent measure among various projects and organizations. (*Note:* different versions of the IFPUG counting standards can yield dramatically different counts for the same system. Know

what version of the rules were used on existing counts and which version is required for new counts.) We recommend using the latest counting rules because IFPUG continues to refine them.

IFPUG Definitions

The IFPUG's *Function Point Counting Practices Manual, Release 4.2* contains the glossary terms listed below. Figure 6.1 illustrates the steps identified in the manual.

Control information — Data used by an application to influence an elementary process.

Elementary process — Smallest unit of activity that is meaningful to the user.

Processing logic— Any of the requirements specifically requested by the user to complete an elementary process: validations, algorithms, calculations, and reading or maintaining a file.

External input (EI) — Elementary process that processes data or control information that comes from outside an application's boundary.

Internal logical file (ILF) — User-identifiable group of logically related data or control information maintained within the boundary of an application.

External inquiry (EQ) — Elementary process that sends retrieved data or control information outside an application boundary.

External output (EO) — Elementary process that sends derived data or control information outside an application's boundary.

External interface file (EIF) — User-identifiable group of logically related data or control information referenced by an application and maintained within the boundary of another application.

Data functions — Internal local files and external interface files.

Transactional functions — External inputs, external outputs, inquiries.

Derived data — Data that does not necessarily update a file.

Function points — Per IFPUG, a method of estimating costs and resources required for software development and maintenance.

IFPUG Steps

Step 1: Determine Type of Function Point Count

The first step in the function point counting procedure is to determine the type of function point count. The three types of counts described in the manual are:

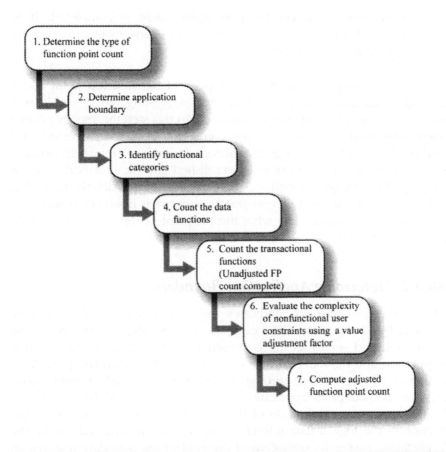

Figure 6.1   IFPUG function point counting process.

1. *Development project function point count* — A measure of the functions provided to the user with the first installation of the software delivered when the project is complete.

2. *Enhancement project function point count* —A measure of modifications to an existing application that add, change, or delete user functions delivered when the project is complete. When the functionality from an enhancement project is installed, the application function point count must be updated to reflect changes in the application's functionality.

3. *Application function point count* — A measure of an installed application. This measure, often called the baseline or installed function point count, provides a measure of the current functions the application provides the user. This number is initialized when the

development project function point count is completed. It is updated every time completion of an enhancement project alters the application's functions.

This initial step documents the purpose of the function point count through interaction with the organization requesting the count. Project assumptions are clarified and documented. In this step the specific source documents used as a basis for the count are identified, collected, and evaluated. Traceability of logical functions included within the functional requirements at a point in time is established and the historical base for gauging future projects is defined. This step results in a definition of what is to be included in the function point count, what information serves as the basis for the count, and what the recipient of the count or estimate expects to receive.

Step 2: Determine Application Boundary

The application boundary indicates the border between the software measured and the user. The boundary defines what is external to the application and serves as the conceptual interface between the internal application and the external user environment. The boundary provides a definition of the interface through which data processed by transactions pass into and out of the application and bounds the logical data maintained by the application. Definition of the boundary is one step in the identification of the logical data referenced by, but not maintained within, the application. Successful definition of the application boundary requires an understanding of the user's external business view of the application that is independent of technical and/or implementation considerations. This application boundary is also referred to as the counting scope.

A project may include one or more applications or subsystems. The purpose of this step is to define specifically the applications or subsystems as they will ultimately be used. The application boundary is the logical boundary that envelops self-contained user functions that must exist to deliver the user requirements. This boundary separates the software from the user domain (users can be people, objects, other software applications, hardware devices, departments, and other organizations). Software may span several physical platforms and include batch and online processes, all of which are included within the logical application boundary.

As illustrated in Figure 6.2, the boundary definition encapsulates the estimate to a defined set of functions executing within a given space. Everything within that space is part of the estimate, including all code

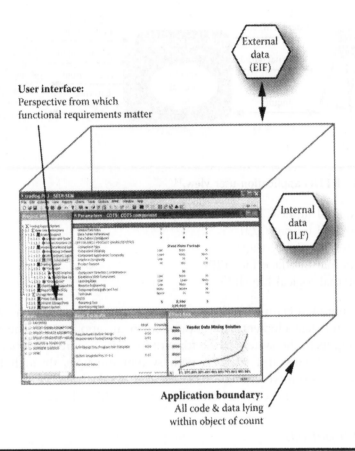

Figure 6.2 Application boundary.

and data residing within the boundary. All data and functions residing outside the boundary are external to the estimate.

Data stored within the application's boundary is considered an internal logical file. Data stored outside the boundary and referenced by the application is considered an external interface file. Data crossing the boundary constitutes a transaction (external input, external output, or external inquiry).

Step 3: Identify Functional Categories

The next step is to identify which functions of the system belong in which categories. There are five categories of functions and all are described in detail below.

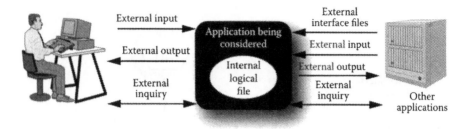

Figure 6.3   IFPUG application user view.[14]

- External input (EI)
- External output (EO)
- External inquiry (EQ)
- External interface file (EIF)
- Internal logical file (ILF)

As illustrated in Figure 6.3, these functional categories map to the ways functions and data elements are supported in an application. The user provides inputs to the system in the form of EIs. The user receives outputs in the form of EOs and interacts with system functions through EQs. Inputs are transformed through ILFs and the system interoperates with other applications and external systems through EIFs, EIs, and EOs.

External Input (EI)

An EI is any function or transaction that moves data into an application. Generally, this data is used to update an ILF in an application. An EI should be considered unique if the logical design requires input processing that is different from other EIs. During EI identification, all items that update ILFs are identified. For each item identified: (1) consider each unique format a separate EI; in some cases the same data can be received in more than one format; (2) count one EI for each data maintenance activity (e.g., add, change, and delete) performed.

To identify multiple EIs generated by one physical file, look at the record types on the file. Exclude header and trailer records (unless required for audit purposes) and record types required due to physical space limitations. Look at the remaining record types for unique processing requirements and associate an EI for each unique process. Data received from outside the subsystem boundary that either maintain (add, change, maintain, populate, or delete data in) an ILF or provide control functions are identified as EIs. Data with unique processing requirements are counted as separate EIs.

EI Examples

In a banking system, customer data that is input into a customer account file is an example of an external input. In a satellite surveillance system, an example is the input from a ground system commanding a new pointing position.

Duplicate EIs

Each different input process for the same operation is counted. An example might be a banking system that accepts two identical deposit transactions, one through an automated teller machine (ATM) transaction and a second through a manual teller deposit transaction. Each transaction would be counted as a separate EI.

Suspense File Updates

Input processes that maintain either ILFs or suspense/carry-around files should be counted based on the following. If they are updateable by the user, count them as ILFs and count an EI for each data maintenance activity performed on an ILF. If a suspense/carry-around file cannot be updated, count an EI for each data maintenance activity that the program itself performs on the original ILF. In either case, the process of reapplying data from a suspense/carry-around file to the ILF is not counted. Multiple methods of invoking the same input logic, for example, entering either *A* or *Add* on a command line and also using a function key for *Add*, should be counted only once.

Not External Inputs

The following examples are not EIs: (1) reference data; EIFs utilized by an application but not maintained by it; (2) input side of an external inquiry; data input used to drive selection for data retrieval (see external inquiry section below); (3) menu screens that simply facilitate navigation; (4) log-on screens that facilitate entry into an application but do not maintain ILFs.

Rating Complexity for External Inputs

Each EI is assigned a low, average, or high complexity rating based on the number of file types referenced (FTR) and data element types (DETs). DETs are usually unique, user-recognizable, nonrepeating fields or attributes, including foreign key attributes that enter the boundary of the subsystem or application.

Data element type identification — The DET count is the maximum number of user-recognizable data elements that are maintained as ILFs by the EIs. Each data element maintainable as an ILF by the EI is a DET with the following exceptions:

- Duplicate fields created by the same user input. For example, an account number or date that is physically stored in multiple fields should be counted as one DET.
- Fields that appear more than once in the ILF because of technology or implementation techniques should be counted only once; for example, if an ILF is comprised of more than one table in a relational database, the keys used to relate the tables would be counted only once.

Additional DETs are credited to the EI for the following:

- Command lines or function keys that provide the capability to specify the action to be taken by the EI — one additional DET per EI, not per command or function key; navigational keys, however, are not counted.
- Fields not entered by the user but maintained as ILFs through EIs should be counted; for example, a system-generated sequenced key maintained as an ILF would be counted as a DET.
- Error or confirmation messages resulting from input are each counted as an additional DET for the input.

File type referenced identification — An FTR is counted for each ILF item or file maintained or referenced and all EIF items or files referenced during the processing of the EI. File types referenced, or more simply, files referenced, totals the number of ILFs maintained, read, or referenced and the EIFs read or referenced by the EI transaction. Rate the complexity of each EI using Table 6.1.

Table 6.1   Complexity Rating Table for External Inputs

	1 to 4 DETs	5 to 15 DETs	16 or More DETs
0 to 1 FTRs	Low	Low	Average
2 FTRs	Low	Average	High
3 or More FTRs	Average	High	High

External Output (EO)

An EO is any function or transaction that manipulates data and presents it to a user. Weapons firing solutions, status reports, commands to other systems, or outgoing e-mail can be counted as EOs. The key feature of an EO is that the information presented outside the boundary must contain derived or calculated information or update an ILF. Otherwise, the transaction is categorized as an external inquiry (EQ).

External Output Examples

An example of an EO in a banking system is a customer's monthly statement. A map sent back to the ground is an example from a satellite surveillance system.

Reports

Each report produced by an application is counted as an EO. Two reports that are identically formatted, but contain different information are counted as two EOs because each requires unique processing logic and unique calculations.

Duplicate Reports

Identical reports produced on different media due to specific user requirements are counted as separate EOs. The processing required to produce different output media is considered unique processing logic. For example, identical reports on paper and on microfiche are counted as two EOs. (*Note:* This counting practice is undergoing review and may change in future IFPUG releases.)

Graphical Formats

Graphical outputs should be counted as if presented in textual format. Each different graphical display requested by the user should be counted as an EO. Statistical data presented in a table, bar chart, pie chart, and exploded pie chart should be counted as four EOs.

Report Generator

External output developed for the user with a report generator should be counted as an EO for each specified unique report. If a report generator facility is requested by the user as part of an application for do-it-yourself report generation, one EI should be counted for each report definition parameter or unique command (e.g., select, compare, sort, merge, extract, calculate, summarize, or format) requested by the user to control report generation; one EO should be counted for the total report program; and one ILF should be counted if a new file is created and saved.

Not External Outputs

The following are not EOs:

- Help. See EI identification section.
- Error or confirmation messages; these generally are counted as additional DETs for the transaction (external input, output, or inquiry) with which they are associated.
- Multiple reports with unique data values; identical reports with the same format and processing logic but unique data values are not counted as separate EOs. For example, two reports, the first containing customer names A through L and the second, customer names M through Z, are counted as only one EO.
- Summary fields (column totals) in a detail report do not constitute unique EOs.
- Ad hoc reporting. When a user is responsible for creating reports through the use of a language such as FOCUS or SQL, no EOs are counted.

Rating Complexity for External Outputs

Each EO function is assigned a low, average, or high complexity rating based on the number of FTRs and DETs. EOs should be generated by the application in a format that can be used by an external source. Identify each unique format under which data will be output, whether to a screen, external application, hard drive, or other device. (*Note:* This counting practice is undergoing review and may change in future IFPUG releases.)

Data element type identification — A DET should be counted for each user-recognizable, nonduplicate field that appears in the EO. Each field in the EO is a DET within the following guidelines:

- User-recognizable duplicate fields (for example, account numbers or dates physically stored in multiple fields) are counted as one DET.
- Count a DET in the EO for each unique command or parameter in a report generator facility requested by the user for do-it-yourself report generation.

Table 6.2 Complexity Rating Table for External Outputs

	1 to 5 DETs	*6 to 19 DETs*	*20 or More DETs*
0 to 1 FTRs	Low	Low	Average
2 to 3 FTRs	Low	Average	High
4 or More FTRs	Average	High	High

- Count a DET for each type of label and each type of numerical equivalent in a graphical output; for example, a pie chart might have two DETs, one for designating the category and one for the applicable percentage.
- Do not count literals as DETs.
- Do not count paging variables or system generated date-time stamps.

Additional DETs are credited to the EO for the following:

- Count additional DETs for each summary or total field on the EO.
- Count a DET for each distinct error or confirmation message associated with the transaction.

File type referenced identification — An FTR should be counted for all ILFS and EIFs referenced or maintained during the processing of the EO. Rate the complexity for each EO using Table 6.2.

External Inquiry (EQ)

An EQ is a unique request that results in the retrieval of data. An EQ request does not update or change any of the software ILFs. An EQ response does not contain derived data; it simply retrieves existing information. An EQ should be considered unique if the logical design requires processing logic different from other EQs. For example, clicking on a drop-down box invokes a response that reveals a dynamic list of items. This is an EQ. The request is the mouse click on the drop-down box, and the response is the display of the list of items. Processes other than direct retrieval of information from ILFs or EIFs are not EQs. In order to identify EQs, identify all processes by which an input triggers the retrieval of data not derived by that process. For each process identified: (1) verify that each input–output combination is unique and consider each unique input–output combination a separate EQ; and (2) credit an EQ for each process.

External Inquiry Example

Retrieval of data: Selection of data retrieval based on data input.

Implied External Inquiries: Change or delete screens that retrieve data prior to change or delete functionality are credited with an EQ, provided the EQ capability can be and is used as a stand-alone function.

Duplicate Output Side: Identical queries produced on different media due to specific user requirements are counted as separate EQs. (*Note:* This counting practice is under review and may change in future IFPUG releases.)

Graphical Formats: Each different graphical display requested by the user should be counted as an additional EQ. A log-on screen that provides security functionality is counted as an EQ. Menu screens that provide screen selection and data retrieval selection input for the called screen are considered EQs, the menu being the input side of the EQ and the called screen being the output side. *Help* involves an EQ pair in which the input and output (explanatory text) are both unique. Credit help text that can be accessed or displayed through different request techniques or from different areas of an application only once. Two categories of help are considered EQs:

- Full screen help. A help facility that depends on the application screen to display help text relating to the calling screen.
- Field-sensitive help. A help facility, dependent on the location of the cursor or some other method of identification, that displays help documentation specific to that field. Credit this as one EQ per screen.

Not External Inquiries

The following are not EQs:

- Error or confirmation messages. Counted as DETs on transaction functions.
- Multiple methods of invoking the same EQ logic. Multiple methods such as entering *I* or *Ins* on a command line or using a function key are counted only once.
- Help text that can be accessed from multiple areas or screens of an application or can be accessed and browsed independently of the associated application is counted only once.
- Menu screens that provide only navigational selection functionality are not counted.
- Derived data. A transaction containing derived data should be categorized as an EO. System documentation that is available online, in lieu of, or in addition to that available in hard copy is

not counted. Online documentation alone should not be considered a delivered software function.

- Test systems. Nondelivered, developer-only test systems are included in system development only and should not be counted; delivered test systems should be counted as normal.
- User-maintained help facility. This facility should be counted as a separate application.
- Independent teaching (tutorial) systems. Computer-aided instruction (CAI), computer-based training (CBT), and other independent software teaching systems that are different from the production system and maintained separately should be counted as separate applications; training systems identical to the production system should be considered as additional sites; do not count them as separate functions.

Rating Complexity for External Inquiries

Each EQ is assigned a low, average, or high complexity rating based on the number of FTRs and DETs:

Data element type identification (input side) — A DET is counted for fields entered that specify the EQ to be executed or specify data selection criteria.

Data element type identification (external output side) — A DET is counted for each user-recognizable, nonduplicate field that appears on the output side of the EQ.

Each field appearing in the EQ is a DET with the following exceptions:

- Fields should be considered from the user's perspective. For example, an account number or date that is physically stored in multiple fields but displayed as one is counted as one DET.
- Fields that, because of technology or implementation techniques, appear more than once in the ILF should be counted only once.
- Do not count literals (fixed information within the program) as DETs.
- Do not count paging variables or system generated date-time stamps.

Additional DETs are credited to the EQ for the following:

- For full-screen help, credit a low complexity EQ per calling screen regardless of the number of FTRs or DETs involved.
- For field-sensitive help, classify an EQ, using the input side, based on the number of fields that are field-sensitive and the number of FTRs. Each field-sensitive field corresponds to a DET.
- Count a DET for each distinct error or confirmation message associated with the transaction.

Table 6.3   Complexity Rating Table for External Inquiries

	1 to 5 DETs	*6 to 19 DETs*	*20 or More DETs*
0 to 1 FTRs	Low	Low	Average
2 to 3 FTRs	Low	Average	High
4 or More FTRs	Average	High	High

File type referenced identification — An FTR is counted for each ILF and EIF read during the processing of the EQ.

Rate the complexity for each EQ using Table 6.3.

External Interface File (EIF)

An EIF is a user-identifiable group of logically related data (data related at such a level that an experienced user would identify the data as fulfilling a specific user requirement of the application) or control information utilized by the application but maintained by another application. EIFs might be used by an application's EOs or EQs. For example, when a program references a file that contains data that is important to the operation of the application but is not updated or maintained by the application itself, it uses an EIF. In order to identify EIFs, identify all data that is:

- Stored externally to the application's boundary
- Not maintained by the application
- Identified as a requirement of the application by the users

Group the data logically based on the user's view:

- View data at the level of detail at which the user can first categorize the data as satisfying unique requirements of the application.
- View the data logically. Although some storage technologies such as tables in a relational database or sequential flat files relate closely to EIFs, do not assume that one physical file equals one logical file.

Each type of data on the following list can relate to one or more EIFs, depending on the user's view.

External Interface File Examples

Examples of EIFs include reference data (data used by the application but not maintained by the application), help messages, error messages, and edit data (criteria).

Not External Interface Files

The following are not EIFs:

- Data received from another application that adds, changes, or deletes data in an ILF (counted as an EI)
- Data maintained by the application being counted but accessed and utilized by another application
- Data formatted and processed for use by another application (counted as an EO)

Rating Complexity for External Interface Files

Each EIF is assigned a low, average or high complexity rating based on the number of RETs and DETs:

Data element type identification — These are user-recognizable, non-duplicate fields residing in the EIF. Each field in an EIF may be a DET, with the following exceptions:

- Fields should be viewed from the user's perspective. For example, an account number or date physically stored in multiple fields but displayed only once should be counted as one DET.
- Fields that appear more than once in an EIF because of the technology or implementation techniques should be counted only once. For example, if an EIF is comprised of more than one record type in a file, the record ID field used to identify the records would be counted only once.
- Repeating fields that are identical in format and exist so that multiple occurrences of a data value can occur are counted only once. For example, EIFs containing 12 monthly budget amount fields and an annual budget amount field would be credited with two DETs: a DET for the monthly budget amount fields and a DET for the annual budget amount field.

Record element type identification — These are logical subgroupings based on the user's view of the data. If there are no further logical groupings to fields, then there is only one RET.

One way to identify different RETs is by record types. Exclude header and trailer records, unless specifically requested for audit purposes, as well as record types required by physical space limitations. Each unique record type corresponds to a RET. Rate the complexity for each EIF using Table 6.4.

Table 6.4 Complexity Rating Table for External Interface Files

	1 to 19 DETs	20 to 50 DETs	51 or More DETs
0 to 1 RETs	Low	Low	Average
2 to 5 RETs	Low	Average	High
6 or More RETs	Average	High	High

Internal Logical File (ILF)

An ILF is a user-identifiable group of logically related data or control information utilized and maintained by an application. ILFs might be accessed by the EIs, EOs, or EQs of an application. As illustrated in Figure 6.4, ILFs convert inputs or inquiries based on user-identifiable groups of logically related information or visible data linked to a requirement.

The ILFs store information processed by an internal function resulting in an EO. For example, the SEER-SEM knowledge bases are ILFs because they are both used and maintained by the application. There are two steps to identifying ILFs. First, identify all data that is:

- Stored internal to the application
- Maintained through a standardized process of the application
- Identified as a requirement of the application by the user.

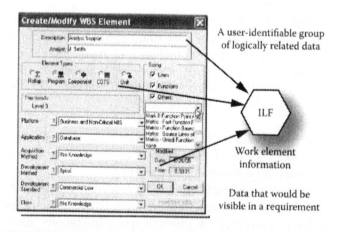

Figure 6.4 ILF relationships.

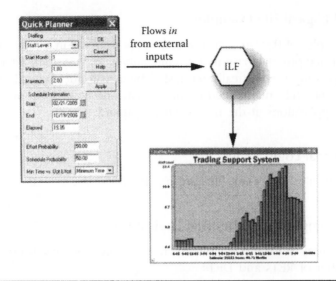

Figure 6.5 Relationship of EI, ILF, and EO.

Next, group the data logically based on the user's view:

- Group data at the level of detail at which the user can first categorize the data as satisfying unique requirements of the application.
- View the data logically. Although some storage technologies such as tables in a relational database or sequential flat files relate closely to ILFs, do not assume that one physical file equals one logical file.

Figure 6.5 shows the relationship of an EI, an ILF, and an EO. To identify potential ILFs, look at the type of data stored and how a user would view or group the data (storage technologies such as tables, flat files, indexes, and paths are irrelevant). Each type of data on the following list can relate to one or more ILFs, depending on the user's view:

- Application data (master files like tax information and personnel information)
- Application security data
- Audit data
- Help messages
- Error messages
- Edit data

Internal Logical File Examples

Two examples of ILFs are a customer account database in a banking system and a topography database in a satellite surveillance system. Backup data is counted only if specifically requested by a user due to legal or similar requirements. ILFs maintained by more than one application are credited to both applications at the time each is counted.

Not Internal Logical Files

Temporary files and work files are not ILFs.

Rating Complexity for Internal Logical Files

Each ILF item is assigned a low, average, or high classification based on the number of RETs and DETs.

Data element type identification — These are user-recognizable, non-duplicate fields residing in the ILF. Each field in an ILF may be a DET, with the following exceptions:

- Fields should be considered from the point of view of the user. For example, an account number or date that is stored physically in multiple fields but displayed only once is counted as one DET.
- Fields that appear more than once in ILFs because of technology or implementation techniques should be counted only once. For example, if an ILF is comprised of more than one table in a relational database, the keys used to relate the tables are counted only once.
- Repeating fields that are identical in format and exist to allow multiple occurrences of a data value are counted only once. For example, ILFs containing 12 monthly budget amount fields and an annual budget amount field would be credited with two DETs: a DET for the monthly budget amount fields and a DET for the annual budget amount field.
- Each unique command or parameter is counted as a DET if ILFs are created and saved in a report generator facility requested by the user for do-it-yourself report generation.

Record element type identification — These are logical subgroupings based on a user's view of the data. (The data analysis equivalents to such logical groupings are data entities.) If there are no further logical groupings to fields, then there is only one RET.

Table 6.5   Complexity Rating Table for Internal Logical Files

	1 to 19 DETs	*20 to 50 DETs*	*51 or More DETs*
0 to 1 RETs	Low	Low	Average
2 to 5 RETs	Low	Average	High
6 or More RETs	Average	High	High

One way to identify different RETs is by record types. Exclude header and trailer records, unless specifically requested for audit purposes, as well as record types required by physical space limitations. Each unique record type corresponds to a RET. Rate the complexity for each ILF using Table 6.5.

Step 4: Count Data Functions (ILFs and EIFs)

This step counts the ILFs and EIFs identified in Step 3. It considers internal and external data entities and identifies logical data stores maintained or stored within the subsystem. External data, transactions, messages, and controls (external inputs) populate, revise, update, change or add to the data stores. These logical data elements support EOs and/or EQs. A data group should not be dependent upon or attributive to another data group for its existence. Data groups are classified as either EIFs or ILFs. An ILF is counted once per subsystem. When identifying ILFs, the data must actually exist or may exist when the software is in use and it is dynamic, not hard coded.

Identify, categorize, and count the ILFs that are persistent, logical entities or data groups to be maintained through a standard function of the software.

Identify, categorize, and count the EIFs that are persistent, logical entities referenced from other applications but not maintained by this application. Typically these data are used in editing, validation, or reporting types of software processes.

When identifying and classifying the persistent logical entities as internal (maintained) and external (referenced only), it is helpful to draw circles around the entities and their included subentities on a data model or entity relationship diagram. If there is no data model or entity relationship model, one is essentially created in this step by building on the context diagram created in the previous application boundary step.

Note that hard-coded data or any tables and files created only because of the physical or technical implementation are not counted. This step records the numbers and types of logical data elements if they are known and if they are not already identified in the requirements. This provides a checklist of data entities to gauge the consistency and completeness of transactional (manipulation of data) functions.

Clarifications can be made by reviewing the entities to determine whether they are on a data model or hand-drawn context diagram and whether they are inside the application boundary (i.e., to be maintained by the software) or external to the boundary (i.e., to be referenced only). A typical question might be: "Why is that entity external? I thought we needed to be able to update that entity." Such questions could lead to a discussion that either confirms the original requirements or reveals an inconsistency in understanding and leads to a change in the diagram. When the review is combined with the transactions outlined in the next step, the majority of potential requirements mismatches are identified.

Step 5: Count Transactional Functions (EIs, EOs, and EQs)

Use the following information to count transactional functions identified in Step 3. You should count:

- **EIs** that are the elementary processes whose primary intent is to maintain the data in one or more persistent logical entities or to control the behavior of the system. Note that these EIs are functional unit processes and not physical data flows or data structures.
- **EOs** that are the elementary processes whose primary intent is to deliver data out of the application boundary, and which include at least one of the following: mathematical calculation(s), derive new data elements, update an ILF (via calculations required to compute outputs), or direct the behavior of the system.
- **EQs** that are the elementary processes whose primary intent is to deliver data out of the application boundary purely by retrieval from one or more of the ILFs or EIFs.

In this step, the majority of missed, incomplete, or inconsistent requirements are identified. The list below provides some examples of the types of discoveries that can be made using function point analysis:

1. If a persistent, logical entity has been identified as an ILF, i.e., maintained through a standard maintenance function of the application, and has no associated EIs, there are one or more mismatched requirements: (1) the entity is actually a reference-only entity (in which case it would be an EIF), or (2) there is at least one missing requirement to maintain the entity, such as add entity, change entity, or delete entity.

2. If there are data maintenance (or data administration) functions identified for data, but there is no persistent logical entity to house the data (ILF), the data model may be incomplete. This would indicate the need to revisit the data requirements of the application.

3. If there is a data update function present for an entity identified as reference only (EIF), this would indicate that the entity is actually an ILF. The data requirements are inconsistent and need to be reviewed.

4. If there are data entities that need to be referenced by one or more input, output, or query functions, and there is no such data source identified on the data model/entity-relationship diagram/context diagram, the data requirements are incomplete and need to be revisited.

5. If there are output or query functions that specify data fields to be output or displayed that have no data source (i.e., no ILF or EIF), and the data is not hard-coded, there is a mismatch between the data model and the user functions. This indicates a need to revisit the data requirements.

6. Most maintained entities (ILFs) follow the AUDIO (add, update, delete, inquiry, output) convention; each persistent logical entity typically has a standard set of functions associated with it. Not all entities will follow this pattern, but AUDIO is a good checklist to use with ILFs.

7. Is this group of data visible to the user via an EI or EO? Because groupings of data are evaluated at the EI or (provisionally) internal layer, they naturally must be evident there.

8. Does this group of data logically belong together? If certain data items are always associated, then they belong in a single group. This categorization scheme reinforces the idea that function points are based on specifics of design rather than implementation. Given this condition, physical attributes (tables, flat files, etc.) often but do not always delineate logical groupings of data.

9. Has this group of data been counted before? An ILF may be encountered in a system many times, but it is designed — and so counted — only once.

Step 6: Evaluate Value Adjustment Factors

This step applies to adjusted function point counts only. Skip this step and go on to step 7 if you are computing an unadjusted function point count.

Evaluate the complexity of nonfunctional user constraints using a value adjustment factor (IFPUG only; not an ISO standard). Through an evaluation of the 14 general systems characteristics (GSCs shown in Table 6.6 include performance, end-user efficiency, transaction volumes, and other factors),

Table 6.6   Value Adjustment Factor Components

Value Adjustment Factor Element	Degree of Influence					
	0	1	2	3	4	5
1. Data communications	Application is pure batch processing or stand-alone application	Application is pure batch processing or stand-alone application	Application is batch but has remote data entry or remote printing	Application includes online data collection or TP (teleprocessing) front end to a batch process or query system	Application more than a front end and supports only one type of TP communication	Application more than a front end and supports more than one type of TP communication protocol
2. Distributed data processing	Data is not transferred or processed on another component of the system	Data prepared for transfer, then transferred and processed on another component of system for user processing	Data prepared for transfer, then transferred and processed on another component of system; not for user processing	Distributed processing and data transfer online and in one direction only	Distributed processing and data transfer online and in both directions	Distributed processing and data transfer online and dynamically performed on most appropriate component of system

3. Performance	No special performance requirements stated by user	Performance and design requirements stated and reviewed but no special actions required	Response time or throughput critical during peak hours; no special design for CPU utilization required; processing deadline is for next business cycle	Response time or throughput critical during all business hours; no special design for CPU utilization required; processing deadline requirements with interfacing systems are constraining	Stated user performance requirements stringent enough to require performance analysis tasks in design phase	Performance analysis tools used in design, development, and/or implementation phases to meet stated user performance requirements
4. Heavily used configuration	No explicit or implicit operational restrictions included	Operational restrictions exist, but are less restrictive than a typical application; no special effort needed to meet restrictions	Operational restrictions exist and are typical for an application; special effort through controllers or control programs needed to meet restrictions	Stated operational restrictions require special constraints on one piece of application in central processor or dedicated processor	Stated operational restrictions require special constraints on entire application in central processor or dedicated processor	Special constraints on application in distributed components of system

Table 6.6 (continued) Value Adjustment Factor Components

Value Adjustment Factor Element	Degree of Influence					
	0	1	2	3	4	5
5. Transaction rate	No peak transaction period anticipated	Low transaction rates have minimal effect on design, development, and installation phases	Average transaction rates have some effect on design, development, and installation phases	High transaction rates affect design, development, and/or installation phases	High transaction rate(s) stated by user in application requirements or service level agreements high enough to require performance analysis tasks in design, development, and/or installation phases	High transaction rate(s) stated by user in application requirements or service level agreements high enough to require performance analysis tasks and require use of performance analysis tools in design, development, and/or installation phases
6. Online data entry	All transactions processed in batch mode	1 to 7 percent of transactions interactive	8 to 15 percent of transactions interactive	16 to 23 percent of transactions interactive	24 to 30 percent of transactions interactive	More than 30 percent of transactions interactive

	None of the items listed	One to three of the items listed	Four or five of the items listed	Six or more of the items listed, but no specific user requirements related to efficiency	Six or more of the items listed; stated requirements for user efficiency strong enough to require design tasks for human factors to be included	Six or more of the items listed; stated requirements for user efficiency strong enough to require use of special tools and processes to demonstrate that objectives have been achieved
7. End-user efficiency made up of navigational aids, menus, on-line help and documents, automated cursor movement, Scrolling, Remote printing (via online transmissions), preassigned function keys (e.g., clear screen, request help, clone screen), batch jobs submitted from on-line transactions, drop-down list box, heavy use of reverse video, highlighting, colors, underlining, and other indicators, hard-copy documentation of online transactions						

Table 6.6 (continued)   Value Adjustment Factor Components

Value Adjustment Factor Element	Degree of Influence					
	0	1	2	3	4	5
(e.g., screen print), mouse interface, pop-up windows, templates and/or defaults, bilingual support (two languages: count as four items) or multilingual (more than two languages: count as six items)						
8. Online update	None	Online update of one to three control files included; volume of updating low and recovery easy	Online update of four or more control files included; volume of updating low and recovery easy	Online update of major internal logical files included	Protection against data loss essential; has been specially designed and programmed in system	High volumes bring cost considerations into recovery process; highly automated recovery procedures with minimum human intervention included

	None of the items listed	Any one of the items listed	Any two of the items listed	Any three of the items listed	Any four of the items listed	All five of the items listed
9. Complex processing including sensitive control and/or application-specific security processing, extensive logical processing, extensive mathematical processing, much exception processing, resulting in incomplete transactions that must be processed again or complex processing to handle multiple input/output possibilities						

Table 6.6 (continued)   Value Adjustment Factor Components

Value Adjustment Factor Element	Degree of Influence					
	0	*1*	*2*	*3*	*4*	*5*
10. Reusability	No reusable code	Reusable code used within application	Less than 10 percent of application code developed is intended for use in more than one application	Ten percent or more of application code developed intended for use in more than one application	Application specifically packaged and/or documented to ease reuse; application customized at source code level	Application specifically packaged and/or documented to ease reuse; application customized for use by means of user parameter maintenance
11. Installation ease	No special considerations stated by user; no special set-up required for installation	No special considerations stated by user; special set-up required for installation	Conversion and installation requirements stated by user; conversion and installation guides provided and tested; impact of conversion on project not considered important	Conversion and installation requirements stated by the user; conversion and installation guides provided and tested; impact of conversion on project is considered important	In addition to requirements for 3, automated conversion and installation tools provided and tested	Same as 4

12. Operational ease	No special operational considerations other than the normal back-up procedures stated by user	[One, some, or all of the following items apply to application. Select all that apply. Each item has a point value of one, except as noted otherwise.] ■ Start-up, back-up, and recovery processes were provided, but human intervention is required. ■ Start-up, back-up, and recovery processes were provided, but no human intervention is required (count as two items). ■ The application minimizes the need for tape mounts and/or remote data access requiring human intervention. ■ The application minimizes need for paper handling.				Application designed for unattended operation (no human intervention required to operate system other than to start or shut down application); automatic error recovery is feature of application
13. Multiple sites	Needs of only one installation site considered in design	Needs of more than one installation considered in design; application designed to operate only under identical hardware and software environments	The needs of more than one installation site were considered in the design; application designed to operate only under similar hardware and/or software environments	Needs of more than one installation site considered in design; application designed to operate under different hardware and/or software environments	Documentation and support plan provided and tested to support application at multiple installation sites; application is as described by 2	Documentation and support plan provided and tested to support application at multiple installation sites; application is as described by 3

Table 6.6 (continued)   Value Adjustment Factor Components

Value Adjustment Factor Element	Degree of Influence					
	0	*1*	*2*	*3*	*4*	*5*
14. Facilitate change; the following characteristics can apply for the application:	None of the items on the list	Total of one item from list	A total of two items from list	A total of three items from list	A total of four items from list	A total of five items from list
A. Flexible queries:						
1. Flexible query and report facility is provided that can handle simple requests. (count as 1 item)						
2. Flexible query and report facility is provided that can handle requests of average complexity. (count as 2 items)						

3. Flexible query and report facility is provided that can handle complex requests. (count as 3 items)

B. Business control data:

1. Business control data is kept in tables that are maintained by the user with online interactive processes, but changes take effect only on the next business cycle. (count as 1 item)

2. Business control data is kept in tables that are maintained by the user with online interactive processes, and the changes take effect immediately. (count as 2 items)

a software complexity assessment can be made. The impact of user constraints in these areas is often not enunciated or even addressed until late in the software development life cycle, even though their influence on the overall project can be significant.

The reason models like SEER-SEM that apply effort adjustments for technology and complexity use unadjusted function points rather than adjusted points is because the IFPUG GSCs would double count the impacts of many of the complexity factors. For example, SEER-SEM accounts for effort impacts of multiple site development which is one of the GSCs.

Determine the Value Adjustment Factor (VAF). The VAF quantifies the general functionality provided to the user of the application. It consists of the 14 GSCs that are used to assess the general functionality of the application. Each characteristic includes descriptions that help determine the degree of influence of the characteristic. The degrees of influence range on a scale of zero (no influence) to five (strong influence). The 14 GSCs are summarized into the value adjustment factor. When applied, the value adjustment factor adjusts the unadjusted function point count within ±35 percent to produce the adjusted function point count. Determining the value adjustment factor requires several steps:

1. Evaluate each of the 14 GSCs on a scale from zero to five to determine the degree of influence (DI).
2. Add the degrees of influence for all 14 GSCs to produce the total degree of influence (TDI).
3. Insert the TDI into the following equation to produce the VAF:

$$VAF = (TDI \times 0.01) + 0.65$$

For example, the following value adjustment factor is calculated if the degree of influence for each of the 14 GSC descriptions is three:

$$(3 \times 14) = 42$$

$$VAF = (42 \times 0.01) + 0.65$$

$$VAF = 1.07$$

Table 6.6 summarizes the information used to calculate the value adjustment factor.

Step 7: Compute Unadjusted and Adjusted Function Point Counts

The unadjusted (raw) function point count adjusts the counts of the unique function types (external inputs, external outputs, external queries, external interface files, and internal logical files) identified through the steps described above. The unique function types that were individually assessed for complexity (low, average, or high) are now given weighting values that vary from 3 (for simple external inputs) to 15 (for complex internal files).

Unadjusted function points (UFPs) are calculated as follows. The sum of all the occurrences is computed by multiplying each function count with a weighting and then adding all the values. The weighting is based on the complexity of the feature counted. Table 6.7 shows weighting values.

$$EI_{(total)} = EI_{(low)} \times 3 + EI_{(average)} \times 4 + EI_{(high)} \times 6$$

$$EO_{(total)} = EO_{(low)} \times 4 + EO_{(average)} \times 5 + EO_{(high)} \times 7$$

$$ILF_{(total)} = ILF_{(low)} \times 7 + ILF_{(average)} \times 10 + ILF_{(high)} \times 15$$

$$EIF_{(total)} = EIF_{(low)} \times 5 + EIF_{(average)} \times 7 + EIF_{(high)} \times 10$$

$$EQ_{(total)} = EQ_{(low)} \times 3 + EQ_{(average)} \times 4 + EQ_{(high)} \times 6$$

$$\text{Unadjusted function point (UFP) count} =$$
$$EI_{(total)} + EO_{(total)} + ILF_{(total)} + EIF_{(total)} + EQ_{(total)}$$

At this point, the unadjusted function point count is complete. The next calculation is required only if the goal is to calculate an adjusted function point count.

The adjusted function point count is calculated using a specific formula for a development project, enhancement project, or application (system baseline) function point count. It is derived by multiplying the unadjusted function point count by the VAF. As illustrated in Figure 6.6, offsetting the unadjusted (raw) function point count by the functional complexity rating and value adjusted factor yields the adjusted function count.

Table 6.7 Function Complexity Table

Function Type	Low	Average	High
External Input (EI)	×3	×4	×6
External Output (EO)	×4	×5	×7
Internal Logical Files (ILF)	×7	×10	×15
External Interface Files (EIF)	×5	×7	×10
External Inquiry (EQ)	×3	×4	×6

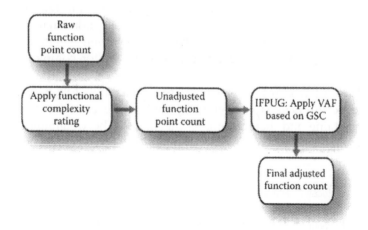

Figure 6.6 Computing final adjusted function count.

In order to find the adjusted function point (AFP) value, the UFP (the raw function count weighted by the appropriate complexity shown in Table 6.7) is multiplied by the VAF.

In other words, the UFP is adjusted by measuring it against the VAF. The final AFP figure can then be calculated as:

$$AFP = UFP \times VAF$$

The VAF can range from 0.65 to 1.35: a VAF of 0.65 would result if all the complexity factors had no influence, and a VAF of 1.35 would indicate all the complexity factors had significant influence. Therefore, if a system is relatively simple, with few constraints and a simple architecture, the VAF would be lower than 1 because the majority of complexity factors would have little influence. On the other hand, if the system to be developed was complex and included stringent performance and reliability requirements, the VAF would likely be greater than 1.

SEER-Function-Based Sizing (SEER-FBS)

SEER-FBS was developed to allow nonfunction point trained users to (1) develop function-based estimates, (2) attribute cost and schedule to end user items such as "one report," and (3) to simplify use on scientific and embedded software. Inputs can be entered using normal function point complexities (low, average, or high).

SEER-FBS output approximates a range (least, likely, and most) of function points and has two modes: (1) the traditional IFPUG mode that

Table 6.8 Comparison SEER-SEM Function Modes: IFPUG and SEER-SEM

Functions	IFPUG Compatible Mode	SEER-SEM Extended Mode
External inputs (EIs)	X	X
External outputs (EOs)	X	X
External inquiries (EQs)	X	X
External interface files (EIFs)	X	X
Internal logical files (ILFs)	X	X
Internal functions		X

Note: SEER-SEM, the cost model containing SEER-FBS, will also accept unadjusted function point counts performed by traditional counting.

supports the five function point categories and (2) the SEER-FBS extended mode that supports the five IFPUG categories and adds a sixth titled *internal functions*, supporting highly algorithmic processing often associated with real-time and embedded systems. The resulting function point approximations are compatible with IFPUG counting rules. There are six categories of functions as shown in Table 6.8.

SEER-FBS is available for use in estimation where rigorous function point counts have not been completed, and to allow nonfunction point-trained users to perform trade-offs, for example, determining the effort to add one additional complex report. Because SEER-FBS is an approximation of function points and does not profess to be an exact function point count, and because it generates a range of function point estimates rather than a single point estimate, it does not expect a user to be expert on function point rules.

Users may classify functions as low, average, or high complexity using function point-defined DETs, RETs, etc., or may simply assume all are average if time is at a premium or if this detail is not known. Some organizations use SEER-FBS as their ongoing size metric. Others perform traditional function point counts later in their development cycles for critical projects.

SEER-FBS External Inputs (EIs)

An EI is any function or transaction that moves data into an application. Generally, this data is used to update an ILF in the application. An EI

Table 6.9   SEER-FBS Uses IFPUG Complexity Rating Table for External Inputs

	1 to 4 DETs	*5 to 15 DETs*	*16 or More DETs*
0 to 1 FTRs	Low	Low	Average
2 FTRs	Low	Average	High
3 or More FTRs	Average	High	High

should be considered unique if the logical design requires input processing different from other EIs.

SEER-FBS Subcategories for External Inputs

Input Screens — Logical screens used to add, edit, or delete internally stored data. Count one screen for each transaction type (add, change, or delete). Input screens may be textual or graphical. One or more physical screens may be processed as one transaction. Conversely, one physical screen when viewed by processes can encompass multiple external inputs.

Interactive inputs — Single inputs by a user, such as selecting an item from a list, that cause action to be taken by the software system.

Hardware inputs — Inputs from hardware devices (e.g., radar data, analog signals, sensor readings) that are directly received and processed by the software.

Batch input streams — Noninteractive inputs such as add, change, or delete that provide a unique process to maintain ILFs. Batch inputs should be identified based on their processes. One physical input can, when viewed logically, correspond to a number of EIs. Conversely, two or more physical inputs can correspond to one EI if the processing logic and format are identical for each.

Rating Complexity for External Inputs

Each external input is assigned a low, average, or high complexity rating based on the number of file types referenced (FTRs) and data element types (DETs). See Table 6.9.

SEER-FBS External Outputs (EOs)

An EO is any function or transaction that manipulates data and presents it to a user. Weapons firing solutions, status reports, commands to another system, or outgoing e-mail could be counted as EOs. The key feature of an EO is that the information presented outside the boundary must contain

Table 6.10 SEER-FBS Uses IFPUG Complexity Rating Table for External Outputs

	1 to 5 DETs	*6 to 19 DETs*	*20 or More DETs*
0 to 1 FTRs	Low	Low	Average
2 to 3 FTRs	Low	Average	High
4 or More FTRs	Average	High	High

derived or calculated information or update an ILF. Otherwise, the transaction is categorized as an external inquiry (EQ). See Table 6.10.

SEER-FBS Subcategories for External Outputs

Screen reports — Each unique report generated by the software that is displayed on screen; they include text reports and 2-D or 3-D graphic reports.

Printed reports — Each unique report generated by the software that is printed by a printer or plotter; they include text reports and 2-D or 3-D graphic reports.

Media external outputs — Each unique report generated by the software that is directed to some output media other than a screen or printer. External Output media types include microfiche, magnetic tapes, audios, photographs, and videos.

Software external outputs — Data formats or messages to be output for use by another software package.

Hardware external outputs — Types of messages sent or transmitted to external hardware devices (e.g., calibration data, navigation solutions, and signal requests).

Rating Complexity for External Outputs

Each external output is assigned a low, average, or high complexity rating based on the number of file types referenced (FTRs) and data element types (DETs). See Table 6.10.

SEER-FBS External Inquiries (EQs)

An EQ is a unique request that results in the retrieval of data. An EQ request does not update or change any of the software ILFs. An EQ response does not contain derived data; it simply retrieves existing information. An EQ should be considered unique if the logical design requires processing logic different from other EQs.

Table 6.11   SEER-FBS Uses IFPUG Complexity Rating Table for External Inquiries

	1 to 5 DETs	*6 to 19 DETs*	*20 or More DETs*
0 to 1 FTRs	Low	Low	Average
2 to 3 FTRs	Low	Average	High
4 or More FTRs	Average	High	High

Rating Complexity for External Inquiries

Each external inquiry is assigned a low, average, or high complexity rating based on the number of file types referenced (FTRs) and data element types (DETs). See Table 6.11.

SEER-FBS Subcategories for External Inquiries

Request–response — A transaction in which entered data invokes immediate retrieval of other data.

Menus — Menu screens that provide screen selection and data retrieval selection input for a called screen are counted as EQs; the menu is the input side of the EQ and the called screen is the output side.

Context-sensitive help — Help text that can be accessed or displayed for a particular screen or field that is selected.

Embedded computer external inquiries —Unique types of requests for information from hardware devices (different from hardware inputs in that they require responses).

SEER-FBS External Interface Files (EIFs)

An EIF contains data needed by the system to perform its required functions. An EIF is a user-identifiable group of logically related data (data related at such a level that an experienced user would identify the data as fulfilling a specific user requirement of the application) or control information utilized by the application but maintained by another application.

SEER-FBS Subcategories for External Interface Files

Reference data — Data groupings utilized by software but not changed, e.g., look-up tables, read-only data files, and master lists.

Fixed messages — Messages used by software but not changed, e.g., error messages, help messages, and system status messages.

Shared data files — Data files or databases created externally to an application but used by it.

Table 6.12   SEER-FBS Uses IFPUG Complexity Rating Table for External Interface Files

	1 to 19 DET	*20 to 50 DET*	*51 or More DET*
1 RET	Low	Low	Average
2 to 5 RET	Low	Average	High
6 or More RET	Average	High	High

Rating Complexity for External Interface Files

Each external interface file is assigned a low, average, or high complexity rating based on the number of file types referenced (FTRs) and data element types (DETs). See Table 6.12.

SEER-FBS Internal Logical Files (ILFs)

An ILF is a user-identifiable group of logically related data or control information utilized and maintained by the application. ILFs may be accessed by an application's EIs, EOs, EQs, or IFs.

SEER-FBS Subcategories for Internal Logical Files

Application data groups — Number of data files or other logical groupings of data that are used, processed, derived, obtained, or changed by the application. A mission planning system might have the following application data groups: target data, weapon descriptions, aircraft data, weather data, pilot preferences, and security access level. Input to SEER-FBS for this example would be 6. The determination of low, average, or high would depend on the number of data elements or parameters in the group. If the target data contained 25 specific parameters (DETs), it would be average.

Data tables — Number of data tables that must be created by the software application. For example, in a mission planning system, an aircraft configuration may be stored in a data table for future use.

Database files — Number of internal data groups or record groupings that would be maintained as a database or record group within a database, for example, a customer list, a mailing list, or an accounts receivable list.

Rating Complexity for Internal Logical Files

Each internal logical file is assigned a low, average, or high complexity rating based on the number of file types referenced (FTRs) and data element types (DETs). See Table 6.13.

Table 6.13   SEER-FBS Uses IFPUG Complexity Rating Table for Internal Logical Files[18]

	1 to 19 DETs	20 to 50 DETs	51 or More DETs
1 RETs	Low	Low	Average
2 to 5 RETs	Low	Average	High
6 or More RETs	Average	High	High

Table 6.14   Guidelines for Internal Function Classification

Complexity	Function
Low	Sorting routines
Average	Reasonably complex functions such as commercial data compression algorithms
High	Signal processing or data reduction algorithms; other functions of high logical complexity

SEER-FBS Extended Category: Internal Functions

Internal functions represent SEER-SEM extensions to IFPUG methods. This unique type is intended to account for functions that manipulate data entirely within an application, or that for other reasons never crosses the application boundary and thus are not EIs, EOs, or EQs.

Internal functions are basic processes performed by a program, for example, data reduction, data analysis, monitoring, data compression, encryption, and application-specific calculations. As an example, in a route-planning program of a mission planning system, the application-specific calculations might include automatic routing, take-off and landing calculations, aircraft deconfliction, and fuel consumption. Low, average, or high complexity ratings for internal functions are based on the guidelines shown in Table 6.14. If the actual classification cannot be determined from these guidelines, consider the function to be of average complexity.

Effective Function Points

Galorath Incorporated's method of computing effective size is applicable to function points and provides an "amount of work" versus the total value view provided by development or application function point counts. This method applies traditional reuse factors to function point counting to compute the effective function points.[15] This method is different from but complementary to IFPUG's enhancement project function point count and provides a measure of how much work in effective function points is required rather than determining the total function point count when complete.

Effective function point counts capture the work of redesigning, reimplementing, and retesting function points when a system is developed in multiple builds or undergoes major or minor enhancements or other changes. (See Chapter 8, titled "Software Reuse and Commercial Off-the-Shelf Software," for detailed definitions of computing effective size for any size metric including function points.)

The following worksheet can be used when performing a function point count to be used with SEER-SEM:

SEER-FBS Function-Based Sizing Detailed Inputs

Project Name: _____ File Name: _____
Program Name: _____ Date: _____

- ■ New Functions
- ■ Pre-Existing Functions, Not Designed for Reuse
- ■ Pre-Existing Functions, Designed for Reuse

Parameter	Low	Average	High	Rationale
+ External Inputs (EIs)				
Input screens (may be textual or graphic; used to add, edit, delete; count one screen for each transaction type, i.e., add, edit, delete)				
Interactive inputs (single inputs by a user that cause an action to be taken by software, e.g., pick an item from a list)				
Hardware inputs (different types of inputs from hardware devices, e.g., radar sensor)				
Batch input streams (non-interactive inputs)				

Parameter	Low	Average	High	Rationale
+ External Outputs (EOs)				
Screen reports				
Printed reports				
Media outputs (unique outputs to magnetic tape, audio, video)				
Software outputs (different data format/message output to be used by another software package)				
Hardware outputs (different types of messages sent to external hardware devices, e.g., calibration data, navigation solutions)				
+ External Inquiries (EQs)				
Request–response (entered data invokes immediate retrieval)				
Menus (menu screens that provide screen selection and data retrieval)				
Context-sensitive help				
Embedded computer inquiries (unique types of requests for information from hardware; this is a request for a hardware input; the actual input was counted above)				
+ External Interface Files (EIFs)				
Reference data (data groupings that are used but not changed, e.g., look-up tables)				
Fixed messages (messages used but not changed by software, e.g., help, errors, system status)				
Shared data files (data files or databases created external to this application, but used by this application)				

Parameter	Low	Average	High	Rationale
+ Internal Logical files (ILFs)				
Application data groups (data files or other logical groupings of data that are used, processed, derived, obtained, or changed by the software, e.g., target data, weather data, security access level)				
Data tables (must be created by this application)				
Database files (internal data groups or record groupings that would be maintained as a database or record group, e.g., customer list, mailing list)				
Internal functions (basic processes performed by software, e.g., data reduction, encryption, other calculations)				

Using Function Points

Function point analysis should be performed by trained and experienced personnel. If function point analysis is conducted by untrained personnel, it is reasonable to assume the analysis will be performed incorrectly. The personnel counting function points should utilize the most current version of the *Function Point Counting Practices Manual*.[13]

Organizations use function points to satisfy many objectives. Consistent use of the metric facilitates tracking and monitoring of scope creep by counting function points at the various stages in a project and comparing the count to the function points actually delivered. If the number of function points increases, scope creep has occurred. An organization may also use function points to track aggregate productivity across similar project types. According to David Longstreet:

> Current application documentation should be utilized to complete a function point count. For example, screen formats, report layouts, listing of interfaces with other systems and between systems, logical and/or preliminary physical data models will all assist in function points analysis. The task of counting function points should be included as part of the overall project

plan. That is, counting function points should be scheduled and planned. The first function point count should be developed to provide sizing used for estimating.[16]

Although much can be gleaned from system documentation, the most accurate function point counts involve systems analysts who are able to answer any questions the function point counters may have. They can also provide system expertise where the documentation might leave gaps and the function point counters would otherwise have to interpret or make assumptions.[17]

Wise use of resources is a key factor when developing a software development plan. The following information from David Consulting Group (DCG) can be useful as a guideline.[18]

Function point approximation will quickly and effectively size your current software application portfolio based upon the accuracy level the client seeks. DCG conducted a detailed study during 1999 to determine the cost and accuracy of various counting techniques including full function point counting, approximation, estimating and backfiring. The results illustrated [in Table 6.15] indicate that it is not always practical or necessary to invest in full counting for a given project or application.

Table 6.15   Cost Comparisons for Function Point Counting[18]

Count Type	Accuracy (Percent)	Effort (Time)
IFPUG	±5	1 to 3 days
IFPUG Limited	±25	1 to 3 days
Approximation	±35	1/2 day
Ratio	±50	<1/2 day
Expert	±50	<1/2 day
Delphi	±100	<1/4 day
Backfire	±100 to 400[a]	Varies

Note: Cost is based on an average size application (250 to 1200 function points) and will vary for applications outside that size range.

[a] Variation based upon language levels.

The study, conducted in 1999, was supported and participated in by several client companies. As a result of the study, DCG has recommended to clients that all baseline counts be accomplished with full disclosure as to the accuracy of the method being utilized. The following high level overview of counting criteria can be used by organizations to discuss and determine which counting method is right for a given application.

IFPUG Detailed — A complete and detailed count; typically performed on highly visible systems, systems that are core to the business or systems that may be undergoing frequent change requests.

IFPUG Limited — Similar to Detailed in that accuracy is a primary concern, but average weightings are applied.

Approximation — The most robust of the many approximation methods, used when accuracy is not of primary concern, but full functionality needs to be recognized.

Ratio — Typically used in instances where all data can be identified and logically parsed into user identifiable groupings.

Expert — Used in cases of commercial off-the-shelf packages or with common applications where the consultant is familiar with similar types of applications.

Delphi — The least effective of the approximating and estimating techniques, Delphi can be used when an organization's portfolio has a certain percentage of Detailed or Limited counts available.

Backfire Calibration — A backfire method that utilizes a customized backfire value; used when accuracy is not an issue, but a sense of overall functionality being supported is necessary.

Backfire Calculation — Same as Calibration; only industry backfire values are used.[18]

In using and applying a function point count, the general guidelines in Table 6.16 can be a useful crosscheck or approximation method if counting one or more components.

Using function points for estimating the effort and schedule of a new system has all the hazards of SLOC and other size metrics. Merely using function points per staff month as a productivity measure is insufficient for estimating new systems unless the new systems have nearly the same technology, people, process, and size. See Chapter 3 for discussion of productivity issues.

Table 6.16 Using Historical Function Point Ratios for Estimating New Systems

Total Unadjusted Function Count	IFPUG 1996 (Percent)	Total Metrics[19] (Percent)	IFPUG[20] (Percent)	GTE[21] (Percent)	ISBSG Benchmark[22] (Percent)
Contribution to total count from ILFs	24	24	23	40	22.3
Contribution to total count from EIFs	4	12	8	5	3.8
Contribution to total count from EIs	39	26	30	20	37.2
Contribution to total count from EOs	22	24	23	25	23.5
Contribution to total count from EQs	12	14	15	10	13.2

Early Function Point Counting (Estimating)

Function point counting requires "the availability of a complete and detailed set of descriptive documentation of the user functional requirements for any software application to be measured."[23] As discussed earlier in this book, an estimate is often required before this level of documentation is available. Various methodologies are available for estimating function points. The author recommends using a tool such as SEER-AccuScope when an early function point estimate is required.

"*Counting function point* should mean measuring software size through the use of the standard IFPUG practices, while *estimating function point* should denote an approximate evaluation of the same size through other different means."[23]

Analysis of Function Point Rules in Tree-Based Framework[24]

Lee Fischman's analysis of function point rules yielded a tree framework that helps explain many counting rules. The basis for function point counting is its rules that delineate the model into a set of closely linked metrics. They give function points uniformity and they also give function points the characteristics that correlate them well with a variety of outcomes. The function point counting rules (FPCR) project sought to assemble these rules into a common tree in which all potential outcomes are represented, including those of all currently valid non-file function points.

Description of Tree and Results

The tree was synthesized in a relatively ad hoc manner. The design goal was to include all rules and capture all valid outcomes, so alternate arrangements of the rules tree may be possible. Some reduction in rules has occurred so that commonality could be achieved, for instance, the "unique processing" requirement refers either to unique logic or to unique data requirements.

Ten separate rules were isolated, of which four are shared by all function points. These may be considered core definitional rules of function points. The rules tree is at least four branches deep. A primary branch occurs at the *update ILF* rule, resulting in one rich set of additional rule lineages and another quite limited one.

All non-file function point outcomes are represented in the tree, although not all outcomes correspond to formally recognized function points. The simplest valid outcome corresponds to the definition of an external input and requires five rules. The most complex outcome requires eight rules and results in the finding of an external inquiry. The external input and external output function points, perhaps notably, exist at similar depths in the rules tree illustrated in Figure 6.7.

The established heuristics may permit the development of an automated function point counting tool for already-developed code. These heuristics would have to be mated with grammatically specific knowledge of particular programming languages.

Backfiring

Simply stated, backfiring is converting lines of code to function points by dividing the line count by a conversion ratio. The author does not recommend backfiring as an approach to generating function points for reasons discussed in this section. The SEER estimation models equate function points to the number of effective work units to implement them, not the number of lines to develop them. The David Consulting Group concurs but for slightly different reasons:

> (We) do not consider backfiring as a recommended approach for sizing .... We would use backfiring only when sizing an organization's installed applications. ... we would validate our numbers by sampling (performing actual function point counts

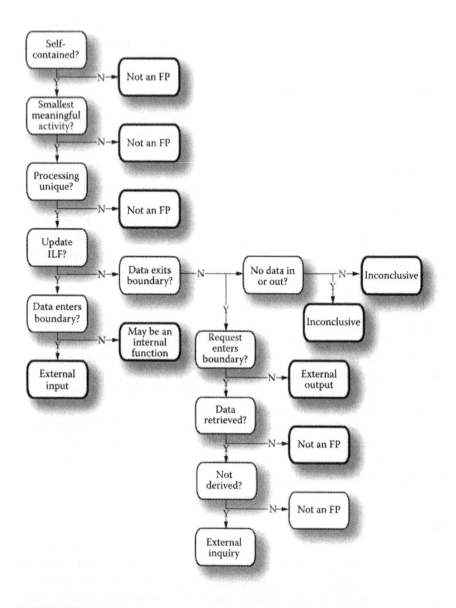

Figure 6.7 Function point rules tree.

and comparing them to lines of code) and validating applications within the installed base at that organization.[24]

Table 6.17 illustrates why backfiring does not work well. Note the large variance in lines of code per function point. The differences in lines to functions may be attributed to several factors:

Table 6.17 Conversion Ratios: Lines of Code per Function Point

Source Code Language	DCG Likely	Capers Jones			Galorath Likely
		Low	Mean	High	
Basic Assembly	575	200	320	450	320
C	225	60	128	170	61
FORTRAN	210	75	107	160	58
C++	80	30	53	125	59

1. The definitions of lines of code (physical lines, logical lines, etc.) were not consistent (see Chapter 5, "Source Lines of Code").
2. The origins of the lines of code (hand coded, autogenerated, etc.) were not defined or unclear (see Chapter 5, "Source Lines of Code").
3. Galorath's numbers attempted to define effective effort units to specific languages to use for estimating, not to estimate gross lines of code.
4. The function point counting rule versions may be different.

Backfiring creates certain problems because expert findings and research vary so widely on the conversion ratios and also because the definitions of lines are not always clear, and if you are working with generated lines of code, the problem becomes more difficult.

Possible Errors in Function Point Counting

While function points can potentially be used to accurately size a software application based on functional characteristics, several factors can cause errors in the count or in the projection:

Developers want "credit" — Some of the most obvious causes relate to the estimate itself. When developers are involved in counting, they tend to overestimate (or overcount existing systems) to "get credit" for their work. (Recently, Galorath Incorporated worked with a manager who tried to take credit for 20,000+ function points when in reality only 2,800 existed. In this case, the requirements volatility and complexity of the application were misconstrued as size.) Managers also often fail to understand the "logical" nature of function points.

Low counts due to forgotten functionality — Galorath analysts found low function point counts calculated for existing systems in the course of modernization because counters were not made aware of "forgotten" functionality (typically up to 20 percent in very old legacy systems).

Errors in counts based on incomplete information — Two function point counters working on the same system will normally produce similar counts. However, Galorath noted counts in which the counts of two competent individuals counting the same system independently showed a 70 percent difference. Upon enquiry, it was found that the system lacked formal requirements documents and each counter interviewed a separate group of development personnel maintaining the existing system.

Function points can overlook system growth — Function points often count a system early in its conceptual phase, before the system has been completely defined and before requirements creep has emerged. Such problems may be dealt with by providing function point ranges that account for possible growth rather than single point counts.

Inconsistent function point counting rule application — Many organizations perform make-your-own-rules function point counting. For example, the author witnessed a large system development in which one of the development organizations counted more than ten times as many function points as the other organizations. This was openly attributed to counters who made their own rules. Perhaps this wouldn't be so bad if they hadn't called their results function points. In doing so, they caused severe confusion.

Difficulty comparing function point counts from different counting rule versions — The rules for IFPUG counting have changed dramatically over the years. An older IFPUG count could be twice as large as one performed under current IPFUG rules. For example, one of the author's customers was livid because his system had half the function points as a similar system. The customer refused to accept the count and fired the counters. What no one realized then was the system that was being compared was counted with older rules. The customer insisted that the function point count was much bigger.

Pros and Cons of Function Points

Pros of Function Points

Function points are valuable measures of application size because:

- IFPUG function points constitute a widely used, accepted method.
- Many certified IPFUG function point counters are available.
- The calculation is objective.
- Unadjusted function points are independent of the technology used to develop the application. Thus, they provide a single, consistent measure of application size, which allows comparisons of productivity

across applications regardless of their size, technology, or development approach.

▪ Function point counts can be used early in the development cycle, which allows the project schedule and effort to be estimated.

▪ Productivity history on completed projects with similar characteristics can be used to refine the estimating process for future projects.

▪ Function point counting standards and their application are supported by an active, worldwide user organization, the International Function Point Users Group (IFPUG).

▪ Function points are successful in describing software size for cost models. Models like SEER-SEM achieve the same high accuracy using properly prepared function point counts as they do with SLOC.

Cons of Function Points

Function points have a number of limitations. For example, managers, customers, and others who are not trained function point counters have difficulty grasping what a function point count tells them (the number of function points for "one more report" gets lost in the count).

In an *IEEE Software* article, Kitchenham[25] stated, "You cannot compare function point counts numerically. An application of 1000 function points is not twice as big, complex or functional as an application of 500 function points. The first application is not *twice* the second in any meaningful sense."

▪ Semantic difficulties — Function point standards were codified in the early 1980s by a standards body hailing from a traditional management information system world. Since then, the standards document has not been drastically overhauled. Its language reflects this with seemingly arcane terms such as *record element types* and *external inputs*. While such careful language insulates a relatively complex metric from everyday misunderstanding, it also impedes learning and acceptance by a wider audience.

▪ Incompleteness — Function points were defined from a user interface vantage. Although a clever angle, this led to the major criticism that all the functionality built into a software system might not be captured. Many argued that substantial internal functionality, without much manifestation at the user interface, might be missed.

▪ Lack of automatic count — No generally automated method is available for counting function points, even in completed systems.

In contrast, lines of code counts can be obtained using simple line counting utilities.

■ Limited domain applicability — In a paper presented at a 1999 meeting, Nihal et al. stated, "Function point analysis uses the amount of stored data as a significant factor in determining the functional size of the application. Where data stored is simple but the processing of stored values is complex, the functional size of the application is underestimated."[26]

Despite a long list of complaints concerning function points, the system has proven to be a definitive indicator of development effort, and it is still fundamentally sound.

When to Use Function Points

Use function point-based estimates on information technology and other systems whenever you can afford to conduct a proper function point count or when you can use analogy, sizing models, or other means to estimate function points. In addition, you should use function points when sizing by SLOC could be misleading. For example, code generators may automatically generate many lines of code, but this may not correspond to substantial manual contributions by programmers. For the analyst, the great strength of function point counts is that they are developed *directly* from specifications, independently of implementation, which means:

■ Early estimates of project size are more likely to resemble the project scope.
■ Estimates of project scope are more comparable across projects.

Because function point counts are more sophisticated metrics that cannot be handled automatically, you must make sure ahead of time that counts *will be done correctly.* Make sure that whoever does the counting is adequately trained and experienced. If prior counts have been performed on projects that may later be related or compared in some way, those counts should be carefully studied so that new work is consistent or the prior counts are normalized to the current standard. Although counts can eventually be done fairly quickly and efficiently, correct methods and consistency are important.

Function Point Risk Management

Even though function point counts are commonly used as a sizing metric, they can potentially be highly inaccurate, especially during the early phases of a software project when the application itself is not well understood. Function point size estimation errors generally result in three major areas of risk (note that these are essentially the same risk areas presented by SLOC):

1. Errors in function point counts can prevent scaling the development environment to reflect reality, which can lead to defining cost drivers that may be inappropriate, underestimated, or overestimated.
2. Incorrect sizing of the application can lead to a misalignment of skills to tasks, miscalculation of schedules and level of effort required, and either underestimation or overestimation of project staffing requirements.
3. Unrealistic customer expectations, poorly defined objectives, requirements, and specifications, or unconstrained requirements growth during the software development life cycle can result in changing counts, cost, and schedule overruns.

Function Point Counting Risk Checklist

An underlying set of error sources will affect the accuracy of the estimation process and the ability of an organization to consistently count or estimate using function points. These error sources can be grouped into five categories: (1) estimation process integration and planning; (2) estimation staffing and support resources; (3) information currency; (4) process integrity; and (5) estimation scope. In order to implement effective counting practices, it is imperative to learn how to deal with these issues, which are not addressed in the baseline function point counting specifications. Table 6.18 is a checklist that can be used to identify and thus prevent potential errors and reduce the risk in the function counting process.

Summary

Function points serve as a viable method of describing software size but require strict adherence to predefined counting rules to ensure validity. Function point counts for completed systems may be kept in a sizing database and used as analogy for new systems, even before detailed function point count can be performed.

Merely using function points per staff month as a productivity measure is insufficient for estimating new systems unless the new systems have nearly the same technology, people, process, and size. Function points are excellent for describing size to a cost model. While function points are not a panacea, their use has proven to help organizations better control their software projects and successfully deliver systems to their customers.

Table 6.18   Function Point Counting Risk Checklist

Major Issue Area	Potential Error	Risk	Risk Effect
Estimation Process Integration and Planning			
	Was the task of counting function points included in the overall project plan?	Inconsistent estimation process not integrated into standard process.	Estimate may not reflect project standards, common process or required management, engineering, assurance, or reporting processes.
	All activities of the project team should be items in the project plan. Ensure that adequate time has been dedicated to completing the task.	Estimates may not include sufficient time, staff or other resources to accomplish task.	Resources projected may be insufficient, precluding a successful project result.
	Were current *IFPUG Counting Practices* followed?	Estimate is developed using inconsistent or home-grown technique that may not adequately consider critical factors in relationships.	Any projections based on function point count may be based on incorrect information and prove inadequate.
	Is this a function point count (completed code) or a function point estimate (code yet to be developed)? Has the count been reviewed by an independent certified function point specialist?	Individual performing count or estimate may incorrectly apply process or not adequately consider essential information.	All estimates based on function point count may reflect undocumented estimator bias or problems based on incorrect application of counting process.

Table 6.18 (continued)   Function Point Counting Risk Checklist

Major Issue Area	Potential Error	Risk	Risk Effect
Estimation Staffing and Support Resources			
	Are the individuals performing the function point count trained in function point counting? Are they certified? Have they ever used the process? The individuals conducting counts should be familiar with IFPUG counting rules as applied to their task. If the person completing the count passed the IFPUG certification exam, one has an added degree of certainty that, at a minimum, the person understands the counting or estimating process. While passing an exam does not guarantee accurate counts, it does guarantee a minimal level of competency which, coupled with a proven track record of producing function point counts or projections using	Function point count or estimates based on a count done by an untrained individual or one with limited credentials may have limited accuracy and may not be consistent with established counting processes.	All estimates based on function point count may reflect undocumented estimator bias or problems based on incorrect application of counting process.

Table 6.18 (continued)   Function Point Counting Risk Checklist

Major Issue Area	Potential Error	Risk	Risk Effect
	the process, can lower the risk of an incorrect estimate.		
	Has the arithmetic been reviewed?	Arithmetic errors in the count may not be caught, resulting in significant counting errors.	Simple errors in a count may result in significant errors or inconsistencies in the count or the estimates based on it.
	Has an independent review of the estimate and estimation process been conducted? Have identified issues been documented and resolved?	Counting process does not include essential checks and balances to ensure that standard process was followed and that critical issues, risks, and assumptions are documented.	Count may prove invalid due to process issues in performing the count or undocumented realities that limit its accuracy or applicability.
Information Currency			
	Did the function point counter use current project documentation to count function points? If not, how old was the documentation? Were adjustments made to the function point count based on the phase in the development life cycle when the count was done?	Information used as the basis for the function point count may not reflect the current, documented state, or current technical baselines of system.	Users of function point count may assume the basis of the count reflects current system baselines and thus decisions or estimates that are based on it may be incorrect.

Table 6.18 (continued) Function Point Counting Risk Checklist

Major Issue Area	Potential Error	Risk	Risk Effect
	Do the individual function point component (ILF, EIF, EI, EO, and EQ) percentages conform to industry ranges? If not, is there a valid reason?	Resultant counts may be incorrect or inconsistent with similar system counts.	Function point counts may be biased and may not reflect the true size of the application based on established industry numbers.
	Has an inventory of transactions (EI, EO, and EQ) and files (ILF and EIF) been reviewed by the project team? The greatest error in counting function points is omission (not including everything). It is important that the application team review the function point count for completeness and accuracy.	Not including the application team in function point counts may result in failure to include known issues and concerns in the count.	The function point count may not reflect the understanding of the team and there may be limited team support of any estimates based on the count.
	Are value adjustment factors needed for use with the chosen estimation methodologies? Unadjusted function points used with models like SEER-SEM and ISOSTD do not include value adjustment factors.	Value adjustment factors (VAFS) used must accurately reflect the conditions in the enterprise and must be consistent with applications made by the organization.	Inconsistent or incorrect VAFs incorrectly offset counts and have a consistent and incorrect basis for estimates based on adjusted counts.

Table 6.18 (continued) Function Point Counting Risk Checklist

Major Issue Area	Potential Error	Risk	Risk Effect
	Have all the assumptions associated with the function point count been documented?	If critical issues, risks, and assumptions that need to be carried with the estimate are not documented, use of the count may be based on an incorrect assumption that all critical factors have been addressed.	Count may prove invalid due to undocumented realities that limit its accuracy or applicability.
	Are the assumptions consistent with other projects?	Assumptions used in estimate must be credible, consistent with the realities of the enterprise, and the historical experience of the organization, or should be evaluated for consistency with the experiences of similar projects.	By not addressing common assumptions used by other projects, issues, problems, and risks resulting from organizational factors may not be considered when counting or estimating size using function points.
	Have all the assumptions impacting function point counting been forwarded to a central function point group? All assumptions should be reviewed by the central function point group.	By not having a central place that coordinates use of function points, different interpretations of critical factors relating to the count or estimate may occur and information needed for the count or estimate may not be available.	Function point count and estimates that result from it may not reflect assumptions and experiences of other projects, causing the count or estimate to be invalid.

Table 6.18 (continued)   Function Point Counting Risk Checklist

Major Issue Area	Potential Error	Risk	Risk Effect
Process Integrity			
	Did the project team participate in the function point count? The project team should include the most knowledgeable individuals regarding the functionality being delivered to the user. They are the best source of information about the project. Frequently the project team is not involved when a function point count is completed. The function point counter will evaluate some documentation, eventually generating a function point number.	By not adequately involving the project team in the counting of function points or their use in subsequent estimation activities, critical insights and undocumented information may not be factored into the count or the estimates.	The function point count and estimates that result from it may not reflect assumptions and experiences of the project team, causing the count or estimate to be invalid.
	Were internally developed function point counting guidelines followed?	Count or estimate is developed using a project-specific process reflecting biases and local offsets that may not adequately consider critical factors or relationships.	Projections based on function point count may be based on incorrect information and may prove inadequate.

Table 6.18 (continued) Function Point Counting Risk Checklist

Major Issue Area	Potential Error	Risk	Risk Effect
	Was the application counted from the user's point of view?	Count or estimate does not reflect the user's view, reflecting biases and offsets that only consider project factors, and critical user related factors or relationships may not be adequately considered.	Projections based on function point count may be based on information that does not consider essential user information and requirements and may prove inadequate.
	Was the system counted from a logical and not a physical point of view?	System count does not consider the actual size of the application, but only interpretations of information used to extrapolate size metrics.	Function point count and estimates that result from it may not be consistent with actual size of application.
Estimation Scope			
	Does the established boundary for the function point count match the boundaries of other metrics (time reporting, defect tracking)? If not, why?	Inconsistencies in system boundaries or boundaries of the count may result in metrics that do not reflect a common baseline.	Function point counts and estimates derived from it may not be based on a common system scope, precluding consistency of related metrics.
	If the function point count was for an enhancement, was the boundary the same as the boundary for the application? If not, why?	Enhancement boundary may differ from the full system boundary, resulting in incorrect assumptions concerning the	Function point counts and estimates derived from it may not be based on a correct system boundary.

Table 6.18 (continued)   Function Point Counting Risk Checklist

Major Issue Area	Potential Error	Risk	Risk Effect
		scope of the count or the boundary of future estimates using the count.	
	Has the boundary changed? If so, why?	If the boundary of the count changes, the resulting count may be based on incorrect designation of key factors and offsets.	Function point counts and estimates derived from it may not be based on correct designation of functions or offsets.

Endnotes

1. Garmus, David and David Herron. *Function Point Analysis*. Boston: Addison-Wesley, 2001.
2. Albrecht, A.J. "Measuring Application Development Productivity." *Proceedings of IBM Applications Development Symposium*. Monterey, 1979.
3. Jones, Capers. *Programming Productivity: Issues for the Eighties*. New York: IEEE Press, 1981 (Revised 1986).
4. International Function Point Users Group. *Function Points Counting Practices Manual, Release 4.1*. Princeton Junction: IFPUG, 1999.
5. Jones, T.C. *The SPR Feature Point Method*. Boston: Software Productivity Research Inc. 1986.
6. Symons, C.R. "Function Point Analysis: Difficulties and Improvements." 14.1. *IEEE Transactions: Software Engineering*, January 1988.
7. Whitmire, S.A. "3D Function Points: Scientific and Real-time Extensions to Function Points." *Pacific Northwest Software Quality Conference*. Portland, 1992.
8. Netherlands Software Metrics Users Association (NESMA). *Definitions and Counting Guidelines for the Application of Function Point Analysis*. Netherlands: NESMA, 2002.
9. Abran, Alain. *Full Function Point Method*. <http://www.dpo.it>
10. Fischman, Lee. "A Full Service Function Metric, Open for Business: Evolved Function Points." *Software Technology Conference*. Salt Lake City, 2001.
11. Galorath, Dan. "Parametric Cost Application to Function Points." *IFPUG User Meeting*, 1996.
12. International Function Point Users Group. *IT Measurement: Practical Advice from the Experts*. Boston: Addison-Wesley, 2002.

13. International Function Point Users Group. *Function Point Counting Practices Manual, Release 4.2.* Princeton Junction: IFPUG, 2004.

14. IFPUG standard briefing, IFPUG, 1999.

15. International Function Point Users Group. *IT Measurement: Practical Advice from the Experts.* Boston: Addison-Wesley, 2002.

16. Longstreet, David. "Fundamentals of FPA." Longstreet Consulting: Function Point Counting, 2000. <http://www.softwaremetrics.com/fpafund.htm>

17. Brown, Ian. Personal correspondence, 2005.

18. The David Consulting Group. "Industry Data." 9 Sept. 2005. <http://www.davidconsultinggroup.com/indata.htm>

19. Desharnais, Jean-Marc and Pam Morris. "Post Measurement Validation Procedure for Function Point Counts." *Software Engineering Standards Issues.* Montreal, 1996. <http://www.lrgl.uqam.ca/sponsored/ses96/paper/desharna.html>

20. Galorath, Judy. Personal interview, July 2000.

21. Longstreet, David. "Fundamentals of FPA." Longstreet Consulting: Function Point Counting, 2000. <http://www.softwaremetrics.com/fpafund.htm>

22. Meli, Roberto and Luca Santillo. "Function Point Estimation Methods: A Comparative Overview." DPO Resources: Papers, 1999. <http://www.dpo.it/english/resources/papers/1999-fesma-fpestmet-en.pdf>

23. Fischman, Lee, Personal interview, 2000.

24. The David Consulting Group. "Industry Data." 9 Sept. 2005. <http://www.davidconsultinggroup.com/indata.htm>

25. Kitchenham, B. "The Problem with Function Points." *IEEE Software,* March/April 1997.

26. Nihal, Kececi, Ming Li, and Carol Smidts. "Function Point Analysis: An Application to a Nuclear Reactor Protection System." *International Topical Meeting on Probabilistic Safety Assessment.* Washington, D.C., 1999.

Chapter 7

Object-Oriented Sizing: Object and Use-Case Sizing

Nothing is particularly hard if you divide it into small jobs.

Henry Ford

Introduction

Whenever a new or different method of software development appears, many people denounce existing methods of sizing and costing. They look for new methods consistent with the latest revolution in software development and believe that everything learned from the past is obsolete. This was the original thinking of many in dealing with object-oriented systems. One of the difficulties of object-oriented systems in general is the belief of many people that they are building an object-oriented system when they use a language like C++, independent of using object-oriented design techniques.

Object-oriented design methodologies are true discriminators of object-oriented systems. As early as the introduction of Ada in the early 1980s, people claimed that object development was revolutionary and existing estimation techniques were not viable. However, time has shown that lines of code and function-based sizing perform just as well on object-oriented systems as on others. The reason organizations such as Galorath Incorporated explore object-oriented and use-case-oriented size metrics is not because existing metrics do not work. It is because the closer we can get to the actual artifacts the developers produce, the simpler it is to obtain definitions of size that can be understood and measured easily.

This chapter examines object-oriented and use-case sizing. It also reveals how to address risk and uncertainties associated with the use of these alternative methods and describes methods for managing the risk of using new or unproven estimation methods.

Background of Object-Oriented Design

Before exploring object-oriented (OO) metrics, it helps to appreciate the background of OO design methodology. The origins of OO design and development reaches back to the 1960s and 1970s when OO programming languages such as Simula[1] and Smalltalk[2] were essential components in the development of these methodologies. Developments remained informal until 1982 when Grady Booch devised the *object-oriented design* term.[3] During the 1980s other OOA/D (object-oriented analysis and design) pioneers developed their ideas: Kent Beck, Peter Coad, Don Firesmith, Ivar Jacobson, Steve Mellor, Bertrand Meyer, Jim Rumbaugh, and Rebecca Wirfs-Brock, among others. Coad created a complete OOA/D method in the late 1980s and published twin volumes titled *Object-Oriented Analysis*[4] and *Object-Oriented Design*[5] in 1990 and 1991.

As the methodology matured and its use expanded, Wirfs-Brock and others described the responsibility-driven design approach to OOD in their popular *Designing Object-Oriented Software*[6] published in 1990. During the 1990s and early 21st century, OO methodology matured and experienced a surge of interest from software engineers applying the methodology, researchers and practitioners who expanded and clarified the methodology, and academics who promulgated its use and trained the next generation of practitioners.

As might be expected, the long history of OO research and development produced a corresponding cornucopia of proposed metrics. In 1993, Chidamber et al.[7] presented a suite of OO metrics, including some that measure size. In 1996, Basili et. al.[8] published 11 design metrics that include some well suited for measuring size.[9] Henderson-Sellers[10] also identified many metrics potentially able to measure the various dimensions of OO software development effort. These early papers provided a foundation for future metric proposals.

In 1994, Booch and Rumbaugh combined their two methods — the Booch and OMT methods — to create a common notation known as Unified Modeling Language™ (UML). The common notation eventually incorporated the objectory method developed by Ivar Jacobson. Booch and Rumbaugh decided to reduce the scope of their effort by focusing on a common diagramming notation — the UML — rather than a common method. This scope-reducing effort in 1997 resulted in the formation of an industry body for devising OO-related standards. Known as the Object Management Group (OMG), it developed an open standard leading to the initial UML Version 1.0. Since then, the standard has been subject to ongoing refinements, with UML Version 2.0 released in 2004. The UML has emerged as the *de facto* standard diagramming notation for OO modeling and continues to be refined by the OMG.

Overview of Object-Oriented Techniques

Object-oriented techniques differ from traditional structured programming. Data and the procedures that act on them are combined in objects but kept separate in other development methodologies. Figure 7.1 illustrates this for the case of three classes of objects (Program, Current_Config, and Event_Log). The attributes associated with each class are shown in the middle of each box (Program has none; Current_Config: sensorsettings, activated; Event_Log: events). The methods are shown in the bottom of each box (user_program, set_config, eval_event, reset, record_event, and monitor).

As might be expected, the most natural thing to count is the number of classes, as most proposed OO metrics do. Classes do vary in their number of methods, attributes, and in the complexity of both methods and attributes. These can be seen in detail in the methodology described later in this chapter.

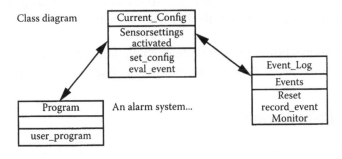

Figure 7.1   Class diagram.

Object Points

As with other systems, objects typically are composed of screens, reports, and modules. While not directly related to objects, some parallelism exists between what is counted for function points versus object points. Getting an object point is very similar to the function point counting method described in Chapter 6 of this book. Adjustments are made to the raw count for complexity and summed to achieve a final count — just like for function points. Object points have a number of advantages. They usually require less effort to count than function points, the results are comparable, and object points better suit OO-based systems.

Counting object points is in some ways easier than counting function points because less judgment is involved and less experience is required. OO artifacts such as classes can be counted directly, while services (methods) are evaluated using standard IFPUG rules. It can take less time to obtain comprehensive sizing information from an OO system than from a similar nonobject system.

Performing Object Point Counts

Three steps are involved with performing an object point count:

1. Determine whether you have been supplied with the classes and methods of an OO system.
2. Determine whether the classes lie inside or outside the application. Count the number of unique subclasses for each class, then count the number of attributes in each class, including those defined in subclasses. Use these subclass and attribute counts to determine the complexity of each class.
3. Note the methods (service) in each class. Count the number of classes referenced by each method and the number of attributes referenced by each method. Use these class and attribute counts to determine the complexity of each method (service).

Table 7.1 shows how to incorporate each element of OO technology into an object point count. Parentheses indicate analogous function point terms.

Object Point Definitions

Classes

A class includes one or more objects with a uniform set of attributes and services. Objects are defined as members of a class of objects.

Table 7.1 Object Points and Function Points

Object Point	Corresponds To	Complexity	Corresponds To
Internal class	(Internal logical files)	Total subclasses	(Record element types)
		Total attributes	(Data element types)
External class	(External interface files)	Total subclasses	(Record element types)
		Total attributes	(Data element types)
Inquiry service	(External inquiries)	Total classes	(File types referenced)
		Total attributes	(Data element types)
Output service	(External outputs)	Total classes	(File types referenced)
		Total attributes	(Data element types)
Input service	(External inputs)	Total classes	(File types referenced)
		Total attributes	(Data element types)

Classes are essentially templates for the creation of objects. Classes exist as hierarchies; the top level of the hierarchy can be considered the base class; unique variations of the base class are descendants. Objects created from a base class or descendant class are termed instances.

Classes may be sized into either internal or external classes, depending on which side of the application boundary they lie. In IFPUG terminology, classes can be compared to external interface files or internal logical files.

You should count base (highest level) classes only, and not descendant classes. Descendant classes are those that inherit the properties of higher level classes while adding additional attributes or services. Remember that you should count a class but not its instances, (i.e., objects created from the class).

The application boundary defines what is and is not a part of any application; it is an important concept for classifying function point counts and object counts. Application boundaries are determined by the designer and depend secondarily on the goal and scope of development. When counting in an OO environment, the application boundary may correspond to the subject. In OO design, the subject is defined as:

> A mechanism for guiding a reader (analyst, problem domain expert, manager, client) through a large, complex model. Subjects are also helpful for organizing work packages on larger projects, based upon initial OOA investigations.[11]

Internal Class

Each class of objects residing inside the application boundary is treated analogously to an IFPUG standard internal logical file (ILF). See Chapter 6 for details on IFPUG standards.

External Class

Each class of objects residing outside the application boundary is treated analogously to an IFPUG standard external interface file (EIF).

Class Complexity

To determine the complexity of a class, you must evaluate the characteristics described below: attributes, and descendant classes. These characteristics will then be translated to standard function point measures.

Attributes — Count the number of unique attributes in the class, including attributes that may be defined in its instances but not in the parent class itself. Each attribute should be considered a DET.

Descendant classes (subgroups, subclasses) — Descendant or child classes inherit many of their properties from a base class. In IFPUG terminology, each unique instantiation of a base class is counted as a record element type (RET). As with RETs in standard function point counts, descendant classes thus help determine the complexity of function points. Count the number of unique descendant classes for this class; each should be considered an RET. (If the class you are examining actually inherited its properties from a higher class, you should count the higher class as the ILF, not this one.) Descendant classes may also be known as:

- Subgroups (used by IFPUG)
- Subtypes (semantic data modeling)
- Subclasses (some OOPLs)
- Child classes

Count the number of unique subclasses of this class. For example, if the class is "airplane," an object may be a crop duster or jet fighter. Subclasses may also be called subgroups, subtypes or descendant classes. Rate the complexity for each internal class using Table 7.2.

Table 7.2   Object Point Complexity Rating Table for Internal Classes

	1 to 19 DETs	*20 to 50 DETs*	*51 or more DETs*
0 to 1 RETs	Low	Low	Average
2 to 5 RETs	Low	Average	High
6 or more RETs	Average	High	High

Rate the complexity for each external class using Table 7.3.

Table 7.3   Object Point Complexity Rating Table for External Classes

	1 to 19 DETs	*20 to 50 DETs*	*51 or more DETs*
0 to 1 RETs	Low	Low	Average
2 to 5 RETs	Low	Average	High
6 or more RETs	Average	High	High

Services (Methods)

Services, also known as methods, are specific behaviors endowed and expected of an object. This definition should be used when deciding the function point category under which a particular service should be defined. Services essentially are functions contained within an object. A service may be instantiated at the class level or lower, within a specific instance. The complexity of a service is determined on the basis of how many classes (analogous to FTRs) and attributes (analogous to DETs) are referenced.

Inquiry service — This is an IFPUG standard external inquiry that resides as a service (method) within an object class.

Output service — This is an IFPUG standard external output that resides as a service within an object class.

Input service — This is an IFPUG standard external input that resides as a service (method) within an object class.

Determining complexity for input, output, and inquiry services — All descendants of a single base class that are referenced by a service are counted as only one file type referenced (FTR).

Attributes — Count the total number of attributes and messages received by the service. Each is equivalent to a data element type (DET).

Classes — Each base class referenced by a service is counted as one FTR. Include all descendant classes within the base class that are referenced as part of the base class.

Message connection (definition) — The processing dependency of an object, indicating a need for services (from outside the immediate object) in order to fulfill its responsibilities. Message connections involve a sender and a receiver. The sender sends a message to the receiver, asking the receiver to do certain work. Message connections exist only for services.[12]

Message connections should be considered additional, unique FTRs for EIs, EOs, and EQs that employ them. There are processing requirements of both sender and receiver and should be evaluated separately.

Rate the complexity for each inquiry service using Table 7.4.

Table 7.4   Object Point Complexity Rating Table for Inquiry Services

	1 to 5 DETs	6 to 19 DETs	20 or more DETs
0 to 1 FTRs	Low	Low	Average
2 to 3 FTRs	Low	Average	High
4 or more FTRs	Average	High	High

Rate the complexity for each output service using Table 7.5.

Table 7.5   Object Point Complexity Rating Table for Output Services

	1 to 5 DETs	6 to 19 DETs	20 or more DETs
0 to 1 FTRs	Low	Low	Average
2 to 3 FTRs	Low	Average	High
4 or more FTRs	Average	High	High

Rate the complexity of each input service using Table 7.6.

Table 7.6   Object Point Complexity Rating Table for Input Services

	1 to 4 DETs	5 to 15 DETs	16 or more DETs
0 to 1 FTRs	Low	Low	Average
2 FTRs	Low	Average	High
3 or more FTRs	Average	High	High

The unadjusted (raw) object point count is the count of unique objects that were identified through the steps described above. The unique object types counted are:

Internal class
External class
Inquiry service
Output service
Input service

The unique function types that were individually assessed for complexity (low, average, or high) are now given a weighting value that varies from 3 (for simple external inputs) to 15 (for complex internal files). Unadjusted object points (UOPs) are calculated as follows. The sum of all the occurrences is computed by multiplying each function count with a weighting and then adding all the values. The weights are based on the complexity of the feature counted. Table 7.7 shows the weighting values.

Table 7.7   Object Point Function Complexity

Function Type	Low	Average	High
Internal class (IC)	×7	×10	×15
External class (EC)	×5	×7	×10
Inquiry service (QS)	×3	×4	×6
Output service (OS)	×4	×5	×7
Input service (IS)	×3	×4	×6

$$IC_{(total)} = IC_{(low)} \times 7 + IC_{(average)} \times 10 + IC_{(high)} \times 15$$

$$EC_{(total)} = EC_{(low)} \times 5 + EC_{(average)} \times 7 + EC_{(high)} \times 10$$

$$QS_{(total)} = QS_{(low)} \times 3 + QS_{(average)} \times 4 + QS_{(high)} \times 6$$

$$OS_{(total)} = OS_{(low)} \times 4 + OS_{(average)} \times 5 + OS_{(high)} \times 7$$

$$IS_{(total)} = IS_{(low)} \times 3 + IS_{(average)} \times 4 + IS_{(high)} \times 6$$

Unadjusted object point count =
$$IC_{(total)} + EC_{(total)} + QS_{(total)} + OS_{(total)} + IS_{(total)}$$

The unadjusted object point count is now complete.

Predictive Object Points

Unlike traditional measures, predictive object points (POPs) are based on an object-oriented paradigm, encapsulating object behavior and the interactions of objects. POPs combine several contemporary metrics to establish an overall measure suitable for predicting effort and/or tracking productivity.[13] However, the amount of information required may make them difficult to obtain in practice.

Development of Use-Case Metric

Use cases utilize a very simple graphical language. The artifacts in a use-case diagram are its actors (stick figures in Figure 7.2), use cases (circles), and relations (arrows). Relations between use cases, rather than actors, are differentiated by whether they include or extend the functions of another use case. Use cases are deliberately simple and use-case metrics could hardly be any more complex.

The relationship between use cases and project effort was explored by Gustav Karner[14] who identified a relationship between metrics designated unadjusted use-case points (UUCPs) and the effort needed to develop a software project as defined by that use-case model. Galorath Incorporated and others further applied this work to project sizing and estimation.[15]

It is not accidental that use-case points and function points share part of a name. Use-case points took some inspiration from function points, particularly in the application of technical weighting factors to a baseline count of observed artifacts.

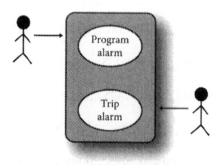

Figure 7.2 Two use cases describing a simple alarm system.

Use Cases

No discussion of OO metrics would be complete without considering use cases. In the object-oriented UML, the use-case view is used alongside class and other diagrams during the design process. The advantage of use cases is that they are developed at the earliest or notional stages of system design, and so afford opportunities to understand the scope of a system early in its life cycle.

When estimating projects that will use object-based methodologies, the starting place is project requirements — just as with other sizing methodologies. In this case, however, the requirements are defined by a use-case model that is used to compute an initial project effort estimate rather than *shall* statements or user-based scenarios. The use-case model defined in UML uses a standardized notational language with defined standards to document project requirements, design, and development. The model is used initially to capture the requirements, then expanded to include design details as the project progresses. Use cases described in UML allow a reasonably accurate initial range estimate to be made and this estimate can become even more accurate as a project progresses.

A set of use cases describes the elemental tasks a system is to perform and the relation between these tasks and the outside world. Each use case is a single task having some useful outcome; it is performed by the end user of a system. An end user could be a person or an automated entity, a subsystem, etc. The nature of the outcome can vary radically from use case to use case, as long as it has perceived value. Jacobson, Booch, and Rumbaugh define a use case as "a description of a set or sequence of actions, including variants, that a system performs that yields an observable result of value to a particular actor."[16]

Use cases help designers elicit desirable system behavior early in development. They allow interactions to be described in forms that are easy for people to understand and remember, e.g., as narratives or dialogues. This lets end users, stakeholders, and other nondevelopers become directly involved in capturing requirements and determining specifications.

Calculation of Unadjusted Use-Case Points

Unadjusted use-case points are calculated in three stages. An optional fourth stage is required to complete an adjusted use-case point count. First, the basic artifacts of a use-case diagram, namely actors and the use cases themselves, are ranked by their complexity. Next, each is separately summed while being weighted for complexity. The sums are then added to arrive at an unadjusted use-case point count. As an optional step, the unadjusted count can be adjusted by technical and environmental factors. Unadjusted use-case points equal the sum of all actors and use cases, each weighted by its complexity:

$$
\text{Unadjusted use-case point (UUCP)} =
$$
$$
\text{Actor\_WeightFactor} + \text{UseCase\_WeightFactor}
$$

Table 7.8 summarizes the calculation of total weighted use case and UseCase_WeightFactor. Table 7.9 describes the calculation of total weighted actor and Actor_WeightFactor.

The weighting factors U1, U2, and U3 in Table 7.8 are normally given the values 10, 15, and 20 while the factors A1, A2, and A3 shown in Table 7.9 are assigned values of 1, 2, and 4. However, these factors may vary, depending on the type of application, use-case specifying style, etc. Weights should be reevaluated based on circumstances.

Table 7.8 Calculation of Total Weighted Use Case

Use-Case Type	Description	Factor	Number of Use Cases	Results
Simple	1 to 3 transactions	U1	N_U1	U1 × N_U1
Average	4 to 7 transactions	U2	N_U2	U2 × N_U2
Complex	8 or more transactions	U3	N_U3	U3 × N_U3
Total Use-Case Weight Factor				UseCase_WeightFactor

Table 7.9 Calculation of Total Weighted Actor

Actor Type	Description	Factor	Number of Actors	Result
Simple	System interface	A1	N_A1	A1 × N_A1
Average	Interactive or protocol-driven interface	A2	N_A2	A2 × N_A2
Complex	Graphical interface	A3	N_A3	A3 × N_A3
Total Actor Weight Factor				Actor_WeightFactor

Adjustment of Use-Case Point Count (Optional)

After the UUCP count is completed, an adjusted use-case point count (AUCP) can be calculated by applying adjustments driven by project-specific technical and development environment considerations. The adjustment is made by multiplying the respective weighting factors by the unadjusted use-case point count:

$$AUCP = UUCP \times TF \times EF \text{ such that:}$$

$$\text{Technical factor (TF)} = 0.6 + (0.01 \times TWF)$$

$$\text{Environmental factor (EF)} = 1.4 + (-0.03 \times EWF)$$

Table 7.10 and Table 7.11 summarize the calculation of these factors. The assessed values in both tables are rated using the following scale:

0 = no influence throughout development
3 = average influence throughout development
5 = strong influence throughout development

Weights given in these tables were suggested by Banerjee and may need significant tuning to represent a particular organization.

Most estimation models such as SEER-SEM use UUCPs and do not use the technical or environmental weighting factors for the same reasons discussed with function points: applying such factors could cause double counting when applying estimation technology factors.

Concluding Comments about Use-Case Points

The lack of clearly accepted weights is one reason that use-case points have not achieved the status of a fully accepted metric. However, they have repeatedly been shown to be significant and consistent estimators of project effort. Recent research at Galorath Incorporated and use of use-case points in its consulting projects confirm this finding.

Sizing Web Development

This discussion is drawn from work done by Don Reifer.[18] The large projects that served as standards in the software engineering community are now being replaced by many small Web developments using different technologies and working against what had been considered impossible

Table 7.10 Calculation of Use Case Points Technical Weighting Factor

Technical Factor[17]	Weight	Assessed Value	Calculated Factor (Weight × Assessed Value)	Comment
1	2	V1	2 × V1	Distributed system
2	2	V2	2 × V2	Response objectives
3	1	V3	1 × V3	End-user efficiency (online)
4	1	V4	1 × V4	Complex internal processing
5	1	V5	1 × V5	Reusable
6	0.5	V6	0.5 × V6	Ease of installation
7	0.5	V7	0.5 × V7	Ease of use
8	2	V8	2 × V8	Portability
9	1	V9	1 × V9	Ease of change
10	1	V10	1 × V10	Concurrent processing
11	1	V11	1 × V11	Security feature
12	1	V12	1 × V12	Third party access
13	1	V13	1 × V13	Special user training requirements
Technical weighting factor (TWF) = sum of calculated factors.				

development schedules. From an estimator's standpoint, the move to agile methods,[19] extreme programming,[20] component-based engineering,[21] and other techniques have changed the expectations of customers and users of the technologies we develop. Web-based applications have significantly lowered the bar in determining time-to-market for Web-based software applications.

Table 7.11 Calculation of Use Case Points Environmental Weighting Factor

Environment Factors	Weight	Assessed Value	Calculated Factor	Comments
1	1.5	V1	1.5 × V1	Familiarity with life cycle process
2	0.5	V2	0.5 × V2	Application experience
3	1	V3	1 × V3	Object-oriented experience
4	0.5	V4	0.5 × V4	Lead analyst capability
5	1	V5	1 × V5	Team motivation
6	2	V6	2 × V6	Requirements stability
7	–1	V7	–1 × V7	Part-time workers
8	2	V8	2 × V8	Programming language difficulty
Environmental weighting factor (EWF) = sum of calculated factors.				

While many differences arise when estimating traditional versus Web-based development projects, the differences seem to center around two primary factors. First, Web development projects now combine components using agile instead of traditional methods that develop or reuse applications. Second, estimates are based on what can be provided for a certain amount of money rather than "building a product of this size will cost X dollars." Considering these differences, the two major challenges are accurately estimating size and duration.[22]

While size remains a viable basis for projecting effort, the traditional metrics of SLOCs and function points do not adequately address the product content without a method of sizing COTS applications and components. Web applications are typically developed by combining objects like shopping carts, Java scripts, and building blocks like cookies, ActiveX controls, and component object model components.[22]

Risk Associated with Object-Oriented Projects

In 1999, we conducted an assessment of a large information technology project that had obvious schedule problems. The managers extended the development duration but were allocating less and less time to testing. We brought this up when interviewing a senior manager and he said, "No worries. I have been assured by my senior technical staff that object-oriented systems need less testing."[23]

OO systems are indeed different; the danger is that they are thought of as either too different or not different enough. This section outlines a few risk areas and other considerations that have been encountered in evaluating OO-based systems. In his excellent article titled "Inherent Risks in Object-Oriented Development,"[24] Peter Hantos discussed certain risk areas that have the potential to impact the ability to complete an OO-based project within the desired cost and schedule constraints.

Fully object-oriented projects require significant shifts in development process and design thinking. They differ dramatically from legacy functional decomposition methods for architecting systems or implementing programming constructs. Teams that have long used structured approaches seem to have the most difficulty moving to OO processes. Passive resistance to OO methods at the team level often precludes "jelling" of a team[25] and results in schedule delays, loss of productivity, and friction within the teams and the project as a whole. Many of the arguments that lead organizations to adopt OO methodologies are often not correct and lead to unrealistic schedules and budgets:[26]

> **Optimistic assumption** — OO is better at organizing inherent complexity and abstract data types make it easier to model the application.
> **Optimistic assumption** — OO systems are more resilient to change due to encapsulation and data hiding.
> **Optimistic assumption** — OO design often results in smaller systems because of reuse, resulting in overall effort savings. This higher level of reuse in OO systems is attributed to the inheritance property.
> **Optimistic assumption** — It is easier to evolve OO systems over time because of polymorphism.

When OO is introduced for the first time, expectations are often exaggerated, while the costs and risks are frequently minimized:

- Building class libraries is time consuming or, in case of purchase, libraries represent major, up-front investments.
- To achieve high returns on investments, reuse must take place in a very large project or on multiple projects.

When using OO methods, the design process becomes more important than it is for non-OO projects. With encapsulation, data hiding, and reuse, design complexity moves out of the code space and into the design space.

Increased design complexity has testing consequences and even if incremental integration is applied, more sophisticated integration test suites need to be created to test systems with potentially large numbers of highly coupled objects.

OO concepts actually make system comprehension easier during analysis and design, which makes testing and debugging consequently more difficult. All debugging methodologies and tools need to work with abstract data types and instances. It is a common myth that only black box testing is needed and OO implementation specifics are unimportant.[27] Inheritance, encapsulation, and polymorphism increase the potential for coding errors when using OO that is not present with conventional languages.

Personnel shortfalls — One cornerstone of any estimate projecting the size or cost of an object-based application is the availability in adequate numbers of trained, capable individuals familiar with the methodologies when required. The success of these projects depends primarily on the people in the organization and, when the specialized skills associated with OO are not available when required, the project impacts, particularly those related to cost and schedule performance, can be significant.

The organization must understand the risks associated with the cost and schedule constraints in relation to the delivery, quality, and operational support commitments of the project. It must strike the correct balance between application domain knowledge and OO knowledge in such a way that the project can perform within constraints while still meeting the organization's commitments. This is not always a straightforward process because it is often difficult to find people skilled in the required disciplines in timeframes consistent with a project schedule and within budgetary constraints.

A second issue involves the number and distribution of available people. While OO knowledge is a requirement for most individuals on this type of project, the depth and distribution of knowledge is critical to the ability to meet the goals and constraints of the project. It is important that all managers, architects, developers, and testers have or acquire via training the appropriate OO skills. The executives who create, manage, or sponsor the development organization in order to chart a reasonable course for the project will authorize resource levels and availability and determine staffing levels and availability for the project.

While OO experience is an asset for managers, it is a necessity for those who will develop the project. Having experienced and trained personnel assigned as system engineers, architects, developers, quality technicians, testers and to other key roles in the project as well as seeding of all teams with OO mentors is essential to jump-start and facilitate OO development and meet the cost, schedule, delivery and operational commitments.

The estimation methodology for OO projects differs somewhat from procedures discussed in earlier chapters. It goes beyond metrics to issues of actual implementation: OO estimates must consider data-based decomposition, new means of reuse, and component-driven development, among other factors.

Earlier chapters explore misconceptions about the estimating process which often contribute to the failure of software projects. OO methods exacerbate these issues:

- *Estimation experience* — Few organizations have extensive experience estimating OO projects. The processes are new to many organizations. Prior size data can be used for OO projects but some people just want to assume everything is completely different.

- *Scope of estimate* — A failure to include essential project activities and products within the scope of the estimates will result in sizing or cost errors and inconsistencies. Every estimate, whether a projection of size or an estimate of the cost of a project, makes assumptions about the scope and boundaries of the application. The OO methodology differs significantly from the more classical structured development models. New technologies such as UML, OO frameworks, OOA/D patterns, OO architectures, and OO components that take advantage of OO design principles result in different process steps and dramatically different documentation and quality assurance steps.[28] If projections of size and cost are to be accurate, the models used and the estimation factors applied must reflect the true nature of the methodology and the products developed.

- *Estimation expectations and assumptions* — Misunderstanding the process requirements and the benefits, restrictions, and capabilities of OO methods leads to unrealistic plans and expectations. Aggressive claims made concerning the levels of productivity, quality, and reuse obtained from OO methods are not always realized. Models such as SEER-SEM and COCOMO incorporate limits that are used to evaluate the reasonableness, risk, and relevance of the estimates they produce.

- *Shortfalls in COTS, external components, and legacy software* — A core component of the OO process is inheritance which relies on the use of COTS and other externally developed or legacy components. This presents some difficulties for structural comprehension and architectural design. These external components, their architecture, interfaces, and documentation may not be consistent with the class and object architecture, communication mechanisms, and view models of the system being developed.

The interface of object database implementations with traditional relational database management systems potentially could cause cost, schedule, and other problems in OO applications where multiple new technologies merge (in the use of Java-specific OO COTS products — Enterprise Java Beans, Java Message Service, etc.) to develop application services on standard IBM, Sun, and Oracle platforms.

■ *Requirements or user interface mismatch* — Use cases are used almost exclusively to develop requirements in OO systems. Use cases only capture functional requirements. Additional process steps are needed to develop and implement quality-related, nonfunctional requirements.

The following looks at Boehm's Consolidated Risk List in relation to OO methodologies.[29]

Shortfalls in architecture, performance, and quality — Data abstraction, encapsulation, polymorphism, and the use of distributed objects increase architectural clarity, but at a price: substantial overhead due to the introduced layers of indirection. There are additional layers of architecture definition. Unless the system is carefully architected and sound performance engineering practices are implemented from the beginning, satisfying both performance and quality objectives becomes difficult. In the case of real-time applications, the system architect must determine the optimal system cohesion. Most real-time performance issues can be resolved if you are willing to suffer increased coupling and the consequent loss of flexibility in the architecture.

"Another sensitive part of OO systems is memory management in general and the implementation of garbage collection in particular. Garbage collection is an integral part of most OO run-time environments. It is a popular technique to ensure that memory blocks that were dynamically allocated by the programmer are released and returned to the free memory pool when they are no longer needed. A typical OO application of this feature is the dynamic creation and destruction of objects. The problem is that in conventional systems, the execution of the main process needs to be interrupted while the garbage collector does its job. This randomly invoked process with variable durations disrupts the real-time behavior of the system."[29]

Most software development organizations that use OO do so because managers feel that they will save money and time through increased reuse. Without an explicit reuse agenda and a systematic, reuse-directed software process, most of these OO efforts do not lead to successful, large scale reuses. OO promises a high level of reuse via the inheritance features and the use of class libraries. However, development teams producing software without explicit reuse objects and criteria do not achieve those savings. Even when functional reuse is accomplished, timing and sizing requirements for embedded systems may not accommodate the reused software.

Continuing stream of requirement changes — While this is primarily caused by customer behavior, the use of OO does tend to support the impression that the systems are more flexible from the perspective of requirements churn than other, more standard approaches. While OO architectural considerations, encapsulation, and data hiding increase the resiliency of the developed system to requirements volatility, any change in requirements during development increases the cost of the application, increases the risk, and stretches the schedule, particularly if the change comes late in the development.

Shortfalls in externally performed tasks — This risk, while caused by contractor behavior, is often exacerbated by the unavailability of trained OO personnel, a lack of OO knowledge on the part of estimators and schedulers who lay out the project structure, and inexperience in applying the methodologies to real project environments.

Straining computer science capabilities — The appeal of the OO concepts that are theoretical in nature inspires system architects to use OO in designing complex systems. This risk item refers to the persistent tension between the theoretical concepts and their implementation, and the delicate balance that must be maintained among programming languages, developing environments, and analysis and design methods.[29]

These elements have to be continually verified against the developed system's architecture and the cost, schedule, quality, and operational commitments of the project to assure sufficient "bench strength" within the development organization to meet them.

Summary

OO is not new; it has been around for over 20 years. However, many organizations today are trying OO for the first time. Traditional sizing measures work for OO systems. Additional size metrics are available and are being refined to work with OO artifacts. OO is not a silver bullet. Beware of estimates that are significantly (and artificially) reduced based on the use of OO. Most first-time projects using OO experience significant cost and schedule growth.

Endnotes

1. Sklenar, J. (jaroslav.sklenar@um.edu.mt) 1997.
2. Kay, Alan. *The Early History of Small Talk*. New York: ACM Press, 1993. 69.
3. Booch, G. "Object-Oriented Design 1.3." *Ada Letters*, March–April 1982, 64.
4. Coad, P. and E. Yourdan. *Object-Oriented Analysis*. Englewood Cliffs: Yourdan Press, 1990.
5. Coad, P. and E. Yourdan. *Object-Oriented Design*. Englewood Cliffs: Yourdon Press, 1991.
6. Wirfs-Brock, Rebecca, Brian Wilkerson, and Lauren Wiener. *Designing Object-Oriented Software*. Upper Saddle River: Prentice-Hall, 1990.
7. Chidamber, Shyam R. and Chris F. Kemerer. *A Metrics Suite for Object-Oriented Design*. Cambridge: Massachusetts Institute of Technology, Sloan School of Management, E53-315, 1993.
8. Basili,Victor, Lionel Briand, and Walcelio Melo. "A Validation of Object-Oriented Design Metrics as Quality Indicators." 22.10. *IEEE Transactions on Software Engineering*, October 1996.
9. Lorenz, M. and J. Kidd. *Object-Oriented Software Metrics*. Englewood Cliffs: Prentice Hall, 1994.
10. Henderson-Sellers, Brian. *Object-Oriented Metrics: Measures of Complexity*. Upper Saddle River: Prentice Hall, 1996.
11. Coad, P. and E. Yourdon. *Object-Oriented Analysis*, 2nd ed., Englewood Cliffs: Prentice Hall, 1990.
12. Coad, P. and E. Yourdon. *Object-Oriented Analysis*, 2nd ed., Englewood Cliffs: Prentice Hall, 1990.
13. Minkiewicz, A. *Measuring Object-Oriented Software with Predictive Object Points*. Price Systems LLC, 1998.
14. Karner, Gustav. Metrics of Objectory, Thesis. Linkoping University, 1993.
15. Ferens, D., L. Fischman, T. Fitzpatrick, D. Galorath, and D. Tarbet. *Automated Software Project Size Estimation via Use Case Points*. El Segundo: Galorath Incorporated, 2002.
16. Jacobson, Ivar, Grady Booch, and James Rumbaugh. *The Unified Software Development Process*. Boston: Addison-Wesley, 1999.
17. Banerjee, Gautam. Use Case Points: An Estimation Approach, 2001. http://www.bfpug.com.br/Artigos/UCP/Banerjee-UCP_An_Estimation_Approach.pdf
18. Reifer, Donald J. "WEBMO: Estimating the Cost of Web Software Developments." Software Technology Conference, Salt Lake City, 2001.
19. Highsmith, Jim and Alistar Cockburn. "Agile Software Development: The Business of Innovation." *IEEE Computer*, November 2001. 120.

20. Beck, Kent. *Extreme Programming Explained.* Boston: Addison-Wesley, 2000.
21. Heineman, George T. and William T. Councill. *Component-Based Software Engineering.* Boston: Addison-Wesley, 2001.
22. Reifer, Donald J. "Estimating Web Development Costs: There Are Differences." *CrossTalk: The Journal of Defense Software Engineering*, June 2002.
23. Evans, Mike, interview with software project manager, 1999.
24. Hantos, Peter. "Inherent Risks in Object-Oriented Development." *CrossTalk: The Journal of Defense Software Engineering*, February 2005.
25. DeMarco, Tom and Tim Lister. *Peopleware; Productive Projects and Teams,* 2nd ed. New York: Dorsett House, 1999.
26. Flanagan, E.B. "Risky Business." *C++ Report*, March–April 1995.
27. Binder, R.V. "Object-Oriented Testing: Myth and Reality." *Object Magazine*, May 1995.
28. Jacobson, I. *Object-Oriented Software Engineering: A Use-Case Driven Approach.* Boston: Addison-Wesley, 1992.
29. Boehm, B. *IEEE Tutorial on Software Risk Management.* New York: IEEE Computer Society Press, 1989.

Chapter 8

Software Reuse and Commercial Off-the-Shelf Software

The most radical possible solution for constructing software is not to construct it at all.

Fred Brooks

Introduction

Organizations faced with the difficulties and costs associated with the development of software have turned to the reuse of existing software or using commercial off-the-shelf (COTS) software as an option. Reuse, whether involving home-grown or COTS components, certainly promises lower cost, better quality, a decrease in risk, and the potential for a less stressful development process. Many such efforts succeed, but the promises of decreased cost and risk are not always realized. Requirements, algorithms, functions, business rules, architecture, source code, test cases, input data, and scripts can all be reused. Architecture is a key for reuse.[1]

Many programs that plan substantial reuse find that the assumptions made concerning how much functionality could be achieved were overly optimistic. They are then disappointed when the amount is less than projected or they experience much higher costs for reuse than had been estimated. Reuse is not a panacea, the ultimate saver of schedule, or cost reduction measure that optimistic estimators or zealous managers promise. In reality, reuse or COTS can lower cost, but only partially. COTS application software often satisfies less than 40 percent of the functionality of an application.

Even when functional requirements are reasonably well satisfied, critical nonfunctional requirements such as security, reliability, and performance must be addressed, resulting in schedule and cost impacts. If the functional or interface requirements are not satisfied, wrappers (additional code required to make the new development able to use the existing software) must be planned, designed, developed, and tested.

In all cases, the system or software architecture must be sufficiently mature to allow the detailed design of critical interfaces and the conduct of reasonable trade-offs to enable the evaluation, selection, acquisition, and integration of the capability into the system or software architecture. Only when components are produced like hardware chips, that is, components that are designed for reuse, include appropriate inputs and outputs, and have been fully tested for the environment can the risk of reusing someone else's code be reduced.

When working with embedded systems (software embedded with hardware), critical system, hardware, and operational considerations greatly complicate the evaluation trade-offs and the selection process by forcing the analysis to address external considerations and usability factors at the same depth as internal system and software considerations. The decision to use COTS or reuse a legacy component cannot be made simply because the items "fit in the architecture." The use must be based on a certainty that the components will prove operationally sound across the full range of operational scenarios they must support.

Often reuse decisions are made by defining high level views of what might be needed and identifying off-the-shelf components, preexisting functional designs, and reuse components that roughly satisfy the identified requirement from catalogs or vendors' cost sheets. These decisions then make their way into the estimate only to be reversed later — above the projected cost and outside the projected schedule.

When discussing reuse, it is important to identify the type of reuse. Most reuse falls into one of the following categories: incidental reuse, planned reuse, incremental capability, or COTS.

■ **Incidental reuse** — The most common form of reuse involves an attempt to use software developed for one purpose or application in a new application. This approach is far from cost-free.

The software must be partially redesigned, reimplemented, and then retested to ensure it does what it should do, and does not do what it should not do. This can be a potential minefield that can cause an organization to inherit all the problems of the pre-existing software and reap few of the benefits. Reuse may actually cost more than developing new software because of the poor state or lack of fit of the reused components. Many managers, when planning for software reuse, forget that the reuse software must be tested in the new environment.

- **Planned reuse** — This involves software developed with reuse as a goal during its development. Developers spent extra effort to ensure it would be reusable within the intended domains. The additional cost during development may have been significant but the resulting product can achieve dramatic savings over a number of projects. The SEER-SEM estimation model shows that the additional costs of building software designed for reuse can be up to 63 percent more than building with no consideration for reusability.
- **Incremental capability** — This is the addition of functionality to an existing system, whether through upgrade or incremental deliveries of a system under development. The analysis required is identical to those used for other planned and unplanned reuse; the product is an additional capability added to the existing system.
- **COTS** — The COTS term is applied to almost all retail software. COTS components can be anything from an operating system to a word processor, a language compiler, or a component that is invisibly integrated into a software program.

More systems today take advantage of reuse of preexisting software in the development of new systems. Many like to think of reuse as a silver bullet. In fact, reuse can be Pandora's box if inappropriate assumptions are made about the applicability of the software to be reused or if the reused software has inherent problems.

Reusable Software

Table 8.1 outlines the characteristic differences among types of reusable software.

The effort required for reuse of existing software depends on several factors that must be well understood before a determination to reuse functionality is made. An efficient approach is to convert the preexisting software into an effective (equivalent) number of size units (lines, function points, or other units) using formulas developed from experience.

Table 8.1 Comparison of Types of Reusable Software

	COTS	GOTS	Planned Reuse	Incidental Reuse
Ready to use and documented	Yes	Sometimes	Often	Sometimes
Allows programs to offset rising development costs	Often	Often	Often	Often
Tends to follow open standards, making integration easier	Often	Sometimes	Sometimes	Occasionally
Designed for reuse, generalized and well tested	Usually	Often	Sometimes	Occasionally
Often updated and improved	Usually, due to competitive pressure	Occasionally	Sometimes	Seldom

Reuse involves three activities, each of which has a price: redesign, reimplementation, and retesting. Redesign arises because the existing functionality may not be exactly suited to the new task; it likely will require some rework to support new functions, and will likely require reverse engineering to reveal its current operation. Some design changes may be in order. This will result also in reimplementation, which generally takes the form of coding changes. Whether or not redesign and reimplementation are needed, plan to conduct some retesting to be sure the preexisting software operates properly in its new environment.

The effective size of the existing software can be determined using the formula:[2]

$$\text{Effective size} = \text{existing size} \times (0.4 \times \text{redesign \%} + 0.25 \times \text{reimplementation \%} + 0.35 \times \text{retest \%})$$

The various redesign, reimplementation, and retest components can be estimated by breaking each one down into its several components, then using some additional formulas gained from experience. Table 8.2 shows the components and formulas. The procedure should be tailored for an organization's process specifics. For example, the five components of redesign (as shown in the table) are: (A) architectural design change, (B) detailed design change, (C) reverse engineering required, (D) redocumentation required, and (E) revalidation required.

Table 8.3 illustrates a calculation of reimplementation based on 30 percent recoding required, 32 percent code review, and 35 percent unit testing.

After using the formula provided in Table 8.2 to compute the redesign, reimplementation, and retest percentages, the following equation is used to compute effective size:[2]

$$\text{Effective size = new code + preexisting code} \times$$
$$(0.4 \times \text{redesign \% + 0.25} \times \text{reimplementation \% + 0.35} \times \text{retest \%})$$

For example, if there are 750 preexisting function points and the redesign is 15 percent, reimplementation is 10 percent, and retest is 18 percent, the following formula would be used to determine effective function point rating and the result would be 116 effective function points.

$$750 \times (0.4 \times 15\% + 0.25 \times 10\% + 0.35 \times 18\%)$$

With an additional 140 new function points, the combined effective size would equal the effective preexisting function points (116) plus the number of new function points (140), for a total of 256 effective function points. This effective function point measure quantifies the work to be performed and forms a basis for tracking completion.

Integrating Commercial Off-the-Shelf Software

In hardware design, standardized chips are good examples of standard parts. They are well understood components listed in catalogues and they perform very specific functions: they are the physical building blocks of larger designs. Now imagine preexisting, pretested software components that can be inserted right into new software programs.

These pieces of pretested software are like little black boxes. Just like a standard hardware part, commercial off-the-shelf software is meant to be cheaper and more reliable than a home-grown solution. The following are common subcategories for commercial off-the-shelf software:

Table 8.2 Redesign and Reimplementation Breakdown

Redesign Breakdown		
	Formula to compute redesign percentage:	$0.22 \times A + 0.78 \times B + 0.5 \times C + 0.3 \times (1 - (0.22 \times A + 0.78 \times B) \times (3 \times D + E)/4$
Weight	*Redesign Component*	*Definitions*
0.22	Architectural design change (A)	Percentage of preexisting software requiring architectural design change
0.78	Detailed design change (B)	Percentage of preexisting software requiring detailed design change
0.5	Reverse engineering required (C)	Percentage of preexisting software not familiar to developers; requires understanding and/or reverse engineering to achieve modification
0.225	Redocumentation required (D)	Percentage of preexisting software requiring design redocumentation
0.075	Revalidation required (E)	Percentage of preexisting software requiring revalidation with new design
Reimplementation Breakdown		
	Formula to compute re-implementation percentage:	$0.37 \times F + 0.11 \times G + 0.52 \times H$
Weight	*Inputs*	*Definitions*
0.37	Recoding required (F)	Percentage of preexisting software requiring actual code changes
0.11	Code review required (G)	Percentage of preexisting software needing code reviews
0.52	Unit testing required (H)	Percentage of preexisting software requiring unit testing
Retest Breakdown		
	Formula to compute retest percentage:	$0.10 \times J + 0.04 \times K + 0.13 \times L + 0.25 \times M + 0.36 \times N + 0.12 \times P$
0.1	Test plans required (J)	Percentage requiring test plans to be rewritten

Table 8.2 (continued)   Redesign and Reimplementation Breakdown

Weight	Inputs	Definitions
0.04	Test procedures required (K)	Percentage requiring test procedures to be identified and written
0.13	Test reports required (L)	Percentage requiring documented test reports
0.25	Test drivers required (M)	Percentage requiring test drivers and simulators to be rewritten
0.36	Integration testing (N)	Percentage requiring integration testing
0.12	Formal testing (P)	Percentage requiring formal demonstration testing

Table 8.3   Example of Reimplementation Calculation

	Formula:	$0.37 \times F + 0.11 \times G + 0.52 \times H$
	Reimplementation result:	32.82 Percent
Weight	Inputs	Likely Percent
0.37	Recoding required (F)	30
0.11	Code review required (G)	32
0.52	Unit testing required (H)	35

COTS components — Program parts designed to be included within developed software to provide additional functionality. These parts are designed, developed, tested, documented, and usually maintained by their suppliers. Because COTS components are developed and tested with reuse in mind, they are more generically designed than typical custom software.

COTS applications — Stand-alone applications available for sale to businesses, government, and the general public. For example, word processors such as Microsoft Word or WordPerfect may be considered COTS applications when they are used to fulfill user requirements. COTS applications are clearly tempting because they provide turnkey functionality. However, specific needs may not be perfectly addressed by these general applications.

GOTS (government off-the-shelf) — Similar to COTS, except that the software was developed by or for the government and may not be widely available. GOTS software is generally provided at no cost to government organizations and often to software developers contracting to the government. However, support and updates are not necessarily included or forthcoming. GOTS software may or may not be accompanied by satisfactory documentation. Often it is provided as government-furnished information (GFI) — software without guarantees or warranties — and the developer using it is left with the task of determining how usable it is and what if any of the functionality needed is actually provided.

Examples of COTS software include:

- Stand-alone packages such as word processors, supply chain software, and spreadsheets
- Libraries requiring linkage into application code, for example graphics engines, Windows DLLs
- Development environments with runtime modules, for example, Visual Basic™ and Sybase™
- Vendor-supplied device drivers such as printers, displays, and multimedia
- Information retrieval applications such as hypertext and data mining tools
- Operating system utilities such as file operations and memory management

Use of a COTS product implies a certain trust of its vendor. It is often useful, therefore, to learn as much as possible about the vendor — what are its other business obligations and what is its financial condition — before deciding to use its product.

Fundamental Differences between COTS Software and Custom Development

Here is a list of considerations surrounding any evaluation of COTS versus custom development:

- An "infrastructure" may be required to demonstrate and validate the package.
- The COTS package may dictate standards, architecture, and design.
- Because it has a prespecified design and certain input and output restrictions, COTS may also influence work flow.
- Choosing the wrong COTS package may be more expensive than fixing problems in custom software.

- Resolution of COTS-related issues may be complicated because of the addition of a third party (vendor).
- There may be no source code available and no way to correct a defect.

Items Not Estimated as COTS

When estimating development costs, confusion sometimes arises as to what constitutes COTS and what does not. In general, anything that is purchased for use in a development project is potentially a COTS item. However, software that is used to create software but is not part of a finished product is not COTS; it is a development tool.

Do not cost standard operating systems and development tools as COTS — The impacts of operating systems and development tools are handled explicitly by experience parameters in various estimating models. These items generally are tools that aid in the development of an end product. Other examples include code scanners, code generators, automatic testers, requirements tools, and configuration management tools.

To consider the use of development tools in an estimate, look at the ratings for such parameters as automated tool use, requirements definition formality, function implementation mechanism, and others that relate to the development environment and processes. Acquisition costs associated with these tools must be included in a complete estimate.

Do not estimate modified COTS in the same manner as nonmodified COTS — Just as electronics equipment warranties are no longer valid after a seal is broken, COTS software is no longer COTS after its source code is modified. It may still be estimated as reusable software, but potential COTS advantages are lost:

- The COTS supplier no longer maintains your documentation and source code.
- You no longer know what you are getting because modifications may or may not be consistent with the original software design.
- New updates to the baseline COTS software may not be usable unless modified to suit whatever changes you have made.
- Modified COTS should be handled as incidental or planned reused software (depending on the modifications made); this is still less costly than new development, but not as cost effective as unmodified COTS.

Do not cost incidental and planned reuse software as COTS — Neither of these software types should be treated as COTS software because they are not commercially available and because source code will be worked with.

Weighing Use of COTS

When properly applied, COTS can truly reduce costs, schedules, and development risks. However, several issues related to the use of COTS software must be considered. More than money must often be invested to make a COTS investment work. Listed below are some advantages and disadvantages developers see when evaluating COTS:

Advantages	Disadvantages
Quicker time to market	Use involves learning curve; need for integration and further customization
Better reliability	May not meet all user requirements because it is intended for general use
More end user functionality when compared to custom-developed components	Can be difficult to support because source code may not be provided
Support for components across different hardware and environments	Vendors may discontinue support or cease business
Stricter requirements because of its release for general use	

Case Studies: Real-World Experiences with COTS

The following case studies are actual examples from the authors' experiences. COTS usage has been both a blessing a curse.

Case 1: Components Had Critical Defects and Were Modified by Developer

A COTS library was chosen to store and provide instant access to thousands of items of text data associated with inputs. Defects in delivered COTS and its interaction with the developed application made it necessary for the developer to procure source code and debug and/or correct the previously COTS software. When the COTS vendor moved to a newer version, the developer was stuck with the modified previous version. The result was that the developer had to maintain what was once the COTS portion on its own; the advantages of increased functionality from new versions of the COTS were lost forever. Cost and performance savings over "native" code were still realized, although nowhere near the amounts projected. Fortunately, the COTS vendor made source code available. If source code had not been available (at a price) for this project, the costs would have been even greater, schedule penalties could have been imposed, and development of new solutions would have been required.

Case 2: Powerful (and Defect-Ridden) COTS Component

This project had a graphics display COTS component that was provided as an executable program only, with no source code available. The developer decided to use this COTS package because it provided the best functionality on the market. However, the documentation was poor and the initial releases were defect-ridden. Support was also poor — calls were not always returned. When problems could not be solved, the software requirements were relaxed to make the COTS acceptable. As newer versions of the operating system appeared, however, the COTS software did not always execute properly and vendor support continued to be inconsistent. In addition, the COTS component was available on only one platform. Despite this, the developer assumed that equivalent functionality would be available by the time a second platform was required. The developer also assumed that glue code would be developed to convert calling sequences. No adequate functionality was ever developed for the second platform by the vendor, and the developer was required to develop this functionality from scratch.

Case 3: Application Integrated (Loosely Coupled) without Problems

This application required a simple text editor. There was no requirement for tight data coupling; the only requirement was executing the application. The development team used the operating system's editor. In this case, invoking the stand-alone COTS application was simple, it ran smoothly, and required almost no development time.

Evaluating and Estimating COTS

Imagine that all the work required to integrate a COTS component with the target software is a blob as represented in Figure 8.1. The interface with the COTS functionality appears on the right side. The target software

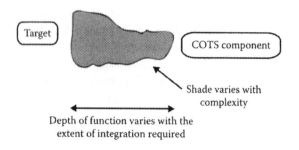

Figure 8.1   Integration of COTS component with target software.

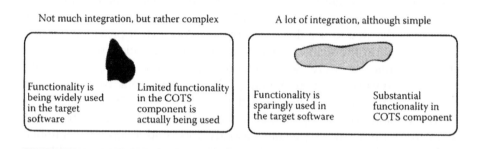

Figure 8.2   Examples of blobs in practice.

interface or resultant functionality impacted is represented on the left side. The area in the middle represents the required work.

The amount of COTS functionality, the impacted target functionality, and integration work together to determine the size of the blob, and thus the job. A lot of integration work means a longer blob and more functionality makes it wider. A fourth factor is complexity, and this is represented by shading. Although complexity is positively correlated with integration work, sometimes a small amount of work will be very complex and vice versa. Figure 8.2 illustrates two examples of blobs in practice. It can be used as a framework to better explain the scope of any COTS integration work.

Three Components of COTS Integration

Figure 8.3 illustrates the three basic components required when estimating the effort involved in integrating COTS software.

Glue code is software that binds COTS software with development software. Glue code can actually serve as an integral part of development software or it can be developed as a separate module inserted between the system being developed and the COTS components. Glue code should

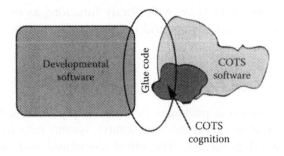

Figure 8.3 Glue code integrating developmental software and COTS software.

normally be modeled as any other coding effort is. It can be sized using either source lines or functions.

Developmental software is generally developed from scratch to meet the stated requirements of a project.

COTS cognition or learning is not a cost-free activity. Even when a developer can directly put a COTS component or application to use, understanding how to use third-party software takes time, effort, and diligence. COTS cognition involves identifying the number of COTS functions that must be learned, used, and tested.

Estimating COTS Integration

This section outlines three different methodologies that can be used to estimate the integration of COTS software: (1) using function points and an estimating model lacking COTS-specific capability; (2) using SEER-SEM cost drivers to estimate COTS; and (3) rules of thumb.

Using Function Points and Estimating Model Lacking COTS-Specific Capability

For the COTS software, perform the following steps:

1. Count the functionality to be learned or used by the developers. In the language of function points, these will usually be internal logical files.
2. Count only the function calls used by the host application as external inquiries.
3. Count any error messages used as external interface files.
4. Count screen, printed, and clipboard outputs individually as external outputs.

5. Count user interactions with library functions as external inputs.
6. In general, count inputs and outputs within the boundary of the host application.

Integration of Stand-Alone COTS Software

What about stand-alone packages that are simply launched from a host application? For example, a mission control system may have an option to launch a word processor. The effort associated with such types of turnkey integration is captured in the host application's development effort. This is appropriate only for COTS packages that are used as-is with no further understanding required. The only required testing would be verification that the host application successfully launches the COTS application with no unwanted side effects.

Stand-Alone COTS Software with Significant Configuration

Some stand-alone packages require significant configuration. For example, a mail system often requires extensive hardware-dependent setup and may involve script and initialization file edits, 4GL code, etc. Configuration should be modeled within a sizing framework, that is, determine the size of each item to be configured. Use the following guidelines for estimating configuration work:

1. Count setup files as internal logical files (function points).
2. If the configuration is performed from scratch, count whatever is created either as SLOC or functions.
3. If configuration templates are provided, count them as preexisting SLOC or functions.
4. For cost drivers when estimating COTS integration without a COTS estimating tool, evaluate the Table 8.4 factors after completing the function point count for the COTS. Even though Table 8.4 expresses the cost drivers in terms of SEER-SEM parameters, they must be evaluated whether using a cost model or simply performing a manual cost study.

Using SEER-SEM Cost Drivers to Estimate COTS

COTS estimation mainly involves sizing the core new developmental code, COTS glue code, and any "cognition" required to integrate and understand the COTS component or application (see Figure 8.3). Sizing the new and the glue code follows the same principles defined in Chapters 5 through 7. COTS configuration can also be estimated based on material in Chapters 5

Table 8.4 Cost Drivers, Descriptions, and Typical Settings

Potential Cost Driver	Description	Considerations
Resource and support location	Degree of access (by proximity) to COTS software vendor resources and support	COTS software vendors are usually geographically remote and support levels can vary tremendously; may be a critical issue if software is complex and challenging to use
Host system volatility	Determines difficulty caused by changes to development virtual machine; impacted by how often COTS software is updated	Volatility may be high if developers want to keep up-to-date with vendor releases
Specification level (reliability)	Level of documentation required	Should be adjusted to reflect specifications that will have to be written to support use of COTS product
Test level	Level to which COTS software will be tested	Stringent internal QA levels may require detailed retesting of vendor-supplied software before internal acceptance
Quality assurance (QA) level	QA level to which COTS software was built	Highly vendor- and product-specific
Requirements volatility (change)	Anticipated frequency and scope of change in requirements once baselined (after preliminary design starts)	Rate based on requirements for COTS portion of the project, not overall project
Language type (complexity)	Difficulty of programming languages used in development; parameter is closely related to function implementation mechanism	Rate COTS software based on complexity of its programming support tools and interface

Table 8.4 (continued) Cost Drivers, Descriptions, and Typical Settings

Potential Cost Driver	Description	Considerations
Memory constraints	Anticipated effort to reduce memory usage	COTS software may use so much memory that conservation measures must be undertaken elsewhere in developed code
Time constraints	Percentage of software that must undergo specific (coding) effort to enhance timing performance	If COTS software is too slow, nothing generally can be done about it; requirements relief or different solution is needed
Real-time code	Amount of software involved in real-time functions driven by a clock external to the software, e.g., gathering data from hardware devices or time-sensitive control of such devices where waiting can alter or lose data	Software that lacks definite and extremely tight time constraints is not real-time code; if COTS has real-time considerations that cannot be met, a different solution is needed
Target system complexity	Complexity of target operating systems, compilers, controllers, and other attached processors	Target system is host development environment; parameter varies with extent of change in that environment
Target system volatility	Determines difficulty caused by changes to virtual machine; may be changes in program editors, compilers or other tools, changes in command languages, or changes in target hardware	Target system is host development environment; parameter varies with extent of change in that environment
Security requirements	Development impacts of security requirements for delivered target system	COTS security levels must usually be accepted as-is; contact vendor for security certification rating

through 7. Table 8.4 illustrates some opportunities and risks, and parameter settings that are associated with COTS software based on SEER-SEM cost drivers. The method of estimating COTS cognition is described below.

A key driver behind COTS estimates is the scope of the integration effort. While traditional size metrics such as lines of code or function points are used to scope traditional work, size is typically not known for COTS integration efforts. In addition, the size of a COTS product is not always correlated with the effort required to integrate it.

For a COTS element, "size" describes the functionality that must be understood by the integrator. This perspective on sizing has been called COTS cognition.

SEER-SEM provides a number of COTS cognition sizing methods: (1) object sizing, (2) feature sizing, and (3) quick sizing which allows an analyst to estimate by drawing analogies. The options for COTS sizing are detailed below:

Object Sizing

If the COTS software is object-oriented, there is no better choice than this metric that was carefully adapted from IFPUG's object-oriented function point specification. Identify the parts of the COTS that will be learned and used, not the entire COTS application. Object points are covered in detail in Chapter 7.

Feature Sizing

This technique was specially developed for use in the COTS WBS element. Developed from function points, feature sizing allows you to model functions as they appear from the developer's perspective. Feature sizing is broken down into three categories: unique functions, data tables referenced, and data tables configured.

> **Unique Functions:** Defined as the number of unique functions that must be understood to integrate the component, functions may reside in APIs, program libraries, etc. A function may pass data, receive data, or both pass and receive data. Count the number of unique functions used or those that must simply be understood.
> **Data Tables Referenced:** This category represents the number of unique data tables referenced including configuration files, databases, external data structures, etc. A single database having several closely related tables should be referenced once only unless those tables are sufficiently different from one another. These data groupings are referenced only and not changed.

Data Tables Configured: The final category includes the number of data tables that must be configured, changed or created in order to integrate the component. Data tables include configuration files, databases, and external data structures. A single database having several closely related tables should be counted once only, unless those tables are sufficiently different from one another. Count each table being created or configured. If an already existing table is being used only to learn how tables should be created or configured, do not count it.

Quick Sizing

This is a method for approximating size by analogy against common application types. Two categories of COTS software are outlined and discussed here: embedded COTS software and components. Embedded COTS software is integrated directly into the delivered software. Embedded COTS software items are broken down further into those that are adapted and those that are components, that is, directly integrated into the computer program.

Components are intended for reuse; source code often is not available and usually requires no modification such as libraries, object classes, and applications.

What distinguishes the COTS WBS element in SEER-SEM is its list of specialized parameters developed after much research into the critical factors underlying the use of COTS software. This section contains a quick overview of COTS WBS element parameter categories.

Off-the-shelf product characteristics — This category of parameters describes issues faced by users of off-the-shelf components. Integration experiences show that these issues differ from standard development issues, and particularly involve product support and integration complexity. Parameters in this category include component type, component volatility, component application complexity, interface complexity, and product support.

Use parameters relate to the quality of the experience developers will have in using these components. Many issues surrounding component integration involve learning how to use components and checking their integrity. The use parameters focus on these factors and include component selection completeness, experience with component, learning rate, reverse engineering, component integration and testing, and test level.

Cost parameters are both recurring (e.g., annual licensing fees) and nonrecurring (e.g., one-time purchasing and training costs) associated with the COTS product.

Evaluating COTS-intensive software goes beyond simple recipes. Foremost are cost-performance trade-offs. As an analogy, imagine a prefabricated

Table 8.5   Rough Scope of COTS Implementation[3]

	Scope of COTS (Effort Months)		
Experience	Limited	Moderate	Complex
Limited	2.3 to 22	19 to 99	143 to 787
Functional	1.5 to 16	13 to 72	96 to 582
Fully proficient	1.4 to 13	11 to 58	84 to 464

house. While such a house can be built economically, the placements of doors and windows are prescribed and customizing such a house can be difficult. The same principle applies to COTS software, where savings of time and effort may be traded for flexibility. Your task is to evaluate the additional costs such losses in flexibility may entail.

Rules of Thumb for COTS Integration

Table 8.5 provides general guidance on COTS integration. Use this table to perform sanity checks on integration efforts from the time necessary to understand the COTS component (cognition) through the time necessary to complete integration (completion of glue code and other necessary configurations). COTS projects vary widely in the level of required integration, the type of integration carried out, the type of product, ease of use, and many other factors. Because of this, this table must be evaluated skeptically; use it only to understand probable ranges for COTS efforts.

Experience with COTS Product

This factor describes the developers' previous experience in integrating developed software with this COTS product:

> **Limited:** nearly no experience with product
> **Functional:** one or two limited instances of dealing with product
> **Fully proficient:** fully knowledgeable and practiced in integration issues with product

Scope of COTS

Scope is the combined functionality and complexity of the COTS product:

> **Limited:** typical desktop-level software products such as a PC-based accounting system or operating system changeover

Moderate: medium-sized company tools such as a human resources system, shop floor automation, shipping, and operating system changeovers

Complex: mainframe-class products such as SAP R/3, a broadly deployed reservations system, or a system with complex real-world interactions that do not become fully apparent except over time

Table 8.5 does not consider outliers. For example, consider a simple fire-and-forget COTS integration of launching a dedicated word processor. This application, called from a host application, may have a great deal of functionality but could be quite simple to integrate. While experience with an application may be limited, integration can be a trivial matter. COTS integration outliers are more pronounced on the downside of the above estimates.

Evaluation and Selection of COTS Products

Although evaluation and selection (E&S) is often a time-consuming process in its own right, no strong methodology that can be used to estimate this task is available. Look to previous E&S efforts to get a sense for how long a particular effort should take. However, E&S cost is more often a function of budget, continuing until either a best selection is found or until funds are exhausted. Table 8.6 provides a starting checklist for selecting and evaluating COTS products.

COTS Risks

Because COTS software is designed to address common needs, the specifications for this software often sound very appealing. However, a number of common assumptions should be questioned:

- **Assumption** — A COTS package is relatively bug-free.
  Reality — Although the marketplace tries to ensure that bugs are discovered and fixed promptly, newer, less tested versions cause defects to reappear. Shop for a mature COTS package (or version).

- **Assumption** — System integrators know the functionality and interface nuances of the COTS packages that they propose to use.
  Reality — Manuals do not always tell the whole story, especially with programming components. Use of almost any COTS involves a learning curve. Look for previous experience with the specific COTS package.

Table 8.6   Checklist for COTS Evaluation and Selection

COTS Characteristic	Estimation Impact
Does developer's organization already have experience with this COTS software?	Yes, reduces cost
Is COTS software vendor an established company or a garage shop operation?	Established firms reduce risk
Is source code available?	Yes, reduces risk if vendor is shaky
Does developer plan to use modified COTS?	Yes, means higher costs of rework
What are licensing terms for COTS?	Difficult licensing agreements can cause delay in delivery of product to development organization; licensing fees can significantly impact life cycle costs of software
What are vendor's commitments to upgrades?	If vendor has no commitment to future upgrades, COTS product can require significant modifications by development team; in a worst case, a new product may need to be purchased or functionality may need to be developed
What are software developer's commitments to upgrades (i.e., is delivered product required to be delivered with most recent COTS version)?	If version 1.0 works well in software development, but you are required to deliver the latest version and it does not work the same as version 1.0, costs increase; if version 1.0 requires development team to design work-arounds when the new version comes out, these may no longer be valid
Quality and reliability of COTS product?	Quality and reliability of COTS product will have a direct correlation to the number of modifications and work-arounds required; unreliable COTS can cause entire application to be unreliable

■ **Assumption** —Glue code is very easy to write. Therefore, only a minimum amount of time is required to design and implement it. *Reality* — Because glue code interfaces independent sets of code, it can be extremely complex.

■ **Assumption** — COTS software works and no special testing beyond integration testing is needed.
Reality — The golden rule behind COTS software is "trust but verify."

■ **Assumption** — User requirements will be met by the finished system.
Reality — In general, COTS packages need to be extended to meet 100 percent of user requirements.

■ **Assumption** — COTS is mass-produced and priced at dramatic economies of scale.
Reality — Keep in mind that although COTS software may be sold to many people, developers must still make decent returns on their investments.

Risk Reduction

Maximize the use of COTS components that:

■ Perform relatively well defined functions.
■ Are mature, replaceable, and have equivalents from alternate, competitive sources. This means studying the market since products are not generally standardized.
■ Have well defined and predictable inputs and outputs. This requires looking at product architecture in some detail.

Minimize the use of COTS components that:

■ Combine many functions in an integrated solution, all of which must be used or purchased and maintained. Ask whether you can use a portion of the COTS product or package.
■ Do not have well defined internal and external interfaces.

Incorporate the other rules of estimation. All the other cautions related to estimation of software projects are applicable to projects incorporating COTS software:

■ Experience levels with languages, tools, and practices are just as important as the languages, tools, and practices being used.
■ Simply having tools available does not mean they will be used.

- The complexity of an application is related to how quickly you can add people to the project.
- There is no such thing as a free lunch! COTS integration is never free.

Risks Associated with Reuse and COTS

While reuse or COTS software can provide the potential to significantly reduce cost, schedule, or quality exposure of a project, opting for reused or COTS software by no means ensures success. Many risks can arise. If not managed and successfully mitigated, they can develop into problems and negate any savings projected. The risks generally fall into three categories:

1. The process used to select the components or criteria used in trade-offs resulting in the selection
2. A need to modify, extend, or upgrade reused or COTS components to support operational or application requirements
3. The need to maintain or sustain the reused or COTS components during periods of operational support

Table 8.7 identifies certain issues that should be considered when selecting COTS or reused components and the risks that may result. Ignoring these issues and failing to manage the risks can quickly preclude meeting the cost and schedule savings.

Summary

The primary difference between reuse and COTS is the origin of the software. COTS is generally purchased. Incidental reuse has been occurring ever since software was invented and has been a hoped for silver bullet. Reuse is not free nor is it generally inexpensive. Planned reuse can reduce cost but costs more to develop.

COTS product integration has expanded dramatically in recent years as an important strategy for achieving cost-effective software systems. Success of this reuse type has been based on the increasing quality of COTS software products and the growth of technologies supporting the integration of architectural styles such as middleware. Financial issues and concerns as well as improved returns on investments resulting from better products have increased the pressure to achieve more with development

Table 8.7   COTS Issues and Risks

Reuse Issue Area	Risk
Component Selection Issues and Risks	
Reuse code or COTS not adequately analyzed at program inception before start of architecture design	Component does not integrate with architecture
Inadequate quantified selection criteria and acceptability thresholds	Components inconsistent with application requirements and must be modified or replaced
Fit of functionality to current application not adequately evaluated prior to selection	Component functionality must be modified or enhanced
Adequate cost analysis or trade-off not conducted to identify specific possible cost savings by minimizing code and design modifications and cost of integration related to selection and use of reused or COTS component	Projected savings may prove unreasonable
Compliance of external and system software interfaces with external engineering interface, application program interface, and data interoperability standards not confirmed prior to selection	Component fails to interoperate with other software components; must be modified
Component Modification Issues and Risks	
Interfaces inconsistent with software architecture operating systems and middleware	Component fails to interoperate with other software components; must be modified
Reuse architecture to which designed is inconsistent with project quality standards or software architecture	Components inconsistent with application requirements; must be modified or replaced
Component will not perform adequately under stress conditions	Components inconsistent with application requirements; must be modified or replaced
Range of values for input variables inconsistent with those required by software architecture	Components inconsistent with application requirements; must be modified or replaced

Table 8.7 (continued) COTS Issues and Risks

Reuse Issue Area	Risk
Security characteristics of component inconsistent with those required for application	Components are inconsistent with application requirements and must be modified or replaced.
Documentation or support elements related to component may be of insufficient quality to be used, may not be current, or may not meet project standards	Documentation or support elements may require modification or replacement; costs may increase for reverse engineering effort required to understand poorly documented COTS
COTS or reuse code may not be a fit with functional requirements it is designed to satisfy	May require design modifications and recoding that will increase cost of integration
No trade study conducted to evaluate reuse or COTS code before or after architecture design	Components inconsistent with architecture requirements; must be modified or replaced
Architecture was designed before reuse or COTS code modules were selected, making integration into architecture with least modification unlikely	Architecture inconsistent with reuse or COTS requirements; component or architecture must be modified or replaced to use it
Need for costly development of "wrappers" to translate reuse or COTS software external interfaces	Unexpected costs or schedule may result from need to develop and qualify wrappers essential to integrate components into software architecture

Sustainment Issues and Risks

Proprietary features of COTS product and positive and negative impacts of all features not identified early	Maintenance of product is impacted or precluded due to proprietary nature of COTS or reused components
Processes used to develop or update COTS or reuse product not sufficiently rigorous to assure that excessive defects do not remain in product	Product may not perform well enough to support needs of application
Applications operating on client–server network must analyze ease of distributing COTS product and its output data on network	Licenses for COTS components may restrict use to limited number of machines

Table 8.7 (continued) COTS Issues and Risks

Reuse Issue Area	Risk
Analysis of sustainment costs for each candidate module not conducted before selection of COTS or reuse software	The cost of sustainment may exceed initial projections
Cost of upgrading to new versions including incorporating previously made modifications and additions not identified before selecting product	Sustainment costs may exceed projected costs and schedule
Costs of licenses not adequately determined prior to selecting COTS component	COTS licensing costs may exceed projections
Costs of replacing product due to proprietary features may not have been calculated or were calculated improperly	Costs for COTS components requiring replacement due to proprietary factors may be excessive
Process used for sustainment of COTS or reused components may not be sufficiently robust to assure long-term integrity of component	As product modifications are applied, integrity of component may degrade
Inadequate funding to keep reuse or COTS current with evolving hardware and system software	It may not be possible to keep components current with technology or application requirements due to resource limitations
Configuration management and control of COTS and reuse products by sustainment organization may prove inadequate to control product releases and changes	COTS and reused component baselines may be lost and unauthorized changes may be applied
Product help desk inadequate to assist users of COTS or reuse components who require assistance	COTS or reuse users may not be able to resolve issues with components
COTS vendor may go out of business	If source code was delivered, development organization may have to take over maintenance of package or new COTS package may need to be purchased, integrated, and deployed

dollars in less time, thus driving system architects to accept and use COTS. These cost factors constitute the primary reason that many organizations are integrating existing systems with new systems and developing software applications that make heavy use of COTS solutions. Only through methodical software reuse, systematic evaluation techniques, and improved understanding of integration can development dollars, time, and effort be more effectively realized with a COTS or reuse development strategy.

Every day, reusing software or applying a piece of COTS software to satisfy an operational or user need becomes easier as more and more vendors offer more and better software products for a dizzying variety of applications.[4] As Northrop Grumman found, COTS effort can be estimated successfully: "The overall effort and schedule predicted were within two percent of the program actuals."[5]

Endnotes

1. Reifer, Donald J. *Practical Software Reuse*. New York: John Wiley & Sons, 1997.
2. Galorath Incorporated. *SEER-SEM User Manual*. El Segundo: Galorath Incorporated, 2004.
3. Galorath Incorporated. *OSD Software Estimation Guidebook*. El Segundo: Galorath Incorporated, 1997.
4. Brooks, Frederick P., Jr. "No Silver Bullet: Essence and Accidents of Software Engineering." *Software Magazine*, 1995.
5. Bradford, Kathy and Lori Vaughan. *Improve Commercial-off-the-Shelf (COTS) Integration Estimates*. Redondo Beach: Northrop Grumman Mission Systems, 2004.

Chapter 9

Performing to Estimate: Managing and Monitoring Development

Preparation precedes performance.

When performance is measured, performance improves. When performance is measured and reported, the rate of improvement accelerates.

Thomas S. Monson

Introduction

The previous chapters discussed the processes used to develop the best possible estimate. When agreed to by the organization funding the effort and the stakeholders who participate in the activity or ultimately will use the product, an estimate becomes more than a projection of what it will take to deliver an acceptable product. The estimate becomes a commitment on the part of the developer to deliver an acceptable product within the defined schedule for the desired cost. This chapter will explore how metrics and measures as well as the use of earned value techniques can help development organizations monitor project performance and productivity against assumptions in the estimate and identify problems before their impacts affect the ability of the developer to meet its basic commitments.

Meeting the productivity commitments should be a concern of software managers from the beginning to the final product delivery. Even though software productivity is highly subject to the skills of the individuals involved in the development life cycle, improved processes and tools can help increase overall productivity. In order to meet productivity commitments and significantly reduce software project productivity risk, it is important to simultaneously evaluate the processes, tools, and skills that characterize a project and its personnel.

Managers must recognize and address the factors that affect software productivity and have a process and metrics in place to monitor productivity and take action when it falls below a predefined threshold. "Measuring provides insights to improve the performance of processes and products."[1]

Years ago, I was asked to straighten out a failing software project. The hardware people and management were convinced that the software personnel were not competent. The hard deadline for release was approaching (the project concerned a consumer printer product targeted for Christmas). I found little documentation, no metrics, and virtually no structure to the entire software effort.

In the course of correcting the project, I first looked for the "meatballs in the spaghetti" by identifying possible units of development that could be tracked. Unit development folders were created for each unit (meatball). Earned value metrics were assigned for the individual activities of each of these units. This established a method for tracking progress. A large wall chart showed expected completion dates for all activities and the amounts of value earned by completing each one.

Weekly reviews were held for each unit. The developers and management started seeing progress and could also see where units were floundering. These units received additional technical review and attention. Additionally, using the limited parametrics available at the time, a cost–benefit analysis was quantified and a change in ROM size was approved. Peer reviews were instituted to improve product quality. These changes, combined with the metric approach, allowed the project to be completed within the schedule constraint.[2]

Metric Reporting

Product and process measurement is a core process component for managing project productivity. As stated by the Software Engineering Institute when describing practical software measurement (PSM): "Measurement is a key element of successful management in every well-established engineering discipline."[3] Despite the importance of metrics, many organizations are reluctant to implement the discipline for a variety of reasons including:

- Difficulty of acquiring information to support the metrics requirement due to the nonquantitative information produced by the project's processes
- Fear that accurate quantitative information will cast a bad light on the project, resulting in the raising of issues that cannot easily be handled
- Concern that accurate metrics information will provide the customer insights into project performance and product quality and progress that cannot be explained away

As a result, projects that follow effective software engineering processes are not always committed to the timely collection and reporting of metrics. Such projects may result in successful development while ignoring all opportunities for improvement provided by metrics.

Projects that do not measure find it impossible to determine the state of software development and quantify progress toward schedule, cost, and quality targets. Alexander's first law states that "Metrics are hard to get on projects which don't keep records."[4] As simplistic and obvious as this statement sounds, the number of projects that do not involve metrics is astounding.

Software measurement is the means by which customers, managers, and developers achieve a common quantitative picture of progress made, issues that must be addressed, risks that are being managed, effectiveness of the process used, and the quality of the products produced. The objective of the measurement process is to provide information required to make informed decisions that impact project cost, schedule, and technical objectives.

The metrics collection process must be a systematic but flexible activity that serves as an integral part of the overall project management structure. Project issues should drive the measurement process.[5] A metric in isolation is not sufficient to determine program status. A set of metrics and their trends are usually needed to make a judgment. For example, when a metric such as testing requirements coverage indicates unacceptable requirements for a given testing period, the metrics process should not only indicate the problem with testing but also the links to related quantitative information and other measurements that can be evaluated to isolate the specific cause or causes of the problem. In this way, the corrective action taken addresses the problem, not simply the symptoms. This process is often called root cause analysis.

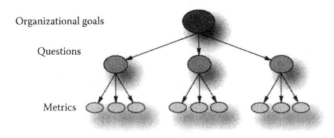

Figure 9.1   Goal–question–metric paradigm.

A useful and effective way to identify metrics and establish a process consistent with the needs and capabilities of the organization is to apply the goal–question–metric (GQM) paradigm defined as part of the PSM process. Figure 9.1 illustrates the relationship of the GQM components.

At its top level, an organization establishes certain goals that should be met to satisfy its commitments and objectives. From these goals, specific questions may be asked related to what is required to meet the goals and metrics are developed from these questions. For example, a project may have a goal of meeting the cost commitments made through the estimate. Several questions that might arise and related metrics are shown in Table 9.1. These questions allow the definition of specific metrics that will provide quantitative answers to the question and insights into how the organization is addressing them.

The spaghetti-and-meatball story above showed that the goal was to meet schedule constraints. The questions were whether the product was too large, whether the product was produced quickly enough, and whether the processes were working. The metrics used were program (ROM) size, earned value, and defect rates.

The GQM paradigm is based on the theory that all measurement should be goal-oriented. An organization should have some rationale for collecting

Table 9.1   Sample Questions and Metrics

Sample Question	Sample Metric
Do I have enough people?	Staffing profile
Are my requirements sound?	Requirements defects
Do I have enough resources available when I need them?	Resource availability

measurements and would have no need to collect metrics simply for the sake of collecting them. Each metric collected is stated in terms of the major goals of the project. Questions are then derived from the goals and help to refine, articulate, and determine whether the goals can be achieved. The metrics collected are then used to answer the questions in a quantifiable manner.

While many approaches for measurement have been presented over the years, the most relevant and perhaps the most consistent with the realities of monitoring productivity is based on the PSM approach developed by the U.S. Department of Defense.[6] The GQM paradigm shown in Figure 9.1 is an integral part of the PSM process.

PSM[7] is built around nine measurement principles:

1. Objectives and issues are used to drive the measurement requirements. Project objectives are goals and requirements: cost, schedule, quality, functionality, and technical performance. Issues are areas of concern that present obstacles: problems, risks and lack of information.
2. Define and collect measures based on the technical and management processes. Measures should be collected as natural by-products of work performed. Consider the processes of other team members and subcontractors along with your own project processes.
3. Collect and analyze data at a level of detail sufficient to identify and isolate problems. Periodically collect, process, and analyze measurement data. Specific data depends on project objectives and issues and the kinds of questions that must be answered.
4. Implement independent analysis capability. An independent group should assess measurement data to ensure objectivity and accurate, unbiased assessment of project status.
5. Use a systematic analysis process to trace the measures related to the decisions. The meanings of the numbers must be understood. There should be a clear flow from the data through the analysis to the conclusions. The analysis process should provide repeatable results.
6. Interpret the measurement results in the context of other project information. No single measurement result is good or bad. A variance between planned and actual indicates a possible problem, not the cause.
7. Integrate measurement into the project management process. Measurement provides insight into the current phase. It also can project consequences of current actions on later phases.

8. Use the measurement process as a basis for objective communications. Involve the entire project in developing the measurement process. All parties should use the same data and have a common understanding of the data definitions and commitment to the value of the measurement program.

9. Focus initially on project-level analysis. Project success means meeting specific objectives. Implement a consistent measurement process on all projects. Organization-level data can be derived from well defined project measures.

When the metrics process is functioning, management and development teams will have quantitative information available to answer the following questions regarding their projects:

■ Is the program still on track to complete within cost, schedule and performance criteria?
■ What are the natures of the problems and issues that adversely affect the project and what can happen if they are not handled?
■ What risks may impede the completion of the program within cost, schedule, and performance criteria?
■ What problems and risks are already being addressed? Are additional adjustments or corrections to the approach required?
■ What indicators will reveal the emergence of future problems and issues?
■ What indicators will reveal the emergence of negative changes?
■ On what issues and in which areas should the program manager focus to ensure the success of the program?

Answers to these questions can serve two primary purposes. First, they provide a record of events that can be used to identify trends related to productivity, project performance, issues or risks, and product quality. The record can be used to determine what occurred, determine issues or impediments to meeting cost or schedule targets, and readjust the probability that a risk or issue will transition into a problem.

The second purpose is using the metric information to make realistic projections of what can potentially occur and determine when predefined corrective actions should be started. By projecting trend information and analyzing the causes of identified shortfalls, a reasonable extrapolation of potential future problems and issues can be made based on current project factors. Both activities provide critical, on-the-ground insights into the cost and schedule performance of a project and reveal why growth is being experienced and what can be expected in the future. Without this data, management is "flying blind."

Metrics Sets

The basic GQM relationship is defined in Table 9.2 within the context of PSM. The table was adapted from information provided from the PSM process.

Table 9.3 lists examples of typical performance measures used on many software projects. Performance measures provide managers specific information concerning the state of the project, the rate of expenditure of resources, and progress toward completion. While the entries under the *Goal/Question* and *Metrics* columns are fairly representative of the measures used by software projects in general, the entries in the *Measure of Success* column vary greatly and should be established specifically for each project.

Productivity

Productivity has one basic definition: productivity = size/effort. However, multiple definitions describe *effort* and *size*. Many of the different size definitions are described in previous chapters in this book. Values used for effort can include or exclude any of the software development activities and labor categories. To ensure apples-to-apples comparisons size and effort definitions need to be standardized. Table 9.4 is useful for computing a productivity value that can actually be used for measurement.

Productivity Monitoring

Earned value (EV) is the gold standard for productivity monitoring used to monitor project performance of both government and commercial projects. While the process can follow different rules, the core process remains the same. Examples of rules include the 50/50 (half credit when the task is started and the balance at completion), binary completion (100 percent credit at completion, no credit until then), and apportioned credit (percentages of credit as the task proceeds).

EV distinguishes true progress from effort or cost expended. Physical measurements are usually made by comparison with some standard. To measure the width of a room, you wold use a yardstick as the basic measure. While a yardstick, for some reason, does not correspond precisely to the official yard designated by the National Bureau of Standards, it will invariably provide a fairly correct measurement of the width of a room.

The same principle applies to measuring the EV of a project. The goal of EV is to measure progress against plan. When performed correctly, it provides useful management information to aid decision making. Many

Table 9.2 Example PSM Issue Areas

Goal–Question–Metric (GQM)		
Goal Areas	*Question Category*	*Metric*
Schedule and progress	Milestone performance	Milestone dates
		Critical path performance
		Requirements status
		Problem report status
		Review status
		Change request status
		Component status
		Test status
		Action item status
	Incremental capability	Increment content – components
		Increment content – functions
Resources and costs	Personnel	Effort
		Staff experience
		Staff turnover
	Financial performance	Earned value
		Cost
	Environment and support	Resource availability
	Resources	Resource utilization
Product size and stability	Physical size and stability	Database size
		Component interfaces
		Lines of code
		Memory size
	Functional size and stability	Requirements
		Functional change workload
		Function points

Table 9.2 (continued) Example PSM Issue Areas

Goal–Question—Metric (GQM)		
Goal Areas	Question Category	Metric
Product quality	Functional correctness	Defects
		Technical performance
	Supportability and maintainability	Time to restore
		Cyclomatic complexity
		Maintenance actions
	Efficiency	Utilization throughput
		Timing
	Portability	Standards compliance
	Usability	Operator errors
	Dependability	Failures
		Fault tolerance
Process performance	Process compliance	Reference model rating
		Process audit findings
	Process efficiency	Productivity
		Cycle time
	Process effectiveness	Defect containment
		Rework
Technology effectiveness	Technology suitability	Requirements coverage
	Impact	Technology impact
	Technology volatility	Baseline changes
Customer satisfaction	Customer feedback	Survey results
		Performance rating
	Customer support	Requests for support
		Support time

Table 9.3   Examples of Performance Measures

Performance Measures			
Goal/Question	*Metrics*	*Purpose*	*Measure of Success*
Schedule Performance	Tasks completed versus tasks planned at a point in time	Assess project progress. Apply project resources	100% completion of tasks on critical path; 90% all others
	Major milestones met versus milestones planned	Measure time efficiency	90% of major milestones met versus number planned during period
	Revisions to approved plan	Understand and control project "churn"	All revisions reviewed and approved
	Changes to customer requirements	Understand and manage scope and schedule	All changes managed through approved change process
	Project completion date	Award or penalize (depending on contract type)	Project completed on schedule (per approved plan)
Budget Performance	Revisions to cost estimates	Assess and manage project cost	100% of revisions are reviewed and approved
	Dollars spent versus dollars budgeted	Measure cost efficiency	Project completed within approved cost parameters
	Return on investment (ROI)	Track and assess performance of project investment portfolio	ROI (positive cash flow) begins according to plan
	Acquisition cost control	Assess and manage acquisition dollars	All applicable acquisition guidelines followed

Table 9.3 (continued) **Examples of Performance Measures**

Performance Measures			
Goal/Question	Metrics	Purpose	Measure of Success
Product Quality	Defects identified through quality activities	Track progress in, and effectiveness of, defect removal	90% of expected defects identified (e.g., via peer reviews, inspections)
	Test case failures versus number of cases planned	Assess product functionality and absence of defects	100% of planned test cases execute successfully (without errors)
	Number of service calls	Track customer problems	75% reduction after three months of operation
	Customer satisfaction index	Identify trends	95% positive rating
	Customer satisfaction trend	Improve customer satisfaction	5% improvement each quarter
	Number of repeat customers	Determine if customers are using the product multiple times (could indicate satisfaction with the product)	"X"% of customers use the product "X" times during a specified time period
	Number of problems reported by customers	Assess quality of project deliverables	100% of reported problems addressed within 72 hours
Compliance	Compliance with enterprise architecture model requirements	Track progress toward department-wide architecture model	Zero deviations without proper approvals

Table 9.3 (continued)   Examples of Performance Measures

Performance Measures			
Goal/Question	*Metrics*	*Purpose*	*Measure of Success*
	Compliance with interoperability requirements	Track progress toward system interoperability	Product works effectively within system portfolio
	Compliance with standards	Alignment, interoperability, consistency	No significant negative findings during architect assessments
	For Web site projects, compliance with style guide	To ensure standardization of Web site	All web sites have the same "look and feel"
	Compliance with Section 508 for use by disabled persons	To meet regulatory requirements	Persons with disabilities may access and utilize the functionality of the system
Redundancy	Elimination of duplicate or overlapping systems	Ensure return on investment	Retirement of 100% of identified systems
	Decreased number of duplicate data elements	Reduce input redundancy and increase data integrity	Data elements are entered once and stored in one database
	Consolidate help desk functions	Reduce $ spent on help desk support	Approved consolidation plan
Cost Avoidance	Easily upgraded system	Take advantage of COTS upgrades	Subsequent releases do not require major glue code project to upgrade
	Avoid costs of maintaining duplicate systems	Reduce IT costs	100% of duplicate systems have been identified and eliminated

Table 9.3 (continued)   Examples of Performance Measures

Performance Measures			
Goal/Question	Metrics	Purpose	Measure of Success
	System is maintainable	Reduce maintenance costs	New version (of COTS) does not require rework of glue code
Customer Satisfaction	System availability (up time)	Measure system availability	100% of requirement is met (e.g., 99% M-F, 8am to 6pm, and 90% S & S, 8am to 5pm)
	System functionality (meets customer's and/or user's needs)	Measure how well customer needs are being met	Positive trend in customer satisfaction survey(s)
	Absence of defects that impact customer	Number of defects removed during project life cycle	90% of defects expected were removed
	Ease of learning and use	Measure time to becoming productive	Positive trend in training survey(s)
	Time needed to answer calls for help	Manage/reduce response times	95% of severity one calls answered within 3 hours
	Rating of training course	Assess effectiveness and quality of training	90% of responses "good" or better
Business Goals/Mission	Functionality tracks reportable inventory	Validate system supports program mission	All reportable inventory is tracked in system
	Turnaround time in responding to Congressional queries	Improve customer satisfaction and national interests	Improve turnaround time from 2 days to 4 hours

Table 9.3 (continued) Examples of Performance Measures

Performance Measures			
Goal/Question	*Metrics*	*Purpose*	*Measure of Success*
	Maintenance costs	Track reduction of costs to maintain system	Reduce maintenance costs by 2/3 over 3-year period
	Standard desktop platform	Reduce costs associated with upgrading user's systems	Reduce upgrade costs by 40%
Productivity	Time needed to complete tasks	To evaluate estimates	Completions are within 10% of estimates
	Number of deliverables produced	Assess capability to deliver products	Improve product delivery 10% in each of the next 3 years
	Number of lines, functions, etc., completed per unit time	Measure developers work rate	Produced product within 10% of forecasted rate

projects have trouble implementing effective earned value processes. The reasons center around the implementation of adequate basic information to support the EV process. To perform effectively, EV requires (1) a current schedule, (2) a current work breakdown structure (WBS), (3) realistic cost projections allocated to task areas, and (4) a nonambiguous process for reporting milestone completion. Many software intensive projects do not have such data available for reasons already discussed, resulting in reported EV that does not reflect the true state of the program.

While there is not a single, consistent, accepted standard against which a project's EV is measured, the project develops this standard with the plan at inception. If this EV standard is flawed due to a poor plan or uncontrolled plan change, the productivity projections measured will be flawed. The standard for measuring EV throughout a system development project is a project activity network with the total project cost estimate allocated among the tasks in the activity network. Creating this activity network is the most difficult part of implementing the EV metric. Once

Table 9.4 Productivity Computation Worksheet

Effort	Included	Excluded
Software requirements analysis +		
Preliminary design +		
Detailed design +		
Code and unit test +		
CSC (component) integration and testing +		
CSCI (program unit) test +		
System integration through OT&E		
For each software life cycle phase marked above, the following labor categories are included:		
Software management +		
System/software engineers +		
Software designers +		
Software programmers +		
Software testers		

Is effort measured in person months or hours? _____

SLOC	Included	Excluded
Handwritten source lines of code +		
Data declaration statements +		
Comment statements +		
Automatically generated lines of code +		
Blank lines		
Continuation lines (if a logical line is physically written on more than one line, count the additional lines)		
New lines +		
Portion of preexisting software to be modified +		
Preexisting software not modified		

Table 9.4 (continued)   Productivity Computation Worksheet

If size is measured in functions:

Functions	Included	Excluded
New functions +		
Existing functions to be used as-is +		
Enhancements made to existing functions +		
Functionality provided by COTS packages +		
Other (define)		

this is done, measuring EV regularly throughout the life of a project is straightforward. According to Hayes and Over:

> A particular task's earned value is based on the percentage of the total planned project effort that the task will take. As tasks are completed, the task's planned value becomes earned value for the project. The project's earned value then becomes an indicator of the percentage of completed work. When tracked week by week, the project's earned value can be compared to its planned value to determine status, to estimate rate of progress, and to project the completion date for the project.[9]

Essential elements of an EV management (EVM) process are the allocation and specification of work to be performed through a work breakdown structure (WBS), a technique that allows you to break a large project into small manageable units of work that can be monitored and whose effectiveness can be tracked. A large project can be partitioned into smaller tasks that in turn can be subdivided, and so on. These tasks can be prioritized and scheduled over time so they can be addressed in a logical order consistent with the labor, material, and other resource constraints. The lowest level tasks in the WBS are known as *work packages*.

EV, WBS, and other techniques discussed here are applicable to any project of sufficient size when a single individual cannot perform it alone. They are just as appropriate for commercial activities such as banking as they are for aerospace projects such as satellite surveillance systems.

Using Earned Value Management

This section is intended as a brief overview of EVM. For readers who want more detail, many books and courses are dedicated to the topic. Earned value project management relies on the concepts of *planned value* and *earned value*. Each work package is assigned a budget along with start and end dates during project planning. The budget is known as *planned value* and is typically expressed in dollars (although it may be expressed in other units such as person hours).

The work package budget represents some portion of the overall resources budgeted to the project and is expressed in units that can be easily measured after work begins. The term *value* is used because it represents the positive contribution the work package makes to the project, as opposed to *cost*, which has the negative connotation — resources leaving the project. Each work package is scheduled and a planned value allocated to each work package. The *budget at completion* (BAC) is the total planned value for all the work packages. It is really a budget for completion.

As a project proceeds, work package progress can be tracked by recording the completed work by work package. This is called *earned value* because it represents the planned value earned by completing scheduled work. EV or completed work can be directly compared with planned value (scheduled work) and with the *actual cost* expended to perform the work in order to obtain a clear indication of how the project is progressing.

As illustrated in Figure 9.2, tracking progress through EV is accomplished through an S curve, a graph that shows cumulatively how a project budget is planned to be spent over time. The curve provides a graphical representation of how much value has been earned based on work completed versus how much money has been spent. The value of the curve is it provides an accurate representation of how the project is performing against plan based on actual progress, not by opinions or "spin." (Note: in standard EV terminology, schedule variance is not calendar time variance but variance in progress, that is, the difference between EV and the baseline plan expressed as hours or costs. Some models such as SEER-SEM have added a time variance as well quantifying variance in elapsed time.)

Figure 9.2 illustrates the actual costs of doing the work over a given period compared to the budget for the work performed and the budget for all work planned. The same graph can show how the value of the product increases over the same period based on work accomplished. Table 9.5 summarizes the values illustrated in Figure 9.2 that will be used in the EV examples.

The three curves on the graph represent:

> **Budgeted Cost for Work Scheduled (BCWS)** — Cumulative, time-phased budgets for all planned activities
> **Actual Cost of Work Performed (ACWP)** — Cumulative, time-phased real costs of work charged against completed activities
> **Budgeted Cost of Work Performed (BCWP)** — Cumulative, time-phased, planned costs of the work; allocated to completed activities

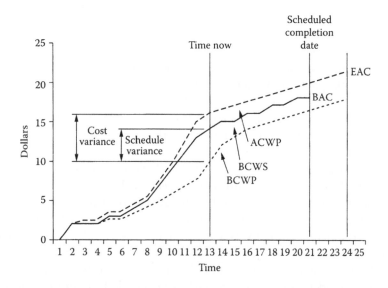

Figure 9.2   Earned value S curve.[10]

Table 9.5   Earned Value Numbers Based on Figure 9.2

Name	Acronym	Value from Figure 9.2
Budgeted cost for work performed	BCWP	10 (time now)
Budgeted cost for work scheduled	BCWS	14 (time now)
Actual cost for work performed	ACWP	16 (time now)
Budget at complete	BAC	17 (time complete)
Estimate at complete	EAC	23 (time complete)

The BCWS curve is derived from the WBS, the project budget, and the project master schedule. The cost of each work package is calculated and the cumulative cost of completed work packages is shown based on the planned completion dates shown in the master schedule.

The ACWP curve is determined by actual measurement of the work completed. Sources could be actual costs recorded from invoices and time sheets. This may appear to be a daunting task but it can be very simple with sufficient planning and organizing.

The BCWP is calculated from the measured work complete and the budgeted costs for that work.

Both schedule and cost variances can be calculated in monetary terms from the data needed to produce the S curves. Schedule variance is the difference between the EV and the planned budget.

$$SV = BCWP - BCWS$$

Cost variance is the difference between the EV and the actual costs of the work.

$$CV = BCWP - ACWP$$

The S curve shown in Figure 9.2 shows that the cost to date (ACWP) is higher than estimated cost (BCWP). Based on this information, what is a reasonable estimate of the cost at project completion? Or in EVM terms, what is a reasonable estimate at completion (EAC)? Is it reasonable for the project manager to take the position that the project cannot make up the cost overrun to date, but that from this point on the project will meet the budget (initial estimated cost) for each task? The cost performance index (CPI) and to-complete performance index (TCPI) quantify the reasonableness of the EAC. The CPI metric is calculated as the following ratio:

$$CPI = BCWP/ACWP$$

The CPI at the report date (*Time Now* on the graph) of Figure 9.2 is 0.625 (CPI = 10/16 = 0.625). This is a measure of productivity in meeting the estimated cost. When CPI is less than 1, actual project productivity is less than that needed to meet the cost estimate. When CPI is greater than 1, actual project productivity is better than that needed to meet the estimated cost. A CPI of 1 means that the productivity to date is exactly what is needed to meet the estimated cost.

The schedule performance index (SPI) is defined as:

$$SPI = BCWP/BCWS$$

If the SPI is less than 1, the project is earning less value than was originally scheduled. In the example, SPI is 0.71 (SPI = 10/14 = 0.71).

The following definitions are provided as a quick summary of the basic concepts and formulas used in the earned value process.

$$\text{Estimate at completion (EAC)}_{min} = (BAC - BCWP) + ACWP$$

EAC_{min} assumes that although there was an overrun to date, the rest of the project will perform to budget.

$$\text{Estimate at completion (EAC)}_{mid} = [(BAC - BCWP)/CPI] + ACWP$$

EAC_{mid} assumes the overrun to date and that the rest of the project will perform at the same level demonstrated to date.

Estimate at completion $(EAC)_{max}$ = [(BAC − BCWP)/(CPI x SPI)] + ACWP

EAC_{max} assumes that the overruns to date are indicative of faulty processes and will continue to degrade throughout the remaining portion of the project.

In our example from Figure 9.2:

$$EAC_{min} = (17 - 10) + 16 = 23$$

$$EAC_{mid} = [(17 - 10)/0.625] + 16 = 27.2$$

$$EAC_{max} = [(17 - 10)/(0.625 \times 0.71)] + 16 = 31.8$$

TCPI is the same productivity measure as CPI, but applies to the remainder of the project where this productivity measure is based on the value chosen for EAC. The equation is:

$$TCPI = (BAC - BCWP)/(EAC - ACWP)$$

$TCPI_{min}$ = (BAC − BCWP)/(EAC_{min} − ACWP) = (17 − 10)/(23 − 16) = 1.*

$TCPI_{mid}$ = (BAC − BCWP)/(EAC_{mid} − ACWP) = (17 − 10)/(27.2 − 16) = 0.625

$TCPI_{max}$ = (BAC − BCWP)/(EAC_{max} − ACWP) = (17 − 10)/(31.8 − 16) = 0.44

EAC_{min} is based on achieving the budgeted productivity from the report date all the way to the end of the development. In this example, the budget productivity is much higher than the actual productivity to date. This sudden, extreme improvement in productivity (from 0.625 to 1) is nearly impossible for a software development team that has performed below planned productivity up to this point in a project.

Estimating EAC_{min} in Figure 9.2 to be $23M by assuming the cost overrun to date would not be overcome and assuming from this point on all tasks will be completed at the allocated budget does not seem reasonable. Experience shows such feats rarely happen. Unless specific measures are put in place immediately to significantly improve productivity, the $27.2M or $31.8M estimate for EAC is much more realistic than the $23M.

---

* By definition, $TCPI_{min}$ will always equal 1 because TCPI is the productivity for the remainder of the project and EAC_{min} is based on performing to budget for the remainder of the project.

When Reality Sets In

Brian Marick, a long-time professional software testing consultant, pointed out the real issue that impacts the ability of an organization to meet its initial productivity projections:

> The real complexity in our jobs is that all planning is done under conditions of uncertainty and ignorance. The code isn't the only thing that changes. Schedules slip. New milestones are added for new features. Features are cut from the release. During development, everyone — marketers, developers and testers — comes to understand better what the product is really for.[11]

Dwight Eisenhower pointed out one issue that defeats planning success: "The plan is nothing; the planning is everything." Many software organizations focus on the physical documents, the project plans, and forget their real value as blueprints to enable a project to meet its commitments. The plans made at the beginning of a project, that select and frame the processes, determine the practices used, and provide management controls establish how the commitments of the program are to be met.

When initial estimates are made and initial plans for development are produced, there is a certainty that "this time we'll get it right, we won't make the same mistakes we made last time." Only when the imprecisions of the real project environment take over does reality set in. If a project cannot produce quickly enough for any reason (act of God, technology shortfall, management or staff attitude or culture, process uncertainty or if its size or complexity grows substantially), the estimate used to develop the plan is compromised and may be largely invalidated.

Despite the desires of managers to plan and implement truly risk-free projects, and deliver products expected by their customers within cost and schedule constraints, a difficult reality must be addressed: software projects can only implement those processes that can be accommodated by the money, time, people, and other resources available.

Organizations must understand their resource limitations and creatively plan the best possible processes that will result in the lowest risk projects. Often, increasing early spending on practices such as inspections may increase the short-term budgets while decreasing the long-term cost exposure of the project by significantly lowering rework. More money and time spent on defining, analyzing, and specifying good requirements lowers potential exposure during implementation, testing, and delivery. Tighter configuration management (CM) processes implemented from the onset minimize the risk of wasted effort. Sometimes, when budget and time are unrealistic, you must invest in the process in order to minimize downstream costs and schedule requirements.

"Shoestring" Project Environments

Few projects have sufficient money or time to implement the processes and schedules they feel are required to satisfy the project commitments and expectations of the users with little or no risk. This is often not the result of poor or flawed estimates, but rather, the result of a flawed negotiation in which management and customer struggle to fit user requirements into a predetermined budget or schedule constraint. Many factors that may contribute to this problem are often not addressed by the negotiation team:

- Management pressure to "get it done"
- Failure of negotiators to understand the reasons for processes that underlie the estimate
- Lack of understanding of software to be produced and the required process steps
- Audits and special tests required prior to delivery
- A host of other factors that drive the estimate

Once agreements on price and schedule are reached, a project takes on a life of its own. A baseline is set and cannot be changed without major difficulty even if the time or available funds prove inadequate when the real requirements of the project become obvious.

When this happens, when project commitments seem to exceed the available money or time, the answer is to renegotiate the commitments, hope for the best, or address and manage the risk through implementation of a project environment that provides the maximum potential of meeting the commitments within the agreed budget and schedule. This "shoestring" project environment requires the management of productivity with as much rigor as is usually applied to the management of the cost, schedule, technical, and contractual aspects of the project.

While productivity management should be the concern of all project managers, it is an absolute requirement of those who are resource- or schedule-challenged. This planning and subsequent tracking against predefined productivity goals must be in place early in a project and pursued vigorously throughout its life. Tom DeMarco, in his novel, *The Deadline*,[12] noted how productivity is lost on a software project:

A day lost at the beginning of a project hurts just as much as a day lost at the end ... There are infinitely many ways to lose a day ... but not even one way to get one back.

Process Performance

Every software project, whether large or small, complex or simple, in-house or supporting a client, follows a process to fulfill its commitments. A process is the integration of:

- **Project rules** — product and process standards
- **Tools** — automated and manual facilities that enable the implementation of the process requirements
- **Procedures** — a specific set of practices that determine how the project implements the process requirements

The various processes used significantly influence and constrain how a project is managed. For example, a project that does not rigorously develop and maintain a schedule will have difficulty tracking earned value against it. Projects that use highly concurrent engineering methods may find it difficult to perform configuration management and maintain traceability between architecture and requirements.

Next to people skills, the processes used are the single most important determinants of productivity and major sources of project risk. The processes must be planned, scaled to the cost, schedule, and customer constraints, and rigorously enforced. They (project rules, tools, and procedures) involve the integration of many disparate methodologies that must work seamlessly to fulfill the objectives of the project within the established constraints and commitments. The project environment must be integrated into a cohesive and seamless process consistent with its specific needs, objectives and constraints and the goals of the organization that has project responsibility.

Many overcommitted projects with serious cost and schedule constraints often try to address the environment needs through bizarre, unproven processes that promise great productivity gains, but allow only limited time, money, and other resources to deal with any productivity impacts when the gains are not fully realized. These impacts can result from needs for staff to receive unplanned training, implementation difficulties, staff resistance, or simply the failure of cutting-edge methodologies to fulfill their promised benefits. Others — worse — rush to the cheapest solution they can find in an attempt to save time and money. This price-first mentality can result in the applications of methods or tools that are worse than nothing. They do not fulfill project needs, they consume significant resources, and they must be replaced during the project to meet requirements or to correct issues related to use of the method or tool.

For example, on an assessment completed some years ago, an inexperienced manager tried to explain at great length that he had no need for testing because he was using object-oriented design. It was obvious to everyone except that manager that the lack of testing would result in unacceptable quality and a product — if one was produced —that would not meet user expectations.[13]

Technology Solutions

Problems related to defining a process such as consistency with basic requirements, ability of staff to implement process, experience of the customer, and availability of essential support infrastructure are often compounded by technology professionals who are asked their opinion by management concerning which method or tool to use but are not well equipped to account for productivity realities related to resource limitations.

A technology-centric focus on technical flash, efficiency of design, and cutting edge technologies can result in projects that are more expensive than they need to be, even though the method or tool promised better performance at lower cost and in a shortened time frame: the silver bullet.

It is very tempting for managers to jump to a "right solution" based on promises made by the developers or vendors of the method or tool, but the right solution is the wrong solution if the project cannot afford to build and support it. Certain questions must be asked to ensure the solution is really appropriate:

- What specifically is the need to be addressed through the selection and use of the method or tool?
- Has anyone in the project used it before and, if so, what was his or her experience?
- Are any other solutions available; if there are, why have we not considered them?
- How will this method deal with the cost, resource, and schedule constraints we face?
- Is there any quantitative evidence that the solution will address the projected resource or schedule shortfalls facing the project?
- Will the methods or tools integrate with other methods and tools used by the project and provide products that can be inspected to reveal and remove defects?

- What resources are available to support the application of the methods or tools; are they the right ones based on the risk of the solution?
- Considering the experience of the staff, the expectations of the customer, and the reality of the constraints, can we creatively define a way to use this method or tool to meet and satisfy the project requirements within acceptable risk?

Understanding Process Selection Constraints

Ideally all process decisions should be definite before completion of the estimate and agreements by the various stakeholders, but this is rarely the case. The organization responsible for the development must address a single, specific issue: what processes, when integrated together, will support the productivity commitments made by the project through the estimate? When selecting and planning, several items constrain the selection:

- Do we have enough money, time, qualified personnel, and other resources to adequately satisfy the commitments made to users if we use this process, method, or tool?
- Do we understand why the technology is needed and how it will better position the project to achieve its commitments within the cost and schedule constraints?
- What are the essential training, installation, and support requirements to fully realize the promised productivity and schedule benefits?
- Do we have evidence that the promised benefits will actually be realized in time to help this project?

It is tempting to start with a technical solution in mind: we need to use XYZ design method and the ABC suite of tools so we can reduce our costs by 10 percent and shorten our schedule by 6 months. This approach, however, specifies a solution before the problem is understood. Using a model like SEER-SEM enables you to make realistic evaluations of such choices.

Perhaps a different approach — evaluating why the estimate and schedule are inadequate and by how much and what risks and obstacles realistically can impact them — will serve your goals as well or better. If you start by defining the specifics of the problem, you can brainstorm many options that fill these needs in different ways. One way to help define the specific problems is by looking at the top ten cost drivers of your program. Some (such as security requirements) will be uncontrollable.

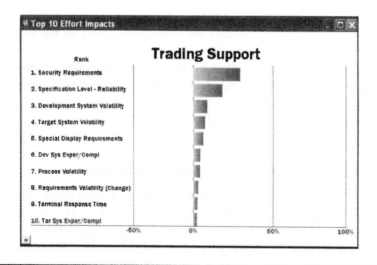

Figure 9.3   Example top ten effort–cost impacts.

Others will be controllable by management decisions. Figure 9.3 is a top ten chart illustrating effort–cost impacts. Note that the top ten drivers will vary from project to project.

Five simple steps that will allow a better selection of appropriate methodologies and help define a process for realistic and responsive software process are listed below.

1. Define high level process considerations that have the potential to negatively impact the project, raise project risk, or delay completion of acceptable deliverables. Projects with significant cost and schedule risk often try to use less mature or unproven processes to satisfy aggressive schedule or cost commitments. Also, a project may consider increasing short-term investments in activities or disciplines such as structured inspections or peer reviews of requirements, plans, and architectures of other project-related products to lower the risk of unplanned for, late stage rework — a genuine productivity killer. Many studies have shown that without early identification and control of defects, late stage rework can exceed 50 percent of total program cost.[14] One study showed the effort required just to find a defect increased from 1.2 hours early in the project to 1.5 hours late in the project for nonsevere defects and 1.4 early in the project to 3 hours in the project for severe defects.[15]

2. Define the user expectations for the system and rigorously control development to meet them. Understanding who will use the system and how it will be used can significantly reduce the difficulty

meeting the needs of the user and controlling the requirements growth. By involving the user in the development process and assuring that they play a primary role in defining and evaluating requirements, the complexity of the system can usually be reduced and delays associated with user-caused rework can be minimized or even avoided.

3. Develop and enforce a management, project monitoring, and reporting process that will provide positive control over the expenditures of resources and allow the anticipation of problems through metrics and rigorous risk management. While all projects should include these processes, the degree of rigor and the expenditure of resources to support them will increase based on how restrictive the cost and schedule constraints become. Project surprises that result in resource or schedule growth must be minimized, particularly if they impact already constrained baselines.

4. Understand and focus on the nonfunctional requirements such as security, performance, and reliability determining whether the user needs 24–7–365 support without failure, the real degree of protection required, and the minimum acceptable response time required based on actual operational needs rather than perceived wants. Is it sufficient if the system is available 95 percent of the time during working hours and casual browsers will not stumble into it by accident? How serious are the impacts of security breaches and availability failures? Does your system contain sensitive or controversial information that would make you a target for attacks? Very reliable and secure solutions are expensive, often exceeding the cost of less secure systems dramatically.

5. As cost and schedule constraints become more stringent, the management of the basic project baseline must move from emphasizing control of productivity to increased control of product size, requirements, and functional capabilities. There is a strong and direct correlation of the size of the product, the costs of developing it, and the time required to develop it. Figure 9.4 illustrates this size–cost relationship. Traceability must be established and maintained and an allocated size budget must be maintained and verified as the architecture and code are developed. As product size grows, the productivity impacts must be addressed and, if required, resolved through the adjustment of product functionality. (Proper size estimates with growth included can reduce the impact of this issue. See Chapter 5.)

You must define a process that matches the reality of the project constraints. Then select specific methodologies and tools that provide the

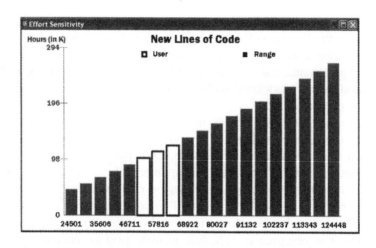

Figure 9.4 Size–cost relationship.

highest potential to support the productivity required to meet the cost and schedule commitments (not arbitrary profit goals — real contractual or agreed-to budgets and schedules). These methodologies must be proven and be consistent with the capabilities of the organization and the project staff. They must be sufficiently mature so that unexpected negative results caused by methodology shortfalls, inconsistencies, or implementation problems do not arise. When planning for and selecting methodologies and defining the software process, keep in mind that as the schedule and budget tighten, management acceptance of more risk in the form of using cutting-edge or less mature methodologies is usually the by-product.

Product Quality and Stability

Richard Stevens (inventor of the DOORS Requirements Tool) once stated, "You want a hundred million dollar system by next month with no defined acceptance criteria. I can build it!"[16] This statement points out the need to negotiate what your customer wants, when your customer wants it, and what the product needs to look like early, before you start to work. If projects are to meet established productivity targets, you must have a clear definition of what products are to be delivered, what they have to look like, and what the acceptable minimum level of quality is.

Quality has a number of different meanings when it relates to a software project. One meaning deals with the conformance of the various deliverables with requirements or expectations of the customer. A second deals with the density of defects in the requirements, architecture, code, or critical project information. A third definition deals with the adequacy of the product to meet the operational needs, expectations, and realities of the user. Every project must decide what *quality* means based on the program objectives. Unplanned rework can destroy any hope a project has to meet or exceed productivity projections that serve as the basis of any software estimate.

Defects

A defect is defined as a situation in which a product does not meet a specified characteristic or as deviations from the expected outcome of a task. Defect removal is costly and it is virtually impossible to remove all defects without unlimited staff and an unlimited schedule. Evidence indicates that a significant number of problems (around 80 percent) in software development such as, defects, rework, changes, and maintenance efforts, are actually caused by a small proportion of modules (around 20 percent). This is known as the 80:20 rule and it allows the early prediction and identification of a small proportion of risky modules.

A corollary to the 80:20 rule is Barry Boehm's 20:80 rule stating that 20 percent of the system executes 80 percent of the time. The risky modules should be selected from this 20 percent. This concept allows software developers to focus quality assurance activities such as testing and inspections on those modules that can result in a significant improvement in the quality of the software products and the presence and density of defects.

Defects should be tracked formally at each project phase or activity. Figure 9.5 is a sample defect tracking chart that can be used to track insertion and removal versus estimated or expected number of defects. If defect discovery is slower than the estimate, it could be a sign of oncoming schedule slippage. Data should be collected to determine the effectiveness of methods used to discover defects and to correct them. This approach will not accommodate a *private defect* —one that is detected and removed without being recorded. Defect tracking allows an organization to characterize error propensity and then focus its resources appropriately.

It is more economical and effective to find and fix defects before they are discovered during testing. Inspections can detect potential defects and focus corrective action toward the work product and the processes that produce the work product. An inspection is a formal facilitated meeting conducted to find defects in software and other products at or near the point of insertion of the defect.

This early identification results in the need for a project to expend significantly fewer resources for rework. Although numbers vary by project and environment, the average cost to fix a defect conforms to what is known as the 1:10:100 rule: a defect that costs $1 to fix in requirements

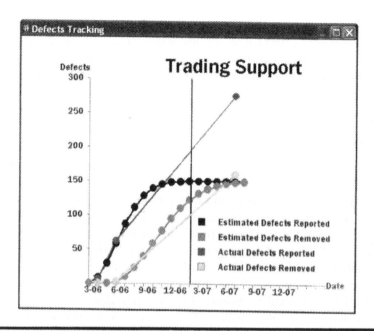

Figure 9.5   Defect tracking chart.

or design costs $10 to fix in a traditional test phase and $100 to fix after the product goes into production (live) use. A number of factors increase defect removal costs as a project progresses; they include:

- The ripple effect of changes throughout a system or application; the ripple leads to essential changes to related components as the product is more completely developed.
- Repeating past tasks (updating requirements, redesigns, recoding) to correct observed defects and updating completed documentation and support products.
- Notifying project workers and users of changes and requalifying releases and installed system configurations.

While some degree of rework is a factor in all estimates, late defect removal is costly and time consuming. Changes at the end of a project add risk and the options available for correcting a defect may decrease greatly as a project moves to completion. Additionally, the developers who produced the defective design or code may no longer be available. The need to find defects as early as possible in a project places an emphasis on defect prevention accomplished through defect measurement and analysis. This measurement and analysis information is then used to modify the processes based on feedback to identify the causes of the existing defect insertion and correct the process to avoid future defect insertion.

Code Inspections

Inspections can be performed on any product (test plans, procedures, users manuals, codes, code fixes) to improve defect detection efficiency of any process that creates the product. Inspections are based on the inspection process developed by Fagan.[17]

Inspections are more rigorous and formal processes than walk-throughs. Users of the method report significant improvements in quality, development costs, and maintenance costs. Capers Jones[18] estimates that the average software company in the United States releases products with 15 percent of the defects still in the product. Companies that rigorously employ inspections are approaching 1 percent defects remaining in released products. Jones noted that a company can never have satisfied customers if it tolerates 15 percent defects in released products. Inspections differ from more classical reviews in several respects:

- Statistical quality control on the document; inspections track a number of metrics designed to improve the inspection process
- Statistical process control of the producing organization
- Emphasis on earliest possible defect detection
- Emphasis on immediate and controlled correction; tracking to assure correction
- Trained and certified inspection leaders (moderators)
- Moderator leadership (chief moderator concept)
- Specialized roles to increase defect total find rate for team
- Specialized checklists for each document type
- Formal entry criteria for inspections start-up
- Formal exit criteria for inspection completion
- Measurable criteria for repeating unsatisfactory inspections
- Pareto analysis: identifying error-prone components
- Experiential optimum rates of work enforced
- Specific devices and techniques for avoiding individual blame
- Restriction of author from leading, reading, explaining, or defending documents
- Prohibition of discussion of defect assertion
- Author-only control over correction
- Subjection of all important documents to inspection
- Peer inspection; everyone learns on the job
- Two-hour maximum duration to combat tiredness factor

The purpose of an inspection is to identify as many potential defects as possible in the work product being inspected. An inspection requires preparation before the meeting, a skilled meeting leader, knowledgeable inspectors, and follow-up after the meeting to ensure that any necessary

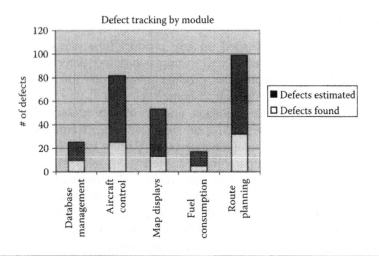

Figure 9.6 Chart of error-prone modules.

rework is accomplished. The author of the work product being inspected has final determination of which potential defects are actual defects. Data captured from inspections can be used to identify patterns in defect detection and prevention. Figure 9.6 illustrates error-prone modules.

Staff members who participate in the inspection process should be trained in the process and in the facilitation skills essential to the success of inspection-based techniques. Many attempts at implementing inspections fail due to damaged relationships caused by inspections, usually because the reviewers have not been trained in giving interactive criticism. In addition, it is easy to drift into critiquing the producer instead of the product.

While it appears on the surface that inspections will take more time, they can actually reduce overall project time by as much as 15 percent. Lower defect rates will reduce costs and increase the quality of the release. Walk-throughs and inspections are certainly affected by cultural issues. While cultural resistance to formal and intrusive processes such as inspections often precludes their acceptance, the obvious benefits and critical role such procedures play in minimizing rework impacts makes management persistence in pursuing their use a critical factor in managing risks.

The use of inspections, the management, and the assurance of the product against quality targets requires that a project follow consistent processes that can accommodate the inspection requirement. Management must reinforce the importance of processes or else participants will ignore them. There are simple and effective ways to dramatically improve the quality of software and reduce the costs and schedule related to rework. Not only is overall quality improved, but project time is reduced. The keys to success are having an inspection process in place and remaining aware of interpersonal issues.

Staffing Levels

One of the easiest metrics to track against plan is the actual number of staff performing the work. If this metric deviates more than 10 percent from the initial plan, immediate steps must be taken to correct the over- or under staffing. When a project falls behind schedule, one of the first places to look is staff level. Figure 9.7 shows tracking of planned against actual staffing. The project illustrated started out in trouble and over the next few months appears to have made no successful attempts to correct the problem.

The use of automated tools such as SEER-SEM PPMC (described in Chapter 12) can greatly increase the effectiveness of these processes in managing large or small software developments.

Team Performance

The equalizer in adjusting productivity projections to unrealistic constraints is for management to focus on the management and "jelling" of teams rather than more classical management techniques that concentrate on individuals. The management processes used to maximize team cohesion differ significantly from the normal, classical approaches but the productivity payoff can be enormous. As discussed in the second edition of

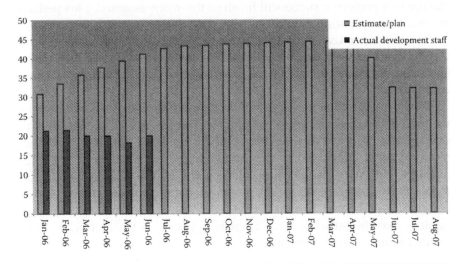

Figure 9.7 Actual staff versus planned staff.

Peopleware by DeMarco and Lister,[19] for virtually any performance metric you define, you can expect the following:

- The best people outperform the worst by about 10:1.
- The best performer is about 2.5 times better than the median performer.
- The half who are better-than-median performers outdo the other half by more than 2:1.

While it is difficult to assure that a team will jell, the productivity benefits, particularly on severely cost- and schedule-constrained projects, make the attempt an essential element in managing a project to achieve productivity commitments. Most managers do not manage as if they have more people worries than technical worries; they manage as if technology is their principal concern. They tend to focus on the technical instead of the human side of work because it is easier. Human interactions are complicated but in organizations with the best chemistry, managers devote their energy to building and maintaining healthy staff chemistries.

Elements of this strategy may include making a cult of quality: only perfect is close enough for us. Quality is one of the strongest catalysts for team formation, setting an effective team apart from the rest of the organization that does not have the same focus. While extraordinary quality does not make good short-term economic sense, it always pays off in the long term. A team takes pride in achieving an extraordinary standard and working as a team to achieve it.

A manager who focuses on team management provides a satisfying closure to a project: a successful finish of the work assigned, plus perhaps an occasional confirmation along the way that everything is on target. Team members must acquire the habit of succeeding together and liking it. Effective team managers take pains to partition the work into pieces and make sure that each piece has a substantive demonstration of its own completion.

While many other management techniques can lead to jelled teams, the goal is to build a sense of teamwork. The essence of successful team management is to have everyone pull in the same direction and then motivate team members to the point where nothing, not even their manager, can stop the progress. One of the hardest management challenges is to provide strategic rather than tactical direction. Teams consist of peers, equals who function as equals. Team-based management recognizes that the structure of a team is network, not a hierarchy. Good teams require little leadership.

Summary

Managing to productivity targets has been a challenge facing software projects for many years. Barry Boehm documented many of today's software management problems[20] in 1976:

> **Poor planning** — Leads to large amounts of wasted effort because tasks are unnecessarily performed, overdone, poorly synchronized, or poorly interfaced.
> **Poor control** — Even a good plan is useless when it is not kept up to date and used to manage the project.
> **Poor resource estimation** — Without a firm idea of how much time and effort a task should take, a manager is in a poor position to exercise control.
> **Unsuitable management personnel** — Software personnel tend to respond to problem situations as designers rather than as managers.
> **Poor accountability structure** — Projects are generally organized and run with diffuse delineation of responsibilities.
> **Inappropriate success criteria** — Minimizing development costs and schedules will generally yield a hard-to-maintain product.

There is little argument that while the dimensions and characteristics of the problems have changed, this core set still applies to today's projects. Applying the processes and techniques detailed in this chapter can make it possible for program managers to manage to productivity targets for successful project completion.

Endnotes

1. Stutzke, Richard D. *Estimating Software-Intensive Systems*. Upper Saddle River: Pearson Education Inc., 2005.
2. Galorath, Dan. Personal experience.
3. Joint Logistics Commanders Joint Group on Systems Engineering. *Practical Software Measurement: A Guide to Objective Program Insight 2.1*, March 1996.
4. Alexander, Ian. "Metrics, Sizing and Cost Estimation Quotations." *Proverbs: Requirements Engineering Proverbs, Sayings, Maxims, and Quotations*, 1997–2004. http://easyweb.easynet.co.uk/~iany/consultancy/proverbs.htm
5. U.S. Department of Defense. *Practical Software Measurement (PSM): A Foundation for Objective Project Management 3.1a*. Washington, D.C., 1998.

6. Florac, William A., Robert Park, and Anita D. Carleton. *Practical Software Measurement: Measuring for Process Management and Improvement.* Pittsburgh: Software Engineering Institute, 1997.

7. Florac, William A., Robert Park, and Anita D. Carleton. *Practical Software Measurement: Measuring for Process Management and Improvement.* Pittsburgh: Software Engineering Institute, 1997.

8. U.S. Department of Energy. *Basic Performance Measures for Information Technology Projects.* Washington, D.C., January 15, 2002.

9. Hayes, W. and J. W. Over. *The Personal Software Process: An Empirical Study of the Impact of PSP on Individual Engineers.* Pittsburgh: Software Engineering Institute, December 1997.

10. Anonymous. "Earned Value Management Part 1." *Project* Magazine, November 2000. http://www.projectmagazine.com/nov00/evm1.html [September 2004]

11. Sehl, Georg. "Quotations." *Software Testing and Quality Assurance: Quotations from Books and Articles.* December 2004. http://gsehl.editme.com/TestingQuotes

12. DeMarco, Tom. *The Deadline.* New York: Dorset House, 1997.

13. Evans, Mike. Personal experience.

14. Boehm, Barry W. and Victor Basili. "Software Defect Reduction: Top Ten List." *IEEE Software,* January 2001.

15. Shull, Forrest et al. "What We Have Learned about Fighting Defects." *Proceedings of Eighth IEEE Symposium on Software Metrics,* 2002.

16. Alexander, Ian. "Metrics, Sizing and Cost Estimation Quotations." *Proverbs: Requirements Engineering Proverbs, Sayings, Maxims, and Quotations,* 1997–2004. http://easyweb.easynet.co.uk/~iany/consultancy/proverbs.htm

16a. http://cs.mwsu.edu/~stringfe/courseinfo/5443lectures/Pareto.ppt#276,3, BasicCodeMetrics

17. Fagan, M.E. "Advances in Software Inspections," SE-12.7. *IEEE Transactions on Software Engineering,* July 1986. 744.

18. Jones, C. "The Pragmatics of Software Process Improvements." *Software Engineering Technical Council Newsletter,* Winter 1996, 1.

19. Demarco, Tom and Timothy Lister. *Peopleware: Productive Projects and Teams.* New York: Dorset House, 1999.

20. Yourdon, Ed. *Classics in Software Engineering.* Indianapolis: Yourdon Press, 1979.

Chapter 10

Risk Management Process

The time to repair the roof is when the sun is shining.

John F. Kennedy

Introduction

The risk management process has long been a means to manage the uncertainty that exists in all endeavors, and more to the point in projects whose goal is to provide a product with significant software content to satisfy some identified set of needs and requirements. In today's world, where profit margins are shrinking, the competition to acquire work is significant, users and customers may have inflated views of what is possible, and the frequency and magnitude of technological change are dramatic and increasing, the management of risk is not an option. It is an absolute necessity if project success must be more than an accident.

This chapter describes the essential relationship between estimation and risk management. It describes the differences between those factors that are actual risks and those that represent problems, issues, and concerns. It describes the birth, life, and death of a risk and explains how this cycle layers on the project cycle. It also describes how realistic, nonbureaucratic, and lean risk management processes can be planned, implemented, and supported to help managers avoid the impacts that flow from estimates.

These risks normally result from estimates that were not representative of the reasonable size and resource realities of the project or became obsolete because of changing product requirements or processes. This chapter also provides examples of worksheets and describes risks and indicators related to size and cost estimation issues, shortfalls, and trade-offs. Finally, it discusses the costs versus benefits associated with the application of risk management in a typical project.

History of Risk Management

While the need to be aware of and avoid risks in software projects has always existed, risk management did not really gain traction within the software community until the late 1980s. Barry Boehm, a leading expert in software processes, developed and published his concept of the *spiral model*[1] — a risk-driven, iterative model that capitalizes on the evolutionary nature of the software development process to define a life-cycle model that allows for requirements evolution and growth while minimizing the risk of uncontrolled change that has plagued software projects since the inception of the industry.[2]

Many initiatives within academia, government, and the private sector have focused on the management of risk in project environments, but risk management gained popularity only through initiatives conducted by the Software Engineering Institute (SEI) at Carnegie Mellon University and the Best Practices Initiative conducted by the Software Program Managers Network (SPMN) for the U.S. Department of Defense (DoD). In 1990, the SEI Risk Program was chartered to develop risk methods and act as a technology transfer agent to bring the discipline to industry. The program led to development of the risk management paradigm and the process of taxonomy-based risk identification that became widely used.

The SPMN chartered a group known as the Airlie Software Council (a group of leading software experts) to identify and document best practices proven to improve productivity while lowering cost and reducing risk.[3] The SPMN then used a variety of methods to bring these practices to academic, government, and private sector organizations intent on improving their processes and the bottom line metrics of cost, schedule, and user satisfaction.

The initial nine best practices were released in 1995 and then updated in 1999 as a set of sixteen. In both the initial and later releases, members of the Airlie Software Council reached an absolute consensus that the number one best practice — the one that had the most significant impact on the success of a project — was risk management. While not implementing risk management did not guarantee project failure, implementing the process effectively went a long way to enabling success. Risk management is now a required discipline both for DoD programs and for many private sector organizations seeking to improve their software processes and gain more predictable and consistent project results.

Why does this book on size and cost estimation have a secondary focus on risk management? Many of the really critical issues that make it difficult for a project to meet budget, schedule, quality, and operational commitments are rooted in the decisions and trade-offs made during the estimation process and in the degree of rigor used. Schedule, cost, and reliability are major risks in and of themselves that must be managed. During the estimation process, future project risks can seem to be little more than issues to be ignored, addressed, or deferred. Such issues include insufficient time to perform the estimate, few or inadequate requirements, volatile system concepts or requirements, lack of user or stakeholder participation, unproven teams or techniques, and unknown or changing predeployment certification requirements.

Over the past years we have been involved with many projects, some large, some small; some in the public sector, and others in the private and academic sectors. Although the risks varied by potential impact, category, type, and specifics, every project involved some risk. A basic thread, however, ran through every one of them: it is much better to know about a risk early than to experience the impact that results when the problem occurs.

Frank Doherty, a senior manager supporting large government programs, in a recent interview[4] discussed how the early visibility of risks can significantly benefit any project. He outlined the key benefits and why the process is essential to a project's health and well-being.

Q. Why do think risk management has worked so well in your organization?

A. We start early. We capture risks before they have a chance to transition to problems. We continuously look for risk in the plans we make, the estimates we produce, the concepts and requirements we develop, and in any other factors that we use to define the constraints of the project and the commitments made by the organization while we can still change them without significant cost or project turmoil. We really take risk management seriously.

Q. Give me some examples.

A. As we define our processes we bring in an objective third party to ask what can go wrong. They often find many issues that we treat as high impact risks. In many cases we change the processes to minimize the potential effects. In others, we track the risk and look for increasing probability of occurrence and the need to mitigate the effect. This early mitigation helps us to avoid associated cost, schedule slips, and potential rework due to excessive defects, all of which can be significant.

Q. Did the organizations interfacing with the project have as high an opinion of the benefits of risk management as you do?

A. Our current project is really unique in that risk management is a priority, not only in my shop, but it is also supported by our current customers, stakeholders, and others interfacing with the project. The attitude toward risk is that risks found and mitigated early are better than risks we don't know about. In my experience, this general acceptance of risk management is not usual. Most managers that I have worked with are not as open to candid views of what can go wrong. It's refreshing and is working well on this project.

Q. Where do you think this will go?

A. I can't see any reason why the emphasis on risk management should change. The process is working well; we have identified and are mitigating significant risks and thus avoiding potential disasters. On a project as complex as this, there are many risks that, if they became problems, the impacts on the project might not be controllable. By identifying risks early and taking steps to mitigate them, we avoid the impact, minimize the problems that we have to deal with, and ensure that most of the commitments we made are realistic.

The commitment to manage risk early in a project — particularly when the initial estimates are produced and during the process of developing the system concepts and initial requirements — and to maintain the process as an integral part of the project culture often means the difference between success and failure. Successful project managers maintain focus on their project's critical success factors.[5]

Despite the many arguments in favor of risk management and its obvious benefits, the myriad of examples of its success, endorsements by organizations that buy or build software, and the obvious need to anticipate and manage the frequency and impact of unexpected problems, it is still a hard sell. Real risk management is not just having a plan and providing some resources to "fill a square." To be effective, risk management must involve proactive participation by all levels in the acquirer and supplier organizations, continuous identification and analysis of risk based on a preplanned process, and a commitment by project management to use the information to make decisions and manage the project.

In performing project assessments over many years, we have observed numerous factors that contribute to a resistance to risk management. Two seem to be most common: the organizational culture and the difficulty in distinguishing between common problems and true risks. We have found that an organization's culture can inhibit project managers from both understanding the true natures of risks and reporting them to higher management, despite the fact that risk management processes and tools are straightforward and easy to plan and implement.

Secondly, the problems that are common to all projects, such as unexpected attrition, loss of funding, and unanticipated requirements do not necessarily in and of themselves constitute risks. The inability to distinguish them can lead to the belief that identified risks translate to immediate problems that require prompt and often dramatic action and to the belief that common problems constitute dire risk. By confusing the two, project managers are often inhibited in honestly reporting actual risks to management, customers, and stakeholders.

Cultural Obstacles to Managing Risk

Many organizations create cultures that emphasize achievement of goals in the face of overwhelming challenges. This is an essential attitude for any successful organization, but if taken to extremes, this attitude makes it very difficult for management to accept risk and believe in and support risk management as an important discipline. There is an underlying belief that all will be well. Management is confident that the software gods will shine on this deserving project.

When managing or participating in a software-intensive project, there is no reason to be optimistic; history doesn't support it.[6] Yet, for many reasons, optimism slips into projects time after time. When a project begins, the team genuinely desires to do well and assumes the lessons learned from the last project will take hold this time. After all, many aspects of the last project went well and it seems reasonable to assume that such success will continue.

Hope always has a way of triumphing over experience. For example, a young programmer was assigned to solve a problem with a critical interrupt handler in a real-time system. Rather than repair it once again, he decided to rewrite about 300 lines of assembler code. He worked day and night for 60 hours straight. When he was done, the interrupt handler was tested and deployed without a flaw. Sweet success! By remembering the success, the programmer believed the next time he could write 300 lines of code in a day (his lack of sleep blurred his perception of time). He forgot that in actuality the project took 60 hours and violated every company quality policy. Once again hope triumphed. Software people in particular need such successes to keep from losing their self esteem because much of their work requires them to confront today the mistakes made yesterday.

It is only human nature (optimism bias) to believe that all will be well, which is why process-based risk management cannot be truly effective without management support and staff acceptance. Management often chooses to dismiss evidence that contradicts its belief that a project is proceeding to plan, even if that evidence results from critical processes such as quality assurance, metrics, and process improvement that provide objective, often quantitative information that accurately describes project status.

This attitude also prevails when management is confronted with the information that results from risk management. To paraphrase Tom DeMarco, there are many individuals and activities within a project organization whose focus is to reinforce what is going right in a project; risk management's job is to point out what can go wrong. Therein lies the problem. Managers and staff who are committed to making the project succeed and who are working long hours under intense pressure do not want to be reminded that one crisis can lead to another. Senior management, customers, and stakeholders often adopt the Nike philosophy: just do it! Their interests lie in minimizing the reality of risk, not in embracing the fact that risk is a normal part of all projects that cannot be ignored. Risk management hands them more reality than they want to deal with.

An organization's culture is also defined by the manner in which its members communicate. Experience shows that many failures in regard to risk management are caused by imperfections in the human communication process. For example, many program managers, especially those facing more problems than they can handle, unconsciously signal to their teams that they do not want to hear about any new risks, even if they explicitly support good risk management processes. Their teams thus become reluctant to identify and report risks even though they could significantly affect the project.

Because "the spouting whale gets the spear," team members become deaf and blind to essential information that would enable them to mitigate long-term threats and are forced to respond to problems as they arise, often in crisis mode. The project manager will tend to assign part or all of the responsibility for mitigating a risk to whoever identifies it. Such a response can communicate to team members that it is dangerous to identify new risks, because they will be stuck with mitigating the risk while performing their regular duties, most often without appropriate resources.

Continuous, proactive risk management can overcome these cultural barriers when it openly involves all members of an organization or participants in a project. It helps managers, staff, and stakeholders make correct, informed decisions by allowing them to anticipate what can go wrong rather than waiting to react to it. When performed correctly, risk management dispels the myth of the no-risk project. To the benefit of the project, it confronts assumptions and projections that do not include contingency factors. It questions commitments and agreements that assume rigid adherence to plans while omitting options to address the reality that a potential risk can occur.

It takes a truly mature manager and a savvy customer to embrace the benefits of risk management because the message is not entirely pleasant. Risk management tells them they must recognize that if risks are not addressed when identified, they are likely to negatively affect a project in the future. That is an unpleasant reality, but a manager ignores that reality at his or her peril. The positive aspect of the message is that it is within a manager's control to determine the degree of impact of a risk based on the actions he or she takes take today.

Risks versus Problems

The concept of risk management is based on a fundamental premise: risk management addresses those factors that have the potential to impact a project; problem management addresses those factors that are already causing impacts. Risk management is strategic in nature because it addresses current realities to identify risks that could cause problems in the future. It therefore enables management to plan and implement both strategic and tactical actions before a problem occurs. Problem management, on the other hand, is tactical in nature because it can only address, using short-term solutions, a situation that is already affecting a project. Both disciplines are essential, but they are different and should be treated as such. For example, fire prevention is risk management versus fire fighting which is problem management.

Risk management — Elaine Hall wrote that, "Risk is a consequence of the uncertainty in our work, not a reflection of our own ability."[7] Risk management is almost exclusively focused on potential threats and their impacts rather than on current project performance or occurring events. Risk management enables project management to anticipate and control events. It provides the means to monitor project indicators such as performance trends and recurring issues and problems, identify, analyze, and document the risk. Project managers can then define appropriate mitigations and implement them when a risk meets a predetermined threshold based on a risk index or occurrence of a predefined event or condition.

In the risk management process the staff, stakeholders, management, and customers are asked where they think the project is headed and what can get in the way. Asking these questions allows management to identify potential risks, and by implementing effective mitigation strategies at the right time, projects can minimize or avoid the impacts should the risks become problems. The best way to look at risk management is to use the bouncing ball analogy[8] noting that every ball bouncing into the street is followed by a child. Likewise, the presence of certain project indicators means you should assume a risk exists. Stakeholders sometimes have their own agendas that may bias the process.

Problem management — Problem management focuses on the current condition of a project and deals with issues the impacts of which are immediate and affect the project to some degree — unexpected attrition, loss of funding, unanticipated requirements, failure of hardware to perform to specifications, excessive defect and rework rates and a host of other factors. Problem management is a four-step process: (1) identify, (2) analyze, (3) implement, and (4) monitor.

Problems are usually identified through the presence of a straightforward indicator, for example, your boss standing over your shoulder with a scowl on his face and papers in his hands or a comment such as "I've got good news and bad news. Which do you want first?" More subtle signs are unexpected indicators in metrics performance, negative project trends that do not improve, and increased management or customer pressure to accomplish tasks not included in task statements or baselines. However the problem is indicated, its successful resolution depends on the timeliness of the attention it receives, the relevance of the actions taken, their effectiveness, and sufficient management focus on implementing a solution. The most essential element is time. By not conducting the risk management activities that could have anticipated the problem, management sacrificed the time required to establish mitigation procedures, negotiate with customers and suppliers in a meaningful way, and vary specifications or change architectures. As a result, the project is overtaken by events and, based on the impact of the problem, it could very well fail altogether.

In order to be effective, problem management must address the underlying cause of the problem rather than its symptoms. For example, staff attrition surely indicates a problem, but by simply reorganizing or hiring new people, management misses the true cause which may be: too much overtime caused by unrealistic schedules fueled by unreasonable customer pressures. Unless management gets to the root of the problem and reduces or eliminates the pressures from the customer, the schedules will continue to be unrealistic, the overtime will continue, and the staff will continue to leave. By taking the time beforehand to identify potential risks, management can add staff attrition to the risk list, monitor the conditions that can cause it, and take appropriate steps to mitigate it should it occur.

Risk Management Success Factors

Risk management requires top-level management support, acknowledgment that risks are realities, and a commitment to identify and manage them. One discriminator of a successful organization or project is the use of risk management to anticipate potential negative conditions, problems, and realities. Ineffective projects are forced to react to problems; effective projects anticipate them. "Your organization will be much better once it moves away from reacting to change, and toward proactive anticipation and management of change."[9]

Formal risk management must be an integral part of the entire program management structure and processes. In fact, risk management should be the program manager's number one priority. Risks that become problems can negatively affect cost, schedule, productivity, product quality, and/or system performance. The program manager must plan and establish formal methods for identifying, monitoring, and managing risks and ensure that sufficient resources are available to conduct related activities. An effective risk management plan helps ensure that a quality system is delivered on time and within budget and that it performs to user requirements — the first time.

Tom DeMarco[10] captured the essence of risk management:

> The most important aspect of managing risks is to face up to uncertainty ... for instance, if you said, 'I can't tell you for sure whether we'll be done June 15 or June 30,' people will accept that as a reasonable window. Now, unfortunately, that's not a reasonable window at all ... saying it will take from 18 to 30 months to get this job done, that would declare uncertainty that is consistent with a kind of uncertainty we've seen in the past. But that would be politically unacceptable ... The truth of the matter of is, there is a lot of uncertainty. And the thing that is really hard about risk management is it forces you to declare your uncertainty, to show the entire range.

As DeMarco indicates, far too many software projects will identify a potential risk and then ignore the possible impacts. Too often, managers do not want to know what risk management tells them, which in effect is that a significant number of issues can get in the way of success and a can-do attitude is not sufficient to overcome them.

"The problem of project management, like that of most management [is] to find an acceptable balance among time, cost and performance."[11] When a project moves out of balance, risk results. For example, schedule performance often becomes most important due to customer pressures, so cost and product performance lose emphasis. Or product performance takes center stage due to a customer review, so the focus drifts away from cost and schedule performance. As a result of this imbalance in priorities, what was once well controlled now becomes less well managed and risk results. Risk management can address such imbalances if they occur throughout a project. "An effective risk management program is dynamic and ongoing throughout the development process and requires the participation of everyone involved."[12]

While every project we assess professes to implement risk management, we have observed two very different focuses in its application. Some managers focus on the process and some focus on making risk management a cultural imperative. A manager who focuses on the process has a risk manager who makes sure that the seven steps of risk management (described later in this chapter) are visible in the project and to all stakeholders.

This focus is certainly a necessary part of risk management, but in a certain respect it is a mechanical approach that can convey a false sense of security. The organizations that focus on the process tend to be more concerned with the appearance of process integrity than the result of the process. In these organizations, the project manager will give "lip service" to how important risk management is to the project but will never use risks to influence decisions or plot a future course. He will build a close-looped system where actual risks never leak out. Indeed, there have been situations where a manager dictated the types of risks that could be identified. During one assessment, an engineer related to us the instructions he had received from the manager of a major commercial program: "Don't give me any cost, schedule, or process risks because, if they get out, they will make the project look bad."

In our experience, we have found that very few projects implement risk management as a cultural imperative where it is at the core of the management process and where the output of the process, the prioritized risk list, drives all project decisions and activities. Where risk management is a cultural imperative, risks serve as the focus of all project reviews and reporting and the process is an open system that encourages all team members and stakeholders to review and comment on a risk list that is kept current.

In addition, the process is linked to predetermined metrics that are continually collected, that indicate an anticipated project state, and that form the basis for mandatory triggering of mitigations and actions. "A pattern of measurement enables projects to establish realistic plans and then gauge where they are against the plan."[13] When the project falls out of balance, plans invariably are compromised, and when plans are compromised, risks result. Where risk management is a cultural imperative, management has documented effective metrics that allow identification of risks and assessment of their likelihood of becoming problems.

Essential Risk Management Definitions

Adequate risk reserve to cover cost — Risks without reserves often cannot be successfully dealt with. A quick and easy method of calculating a required risk reserve is: (1) determine the probability of risk occurrence as a percentage (e.g., the probability of missing an established milestone is 30 percent); (2) determine what such a schedule slip would cost (e.g., $50,000 in penalties or additional labor); and (3) multiply the two figures to arrive at the estimated reserve required to mitigate this risk (30 percent × $50,000 = $15,000).

Likelihood of occurrence — Probability that a particular risk will transition to a problem. Likelihood is often expressed as a grid:

0 to 20 percent: low probability of occurrence
21 to 40 percent: potential for transition
41 to 60 percent: transition to problem probable
61 to 80 percent: transition probable
81 to 100 percent: transition imminent

Metrics-based risk management — Quantitative approach to categorizing, monitoring, assessing, and controlling risks. The use of metrics to track a supplier's progress toward meeting a deadline can serve as an invaluable "trip wire" that affords a program manager ample early warning of impending schedule slippage.

Negative impact — Inability to achieve a part of a plan, including cost and schedule constraints and technical aspects such as safety, utility, efficiency, and mission effectiveness that affects customer acceptance of the product.

Opportunity — Event, tendency, or situation that may open an opportunity to improve on the project plan (emphasis on *may* — if the opportunity is staring you in the face right now, it's a decision problem, not a risk problem).

Parametric risk estimation — Quantitative approach to estimating uncertainty in which a higher probability of occurrence requires increases in cost and extensions in schedule to mitigate. The most sophisticated parametric models allow the specification of cost and schedule probability separately.

Problem — Risk that has occurred and negatively affects a project.

Risk — Any potential situation or event that could negatively affect a project's ability to achieve objectives within defined cost and schedule constraints if it is not mitigated. Risk occurs in every project and can include effects that are beyond the manager's control. An event that is certain to occur is not a risk and should be addressed by normal planning and management activities.

Risk aggregation — Risks that occur together to cause a negative impact.

Risk avoidance — Choice of not acting to try to prevent a risk from occurring, such as choosing not to build a component that is critical to the safety of the system to avoid the risk of failure to deliver a safe system.

Risk chaining — One risk may create another risk, which may create another risk, until eventually cost, schedule, and technical impacts are felt. For example, a key person's resignation (Problem 1) may cause a project to be understaffed (Problem 2), which may cause a late delivery of a component (Problem 3), which may lead to late product delivery (schedule impact) that may be unacceptable to the customer (impact). The strategy of mitigating the effects of risks is to interrupt the chain, thereby minimizing or eliminating the impacts. Each risk should be addressed on its own to forestall the chain from continuing.

Risk containment — Process of mitigation to control the effects of a risk that has occurred.

Risk evasion — Failure to establish the reserves and conduct the planning necessary to mitigate risks in order to save resources.

Risk index — Prioritized list of risks that are identified and tracked by the program. Priority is determined by calculating impact × probability of occurrence.

Risk management — Practices and procedures that enable managers to identify, assess, categorize, monitor, control, and mitigate risks.

Risk mitigation — Process of planning responses to specific risks, such as identifying a second supplier that can deliver if a primary supplier cannot meet a deadline.

Risk trigger; risk transition — Measured event or circumstance that causes a risk to become a problem. In the risk management process, specific risk triggers with metrics and thresholds are identified. This enables the project manager to determine when the risk can transition to a problem and thus act to mitigate its effects.

Introduction to Risk Management Concepts

Both success and failure in software-intensive projects can have different definitions. Whenever an organization commits to buy or build a product with significant software content, that choice will either have a successful outcome or become a failure. The outcome depends on numerous factors and can be subjective, as the customer and user community determine, even if all the cost, schedule, and technical objectives have been met. For example, a project may deliver a product on time, within budget, and with full functionality, but an overlooked security flaw may prevent deployment. Or a project may deliver only 80 percent of promised functionality and still provide the end users what they needed and expected. Which example is a failure and which is a success?

Risk management is a method of identifying and assessing the probability that a risk will occur, determining the severity of its consequences, and prioritizing identified risks based on that data. Using risk management, the project manager can thus distinguish between risks that can cause significant impacts but be mitigated and risks that can cause a project to fail by delivering a product that cannot be used in an operational environment. By doing so, management is prepared to provide the time and resources required to mitigate the risks with the highest potential to cause project failure.

Determining the severity of a risk requires determining its consequences should it occur and also its potential to trigger more severe risks. Although risks are analyzed and rated individually, this method also involves understanding potential consequences of risks by understanding the relationships between them. This enables management to focus on ensuring the commitments made by developer, customers, and end users are accomplished by determining which risks would have the most severe impacts and could preclude the project from meeting its basic commitments. In this way, risk management provides a means of avoiding or minimizing an impact to a project and its associated loss.

The basic commitment of a provider to a customer is to deliver an acceptable product within the cost and schedule constraints established by the customer and assume the risks associated with meeting that commitment. The provider organization has the most defined set of commitments that include delivering a useful product in time to enable its timely planning and installation and doing so with the money and resources provided. The provider organization also commits to producing the required functionality in a manner that enables the product to interact with other systems and satisfies end user requirements. The provider must be as certain as possible that it can deliver a product of sufficient quality that performs properly in its operational environment to the satisfaction of customers, users, and other stakeholders within the cost, schedule, and operational constraints.

The interrelated commitments of customers, users, stakeholders, and providers create a trade space in which goals related to technical requirements (cost, schedule, performance, and quality) can be traded off to ensure the product is delivered. When the constraints created by these relationships form a narrow space (i.e., tight schedules lead to tight budgets which engender more stringent development or quality requirements), the higher the risk that a project will fail to deliver a product that meets customer expectations. Risk accordingly is lowered when these relationships create a broader space. Risk management is a key to setting smart objectives for a project.

The provider uses the risk management process to monitor progress in meeting its basic commitment and track the associated risks using objective, quantitative metrics related to the required development tasks. These metrics are critical to triggering recovery or mitigation procedures that are initiated when pre-established threshold values indicating an increased probability of risk, an increase in its impact, or its proximity to occurrence are approached.

In order to understand the risks involved and deliver a successful product, a developer must not only understand the technical requirements, but just as importantly understand the needs and expectations of the users and stakeholders. Understanding the risks, the developer must ensure that each component of the project organization, especially the user, is involved in defining, reviewing, and monitoring the product during its evaluation for acquisition or during its development.

The developer must establish the means to involve users and stakeholders with requirements development, project management, quality control and assurance, testing, and other aspects of the project and involve them in the conduct of risk management. Their involvement ensures all participants understand each other's needs and expectations and the absolute requirements that must be met to ensure the product can be deployed, operated, and supported in its intended environment. The key lies in clear communication with the user in addressing its requirements to avoid the rework caused by inserted defects when requirements are not clear.

Computing a Risk Index

Risk is expressed both as a measure of the probability of failure to achieve a particular outcome and as a measure of the consequences of failing to achieve that outcome. For processes, the metric is the difference between the results that would occur from the best practice of that process and the results of actual performance.

As risks are identified, they can be categorized by impact (I). A Level 5 risk represents the highest potential loss that results from a risk that occurs and is not mitigated. Risks are also categorized by likelihood of occurrence (LO). A Level 5 risk is defined as the most likely to occur. When these two factors are multiplied, a risk can be characterized as high, medium, or low and prioritized within a risk index (RI) by a single measure that determines its importance to the project and the relative visibility, response, and reporting required.

$$RI = I \times LO$$

This technique provides the ability to prioritize risks by quantitatively describing them. Table 10.1 lists the criteria used to characterize individual risks, determine the impact horizon and LO, and consistently define the RI. The attributes, probability and impact are the basis for computing the RI — a dynamic value that changes as project conditions force changes in either the potential impact or the likelihood that a risk might occur.

Risks are rated at three degrees of urgency:

> **Low** — treated as routine business
> **Medium** — risk can negatively affect or preclude an organization from meeting a commitment
> **High** — risk could preclude delivery or completion of project (see Figure 10.1)

It is important to rate risks because they are analyzed, prioritized, and reported based on their perceived impacts and probabilities. Risks rated medium receive more attention than low risks until the threat to the project commitment is effectively removed. High-rated risks warrant the highest priority, must be addressed before the less severe classes of risks, and should be tracked until they can be downgraded.

When analyzing risks identified through the estimation process, two factors are important to consider. First, these risks are almost always rated high because they usually affect the accuracy or relevance of a basic commitment made by the supplier of the product to its stakeholders and will produce significant effects if they transition to problems. Second, any uncertainties and risks associated with an estimate can limit the options the project has to apply management, engineering, assurance, monitoring, and reporting practices and tools or address issues or problems. Estimates that are too high or low can dramatically change the risk of a project by forcing actions not based on the reality of available resources.

The nature of the risks can change over time; and their impacts may lessen as mitigations are put in place, project conditions change, and the likelihood of occurrence changes. Figure 10.1 provides an overview of the risk assessment process.

Table 10.2 lists impacts that can result in exposure to risk in different areas, including cost, budget, schedule, attrition and staff availability, product quality, and user satisfaction. Every project has unique risk exposure

Table 10.1 Example Risk Characterization Criteria

Attribute	Risk Rating	Value	Description
Probability	1	Remote (L)	Low chance (0 to 20 percent) risk will occur and cause a problem
	2	Unlikely (M)	Medium chance (20 to 40 percent) risk will occur and cause problem
	3	Likely (M)	Medium chance (40 to 70 percent) risk will occur and cause problem
	4	Highly likely (H)	High chance (70 to 90 percent) risk will occur (potential problem)
	5	Nearly certain (H)	High chance (90 to 100 percent) risk will occur (potential problem)
Impact	1	Minimal or no impact (L)	Minor system damage, recoverable loss of operational capacity; internal slips to schedule and budget <10 percent
	2	Small, acceptable with some reduction in margin need dates (L)	Some system damage, recoverable loss of operational capacity; internal slips to schedule and budget <15 percent
	3	Acceptable with significant reduction in margin (M)	Moderate system damage with partially recoverable operational capacity; schedule slip >10 percent; budget slip >10 percent
	4	Large, acceptable, no remaining margin (H)	Loss of system; significant impact to operational support; schedule slip >50 percent; budget slip >50 percent
	5	Significant, unacceptable (H)	Loss of system; failure of project operations; schedule slip >60 percent; budget slip >60 percent

Table 10.1 (continued) Example Risk Characterization Criteria

Attribute	Risk Rating	Value	Description
Impact horizon (when action must be taken to mitigate risk)		Near-term (N)	In next month
		Mid-term (M)	One to two months from now
		Far-term (F)	Three or more months from now

requirements. The analysis team should develop a table based on this example and tailored to project thresholds as a means of normalizing risk impacts based on predetermined criteria and assessing impacts consistently across a range of important or relevant factors.

After risks are assessed, they must be analyzed to determine strategies for monitoring and managing them to resolution or retirement, a risk management strategy and process must be developed, and risks must be monitored using the RI. The RI provides a consistent means of weighting risks based on threats and vulnerability, ranking them in accordance with their exposure levels and relative to one another, and focusing attention on the most critical risks.

Figure 10.2 is a risk grid — a common method of visually representing risk relationships while factoring likelihood of occurrence and impact. The grid provides a consistent means of correlating risk severity and likelihood, allowing both to be considered in regard to their potential to lead to problems.

One consideration in establishing an RI is understanding the impact of a risk if it does occur along with its long-term effects. Not all risks are created equal. For example, if a project goes over budget by 200 percent but the product is delivered on time, deploys properly, and achieves customer and user acceptance, how do you prioritize risks that result in cost overruns but lead to fulfilling projects goals? They thus take on a lower priority than risks that could impact performance. Such factors are used to weight the risk and provide a measure of realism.

Realism is required to distinguish risks that could potentially terminate a project and fail to deliver a product, risks that can lead to a failure to achieve user acceptance, and risks that can cause an impact to a commitment without jeopardizing successful delivery or use. The most severe risks receive the most weight and are prioritized accordingly.

The RI addresses what is known to be unknown and enables a project team to plan accordingly. Donald Rumsfeld observed that, "There are also unknown unknowns — the ones we don't know we don't know."[14] What is not known cannot possibly be predicted as a risk and planned for, such

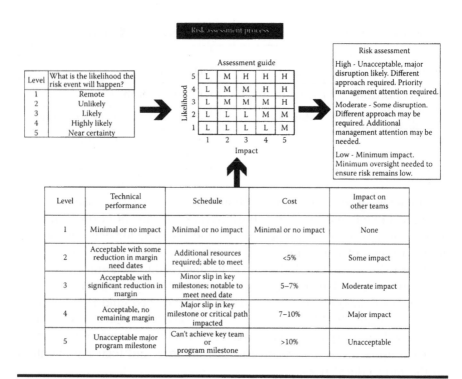

Figure 10.1   Risk assessment process.

as a sudden natural catastrophe. The risk management process focuses on the known unknowns; for unknown unknowns, management can determine a reserve that at best will not be necessary to use. Unknown unknowns generally require the facilitation of additional agreements outside the risk agreed to in the contract.

Risk Management Processes

Risk management is achieved by conducting processes to identify, assess, monitor, and mitigate risk and to provide contingency planning throughout system development, fielding, and postdelivery maintenance and support. The risk management process monitors key development and management practices by implementing the metrics and establishing the risk indicators managers require to identify, prioritize, track, and mitigate risks, and to measure the effectiveness of the risk management plan. The effectiveness of the plan in identifying and managing program risks is in large part determined by management's commitment to conduct continuous risk management.

Table 10.2 Example Risk Normalization Table[a]

Risk Area	Potential Impact
Budget	
0 to 5 percent overrun	1
5.1 to 10 percent overrun	2
10.1 to 15 percent overrun	3
15.1 to 25 percent overrun	4
Over 25 percent overrun	5
Schedule Impact	
0 to 3 month slip	1
3 to 6 month slip	2
6 to 12 month slip	3
12 to 18 month slip	4
Over 18 months	5
Staff and Other Resources	
0 to 5 percent resource shortfall	1
5.1 to 10 percent resource shortfall	2
10.1 to 15 percent resource shortfall	3
15.1 to 25 percent resource shortfall	4
Over 25 percent resource shortfall	5
Quality Impact	
0 to 5 percent quality gate failure	1
5.1 to 10 percent quality gate failure	2
10.1 to 15 percent quality gate failure	3
15.1 to 25 percent quality gate failure	4
Over 25 percent quality gate failure	5
User Satisfaction Impact	
0 to 5 unresolved user comments	1
6 to 12 unresolved user comments	2

Table 10.2 (continued) Example Risk Normalization Table[a]

Risk Area	*Potential Impact*
13 to 25 unresolved user comments	3
26 to 50 unresolved user comments	4
Over 50 unresolved user comments	5

[a] Actual project thresholds vary.

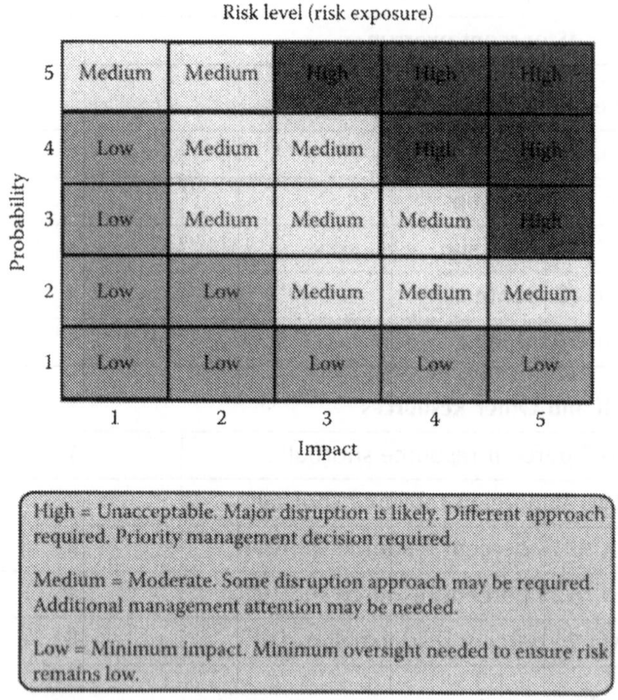
Risk level (risk exposure)
Probability
5
4
3
2
1
Medium
Medium
High
High
High
Low
Medium
Medium
High
High
Low
Medium
Medium
Medium
High
Low
Low
Medium
Medium
Medium
Low
Low
Low
Low
Low
1
2
3
4
5
Impact
High = Unacceptable. Major disruption is likely. Different approach required. Priority management decision required.
Medium = Moderate. Some disruption approach may be required. Additional management attention may be needed.
Low = Minimum impact. Minimum oversight needed to ensure risk remains low.

Figure 10.2 Risk grid.

Failure to act will doom a risk management program, even if management, customers, and stakeholders recognize the need to manage risk and a formal risk management system is put in place. In this situation, the risks identified by the formal process and documented in the risk management plan receive only marginal attention, and thus the project manager is reduced to informal risk management based on intuition and limited information. Because a formal process exists, the customer, stakeholders, and/or higher management assume it is effectively executed. When it is not, the risks as reported do not accurately describe the true risk and as a consequence appropriate actions are not taken.

If risk management measures operate effectively early in a program and then receive inadequate attention and action, risks that do occur can cause problems that compound one another until they reach a critical mass that the project personnel cannot comfortably handle. This dynamic is known as a risk chain. It is more likely to occur where resources are inadequate to mitigate risks and can cause the team to stop identifying significant new risks, which in turn makes program failure more likely.

Seven Steps to Risk Management

The risk management process involving the seven steps described below is straightforward and, from a process standpoint, one of the easier disciplines to plan and implement. A fully functional process including policy, plan, procedures, essential training, an initial risk identification session, and a tool loaded with the initial RI can be established within 30 days. The seven steps do not necessarily occur sequentially. Some overlap as multiple risks are identified, analyzed, mitigated, or retired. The process, if executed in an ongoing and disciplined manner, can greatly increase the probability of success for a software project.

Step 1: Establish Risk Policy, Obtain Commitment to Manage Risk, and Develop Plan

The output of this step is the development and distribution of a risk management policy that empowers management to act. The management and staff must be committed to actively managing risks. This step is achieved by establishing an understanding of the need for risk management and obtaining the commitment of management and the staff to manage risk.

Senior management must commit to risk management as a policy, provide education and training to ensure it is supported continuously throughout the organization, and ensure an effective risk policy and plan are developed, documented, and implemented, with all management levels accountable for its effectiveness. The policy should legitimize risk management as an essential activity, stress effective implementation of the process, and empower program managers and supporting elements to expend resources to manage risks. When effectively implemented, a risk management policy provides the information required to:

- Develop alternatives to achieve cost, schedule, and performance goals
- Establish budget and funding priorities
- Make milestone decisions
- Monitor program status in real time

Project personnel must be trained on the process used to manage risk. An appropriate combination of training, mentoring, and management emphasis is required to implement risk management within an organizational culture. A risk policy concisely delineating basic requirements and signed by the program manager empowers staff to expend resources, assigns responsibility for planning and implementing the risk management process, and establishes a means for training staff. Table 10.3 lists sample policy statements. Each major program component should conduct sessions to identify risks and present findings at regularly scheduled program reviews. To further ingrain the importance of risk management and establish staff buy-in, incentives (financial or otherwise) can be established.

Risk Management Planning

After the policy is agreed to and management and staff are committed to managing risks, a risk management plan will provide structure to the process and comprehensively describe the required procedures, organization, roles, and responsibilities. The plan should define the process and allow change as necessary in response to changing conditions.

A core risk management plan should describe the overall organizational requirements, and each organization should develop a concise risk management plan that is specific to its needs and goals, with appendices added to describe planning requirements specific to the program organization, any waivers or deviations from the core plan, and issues affecting implementation. It should describe required tasks, measures of success, the organizational structure, and associated roles and responsibilities.

It is important to initiate detailed planning early to assure the processes to manage risk are in place, general guidelines for implementing them within the organization are defined, and the project resources are available to support them. Having these issues defined early means that the critical risks associated with sizing, estimation, and scheduling will be identified, characterized, and tracked.

The risk management plan should be updated as planning progresses and as additional information becomes available. It should also reflect changes in the risk management process and it should also describe specific roles and responsibilities.

Table 10.3 Sample Policy Statements

All organizations and programs shall have risk management plans.
All managers shall ensure that risk management is an integral part of a project's defined process.
All organizations shall identify and deal with risk in a positive manner such that identification is recognized and rewarded, and results in positive mitigation actions.
All organizations shall charter entities responsible for coordinating risk management activities.
All organizations shall provide adequate resources for risk management activities.
All organizations shall require training of individuals performing risk management activities.
All organizations shall integrate risk identification, analysis, and mitigation activities into planning.
All organizations shall develop risk management plans according to the program risk management policy.
All organizations shall identify, analyze, and take appropriate software risk mitigation actions during development planning.
All organizations shall track software risk mitigation actions to completion.
All organizations shall make and use measurements to determine the status of risk management activities.
All organizations shall record and track resources expended for risk management activities.
All organizations shall review the risk management activities with senior management on a periodic basis.
All organizations shall review risk management activities with the project manager on both periodic and event-driven basis.
Each project's program manager is responsible for implementing the empowerment policy.
Within any organization, an independent risk officer will serve as the focal point responsible for risk management, implement the policy, and write and implement the plan.

"How-To" Procedures: Essential Planning Elements

The development of a risk management plan is not enough. All specific procedures to be used must be detailed or they will not be implemented consistently. For software projects, the planning and development of specific project requirements that culminate in a risk management plan must be completed earliest, as the requirements provide the framework required to direct the project; procedural development is a continuous activity that refines procedures to reflect changing conditions.

Procedures for conducting sizing and cost estimation risk management should be developed, reviewed, tested, and documented by project start-up, including those required to address risks associated with planning, budgeting, work definition, and scheduling. These procedures guide the activities required to identify, analyze, prioritize, and report risks associated with planning the project. All risk management procedures should be developed in a consistent manner or by following an acquisition model such as IEEE/EIA Standard 12207,[15] which describes the major component processes of a complete software life cycle and the high-level relations that govern their interactions and covers the life cycle of software from acquisition to migration and retirement. It addresses the five primary processes that support the buyers (acquirers) and builders (developers) that initiate or perform the development, operation, and maintenance of software products. The five primary processes are:

- **Acquisition** — The various activities of the acquirer of systems and software products or services.
- **Supply** — The various activities of suppliers of system, software products, or services.
- **Development** — A set of activities performed by the developer defining and developing software products.
- **Operation** — The activities performed by an operator to provide computer system operation in a live user environment.
- **Maintenance** — Software maintenance activities including managing modifications, keeping the product current and operationally sound, migration, and retirement.

The models described in Standard 12207 define common frameworks that facilitate the planning and sequencing of a project. They are intended to facilitate the development of documents such as project plans, work breakdown structures, size and cost estimates, and schedules. The discussion that follows focuses on the acquisition and supply processes.

Table 10.4 lists risks that are common to software projects and relates them to process steps defined in Standard 12207. While the table covers only a small subset of the full set of seven tables, it illustrates the reality that risk encompasses all aspects of a software process and shows how a number of potential areas of risk (risk enablers) associated with a project increases significantly as a project moves forward.

The risk factors were identified from the 350 software project assessments we have conducted for customers in the public and private sectors in the past 12 years, including banking, insurance, defense contractor, government, accounting, and many other applications. We reviewed the results of many representative assessments to identify typical risks. We extracted primary risk data from assessment reports and other information and analyzed the secondary risks and indicators documented as causes in reports provided to customers. We then correlated these risks to the IEEE/EIA 12207 activities.

As seen in the tables, many of the sources of risk become similar as a project moves from activity to activity, but the characteristics of the risk enablers, the specific factors and the means by which these factors are identified and evaluated, differ somewhat between activity areas.

It is essential to identify risk factors for a project because they drive development of the risk management plan and procedures. The types of risk factors identified will indicate what risk identification and analysis techniques should be used, for example, and the organizations that will need to be involved. By identifying the risk factors, specific risk management techniques can be phased into the project as needed and resources can be allocated more effectively. The enablers identified in the tables are representative and must be defined specifically for each project situation.

Management has many choices for setting up a reasonably low risk project structure, but these choices are usually restricted by internal and external realities of the project, for example, pressures from customers, higher management, stakeholders, and vendors, whose expectations can severely undermine the effectiveness of risk management.

The responsible manager faces a "Hobson's choice," which is no choice at all. If he does not plan the project in the aggressive, unrealistic, and high risk way expected by upper management and the customer, his company may not get the work and he may not keep his job. If he proceeds, he may commit his organization to an estimate, schedule, or plan that is high risk at best and not executable at worst. If he realistically identifies risks, he may well hear that:

■ It can't possibly cost that much.
■ What you propose isn't technically elegant.
■ I understand your concerns but I really need it six months earlier.
■ If I had the kind of money you're talking about, I wouldn't need the system you're proposing.

Such pressures can quickly restrict the options available to a manager.

Table 10.4 Standard 12207 Acquisition Process and Typical Risk Enablers

Risk Management Implementation Considerations (Acquirer)		
12207 Acquisition Area	*Procedure Need Date*	*Typical Risk Enablers*
Initiation	Program start	Unrealistic system concept; incomplete, inconsistent system requirements; unrealistic trade-offs; unrealistic expectations; incorrect estimates; customer and stakeholder pressure and bias; unrealistic budget and schedule constraints
Concept description or need definition	Project start	Unrealistic expectations; unrealistic trade-offs; as-is definition shortfalls; limited enterprise models; incorrect estimates; customer and stakeholder pressure and bias; unrealistic budget and schedule constraints
Definition and analysis of system requirements	Prior to start of requirements elicitation	Undocumented expectations; undocumented defects; schedule compression; concept uncertainty; incorrect trade-offs; management optimism; user uncertainty; inadequacy of enterprise models; interface instability; system expectations; understanding of reality; process inadequacy
Schedules for timely completion of tasks	Program start	Unreasonable customer, stakeholder, user, or vendor pressure, bias, and management and/or staff optimism; nonrepresentative or absent historical data; incorrect or inadequate work identification and/or allocation; incorrect or inconsistent estimates; incorrect or inadequate requirements; undefined expectations

Table 10.4 (continued)   Standard 12207 Acquisition Process and Typical Risk Enablers

Risk Management Implementation Considerations (Acquirer)		
12207 Acquisition Area	*Procedure Need Date*	*Typical Risk Enablers*
Estimation of effort	Program start	Unreasonable customer, stakeholder, user, or vendor pressure, bias, and management and/or staff optimism; inadequate, inconsistent, or incorrect requirement; nonrepresentative or absent historical data; incorrect or inadequate work identification and/or allocation; incorrect or inconsistent sizing; undefined expectations
Process implementation	Prior to development of program plan	Incorrect sizing; incorrect estimates; cost, schedule, process, and tool trade-offs; incorrect trade-offs; staff shortfalls; customer expectations; management, customer, and stakeholder pressures; enterprise bias; project complexity

As shown in Table 10.5, each risk enabler is rated as high, medium, or low. The table lists only a small sample of typical 12207 activities but it provides a means for scaling the process- and phasing-specific procedures as needed to effectively identify, analyze, prioritize, track, and report risk as appropriate to its rating.

Several factors must be considered when planning a risk management process:

1. The process must focus on a practical, straightforward implementation that minimizes bureaucracy, simplifies the organizational interaction, and engages staff, management, stakeholders, and other affected organizations in a nonthreatening, effective manner.
2. The process should be structured to be culturally consistent with the project and with the budgets, schedules, and available resources.
3. Whatever process is used, adequate training in procedures is required so that all organizations understand their roles and responsibilities.

Table 10.5   Risk Impact Projection

Initial Evaluation Point	*Activity/Risk Causal Factor*	*H*	*M*	*L*	*Reevaluation Point*	*H*	*M*	*L*
Initiation					At program start			
	Unrealistic system concept							
	Incomplete, inconsistent system requirements							
	Unrealistic trade-offs							
	Unrealistic expectations							
	Incorrect estimates							
	Customer and/or stakeholder pressure and bias							
	Unrealistic budget and schedule constraints							
Request-for-proposal (RFP or tender) preparation					Prior to RFP release			
	Incomplete requirements							
	Incomplete, inconsistent, or unrealistic size and cost estimates							
	Unrealistic trade-offs							
	Customer and/or stakeholder pressure							
	Vendor pressure							
	Customer and/or stakeholder bias							
	Irrelevant boilerplate							

Table 10.5 (continued)   Risk Impact Projection

Initial Evaluation Point	Activity/Risk Causal Factor	H	M	L	Reevaluation Point	H	M	L
Contract preparation and update					Prior to contractor selection			
	Unrestrained customer and/or stakeholder expectations							
	Unrealistic, unjustified trade-offs							
	Incomplete, incorrect work definition and allocation							
	Unrealistic schedules; inconsistent or unrealistic size and cost estimates							
Supplier monitoring					Prior to contract award			
	Nonquantitative supplier reporting							
	Contract inadequacies							
	Vendor pressure							
	User and/or stakeholder pressures and biases							
	Schedule compression							
	Increasing rework							
	Requirements "churn"							
	Unrealistic, unjustified trade-off							
	Contractor performance issues							
	Resource shortfalls							

Table 10.5 (continued)   Risk Impact Projection

Initial Evaluation Point	Activity/Risk Causal Factor	H	M	L	Reevaluation Point	H	M	L
Acceptance and completion					Prior to acceptance test planning			
	Incomplete or untestable requirements							
	Inadequate traceability							
	Customer and stakeholder attitudes and bias							
	Adequacy of concepts and requirements							
	Testing adequacy							
	Issue documentation and resolution							
	Product completeness							
	Trade-off resolution							
	Defect identification and resolution							
	Contractual restrictions and terms							
H = high. M = medium. L = low.								

4. Management should measure the numbers, types, criticalities, and dispositions of risks using predefined metrics and frequently assess the effectiveness of the risk management process.
5. Management should constantly reinforce the need for risk management, provide incentives for its effective application and disincentives for its improper use, and use the results to effectively manage the project.

Step 2: Designate Risk Officer

The output of this step is the assignment of a risk officer — an individual responsible for developing and implementing the risk management process and carrying out the policy for the managers it supports. Risk officer is a staff position in large projects. Risk officers are responsible for identifying, analyzing, prioritizing and reporting risks; tracking risk triggers; and making recommendations for management action. In small projects, the role should be assigned as an additional responsibility.

Every organization involved in a large project is faced with a dilemma: how to ensure risk is consistently and objectively identified, analyzed, prioritized, and reported without funding a disruptive and delaying bureaucracy to do so. The answer is simple. Create an independent staff position, the risk officer, who will handle responsibility for risk management.

Why is designating a risk officer a good idea? The independent status of the risk officer removes the burden from other managers who have little incentive to aggressively pursue risks and objectively assess and report them. Other managers are often reluctant to accept the possibility that other problems can occur when they are already dealing with daily crises. "It can't happen so why should I worry about it'" is a common lament.

Managers often think that if they accurately report risk to higher management, they will invite increased oversight, unwanted help, and excessive management visibility. In situations where risk management is not a priority, this is a valid concern. Organizations often misunderstand risk and believe it is an immediate problem that requires crisis management rather than a potential problem that can be addressed and avoided or mitigated in a timely manner. Still, every project manager has an obligation to inform senior management, stakeholders, customers, and users of the potential for problems as documented in the risks that have been identified in sufficient time to enable them to plan for a problem should it occur. Failure to do this limits the ability of these external organizations to respond to risks as they occur and mitigate their impacts.

Designating a risk officer for each organizational level provides organizational focus and ensures that potential problems are visible to those who are responsible for the project and organization. The risk officer is responsible for implementing risk procedures throughout the organization. To paraphrase Tom DeMarco, most projects have many can-do people; they also need a can't-do person, and that's the risk officer.

While the risk officer must fully understand the technical, administrative, and operational underpinnings of the application and infrastructure, the sole focus is identifying and managing risk within the organization. The independent risk officer should also have the authority to dictate the process. The job involves reporting risks, not initiating mitigation strategies and committing program resources.

The risk officer need not be a full-time position. However, sufficient time must be allocated to maintain a current risk list and advise the manager to whom he or she reports about the most critical risks, potential mitigations, and risks that have transitioned or are about to transition to problems. A risk officer should:

- Identify, along with others, risks by determining what actual and potential risks the program faces.
- Characterize risks.
- Compile a list of past risks to help identify present or future risks.
- Seek out risks by asking project staff members what risks they are aware of or foresee.
- Prioritize risks, establish and maintain a top-ten risk list, and report risks frequently to the appropriate program manager.
- Monitor the progress of risk mitigation activities by individual project team members.
- Ensure consistent risk focus throughout all project organizational levels by fostering open and honest risk awareness among project staff members.
- Have an agreed-to and signed charter with his or her manager that empowers the position and establishes its specific roles, responsibilities, and limitations.
- Not be a manager; should be a nonmanagement individual with an independent reporting chain to his manager, and he should assume a principal leadership role in the risk management process.
- Establish and chair a risk management review board or working group and implement a risk reporting process that allows anonymous risk reporting from all organizational levels and permits monitoring and frequent reporting of risks and risk reserve status to the appropriate manager.
- Use risk tools to document all identified risks.

The risk officer is largely responsible for conducting a continuous process of risk identification throughout the life cycle of a project. He should also ensure a streamlined means of communication exists so that all program participants including developer and customer entities can easily report identified risks to the risk officer to promote and facilitate early risk identification and reporting. A system by which individuals can report anonymously to the risk officer is one option. Anonymity encourages candid reporting of risks without fear of retribution. It can allow identification of obscure risks that might have otherwise gone unnoticed. The risk officer is also responsible for recording and monitoring identified risks and establishing a risk database that should be accessible to all project stakeholders.

In order to effectively achieve this critical function, the individual assigned as the risk officer should be empowered, respected, tenacious, a strong communicator, committed, a comprehensive and integrative thinker, and a good coordinator and facilitator who can balance a variety of interests and strategic demands. Program management must have an open door policy and be willing to listen.

Risk Officer Case Study

We helped a large government project implement risk management across the organization. We helped the agency write policies, plans, and procedures; trained the management, staff, and external organizations affected by the process; and conducted a series of assessments to identify risk. The entire process was effective and began providing useful information within a short time. However, the risk officer assigned proved to be ineffective, spending time attending conferences, writing reports on how good things were, and conducting or attending meetings at which no one took notes. The process quickly became a token that served to placate corporate governance individuals who wanted to cite the process but not deal with the results.

"Black Monday" arrived after an external audit. The risk officer was ill prepared for the result. The audit recommended that the project fix the risk management process or cut off funding and pointed to the risk officer as the cause of the process problems. After much wringing of hands, he was replaced with a committed, aggressive engineer who had a reputation as a comprehensive, integrative thinker, a good communicator, coordinator, and facilitator who balanced a variety of interests and strategic demands. The new risk officer quickly established an independent project risk management group with reporting through an executive steering committee. She reinvigorated the initially established process and reviewed and updated the risk list and tracking procedures. Within 30 days, risk management went from "bust to best." The only variable was the effectiveness of the risk officer.

Relationship of Risk Officer and Management

When his function is performed effectively, the risk officer provides management a critical dimension that is not necessarily available through any other means. A risk manager can provide management with time to react. This can make an organization more effective and reduce the complexity of the problems managers must handle.

Management is obviously the critical coordination point. The managers ultimately own all risks and are responsible for their management. Many administrative, technical, and physical controls used to manage risk are funded and driven through project processes and technologies. While a risk officer provides organizational direction and oversight of risk objectives and programs, the various project organizations must identify, select, and implement the necessary control solutions. Friction between the risk officer and project organizations may arise if the roles are not well defined or if the risk officer tries to replicate functions not within the charter of the position.

The timely and accurate reporting of identified risks is a key problem. Managers naturally wish to ignore or defer reporting critical risks to higher management and try to resolve them locally, even when the risks materially affect the integrity of the risk management process in the external organizations. An effective way of countering this tendency is to establish a reporting chain that allows a risk to be escalated when risk triggers occur. The triggers should be negotiated and approved by the manager to whom the risk officer reports during the risk identification process. This approach ensures that risks transitioning into problems are escalated in a controlled and agreed-to manner and also allows all interested organizations maximum time to address the problem.

Step 3: Identify Risks

The output of this step is a comprehensive list of the potential program risks. Risk identification involves assessing the program to identify critical events that would prevent the program from achieving its objectives. A risk tool should be used to describe the risks and their contexts and any condition or situation causing concern.

Active and continuous risk identification is extremely important because unidentified risks that have not been prepared for can kill a project. Risks can be based on two factors: threats and vulnerabilities. It is important to distinguish them and that requires understanding of a few terms:

> **Critical event** — An event that may serve to change the course of a project.
>
> **Event** — A distinguishable point at which the occurrence of an action or a change in a project condition can be identified as having occurred.
>
> **Threat** — (1) A potential cause of an unwanted event that could cause harm to a project and its assets. (2) A way of harming the project or its assets. The presence of threats indicates that vulnerabilities exist in a process, activity, or information asset.
>
> **Vulnerability** — An observed characteristic of a process, activity, information asset, or group of information assets (including a weakness) that can be exploited by a threat. Vulnerabilities result from weaknesses in processes, controls, environment, assets, and data.

Weakness — A process component that, for some reason, may be prone to not supporting the overall process as expected if certain conditions exist or occur. In the case of a product, a weakness appears when the requirements, architecture, physical product, or other artifacts have not adequately addressed the operational or support needs of the user or where the products were developed without applying a mature, adequate, or effective engineering or assurance process.

Threats can exist to all aspects of a project, including its information assets, processes, organization, infrastructure, and project culture. Information can be vulnerable to threats that result from weaknesses in its consistency, accuracy, currency, or availability. Processes can be vulnerable to management interference, bias, process maturity, staff experience, process integration, or support. Threats to the organization include size, cost and schedule estimation realism, staff morale and attrition, excessive pressure or overtime, management inconsistency or effectiveness, project focus, and requirements churn. The infrastructure can be threatened by availability of IT resources, tool availability, communication resources, network resources, funding shortfalls, schedule constraints, and communication and network, physical, or information security. Finally, the project culture can be threatened when either staff or external stakeholders lose trust in factors such as project cost or schedule performance, quality of deliverables, management failures, performance to agreements and commitments, or otherwise perceive the project to be unsuccessful.

When judged by their probability or potential impact, risks that result from threats and vulnerabilities are about the same. Risks that result from threats are of near-term concern, while risks from vulnerabilities are of concern over the long term, with more time available to mitigate them.

The basic risk identification process entails using a variety of techniques to examine all parts of the organization and determine what critical events would prevent a program from achieving its objectives. Risk indicators include:

- **Lack of stability, clarity, or understanding of requirements** — When requirements change or are not clearly stated, risks to performance, cost, and schedule can result.
- **Failure to use best practices** — The further a developer deviates from best practices, the higher the degree of risk.
- **New processes** — With any new process, whether related to design, analysis, or production, risks decrease as the processes are documented and validated, staff members are trained, and they successfully use the process over time. Process rigor is indicated

by documentation, validation, process maturity, and quality of implementation, which will reduce risk.

■ **Insufficient resources** — Risk to process implementation can result from inadequacies in staffing, including qualifications, funds, schedules, and tools.

■ **Test failure** — Risks can result when a corrective action necessary to address a test failure strains available resources or schedule, for example.

■ **Qualified supplier availability** — Risks can result from the unavailability of qualified outsource suppliers or from their inexperience or lack of qualifications in the specified design and production processes.

■ **Negative trends or forecasts** — Risks can result when the specific actions required to respond to a negative trend or forecast are not taken.

During the risk identification process, you should be attentive to factors that can minimize the visibility or awareness or otherwise mask indicators of critical risk. For example, a schedule risk indicated by a missed milestone can be masked by the fact that all schedules were increased an arbitrary 30 percent as a risk reserve. Schedule risk is less a function of remaining time than it is a function of milestone definition. As Putnam noted, "*Schedule* refers to the elapsed calendar time from the beginning of some phase of development to the end of that phase ... Measuring time is easy, of course. The difficulty lies in establishing unambiguous beginning and ending points."[16] If logical and achievable milestones are not defined, a schedule is already compromised.

Risk Identification Techniques

A risk officer can use a number of techniques to identify risks.

Commitment-Based Risk Management (CBRM)

This technique has two parts: commitment identification and commitment treeing.

Commitment identification — The first step is to identify and document basic organizational commitments by examining basic contractual documentation and amendments and other formal correspondence between developer organizations and between the developer and external organizations. For example, each organization has a basic commitment to its customer to deliver an acceptable product within cost and schedule constraints; and internal developer organizations have commitments with each other.

Commitments are categorized as either formal or informal. Formal commitments are documented obligations the project must meet to fulfill the contract. Informally, a project is committed to the subjective expectations of the customer related to any aspect of the project that carries particular risk. Customer expectations with regard to product performance, the development process, the degree of their involvement, reporting requirements, and the form, structure, quality, frequency and timeliness of deliveries must be fulfilled.

Commitment treeing — This technique creates a commitment tree or taxonomy that maps risks related to failures to meet project commitments, including failures to meet internal organization commitments to fulfill specific delivery, operational product support, schedule, budget, and scope obligations. The risk officer maps risks according to their effects on commitments made throughout all levels of the organization. The project manager can then use this information to assign responsibility for monitoring and/or mitigating risks at all levels in consultation with the risk officer. The risk owner is required to report risk metrics that will enable the likelihood of occurrence of the risk to be quantitatively assessed.

Commitment-based risk management is effective because it provides visibility to the highest impact risks by creating a project-specific taxonomy of commitments related to completing the project and satisfying customer expectations, which are the sources of risk in all its forms, and by enabling project management to use the organizational relationships within the project to mitigate them. It provides program managers, developers, and stakeholders a means to anticipate problems and mitigate their impacts if they occur.

Commitment-based risk management provides structure to the process, thus minimizing the difficulty and reducing the cost and time required to identify and track risks and understand their interrelated effects throughout the organization. It also enables a risk officer to focus attention on the most critical risks and assign risk responsibility to the right owner.

Staff Involvement

This technique involves all staff members in identifying and reporting risks from their own perspectives. The individuals involved with the day-to-day technical, cost, and scheduling aspects of the program are most aware of risks that must be managed. A risk officer can facilitate effective staff involvement by addressing two factors that can inhibit risk reporting: fear of retribution and passivity. Fear of retribution and other undesirable consequences can override any desire or requirement to report risks as they arise. An anonymous system of reporting can counter this fear. Passivity can result when a risk owner does not realize the severity of the consequences of a risk assessed by a risk officer who understands its consequences throughout the organization. Passivity can be overcome by providing incentives to encourage risk reporting.

Staff involvement is the most straightforward way to identify risks, but it has advantages and disadvantages. It is an effective way of identifying real risks that would otherwise not be identified, for example, sliding test schedules, potential design shortfalls, impending attrition, and other issues not visible to higher management or the risk officer. However, it is less effective than commitment-based risk management for identifying relationships between risks. Many risks that are reported are not-yet-visible problems. Their reporting tends to discourage the effective practice of risk management because project management sees a seemingly endless stream of bad news coming from the process. Additionally, the person who goes to the trouble to identify, document, and characterize a risk expects a certain response, and when none is forthcoming, morale can suffer.

Risk Assessments and Surveys

In this technique, an independent assessor uses assessments or surveys that compare a project against a predefined model to identify and characterize risk. This technique is more difficult than the others but it is an effective way to identify risk that requires little setup. Also, it does not assess process effectiveness or rate the capability of an organization to perform the work required except as related to individual risks.

The model selected should provide a comprehensive look at high-risk project areas — an assessment of each area conducted by asking a series of questions designed to identify risks and underlying causes. The types of risks include:

- **Technical risks** — Those associated with developing or modifying a design in an effort to provide improved system performance or interoperability with other systems.
- **Program risks** — Those associated with acquiring and using resources that are not within the control of the system developer or program manager and directly or indirectly affect project success.
- **Maintainability risks** — Those associated with fielding and maintaining the system, including hardware, software, help desk support, training, manpower and resources, and contractor support.
- **Cost risks** — Those associated with project growth and funding instability.

- **Schedule risks** — Those associated with schedule slippage during the system acquisition life cycle, including schedule slippage in interfacing projects and systems.
- **User acceptance risks** — Those associated with overall customer satisfaction and system performance against defined requirements.

We recently captured 195 separate observations during a 3-hour review. These observations revealed 38 previously unidentified risks, 14 of which were high impact, high probability risks that required immediate attention. A risk officer will typically listen for comments that may indicate risk:

- I'm assuming the tool works as you described it.
- There is a 90 percent chance they'll deliver on time.
- The customer really wants this product and I'm sure they'll spread roses at our feet if we give it to them.

The risk officer who hears such comments should ask questions designed to elicit further information:

- What if your perception is wrong?
- How can we plan for things not working out as planned?
- If things don't work out as planned, what mitigations make sense?

The risk officer then works with the person who made the comment to characterize the risk and enter it into the system.

Miscellaneous Other Methods

Many other methods of identifying risks can be applied. These include system safety techniques such as failure modes and effects analysis (FMEA),[17] security assessment techniques such as threat or vulnerability analysis,[18] SWOT analysis,[19] and a host of other quantitative and qualitative methods.

Risk Characterization

Risk characterization is part of the risk identification process. The purpose of risk characterization is to improve understanding of the risk and determine criticality, specific factors involved in gaining such understanding and deciding what can be done to mitigate the problem if the risk transitions to that level. Throughout this process, the information collected as part of the risk identification is translated into a usable form.

Risk characterization involves complex judgments and needs to project the impact and quantify the probability of occurrence. The detailed information essential for determining the best way to address risks is not necessarily available to the people responsible for making the decisions and the people affected by them. Much of this knowledge resides only with the organization that identifies the risk and it needs to be captured while the risk understanding and visibility are fresh.

To characterize risks, a risk officer integrates and assesses two components: the nature of the hazard and the exposure that the potential hazard presents. (A hazard is a threat or vulnerability that may result in a negative impact.) The purpose of this analysis is to determine the impact and probability of the resultant risk and the criticality of potential adverse outcomes. The risk officer works with the person who identified the risk (where possible) and, if assigned, the risk owner, to gather data needed to estimate the hazard and exposure; characterize the risk (combining the factors); and estimate the magnitude and probability of the anticipated adverse effect. The risk officer will work with the appropriate individual to collect the required information and record it on a risk characterization form. Table 10.6 is an example of such a form.

This form is intended to capture the information collected by the risk officer through consultations with technical experts and affected stakeholders who may have essential information or substantial influence over the project. The form should be completed as soon as a risk is identified — before this information is lost. Revising risk characterizations as conditions change facilitates future risk analysis requirements. By consulting with the individuals involved, a project culture of understanding and ownership is created.

"As in all things, ownership is a key component of success. People care more about the things they own, and software development projects are no exception. Fostering a team-wide sense of ownership makes each member accountable for the success of the project."[20]

Potential Risk Identification Activities during Estimation

Risk identification should be an essential part of the project cost estimation process. Risks are identified, characterized, and entered into the risk management system at three points: (1) during planning for the estimate, (2) during development of the estimate, and (3) during the validation and lessons learned phase.

Planning the estimate — The estimation team should collect estimation risks and account for them in the estimation process. The team should identify any item that results in some uncertainty as a risk, for example,

Table 10.6   Risk Characterization Form

Risk Title:	
Description:	
Status:	Risk basis: Threat (T) Vulnerability (V)
Probability:	
Likelihood of occurrence: (1 = very low; 5 = very high)	
Direct impact on organizational commitment? (Y or N)	
Impact (1 = very low; 5 = very high)	Precludes delivery or completion? (1.3 weighted impact)
Risk exposure: Probability × impact (1 = very low; 5 = very high)	
Impact timeframe:	Days-until-impact timeframe:
Earliest and latest dates of timeframe over which risk could occur:	
Impact horizon:	
Date risk first identified:	Critical path:
Person responsible for managing risk:	
Program areas affected by risk:	
Affected phase	WBS
	Development phase
Risk area:	Risk type:
Is responsibility for control of risk internal or external to organization:	
Contingency plan	
Risk mitigation description:	

Table 10.6 (continued)   Risk Characterization Form

Risk Mitigation Steps (Optional):				
Step	*Description*	*Person*	*Due Date*	*Done*

Metrics and Triggers:				
Metrics	*Selection Rationale*	*Analysis Trigger*	*Reporting Trigger*	*Action Trigger*

Date		Person		Event

trade-offs made, unsupported assumptions, management or stakeholder pressures, shortcuts taken, and lack of critical information. The estimation team should designate a member to serve as the risk collector and establish the team's responsibilities and reporting requirements with the risk officer. The team should look for "risk cues" that indicate situations or events that could compromise completion of the project.

Perhaps the most important of the risks listed above is management pressure to meet an unrealistic size, cost, or schedule target. Such pressure can cause a developer to feel compelled to develop an unrealistic estimate that is inconsistent with the available resources. Planning to address this discrepancy will help to minimize but cannot eliminate the risk. Unrealistic estimates assume certain progress and do not account for such risk cues as immature requirements, undefined interfaces, inadequate historical information, absence of standards for sizing the product, and poorly defined objectives, expectations, or goals. All these factors increase the risk that an estimate will not meet expectations. Risks should be resolved or addressed in the estimate as it is evaluated.

Developing the estimate — Most risks during estimate development are caused by inadequacy, incompleteness, and lack of relevant information on which the estimate is based. To ensure a project has a credible chance of meeting its commitments, the estimation team should identify and document any unusual circumstances that cause uncertainty in the estimate, such as trade-offs, assumptions, and inabilities to complete essential activities. The team should capture this information on a risk list in order of priority, with a focus on *core risks* that may cause a chain of other risks to occur. It is important to describe the conditions that could cause an identified risk to become visible and establish risk triggers if possible. It is not essential that these risks be characterized, but to facilitate subsequent analysis and increase its relevance, it is important to capture the risk impact, likelihood of occurrence, potential mitigation strategies, and other information as it is identified.

Validation, lessons learned, and uncertainties — Most risks to an estimate are identified in the validation phase and include shortcuts taken, assumptions, and unresolved issues. It is important that risk identification be pursued rigorously during this phase to provide an objective and forthright assessment of estimate validity. If the process is not followed or is poorly conducted, the estimate released to the customer can contain incorrect assumptions that create a false sense of well-being when in reality the project is set up for disaster. An estimate team member can record risks identified or management may want to assign the risk officer to perform this function to increase their visibility. The risk recorder should meet with the estimation team and document any anomalies or uncertainties they describe and work with them to evaluate the observations, looking for and documenting common threads that could require further analysis.

Step 4: Risk Analysis

The output of this step is the initial risk index. Risk analysis includes evaluating risk areas to determine risk events, assigning likelihood and consequences to each risk event, and creating a risk index. Project components such as systems engineering and personnel should undergo risk analysis. Risk analysis comprises a number of activities:

- Evaluation of identified risk events and determination of possible outcomes
- Identification of critical variances from known best practices
- Determination of likelihoods that the events will occur
- Descriptions of possible consequences

Evaluation — Each identified risk can be rated against the program criteria and assigned a low, moderate, or high rating (see Figure 10.1).

Critical variance — For each risk event related to process, the analysis team must determine the variance of the process from known standards or best practices and rate it. As shown in Figure 10.2, the risk assessment process has five levels (1 through 5). No variance equals no risk.

Likelihood or probability — The likelihood that each risk will occur must also be determined. The subjective criteria are remote, unlikely, likely, highly likely, and near certainty. Zero likelihood of an event means no risk (see Figure 10.2).

Consequence — For each risk identified, the following question must be answered: if the event occurs, what is the magnitude of the consequence? Consequence levels are numbered 1 through 5. A consequence is a multifaceted issue. Most often, four factors are considered when determining consequence: technical performance, schedule, cost, and impacts on other organizations. At least one of the four consequence areas needs to apply for risk to be present. If no adverse consequences are found in any areas, no risk exists.

Use of Metrics

Metrics provide managers with near real-time measures of project status and preclude the need for subjective decision making. They furnish quantitative planning goals and early risk warning triggers that require timely corrective program management action.

Two important elements of an effective metrics program are management support and a knowledgeable software support staff. Management support is required to ensure funding for the metrics effort and to encourage the use of metrics in decision making. A knowledgeable staff understands specific program and software system issues beyond the numbers in the raw metrics data and can translate crude metrics data into valuable information on program and system status.

Key management processes are implemented based on variances in predefined thresholds or trip wires. Metrics program preparation activities include:

- Identification of key metrics based on specific program decision requirements
- Tailoring selected metrics to track identified program risks
- Ensuring that metrics tie closely to the risk management plan
- Definition of metric thresholds
- Determination of a metrics review process and exit criteria

Use of Quantitative Triggers

Each risk should have an indicator that can be tracked against quantitative triggers to determine when action should be taken. When a risk is characterized, a metric is selected to indicate the increase or decrease in risk probability. This metric should be based on underlying risk conditions providing a quantitative measure of the degree of a condition in a project

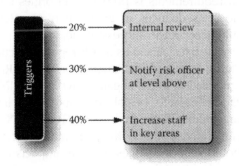

Figure 10.3   Sample risk triggers.

environment, an attribute of a product, or any artifacts that describe it. For example, a metric such as number of tests planned versus number successfully completed over a given period can be used to determine the state of the testing process and the risks associated with failing to meet critical test schedules. Product-based metrics such as defects per thousand lines of code provide indications of the potential quality of a product and accurate predictions of the risks of rework. Figure 10.3 illustrates sample triggers.

The risk officer is responsible for tracking the predefined thresholds (established when the risk was defined and reviewed and approved by the risk owner) tied to specific management-approved quantitative thresholds. As these thresholds are crossed, predefined actions take place automatically. Threshold categories can include:

- Analysis level: conducting secondary analysis using secondary measures and indicators to determine cause of condition
- Report level: reporting risk condition to risk officers in affected organizations
- Action level: initiating staged mitigation based on likelihood of occurrence

Triggers are quantitative. On a frequent basis, a risk officer should evaluate risks in the higher categories (see Step 6: Report Risks) against the assigned metrics to assess trigger status. When a trigger trips, the risk officer should take the assigned action.

Step 5: Prioritize Risks

The output of this step is an updated risk index. From the risk index created in Step 4, a prioritized list of risks weighted by specific offsets to address overarching critical requirements is prepared. Priorities are determined by the severity of the consequences in areas such as safety, security, and reliability that could jeopardize successful deployment. Stand-alone risk tools, such as Microsoft Excel (used as a risk register), Active Risk Manager (ARM), the Risk Rating System, Risk Radar, Risk Matrix, RiskNav, RiskTrak, Technical Risk Identification and Mitigation System (TRIMS), the Program Manager's WorkStation (PMWS), or risk tools integrated into broader, integrated project management tools such as PMTOOLBOX can be used to create and maintain the risk index. Keep in mind that the risk index is dynamic and it should reflect changes in likely impacts or probabilities.

Risks must be prioritized because no project has the resources to mitigate every risk. You therefore need to know which risks pose the greatest threat to a project and should receive priority. In addition, risks must be continuously prioritized because of changing circumstances or external forces that change the priorities of particular risks. The most important risks must be identified because most organizations can only actively mitigate a certain number of risks at a time. The risk officer should focus on actively tracking the highest priority and most likely risks and reporting to management those that may threaten project success.

A risk index can be used to track and prioritize risks based on criticality, the time available for action, their effects on safety, security, critical system operations, and other vital programmatic, operational, deployment, or enterprise factors. The risk index should include means of defining and assigning weights to predefined management factors to track changing priorities. Of course, some risks (designated *opportunities)* can generate desirable results. Such risks should be studied and implemented as appropriate.

Step 6: Report Risks

The output of this step is the reporting of risks to project management and stakeholders at a predetermined frequency based on priority, time to impact, and potential influence on the project should they transition to problems. Effective reporting results in timely mitigation of high priority risks.

Risks must be reported so that appropriate action can be taken. An effective reporting structure should focus on reporting problems so that they can be effectively resolved. The reporting structure should be actively maintained and regularly reviewed to allow the project staff to focus on the risks with the highest impacts.

Reporting Problems versus Risks

It is important to understand the differences between risks and problems when defining a reporting structure so that management understands that not all information in a risk report requires immediate action or that the enterprise, organization, or program has been affected. Risks represent the potential for future problems that have not yet resulted in impacts. An impact will result only if a risk transitions to a problem and is not successfully mitigated. Problems are risks that were not successfully mitigated and thus impacted a project. An organization should therefore have separate processes for both risk management and problem management. The risk officer should scan the risk database to identify risks that will produce problems based on the following criteria:

■ Risk impact is 4 or 5
■ Probability is 5
■ Timeframe is near

Problems and risks require different reporting and management processes. It is important to report the two as distinct categories of events to ensure that project staff members understand that risks are not problems.

Risk Reporting by Exposure

In a typical project of any duration, an effective risk management process will identify many risks, often hundreds of them. This will drown management in risks unless the risk officer maintains the risk list based on priorities and utilizes a consistent and effective process to report risks. The reporting levels are:

■ **Active level for highest priority risks** — The risk officer reports a certain number of highest priority risks — typically no more than 12 — to the manager on a frequent basis, normally several times a week.
■ **Reporting level for medium priority risks** — The risk officer actively tracks and reviews risks at reporting level and they may be evaluated by a risk review board regularly (normally weekly). The number of risks reported typically does not exceed 30.
■ **Archive level for lowest priority risks** — These risks are evaluated regularly but not necessarily frequently (normally every three to four months).

The manager should work with the risk officer to determine how many risks on the active list should be reviewed and how frequently. In our experience, some managers have wanted the top three risks reported daily; others require weekly reports of the top twenty.

Step 7: Establish Risk Reserve

The output of this step is the additional amount of time, money, or personnel required to fund mitigation activities that will take a program to successful completion. A risk reserve may be built into the estimates by setting the probability within parametric models. When the estimate is allocated to specific activities and elements of a project and the associated costs are accounted for and budgeted through the work breakdown structure, a reserve should be established to address potential problems.

The project manager should use a disciplined and comprehensive method to assess project risk in the estimate. Estimates of the required reserve should be defined and quantified throughout a project's life cycle as specific risk elements that can be used to provide adequate risk reserves.

By keeping and managing a risk reserve, an organization can fund mitigation activities and react to risks that transition to problems. Management must understand that the processes and costs associated with risk management are extremely cost-effective, while the cost of mitigation can be significant. When the cost of risk management is balanced against the cost of mitigation, both in dollars and reputation, risk management is a bargain.

A risk reserve should be managed and always address reality. The risk officer should offset the projected cost of mitigation by the number of risks and then recommend a reserve to management based on these calculations. The reserve should account for unanticipated or worst case risks and be stated as one of three ranges: optimistic, most likely, and pessimistic. The risk reserve should include the costs of the resources required to identify and manage critical and high risk areas and also include all projected estimates through risk resolution. The reserve should be a true management asset owned by the manager and it should include funds, resources, and potential staff required to address risks and their potential effects.

Management should frequently reassess the reserve, identify resources allocated to handle contingencies, and adjust the amount to account for mitigation costs. Management should also frequently analyze new requirements for the reserve, manage requirements creep, and account for potential expansion of work and its cost and schedule impacts. The risk reserve should be reevaluated and updated as risk assessments occur and account for such factors as:

- **Time** — Add to the schedule a percent above the estimated time to delivery based on risk of delivery.
- **Money** — Increase budget to include potential additional staff, tools, and time to potential project costs.

- **Staff and potential staff** — The personnel organization should continue to interview for good people and establish second sources for single point staff risks.
- **Resources** — Identify second sources and mitigate key resource risks.

Basic Risk Management Rules

Based on the seven risk management steps and a quantitative approach to dealing with cost uncertainties, we propose six basic risk management rules:

- Rule 1: Projects that fail to manage risk are at risk. All true project risk is plan-centered. If you do not know what your plan is, you face no risk. If your plan is vague, your understanding of risk is at least as vague.[21]
- Rule 2: Risk management is not free. Prepare to commit resources, define a risk management process, and make a risk reserve available.
- Rule 3: Centralize risk management responsibility; distributed responsibility must be coordinated.
- Rule 4: Prioritize risks and deal only with the most critical. All non-negligible risks must have mitigation strategies.
- Rule 5: Program managers are responsible for action; risk managers are responsible for risk identification and follow-up.
- Rule 6: The risk management process must be defined and consistently implemented throughout an organization. Activities must match the organization's risk management policy.

Risk Analysis Viewed as Uncertainty Analysis

According to Evin Stump, a statistical risk (uncertainty) expert, the following measures are popular forms of statistical and other quantitative risk analyses:

> **Qualitative analysis** — This analysis can be expressed in various simple charts (high, medium, or low impact; high, medium, or low probability, etc.). This tends to be performed at a high level of the project. Converting qualitative to quantitative measures is a very crude approximation. Limited accuracy is achieved by this method.
> **Algebraic approach** — Usually calculated as
>
> Risk = probability × consequence or equivalent.

This is a very limited approach that does not provide a great understanding of the risk.

Monte Carlo on work breakdown structure (WBS) cost totals — Each WBS cost total is assigned a distribution (commonly triangular). This is a very common approach.

Monte Carlo on a schedule network — Each task is assigned a time-to-complete distribution. This approach reveals only schedule risks. Schedule risk network analysis requires forward and backward "passes" through the network to characterize the possibly hundreds of paths, identify the critical path, slacks, etc. The approach is similar to minimum path dynamic programming.

Monte Carlo on list of parameters driving cost and schedule estimating relationships — Distributions are assigned to various cost driving parameters. Intervening equations convert these to risk distributions. SEER tools provide simulations of both costs and schedules. This technique is approximately what SEER does at the rollup level.

Monte Carlo simulation of cost and schedule estimating relationships at work element level — This covers costs and schedules and relationships connecting costs and schedules and accommodates "death stars" that fire bullets (big or small) at many work elements, affecting both cost and duration. This approach requires use of a schedule network processor.

The variations on these themes are too numerous to list here.[22]

Establishing Risk Reserve Using Commercial Grade Models

SEER-SEM can identify the amounts of schedule time and/or costs to be held in reserve. Simply prepare the baseline plan at whatever probability is desired — generally 50 percent, which is the most likely. Then set the probability to the higher desired probability — 80 percent is often used. Use the difference as the amount of risk reserve.

The following sections describe how SEER-SEM can help estimate the minimum resources required to satisfy project commitments, deliver a quality product within cost and schedule constraints, and meet the needs and expectations of the end user.

Risk Management Dealing with Cost Uncertainty

Parametric models that are of most value to a project manager provide risk and uncertainty data along with a likely estimate. As discussed

Figure 10.4   Estimate example without uncertainty.

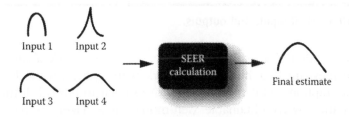

Figure 10.5   Estimate example including project uncertainty.

elsewhere in this chapter, no single number can represent an absolute estimate of the future but rather the result is a range of probable future outcomes. Ranges are natural results of uncertainties specified in inputs. Most parameters are entered in a least–likely–most format.[23]

Calculations made using SEER tools are obtained by running parametric inputs through estimating machinery — equations and historical actuals — to obtain an estimate. Now imagine that you know these parametric inputs with absolute certainty (see Figure 10.4). You will then be able to predict with absolute certainty.

Imagine instead, as is the norm, that you are not absolutely certain of the parametric inputs in your work elements. You have specified each parameter as a range from least to most. SEER uses these inputs to characterize probability distributions. It then sends these probability distributions through its analytic machinery (see Figure 10.5). The resulting estimate is a range of possible outcomes. Just as contributing factors include uncertainties, there will be uncertainties in outcomes.

Risk Analysis at the Work Element Level

SEER-SEM parameters specified as ranges have three inputs: least, likely, and most. SEER uses these inputs to construct a Pert (generalized beta)

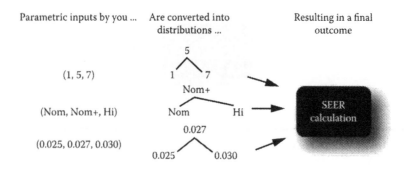

Figure 10.6 SEER inputs and outputs.

distribution. Pert distributions are very common in risk analysis work because they are intuitive, easy to work with, and form the basis of a good assumption. SEER characteristics are similar to normal distributions. Least is the lowest obtainable (left-most) value. Likely is the highest possible (peak) value. Most is the most likely (right-most) value. Figure 10.6 depicts SEER inputs and outputs.

The key to the distributions shown in Figure 10.6 is variation in the least, likely, and most inputs. If the parameter inputs had no variations, the distributions would all be flat lines. The resulting estimate would be a certainty. Estimates at 1 percent probability, 99 percent probability, and all levels in between would be the same as in Figure 10.4.

The more inputs vary, the greater the variation in estimated outcomes. Inputs vary based on a project's uncertainties. For example, the extent of instability in requirements during development may not be well understood when a project is in its early planning stages. The uncertainties are expressed as ranges describing the least (best), likely (expected), and most (worst) cases. These expressions of uncertainty help SEER-SEM bound the ranges of possible outcomes.

Pert Distribution Characteristics

The traditional Pert distribution has the following characteristics:

$$Mean = \frac{Least + 4 \times Likely + Most}{6}$$

$$\sigma = \frac{Most - Least}{6}$$

For a SEER estimate at 50 percent probability, the Pert Mean is used. For probabilities other than 50 percent, the derived standard deviation is used to obtain the alternate probability level. Since the least and most values may not be symmetrical in software development, SEER-SEM computes a separate standard deviation for the positive and negative sides. When the least and most inputs are symmetric about the likely input, this modified Pert is equivalent to the traditional Pert.

$$Right\sigma = \frac{Most - Mean}{3}$$

$$Left\sigma = \frac{Mean - Least}{3}$$

For each input (least, likely, and most), a distribution is generated. The probablity determines which value on the distribution to use for any particular input. This value is then passed through the model for calculation.

To compute an estimate for a given probability, recall that all parameters with least, likely, and most inputs have Pert distributions. With distributions known and specified by the parametric inputs, values at any probability level can be obtained. Imagine that an estimate is desired at the 40 percent level. SEER tools will obtain the estimate via the following steps: (1) all parameter distributions are sampled for their values at the 40 percent level; (2) these values are passed through the SEER estimating machinery. Because all parameters are set to the same probability level, the process is equivalent to fully correlating them.

Correlation is defined as the extent to which two variables vary together. SEER-SEM single WBS element estimates are normally calculated on the basis of factors that are fully correlated with one another. Optionally, users may invoke Monte Carlo analysis and view both correlated and uncorrelated results.

Probability and Intuition

By choosing the estimate probability, you can control precisely the amount of confidence or risk involved in a final estimate. Table 10.7 shows the association between probability and management intuition.

The probability parameters correspond to the probability of successful completion based on the inputs provided. When the probability parameters are high, risk is low; when they are low, risk is high. For example, if probabilities are set to 20 percent, SEER produces an estimate with an

Table 10.7   Probability and Intuition

Management Direction	Probability Level (Percent)
Make sure your estimate is very conservative.	80
Let's be very optimistic about things.	20
Give me a most likely estimate.	50

80 percent chance of being exceeded in reality. If probabilities are set to 90 percent, there is only a 10 percent chance of being exceeded in reality.

Probability-Based Risk Outputs

Figure 10.7 is a cost risk chart showing the full range of probabilistic outcomes.

Project and Roll-Up Risk Calculation

The project and roll-up risk calculation uses a special technique known as Monte Carlo sampling to provide statistically valid estimates at the project and roll-up levels. "The sum of the medians, not usually the median of the sum." Work element estimates are not static points; they are distributions of possible outcomes, as shown in Figure 10.8.

Statistics describing the distribution of outcomes usually cannot simply be added. For instance, if only the median cost of the distributions in Figure 10.8 were known, to say that the sum of the medians is 7 is not correct. The correct method for deriving the median of a combined estimate is to first combine the estimate distributions using Monte Carlo sampling and then derive a new median.

Monte Carlo is a type of statistical summing process by which distributions are combined by drawing from each in a probabilistic manner, adding the results of each draw, and creating a new sample from which statistics will be derived. Each draw is called an iteration; the more iterations, the larger the sample and the more accurate the resulting statistics will be (see Figure 10.9).

When the samples are statistically summed, the new median is 6.6 rather than the expected 7. Apparently the first sample has more weight. What we have done is akin to pulling one estimate from a "black box", another from a second box, summing the two, and thus developing a new combined estimate distribution. Statistics to describe the new distribution can then be derived.

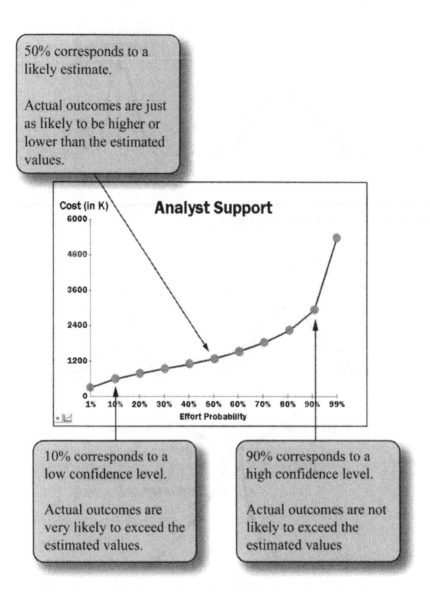

50% corresponds to a likely estimate.

Actual outcomes are just as likely to be higher or lower than the estimated values.

Analyst Support

Cost (in K)

10% corresponds to a low confidence level.

Actual outcomes are very likely to exceed the estimated values.

90% corresponds to a high confidence level.

Actual outcomes are not likely to exceed the estimated values

Figure 10.7 Cost risk chart.

Summary

In the previous sections, we discussed the seven essential steps that enable a project to manage the risks facing the organization. The essential relationships between risks and the size and cost estimates are used to

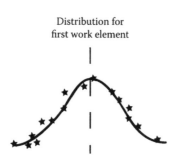

Distribution for
first work element

Median at 3

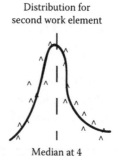

Distribution for
second work element

Median at 4

Figure 10.8 Work element distributions.

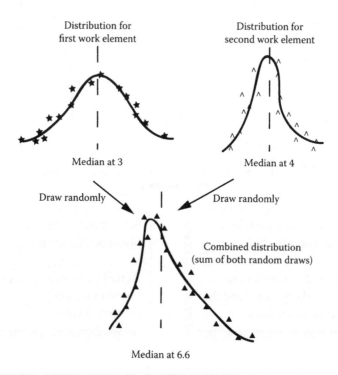

Distribution for
first work element

Median at 3

Distribution for
second work element

Median at 4

Draw randomly

Draw randomly

Combined distribution
(sum of both random draws)

Median at 6.6

Figure 10.9 Combined work element distributions.

project what resources can be made available to the organization to meet its delivery commitments to customers, users, and various stakeholders. If the estimate is too low, the trade-offs and unacceptable shortcuts necessary to keep costs within ceilings may result in unacceptable project risk. If too high, Parkinson's law may kick in, resulting in wasted resources and unnecessary expenditures.

To be effective, risk management must involve proactive participation by all levels of the acquirer and supplier organizations, continuous identification and analysis of risk based on a preplanned process, and a commitment by project management to use the information to make decisions and manage the project.

A project environment should include project-level risk management integrated with software cost estimation techniques. The basic definition of risk is the possibility of an undesirable outcome. Many undesirable outcomes are rooted in estimates that were poorly prepared or were offset by management or stakeholder pressure or bias. Poorly prepared estimates that serve as the basis for building software development plans lead to schedule compression, product compromises for schedule's sake, project shortcuts, and frustrated and overworked staff trying to make up budget shortfalls.

Risk management involves both assessment and control of risks. Cost models can be used in many ways to support both activities and can provide ways to identify risks by providing proven and consistent project descriptors. The cost factors included in models can serve as a checklist of risk items that correlate to cost and schedule overruns. Cost models also support various forms of cost and schedule risk analyses. Models help prioritize risks and support risk management planning in deciding the highest leverage options. Keep in mind though that cost estimation techniques are only subsets of those that can be used in risk management.

All projects involve risks; risk assessment and risk management are intended to address them. Risk management is a program management tool for handling events that might adversely impact a program, thereby increasing the likelihood of success. Risk management is a tool that will:

- Serve as a basis for identifying alternatives to achieve cost, schedule, and performance goals
- Assist in making decisions on budget and funding priorities
- Provide risk information for milestone decisions
- Allow monitoring of the health of a program as it proceeds

Endnotes

1. Boehm, B. "A Spiral Model of Software Development and Enhancement." 21.5. *IEEE Computer*, 1988. 61.
2. Weiss, David. "The Mudd Report: A Case Study of Navy Software Development Practices." Washington, D.C.: Naval Research Laboratory, May 21, 1975.
3. Evans, Michael W. "SPMN Director Identifies Sixteen Critical Software Practices." *CrossTalk: The Journal of Defense Software Engineering*, March 2001.
4. Doherty, Frank. Personal interview, September 2004.

5. Boehm, Barry. "Software Risk Management; Principles and Practices." 8.1. *IEEE Software*, 1991. 32.

6. Evans, Michael, Alex Abela, and Tom Beltz. "Seven Characteristics of Dysfunctional Software Projects." *CrossTalk: The Journal of Defense Software Engineering*, April 2002.

7. Hall, Elaine. *Managing Risk*. Reading: Addison Wesley, 1997. 20.

8. DeMarco, Tom. "Risk Management-Management for Adults." Software Technology Conference, Salt Lake City, 1996.

9. Boehm, Barry, Raymond Madachy, and Chris Abts. "Future Trends: Implications in Cost Estimation Models." *CrossTalk: The Journal of Defense Software Engineering*, April 2000.

10. Dekkers, Carol and Tom DeMarco. "e-Talk Radio: DeMarco, Tom." 22 February 2001. www.Stickyminds.com

11. Norden, P.V. and B.V. Dean, Eds., *Useful Tools For Project Management*. New York: John Wiley & Sons, 1963.

12. Molt, George. "Risk Management Fundamentals In Software Development." *CrossTalk: The Journal of Defense Software Engineering*, August 2000.

13. Putnam, Lawrence H. and Ware Meyers. *Industrial Strength Software: Effective Management Using Measurement*. Washington, D.C.: IEEE Computer Press, 1997. 27.

14. Rumsfeld, Donald. U.S. Department of Defense news briefing, February 12, 2002.

15. Institute of Electrical and Electronics Engineers and Electronic Industries Alliance. *IEEE/EIA Standard 12207*. New York: IEEE, March 1998.

16. Putnam, Lawrence H., and Ware Meyers. *Industrial Strength Software: Effective Management Using Measurement*. Washington, D.C.: IEEE Computer Press, 1997. 71.

17. National Aeronautics & Space Administration. *Software Safety Guidebook*. GB-8719.13. Washington, D.C., March 2004.

18. Information Technology Support Center. *Security Risk Assessment Guidebook*. Washington D.C.: U.S. Department of Labor, September 2001.

19. Osgood, William R. "SWOT Analysis, Where Is My Business Headed and Why? BUZGate: B2B Resources, 1999. http://buzgate.org/nh/bft_swot.html#

20. Holt,George. "Risk Management Fundamentals in Software Development." *CrossTalk: The Journal of Defense Software Engineering*, August 2000.

21. Stump, Evin. Personal correspondence, 2005.

22. Stump, Evin. Personal correspondence, 2005.

23. Galorath Incorporated Technical Note. *Comprehensive Risk Treatment in SEER Tools: How SEER Tools Handle Probability and Risk*. El Segundo: Galorath Incorporated, 2001.

Chapter 11

Applying SEER-SEM to Estimation Processes

Adding manpower to a late software project makes it later.

Frederick P. Brooks[1]

This chapter introduces the SEER Software Estimating Model (SEER-SEM), and provides basic definitions and concepts. The chapter illustrates how SEER-SEM fits into the estimation process described in Chapters 2 through 4; how to use the size information discussed in Chapters 5 through 8; and how it supports the risk management process defined in Chapter 10. (SEER support of Chapter 9 "Performing to Estimate" concepts are covered in Chapter 12.) Much of the information in this chapter was developed from Galorath Incorporated internal documents and other documentation published by Galorath. Therefore we acknowledge contributions by Karen McRitchie (Vice President of Development) and Lee Fischman (Director of Special Projects) who were the primary authors of many of these papers. Mike Ross (Chief Engineer) also provided documents from which this chapter was developed.

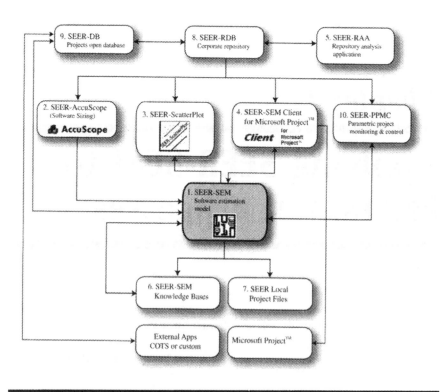

Figure 11.1 SEER Project Manager Edition, basic architecture.

Introduction to SEER-SEM Project Manager Edition Tools

SEER-SEM is the flagship product for software project estimation planning and control. As shown in Figure 11.1, the Project Manager Edition comprises a suite of tools that enable the user to conduct software sizing, software estimation, software project monitoring, and software project control. These functions are all supported by SEER-SEM and its knowledge bases. Additionally, for systems involving embedded software and hardware, SEER-H (the hardware estimation tool with total system vision) integrates software estimation with hardware estimation. It also provides system-level costs such as systems engineering, system project management, and system test operations for complex hardware and software systems producing total ownership costs. The Project Manager Edition includes ten components.

1. **SEER-SEM**™ — This is a powerful decision-support tool that estimates software development and maintenance costs, labor, staffing, schedule, reliability, and risk as a function of size, technology,

complexity, and any project management constraints. SEER-SEM is effective for all types of software projects, from commercial IT business applications to communications, to real-time embedded aerospace systems. It provides the information necessary to make vital decisions about development and maintenance of software products, ensuring project plans that are realistic and defensible.

2. **SEER-AccuScope**™ — This component allows you to ascertain project size using comparative analogy techniques. It is extremely useful for sizing, value assessment, and other quantitative measurements whose estimations of absolute value are difficult. SEER-AccuScope can also work with a repository of historical information that can be automatically transferred to SEER-SEM for cost, schedule, and risk analysis.

3. **SEER-ScatterPlot**™ — This is a repository analysis tool that allows users to view past data, perform regressions, develop and display trends, and compare them to new estimates for cross-checks and confidence. Users may filter datasets to the points of interest based on configurable criteria and may select individual points to examine their values or drop outliers. SEER-ScatterPlot also generates an equation based on the data and shows the correlation and other statistics. It can be configured to work with an SQL or desktop database.

4. **SEER-SEM Client For Microsoft Project**™ — This component transforms Microsoft Project into a tool for planning software development projects. The Client uses SEER-SEM's estimation engine to determine cost effort and schedule. The Client automatically constructs a complete project plan, letting you anticipate every aspect of the development life cycle. You can also have the Client automatically construct a complete project plan from your SEER-SEM project estimate. You can create custom life-cycle templates that build best practices directly into your project plans. You can also customize labor categories to reflect the way that your organization assigns tasks to departments or labor categories to accurately plan staff allocation for a project.

5. **SEER-RAA Repository Analysis Application** — This application allows users to add and edit data in the SEER repository (SEER-RDB). Data may be imported and exported as well.

6. **SEER-SEM knowledge bases** — Contain information regarding various project types and allow a range of estimates to be made with only a few high level inputs. Knowledge bases are divided into six categories for program, component, and unit elements and four categories for COTS elements. The six program, component, and unit knowledge bases are: (1) Platform, (2) Application, (3) Acquisition

Method, (4) Development Method, (5) Development Standard, and (6) Class. A knowledge base is a set of parameter values based on actual project, requirement, and environment data similar to an estimating scenario that can be used to initialize parameter values in WBS elements. Knowledge bases provide a relevant range of values that serve as benchmarks or sanity checks to reference as your project develops. They can be customized to reflect specific factors, and users may also add their own knowledge bases.[2]

7. **SEER Local Project Files** — SEER-SEM may store project files in its own internal format or an open database.

8. **SEER-RDB**™ — This is a corporate repository containing completed software project data. It may be used by SEER-SEM, SEER-AccuScope, and SEER-ScatterPlot.

9. **SEER-DB**™ — This is an open SEER-SEM project database for organizing project estimates, managing configuration, and allowing corporate access. It allows for version control, estimate archiving, and access control of project data. Additional applications may integrate pre- or postprocess data contained in SEER-DB.

10. **SEER-PPMC**™ — The PPMC acronym stands for parametric project monitoring and control (see Chapter 12). This component combines earned value management methods with parametric estimating methods and techniques and provides indications of project health that are timely, accurate, and closely connected to the root cause of potential trouble. The standard metrics are integral parts of the status indications process and include schedule, cost, and time variances, schedule and cost performance, and to-complete performance indices.

The Project Manager Edition is only part of the SEER family of products. Other SEER products worth mentioning in the context of this book are:

SEER-SEM Analyst Edition — This product suite includes a completely data-driven cross-check to a parametric estimate using SEER-ProjectMiner™ technology.

SEER-H™ **with Total System Vision** — SEER-H is a robust decision-support tool that provides a means for estimating the life-cycle cost for hardware projects of any size, from individual components to a variety of complete product assemblies. Using parametric algorithms, extensive knowledge bases, or user-supplied data, SEER-H can reliably and accurately estimate the total cost of ownership for new product development projects. It provides cost and pricing vision from project inception to production, including systems level, product development, production, operations and support, and disposal costs. It also provides detailed insight into the risks, uncertainties, and cost drivers associated with hardware development, acquisition, and integration. SEER-H can also integrate SEER-SEM and SEER-DFM (design for manufacturability) estimates, maintaining full association to the source estimate to provide the most complete and robust roll-up of an entire program or project, complete with system level costs.

SEER-CriticalMass™ — This component makes software sizing, often the most difficult part of software estimation, easier and more accurate, bringing practitioners and estimators closer. It allows you to automatically extract software size from requirements repositories or UML use cases. To accomplish this, SEER-CriticalMass integrates directly with IBM Rational Rose and Rational Modeler tools then exports sizing results directly to SEER-SEM.

Details and Uses

SEER-SEM is composed of a group of models that work together to provide estimates of effort, duration, staffing, and defects. The models can be briefly described based on the questions they can answer:

Sizing — How large is the software project being estimated?

Technology — How productive are the developers?

Effort and schedule calculation — What amounts of effort and time are required to complete the project?

Constrained effort and schedule calculation —How does the expected project outcome change when schedule and staffing constraints are applied?

Activity and labor allocations — How should activities and labor be allocated into the estimate?

Cost calculation — Based on the expected effort, duration, and labor allocation, how much will the project cost?

Defect calculation — Based on product type, project duration, and other information, what is the expected, objective quality of the delivered software?

Maintenance effort calculation — How much effort will be required to adequately maintain and upgrade a fielded software system?[3]

SEER-SEM's most basic concept revolves around Brooks' law[4] (there is an incremental person when added to a software project that increases, not decreases, the duration of a project). Minimum time is achieved by staffing a project as quickly as possible, but not so quickly that the project suffers from having too many people assigned. In this minimum time scenario, effort will be greater but the project will be completed as quickly as possible. The most important concept to understand is that there is a minimum time required to complete a software project. In order to complete a project more quickly, one must (1) build less software, (2) improve the technology and environment so that productivity increases, or (3) accept more risk (and possibly put the project on a death march[5]). Users may then refine the initial estimate by specifying the individual parameters, constraints, and other information. Trade-offs may then be performed until an acceptable project plan is determined.

Summary Input and Output Definitions

SEER-SEM contains numerous parameters defining size, complexity, technology, risk, and uncertainty (see Figure 11.2). The parameters are consolidated into the following categories:

SEER-SEM summary input and output definitions

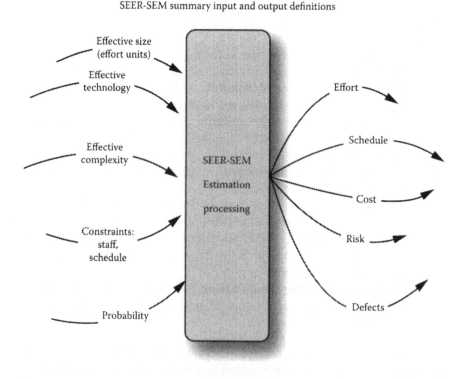

Figure 11.2 SEER-SEM summary inputs and outputs.

Effective size (effort units) — SEER-SEM derives internal size units (sometimes called effective size or effort units) from lines of code, function points, use cases, object points, or proxies that could describe any other size metric, taking into account whether the software is new or reused. Additionally, SEER-SEM tracks total size, that is, the size when the project is completed, independent of the effort required to build the product.

Effective technology — This is the measure of the developer's propensity for productivity based on the requirements of the product being developed. The greater the effective technology, the higher the propensity for productivity and the more productive the development will be. Effective technology is the combined impact of SEER-SEM's 34 technology and environment parameters (detailed later in the chapter). Effective technology may be used as an index to and a benchmark of productivity of the project being estimated, and these can be used to compare the productivity achieved on other projects and by other organizations independent of size and overall application complexity.

Effective complexity — This factor represents the difficulty of the software job. The greater the complexity, the more difficult to staff because of the complexity of the problem of completion in minimum time.

Constraints — SEER-SEM's constraints include user-supplied schedule and staffing constraints.

Probability — The effort and schedule probability (confidence level) at which estimates are calculated.

Effort — A measure of development effort expressed in months, hours, and costs.

Schedule — Development schedule duration in months and by date.

Risk — The range of risk and uncertainty in an estimate.

Defects — The number of defects produced and removed during development and the number of defects latent in the completed software.

Figure 11.3 illustrates SEER-SEM's Quick Estimate screen showing summary inputs and outputs.

SEER-SEM Concept

SEER-SEM is based on the concept that if a user can describe the essential characteristics of a project and range of size, SEER-SEM can provide

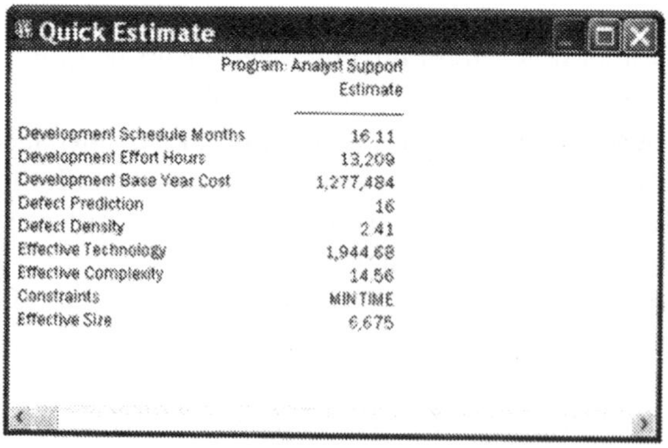

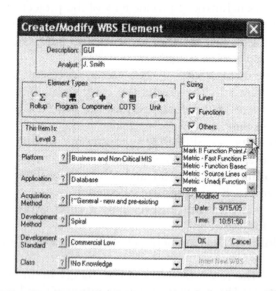

Figure 11.3   SEER-SEM quick estimate showing summary inputs and outputs.

Figure 11.4   SEER-SEM's Create/Modify WBS Element knowledge base selection.

estimates of schedules, efforts, staffing, risks, uncertainties, and defects, characterizing each as a most likely estimate or a risk estimate. Figure 11.4 illustrates the SEER-SEM screen that allows a user to create or modify WBS elements. For initial estimates, users only need to select knowledge bases from a list and input a size range, as follows:

- Platform (mission, e.g., financial processing, ERP, avionics)
- Application (function, e.g., database, business analysis tool, transaction processing)

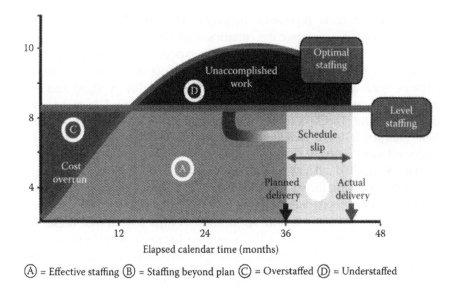

Figure 11.5   Staffing impacts on schedule and effort.

- Acquisition method (source, e.g., new development, concept reuse, major modification)
- Development method (paradigm, e.g., evolutionary, off-the-shelf integration, RUP, Web site construction)
- Development standard (development process, e.g., ISO 9001, ANSI J-016, none)
- Class (optional, user organization defined)
- Size (e.g., lines of code, function points, objects, use cases, screens)

SEER-SEM's initial estimation mathematics then compute the minimum time, effort hours, costs, delivered defects, risks, and uncertainties. The original model worked only with the Raleigh curve models for schedule and staffing. Today SEER-SEM will generate minimum time, optimal effort, and work with real-world staffing constraints imposed on a project.

Optimal effort stretches the schedule in order to achieve a lower cost plan. Constrained staffing uses comparisons to the actual staffing plan and generates the schedule and effort based on that staff. Figure 11.5 illustrates this.

SEER-SEM Sizing

In its initial versions, SEER-SEM used only lines of code as its baseline size input. (See Chapter 5 for a detailed discussion of this topic.) While source lines of code represent an accepted method of measuring size from a developer's perspective, metrics such as function points capture software size functionally, from a user's perspective. SEER-SEM's function-based sizing (FBS) metric extends function points so that hidden parts of software such as complex algorithms can more readily be sized and users can produce estimates even if they do not understand how to count function points. The FBS metric approximates unadjusted function points. (See Chapter 6 for a detailed discussion of function points and SEER function-based sizing.)

With SEER-SEM, all size metrics are translated to effective size, including those entered using function-based sizing. This is not a simple conversion. Rather, the tool incorporates factors including phase at estimate, operating environment, application, and application complexity. All of these considerations significantly affect the mapping between functional size and effective size. After function-based sizing is translated into function points, it is then converted into effective functions as:

$$UFP_e = NewSize + ExistingSize \times$$

$$\left(0.4 \times Redesign + 0.25 \times Reimpl + 0.35 \times Retest\right)$$

Effective functions increase in direct proportion to the amount of new software being developed. They also increase by lesser amounts as pre-existing code is reused in a project, depending on how much rework (classified as redesign, reimplementation, and retest) is required to reuse the code. Effective size is computed from effective functions as follows:

$$S_e = L_x \times \left(AdjFactor \times UFP\right)^{(Entropy/1.2)}$$

where L_x is a language-dependent expansion factor; AdjFactor is the outcome of calculations involving other factors mentioned above (i.e., phase at estimate, etc.); and Entropy ranges from 1.04 to 1.2 depending on the type of software being developed.[7]

SEER-SEM Programmatic Architecture

Open Databases

The full SEER suite includes two open databases that may or may not be used in any particular installation. SEER-DB allows the storage, retrieval, and configuration control of SEER project estimates from diverse locations via Internet, intranet, VPN, etc. SEER-RDB stores data from completed projects that can be accessed by SEER-AccuScope, SEER-ScatterPlot, and other SEER tools as well as Microsoft Office and other third-party tools.

Communicating with SEER-SEM via Microsoft COM

SEER-SEM supports Microsoft COM so that users can have dynamic links between SEER and other programs. For example, an Excel spreadsheet may contain software size data linked into SEER-SEM. In this case, changing the size in the spreadsheet will automatically update the SEER-SEM estimate. The SEER-SEM outputs can also be linked to any other programs that support Microsoft COM.

Server Mode

SEER-SEM has the capability to execute a stream of commands, either from the clipboard, a file, or via Microsoft automation. This feature quickly and automatically allows you to build and edit SEER-SEM project files that have input data coming from other sources. It is known as Server Mode because SEER-SEM can act as an estimating server to other applications.[8] Server Mode has been used for numerous applications, including Excel spreadsheets, SEER-SEM Client for Microsoft Project, Tecolote's Ace-It,[9] Frontier Technologies' ICE,[10] Phoenix's Model Center, and Engineous' Fiper.[11]

Applying SEER-SEM Project Manager Edition to the Estimation Process

The ten project estimation processes introduced in Chapters 2 through 4 can be efficiently executed using the SEER-SEM Project Manager Edition. Steps 1 through 9 will be reiterated throughout this chapter. Step 10 is covered in Chapter 12.

Steps 1 through 3: Establish Estimate Scope and Purpose; Establish Technical Baseline, Ground Rules, and Assumptions; and Collect Data

In Steven Covey's *Seven Habits of Highly Effective People*, we learned to "begin with the end in mind."[12] A SEER estimate also begins with the end in mind — bounded or defined by completing the first three steps of the estimation process. It is best to understand the purpose and scope, the project being estimated, and the ground rules and assumptions before developing a detailed estimate. A SEER-SEM estimate can be developed using only a single line WBS or with a detailed, decomposed WBS. The level of detail of the final estimate is determined by its scope and purpose. For example, if the goal is simply to generate a rough-order-of-magnitude (ROM) estimate, a high level trade-off, or a cross-check to another method, a single line may be sufficient. If an estimate will serve as the basis of a project plan, bid, or another high fidelity use, decomposing the WBS at least to the major computer program level is appropriate.

When using the SEER-SEM Project Manager Edition, you must also determine what activities will be included in the development effort. To that end, SEER-SEM enables you to compose a WBS all the way down to the lowest level component if desired. If the project will include maintenance, you specify the number of years of maintenance to be provided. SEER-SEM can also provide total ownership cost estimates, including estimates of both development and maintenance costs.

In defining the end state of an estimate, you must also determine whether the estimate will be most likely or risk-adjusted. If it will be adjusted for risk, you must determine your tolerance level for risk. Often estimates run at 50 percent probability (most likely), but for risk adjustment, an 80 percent probability may be most appropriate. Schedule and effort risk are controlled separately.

You may also determine the number and scope of releases if the system will be developed incrementally and released in stages. Although this action is not necessary for estimates made early in a project, we recommend separating releases for project plan level estimates.

Additionally, reuse and COTS software should be identified. Using SEER-SEM's ranges, it is possible to identify a blend of project alternatives and obtain most likely project costs and schedules even before detailed project decisions are made. To do so, provide a range of least, likely, and most of the various development alternatives. For example, 100 percent of the code could be developed from scratch or 50 percent could be developed from scratch with the other 50 percent provided by COTS. Once the actual development approach has been determined, it should be modeled using its range in SEER-SEM.

SEER-SEM helps establish and document the ground rules and assumptions upon which the estimate will be based by encouraging you to record notes that describe each WBS element and parameter. This feature also helps you document the source of estimate information and avoid some of the most frustrating aspects of planning a project: reviewing planning information and not remembering why you set your project parameters as you did and not understanding your assumptions. To assist in the data

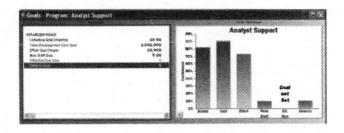

Figure 11.6 SEER-SEM goals and probability of achieving estimation.

collection process, the SEER-SEM knowledge bases provide much of the data needed to develop an initial estimate. In fact, you can use the knowledge bases in conjunction with SEER-AccuScope to quickly generate a viable first estimate.

In order to ensure the estimate you develop will be valid, it is critical to ensure that definitions for each parameter are well understood. You should also confirm that those definitions are being used. For example, you must diligently verify the definition of size you are using, the definitions of labor categories, the phase of the project you are estimating, and other essential inputs. Failure to do so can render an estimate worse than useless. For example, a support contractor once gave us a line of code count and, when asked how a line of code was defined, provided an unclear answer. We then read each definition of lines of code to the contractor and asked whether the definition was the one used to produce the count. Did the contractor use physical lines? Non-comment source lines? Amazingly, the contractor finally said, "We didn't get into that much detail." The contractor provided a size count for a deliverable product, without understanding what it was counting. The company simply made up the count. The Galorath size methodology matrix is designed to feed data into SEER-SEM, with a range of least, likely, and most for each size.

Before actually developing an estimate, it is very useful to identify specific goals in terms of schedules, costs, defects, and other issues. As shown in Figure 11.6, when you enter your goal into SEER-SEM, it provides useful feedback regarding the probability of achieving each goal based on project parameters.

SEER-SEM Software Sizing (Step 4)

Because size is the most important input, SEER-SEM provides numerous sizing tools and methods. Size can be described as lines of code, function points, SEER function-based sizing, use cases, etc. SEER-AccuScope performs relative sizing and numerous other alternatives using proxy features; and a host of other methods are available.

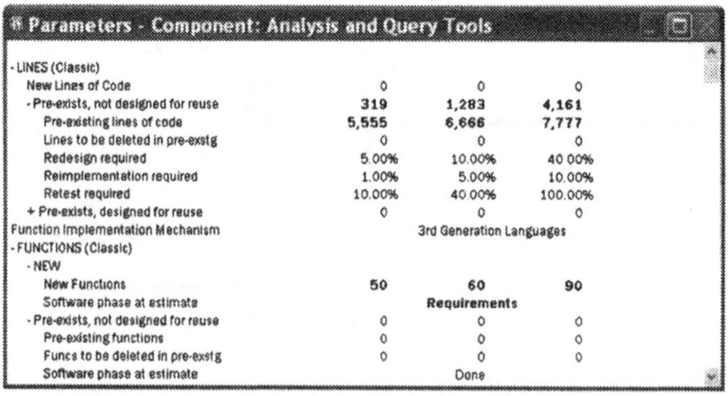

Parameters - Component: Analysis and Query Tools

- LINES (Classic)			
New Lines of Code	0	0	0
- Pre-exists, not designed for reuse	319	1,283	4,161
Pre-existing lines of code	5,555	6,666	7,777
Lines to be deleted in pre-exstg	0	0	0
Redesign required	5.00%	10.00%	40.00%
Reimplementation required	1.00%	5.00%	10.00%
Retest required	10.00%	40.00%	100.00%
+ Pre-exists, designed for reuse	0	0	0
Function Implementation Mechanism		3rd Generation Languages	
- FUNCTIONS (Classic)			
- NEW			
New Functions	50	60	90
Software phase at estimate		Requirements	
- Pre-exists, not designed for reuse	0	0	0
Pre-existing functions	0	0	0
Funcs to be deleted in pre-exstg	0	0	0
Software phase at estimate		Done	

Figure 11.7 Partial SEER-SEM input view showing lines and functions.

In the SEER context, software sizing refers to the estimation of (1) developed size; (2) amount of reuse; and (3) COTS components. As shown in Figure 11.7, users can enter lines of code and function points in the same estimate. This is extremely useful for estimating enhancements to an existing system. A code counter can be used to count the preexisting lines of code, and then the estimate for new functionality can be expressed in function points or SEER function based sizing.

Manual Sizing

Manually sizing (without a software sizing tool like SEER-AccuScope) involves counting or estimating lines of code, function points, SEER function-based sizing, etc., and determining how much is new, and how much is preexisting. Additionally, preexisting should be designated as *designed for reuse* and *not designed for reuse* so that the SEER-SEM reuse factors can operate with most precision (SEER-SEM knowledge bases provide different reuse factors for the preexisting code designed and not designed for reuse). Specific techniques for manual sizing were discussed in preceding chapters.

Automated Sizing with SEER-AccuScope

SEER-AccuScope enables you to automate the software sizing process at an early stage when relatively little is known about size. It uses a relative sizing process by which you can estimate project size by making judgment comparisons regarding the size of other known items and other unknown

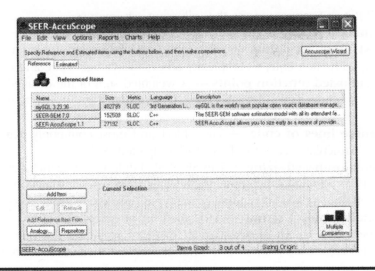

Figure 11.8   SEER-AccuScope sample screen.

items. As shown in Figure 11.8, SEER-AccuScope also includes a repository of past projects and analogies (domain specific functional patterns of your organization) that make relative sizing easier.

SEER-AccuScope's central focus is its estimated and reference items lists. It also accesses SEER-RDB for completed sizes and analogies. Initially, SEER-AccuScope includes three software-specific analogy sets: (1) functional; (2) desktop application; and (3) data-centric.

Functional analogies — The analogies in this set represent very specific items that could be built into desktop software, such as input screens, reports, and other items. This set is comprised of examples that are closely associated with function points. Functional analogies let you specify what an item under development most closely matches, and your entry will directly result in a function point count.

Desktop application analogies — The analogies in this set correspond to whole software applications of varying sizes. They let you compare the software you are building to complete applications. They are most useful if the modules you specify are relatively inclusive of functionality, such as entire subsystems, rather than much smaller functional elements.

Data-centric analogies — These analogies are based on the idea that you can anticipate system size by counting the number of key internal data structures around which the system is being designed. Research has provided some support for this idea, although these analogies are most appropriate for more data-driven systems rather than those that are more algorithmic. In industry parlance, counting data structures is sometimes called *sizing by inference.*

SEER-AccuScope supports the following size metrics:

Function points — The standard list of detailed function point entries.

Fast function points — The same set of detailed function point entries, with each entry's complexity all set to average, speeding entry.

Unadjusted function points — A weighted sum of the detailed function point entries that constitutes a useful summary form for function point entry.

Source lines of code — The oldest and most commonly accepted metric; particularly easy to obtain for completed code.

Function-based sizing — This SEER-SEM unique metric includes more detail than traditional function points. This makes size estimation easier while offering a clear accounting of the types of software artifacts counted.

Detailed object sizing — A detailed list of object points.

Base class — An object-oriented metric constituting the number of base classes; a class from which other classes are derived through inheritance.

Top level classes — A class is a category of objects. A top level class is another object-oriented metric that constitutes the number of top-level classes.

Use cases — Another object-oriented metric that enables you to estimate size at a very early stage of development.

User-defined metrics — Along with the standard list provided above, you can create your own metrics.

SEER-AccuScope will send its resulting sizes and WBS directly back into SEER-SEM for estimation processing, if desired. Figure 11.9 illustrates the comparison capability of SEER-AccuScope.

Choosing Knowledge Bases for Reuse Estimation

Because reuse is an important consideration in software sizing, SEER-SEM includes a wide range of reuse knowledge bases, each of which estimates the amount of redesign, reimplementation, and retesting required for reused software and categorizes the estimate as least, likely, and most. These knowledge bases also include, as a separate item, percentages for software designed for reuse and not designed for reuse. The following descriptive list of SEER-SEM reuse knowledge bases (which is not all inclusive) shows their associated amounts of estimated redesign, reimplementation, and retesting to provide indications of how useful these knowledge bases can be. Additionally, to provide further detail, the reengineering and modification categories show percentages for both code designed for reuse and code not designed for reuse. Note these values may be changed from time to time based on data.

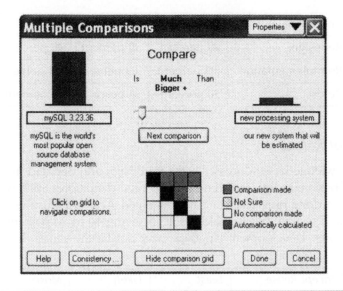

Figure 11.9   SEER-AccuScope relative sizing comparisons.

General — New and Preexisting

This knowledge base covers a combination of new and preexisting software. It describes the amount of rework estimated to be required for a wide range of preexisting software.

General — New and Preexisting	Least	Likely	Most
Redesign	5 percent	10 percent	40 percent
Reimplementation	1 percent	5 percent	10 percent
Retest	10 percent	40 percent	100 percent

Code Generator

This knowledge base addresses code developed via an automatic code generation tool. Although automatically generated code does not require detailed unit level testing and design, it does require the completion of architecture, interface, and other design tasks. A system based on automatically generated code also requires extensive testing, the estimation of which this knowledge base is designed to facilitate. Normally the size of generated code is expressed in terms of artifacts other than lines of code because the number of lines is not the key effort driver. However in cases where generated lines are the only size metrics available, the estimate of generated code should be entered as preexisting lines.

Code Generator	Least	Likely	Most
Redesign	20 percent	30 percent	40 percent
Reimplementation	.01 percent	.01 percent	.01 percent
Retest	50 percent	65 percent	80 percent

Concept Reuse

This knowledge base addresses software design appropriated from a well defined basic concept, including architectural definitions. Such work may have been done previously and then shelved. Concept reuse requires full coding and testing, but it could result in saving 10 to 20 percent in basic design costs. Development language may not be the same.

Concept Reuse	Least	Likely	Most
Redesign	80 percent	85 percent	90 percent
Reimplementation	100 percent	100 percent	100 percent
Retest	100 percent	100 percent	100 percent

Full Design Reuse

This knowledge base is for software utilizing a completely preexisting design that was successfully implemented and that is now being abstracted for reuse. Although this job is more like renovation than reuse, at least some low level design can be reused. Full recoding and testing are required, although design tasks are reduced 30 to 40 percent.

Full Design Reuse	Least	Likely	Most
Redesign	20 percent	30 percent	40 percent
Reimplementation	100 percent	100 percent	100 percent
Retest	100 percent	100 percent	100 percent

Integrate As-Is

This knowledge base supports integration as is, where no design or coding is required — well built code that is considered reliable and was delivered to the developer for virtually turnkey integration with the rest of the system. The software also may originate from a commercial library and be designed for full reuse. While some testing is required to ensure compliance and proper functioning, heavy internal testing of the delivered code is not necessary. This knowledge base assumes that testing will exercise about 10 to 30 percent of the delivered code.

Integrate As-Is	Least	Likely	Most
Redesign	0.01 percent	0.01 percent	0.01 percent
Reimplementation	0.01 percent	0.01 percent	0.01 percent
Retest	10 percent	20 percent	30 percent

Integrate with Configuration

This knowledge base supports use of an off-the-shelf software item intended to be customized, either through code patches or through extensive tables. The software must be customized (perhaps about 5 percent of the total delivered) in order to be useful. Testing will exercise about 10 to 30 percent of the delivered code.

Integrate with Configuration	Least	Likely	Most
Redesign	4 percent	5 percent	7 percent
Reimplementation	0.01 percent	0.01 percent	0.01 percent
Retest	10 percent	20 percent	30 percent

Language Conversion, Automated

Use this knowledge base for estimating the effort required to convert software from one language to another (e.g., from Fortran to C++) using an automated tool. This knowledge base assumes that no change need occur in the software design beyond what is dictated by the language change. The basic application and mission will remain intact. If there are further design changes beyond language conversion, rework should be examined and updated manually. While the automated tool used for conversion will account for the coding effort, some manual reimplementation effort is assumed.

Language Conversion, Automated	Least	Likely	Most
Redesign	2 percent	6 percent	13 percent
Reimplementation	1 percent	3 percent	6 percent
Retest	44 percent	49 percent	61 percent

Language Conversion, Manual

Use this knowledge base for estimating the effort required to convert software manually from one language to another (e.g., from Fortran to C++). It assumes that no change need occur in the software design beyond what is dictated by the language change. The basic application and mission remain intact.

Language Conversion, Manual	Least	Likely	Most
Redesign	2 percent	6 percent	13 percent
Reimplementation	100 percent	100 percent	100 percent
Retest	44 percent	49 percent	100 percent

Modification, Major

This knowledge base supports a major modification to existing software. Typically, the existing software will be used for a new application or mission. It often involves a target environment change and assumes the programming language will not have any significant changes.

Modification, Major	Least	Likely	Most
Redesign (code not designed for reuse)	10 percent	25 percent	91 percent
Reimplementation (code not designed for reuse)	6 percent	11 percent	22 percent
Retest (code not designed for reuse)	38 percent	59 percent	100 percent
Redesign (code designed for reuse)	2 percent	13 percent	23 percent
Reimplementation (code designed for reuse)	6 percent	2 percent	11 percent
Retest (code designed for reuse)	19 percent	15 percent	100 percent

Modification, Minor

This knowledge base supports a minor modification to existing software. Typically, the existing software is used for the same mission, with some changes in functionality. The target environment and programming language will not have any significant changes.

Modification, Minor	Least	Likely	Most
Redesign (code not designed for reuse)	2 percent	7 percent	15 percent
Reimplementation (code not designed for reuse)	1 percent	3 percent	7 percent
Retest (code not designed for reuse)	1 percent	6 percent	12 percent
Redesign (code designed for reuse)	0.01 percent	3 percent	4 percent
Reimplementation (code designed for reuse)	1 percent	1 percent	3 percent
Retest (code designed for reuse)	1 percent	1 percent	12 percent

Redocumentation

This knowledge base is for estimating the effort required to make major revisions to the software specifications and manuals. No change is made to the software. It assumes some familiarity with the software, and that some existing documentation (up to 25 percent) can be reused.

Redocumentation	Least	Likely	Most
Redesign	17 percent	29 percent	48 percent
Reimplementation	0 percent	0 percent	0 percent
Retest	0 percent	0 percent	0 percent

Reengineering, Major

This knowledge base supports major rework of an existing application to improve program structure, documentation, and maintainability. This effort will include moderate amounts of reverse engineering to ascertain the program design. The knowledge base assumes the basic functionality of the application will remain intact, and that the programming language will stay the same.

Reengineering, Major	Least	Likely	Most
Redesign (code not designed for reuse)	30 percent	47 percent	104 percent
Reimplementation (code not designed for reuse)	13 percent	50 percent	85 percent
Retest (code not designed for reuse)	44 percent	59 percent	100 percent
Redesign (code designed for reuse)	5 percent	23 percent	26 percent
Reimplementation (code designed for reuse)	13 percent	10 percent	43 percent
Retest (code designed for reuse)	22 percent	15 percent	100 percent

Reengineering, Minor

This knowledge base supports minor rework of an existing application to improve program structure and documentation. It assumes the basic functionality of the application will remain intact, and that the programming language will stay the same.

Reengineering, Minor	Least	Likely	Most
Redesign (code not designed for reuse)	15 percent	25 percent	84 percent
Reimplementation (code not designed for reuse)	7 percent	15 percent	65 percent
Retest (code not designed for reuse)	28 percent	39 percent	61 percent
Redesign (code designed for reuse)	3 percent	12 percent	21 percent
Reimplementation (code designed for reuse)	3 percent	7 percent	32 percent
Retest (code designed for reuse)	10 percent	14 percent	61 percent

Rehost, Major

This knowledge base supports rehosting software from one target environment to another. It assumes a change in operating systems, target hardware, and development tools (e.g., a port of an application from Windows to a Macintosh environment), that the basic functionality of the application will remain intact, and that the programming language will stay the same.

Rehost, Major	Least	Likely	Most
Redesign (code not designed for reuse)	3 percent	12 percent	25 percent
Reimplementation (code not designed for reuse)	1 percent	7 percent	13 percent
Retest (code not designed for reuse)	42 percent	50 percent	60 percent
Redesign (code designed for reuse)	1 percent	6 percent	6 percent
Reimplementation (code designed for reuse)	1 percent	1 percent	7 percent
Retest (code designed for reuse)	21 percent	12 percent	60 percent

Rehost, Minor

This knowledge base supports rehosting software from one target environment to a similar environment. It assumes no major operating system changes but accommodates differences in development tools between the platforms (e.g., a port from an SGI Unix workstation to a Sun Unix workstation). It also assumes the basic functionality of the application will remain intact, and that the programming language will stay the same.

Rehost, Minor	Least	Likely	Most
Redesign (code not designed for reuse)	2 percent	7 percent	15 percent
Reimplementation (code not designed for reuse)	1 percent	3 percent	7 percent
Retest (code not designed for reuse)	20 percent	25 percent	35 percent
Redesign (code designed for reuse)	0.01 percent	3 percent	4 percent
Reimplementation (code designed for reuse)	1 percent	1 percent	3 percent
Retest (code designed for reuse)	6 percent	10 percent	35 percent

Salvage Code

This knowledge base supports code that is being salvaged from another application where heavy redesign and coding must be applied to renovate the system successfully. The percentage of redesign and recoding required is probably more than half, and nearly full retesting is required. Salvaging code requires major changes to design, development environment, and even programming language.

Salvage Code	Least	Likely	Most
Redesign	40 percent	55 percent	70 percent
Reimplementation	40 percent	55 percent	70 percent
Retest	90 percent	95 percent	100 percent

Subsequent Incremental Build

Use this knowledge base for estimating a deliverable incremental releasable build other than the initial release. It assumes no requirements work after the development of the baseline. Maintenance estimates of subsequent builds or releases refer only to the portion of software being added and modified in this build.

Subsequent Incremental Build	Least	Likely	Most
Redesign	1 percent	5 percent	10 percent
Reimplementation	1 percent	1 percent	5 percent
Retest	5 percent	10 percent	50 percent

Using SEER Function-Based Sizing for Size Estimates

As discussed in Chapter 6 titled "Function-Based Sizing," SEER function-based sizing is often the quickest and easiest method of sizing, especially when it is employed interactively with sophisticated users or program managers who can usually provide ad hoc but valid estimates of the anticipated numbers of screens, databases, etc.

Using Number of Programs Included in Size

The number of programs included in the size estimate is an important parameter when the WBS has multiple computer programs in a single

WBS element. The number of programs included in size essentially takes the effective size and divides it by the number of programs included, estimates one of those programs, then multiplies by the number of programs. The schedule estimate is based on the time required for one program with schedule assuming parallel development. It is more precise to estimate each program individually. However, before such details are available, this allows reasonable effort estimates to be performed.

SEER-SEM Estimation Process (Step 5)

Figure 11.10 illustrates how SEER-SEM provides the functions needed to prepare a baseline estimate. Designing a project work breakdown structure (WBS) in SEER-SEM is the process of translating the technical baseline, established in Step 2 of the ten-step estimation process and entering this into SEER-SEM. To generate an estimate, you must create at least one WBS element to represent a stand-alone program.

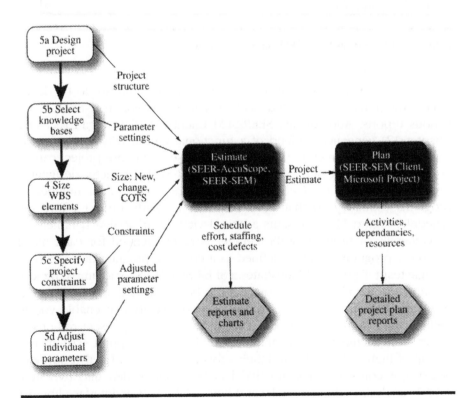

Figure 11.10 SEER-SEM estimation process. Steps 4 and 5 (size software and prepare baseline estimate).

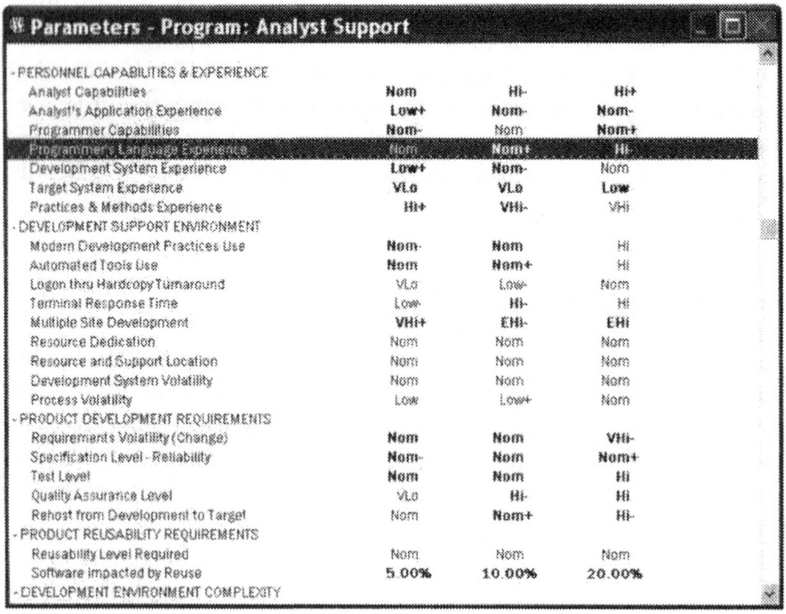

Parameters - Program: Analyst Support

- PERSONNEL CAPABILITIES & EXPERIENCE			
Analyst Capabilities	Nom	Hi-	Hi+
Analyst's Application Experience	Low+	Nom-	Nom-
Programmer Capabilities	Nom-	Nom	Nom+
Programmer's Language Experience	Nom	Nom+	Hi-
Development System Experience	Low+	Nom-	Nom
Target System Experience	VLo	VLo	Low
Practices & Methods Experience	Hi+	VHi-	VHi
- DEVELOPMENT SUPPORT ENVIRONMENT			
Modern Development Practices Use	Nom-	Nom	Hi
Automated Tools Use	Nom	Nom+	Hi
Logon thru Hardcopy Turnaround	VLo	Low-	Nom
Terminal Response Time	Low-	Hi-	Hi
Multiple Site Development	VHi+	EHi-	EHi
Resource Dedication	Nom	Nom	Nom
Resource and Support Location	Nom	Nom	Nom
Development System Volatility	Nom	Nom	Nom
Process Volatility	Low	Low+	Nom
- PRODUCT DEVELOPMENT REQUIREMENTS			
Requirements Volatility (Change)	Nom	Nom	VHi-
Specification Level - Reliability	Nom-	Nom	Nom+
Test Level	Nom	Nom	Hi
Quality Assurance Level	VLo	Hi-	Hi
Rehost from Development to Target	Nom	Nom+	Hi-
- PRODUCT REUSABILITY REQUIREMENTS			
Reusability Level Required	Nom	Nom	Nom
Software impacted by Reuse	5.00%	10.00%	20.00%
- DEVELOPMENT ENVIRONMENT COMPLEXITY			

Figure 11.11 Partial SEER-SEM parameter view.

The SEER-SEM WBS is functional, involving the software to be developed. Additional task-oriented WBS activities are noted in SEER-SEM's various reports. Additionally, SEER-SEM Client for Microsoft Project (see Chapter 12) generates a blend of a functional and activity levels for the work breakdown structure. In a minimum case, the entire project can be estimated as a single WBS element. The SEER-SEM parameter designated *programs included in size* must be set to reflect the total number of programs estimated so that SEER-SEM can properly project effort and schedule. Figure 11.11 presents a partial view of SEER-SEM parameters.

Generally, a program WBS element is recommended for each major computer program, which is defined as a cohesive program developed by a single team. Figure 11.12 illustrates a SEER-SEM WBS for a sample project. As shown in the illustration, programs can be subdivided into components or elements such as language, reuse, and complexity that enable you to define a project more accurately. The sigma symbols represent roll-ups of lower work elements. For example, Item 1 (trading support system) is a roll-up of Items 1.1 and 1.2 and their subitems. Item 1.1.1 (analyst support) is a major computer program that has been subdivided into two Item 1.1.1.1 (analysis and query tools) and Item 1.1.1.2 (screen interface library).

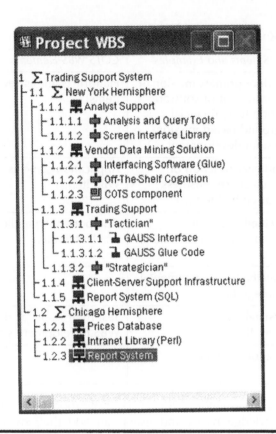

Figure 11.12   Sample SEER-SEM functional work breakdown structure.

SEER-SEM Estimation Process Step 5b: Select Knowledge Bases

The SEER-SEM user's manual defines a knowledge base as "a set of parameter values, based on actual project, requirement, and environment data similar to your estimating scenario, which can be used to initialize parameter values in your WBS elements. Knowledge bases provide a relevant range of values that serve as benchmarks or sanity checks to reference as your project develops, and they can be customized to reflect specific factors."

Knowledge bases provide ranges for all parameters as well as specific calibration information based on industry ranges of data. The first category (Platform) is the most general knowledge base of the set and contains information regarding every parameter. Application and the other knowledge bases refine the input contained in the Platform knowledge base. In general, Application knowledge bases include specifics on complexity

Table 11.1   Knowledge Base Categories

Developed WBS Items and Examples	*COTS WBS Elements and Examples*
Platform: describes primary mission or operating environment of software under estimation (e.g., financial processing, ground-based mission-critical, or intranet development ...)	Platform (same as developed WBS items)
Application: primary function of software (e.g., database, business analysis tool, or embedded ...)	Application(same as developed WBS items)
Acquisition method (e.g., new development, concept reuse, major modification ...)	Component type (database, plug-in, class library)
Development method (e.g., incremental, spiral, COTS integration ...)	
Development standard (e.g., commercial low, IEEE, ISO ...)	Test rigor (same as developed WBS development standard)
Class (organization-specific knowledge)	

and calibration information relevant to application type. SEER-SEM has numerous knowledge bases and users can add their own in the final category (Class). This category is designed specifically to hold information that is specific to the user's organization, such as labor rates, tool and practice ratings, etc. Organization-specific information will override information obtained from the five other knowledge bases.

You may have to choose between two close candidates. Pick the one that best represents or best describes the project. In some cases, you may be able to break down Program into lower level elements in order to pick individual knowledge bases (see Table 11.1 and Figure 11.13). You can fine-tune parameters to account for other situations.

SEER-SEM Estimation Process Step 5c: Specify Project Constraints

A software development project often has one overriding constraint: get it done as quickly as possible. SEER-SEM can support this need by estimating the minimum time, recommended staffing, and associated effort. When constraints such as staffing, schedule, and acceptable risk exist, SEER-SEM can be used to analyze trade-off scenarios between known

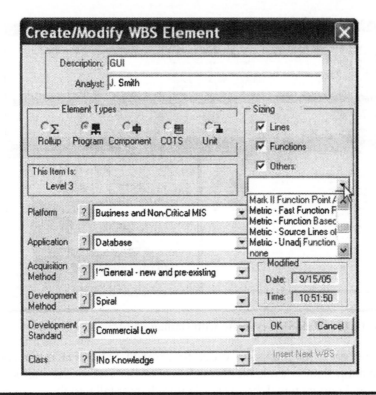

Figure 11.13 Selecting knowledge bases.

constraints, for example, determining whether it is worth adding an additional person to the effort or relaxing the schedule. Figure 11.14 illustrates a schedule constraint and trade-off. Figure 11.15 shows one method by which users may perform staffing and other trade-offs.

SEER-SEM Estimation Process Step 5d: Adjust Individual Parameters

If your goal is to establish a rough-order-of-magnitude estimate or perform a sanity check of an existing estimate, it is probably sufficient to enter size, knowledge bases, and use the output ranges of probability. While these actions may be sufficient to your purpose, Galorath recommends that you examine at least the top ten drivers to see whether you can extract more specific information to use in SEER-SEM to achieve more precise results.

If your purpose is to develop more detailed estimates to achieve effective project planning and control, Galorath recommends that you

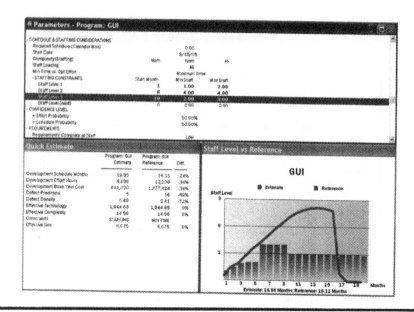

Figure 11.14   SEER-SEM estimate with staffing constraints.

examine each parameter in order to provide SEER-SEM more specific information than is available through use of the knowledge bases alone. Individual parameters defined later in this chapter fall into these categories:

- Lines
- Programs included in size
- Proxy sizing
- Development support environment
- Product reusability requirements
- Target environment
- Confidence level
- System integration
- Software maintenance
- Goals
- Functional implementation mechanism

- Functions
- Personnel capabilities and experience
- Product development requirements
- Development environment complexity
- Schedule and staffing considerations
- Requirements
- Economic factors
- Software metrics

SEER-SEM Estimation Process Step 6: Quantify Risks and Risk Analysis

The information provided in this section originated from material Galorath Incorporated (primarily Lee Fishman) developed, including the *OSD Software Estimation Guidebook*.[13] In quantifying risks and performing risk

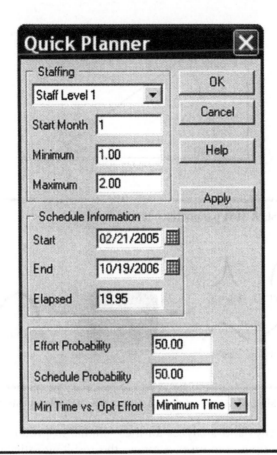

Figure 11.15   SEER-SEM Quick Planner for applying constraints.

analysis, two essential issues must be addressed: (1) SEER-SEM's least, likely, and most inputs and how they are processed, and (2) how SEER-SEM handles correlations at the parameter and program levels.

Distributions

Most parameters are entered into SEER-SEM using a least, likely, and most format as illustrated in Figure 11.16:

> **Least:** value at which 99 percent of actual outcomes are likely to lie above.
> **Likely:** 50 percent actual outcomes are likely to lie above this point and 50 percent below it.
> **Most:** value at which 99 percent of actual outcomes are likely to lie below.

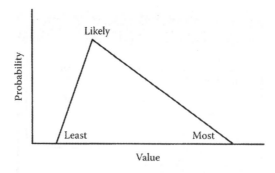

Figure 11.16 SEER-SEM parameter uncertainty range.

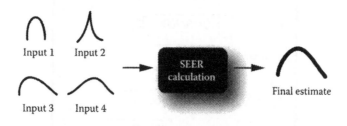

Figure 11.17 SEER-SEM uncertainty ranges generate risk-adjusted result.

SEER-SEM surveys and analyzes all these inputs to produce an estimate. Because each input comprises a range, the resulting estimate provides a range of outcomes, as illustrated in Figure 11.17.

All SEER-SEM's risk-based outputs rely on the distribution of inputs. SEER-SEM obtains estimates by collectively modulating parameters from their lowest to highest settings, from 1 through 99 percent probability. At each probability level, a new estimate is generated.

At the roll-up level, SEER-SEM will also perform a Monte Carlo analysis of a project comprised of multiple programs and report the aggregated results for schedule and costs. Figure 11.18 illustrates a representative Monte Carlo output for schedule. The Monte Carlo analysis is performed both with full correlation (dependent) and with no correlation (independent). Partial correlation and other risk enhancements are planned.

Probability Distribution of Output Ranges

Probability distributions of output ranges vary, depending on the input ranges the user has specified or the values in the knowledge bases if the user has not varied the parameters from their knowledge base values.

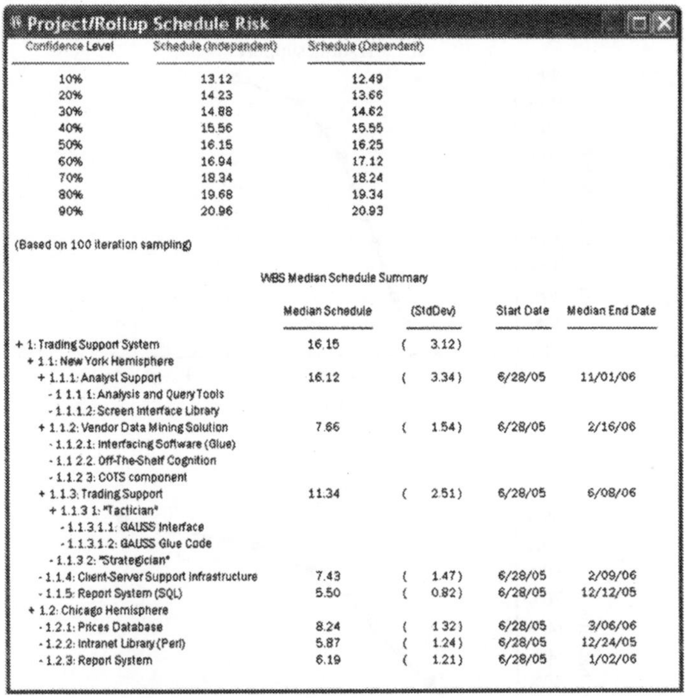
Project/Rollup Schedule Risk

Confidence Level	Schedule (Independent)	Schedule (Dependent)
10%	13.12	12.49
20%	14.23	13.66
30%	14.88	14.62
40%	15.56	15.55
50%	16.15	16.25
60%	16.94	17.12
70%	18.34	18.24
80%	19.68	19.34
90%	20.96	20.93

(Based on 100 iteration sampling)

WBS Median Schedule Summary

	Median Schedule	(StdDev)	Start Date	Median End Date
+ 1: Trading Support System	16.15	(3.12)		
+ 1.1: New York Hemisphere				
+ 1.1.1: Analyst Support	16.12	(3.34)	6/28/05	11/01/06
- 1.1.1.1: Analysis and Query Tools				
- 1.1.1.2: Screen Interface Library				
+ 1.1.2: Vendor Data Mining Solution	7.66	(1.54)	6/28/05	2/16/06
- 1.1.2.1: Interfacing Software (Glue)				
- 1.1.2.2. Off-The-Shelf Cognition				
- 1.1.2.3: COTS component				
+ 1.1.3: Trading Support	11.34	(2.51)	6/28/05	6/08/06
+ 1.1.3.1: "Tactician"				
- 1.1.3.1.1: GAUSS Interface				
- 1.1.3.1.2: GAUSS Glue Code				
- 1.1.3.2: "Strategician"				
- 1.1.4: Client-Server Support Infrastructure	7.43	(1.47)	6/28/05	2/09/06
- 1.1.5: Report System (SQL)	5.50	(0.82)	6/28/05	12/12/05
+ 1.2: Chicago Hemisphere				
- 1.2.1: Prices Database	8.24	(1.32)	6/28/05	3/06/06
- 1.2.2: Intranet Library (Perl)	5.87	(1.24)	6/28/05	12/24/05
- 1.2.3: Report System	6.19	(1.21)	6/28/05	1/02/06

Figure 11.18 SEER-SEM Monte Carlo analysis result.

SEER-SEM's risk evaluation capability falls into two basic categories: probability distributions and sensitivity evaluation. Probability distribution charts give estimates that range from 1 through 99 percent. Sensitivity analyses show how the entire estimate will vary as specific parameters are modulated. Most probability estimates are presented graphically, for management review and analysis. Figure 11.19 is a representative probability estimate.

Risk profiles that are relatively level indicate that program risk is slight. By contrast, a sharply increasing profile indicates the presence of substantial risk where quite different outcomes are possible. Note that parameter settings directly drive risk. If a risk profile sharply increases, it has parameters with inputs that are set wide apart. The sensitivity charts in the following section provide more information regarding risk.

Risk Factor Analysis with Sensitivity Charts

Sensitivity charts, such as those illustrated in Figure 11.20, allow you to further examine the impacts of specific parameters to more accurately identify the sources of risk.

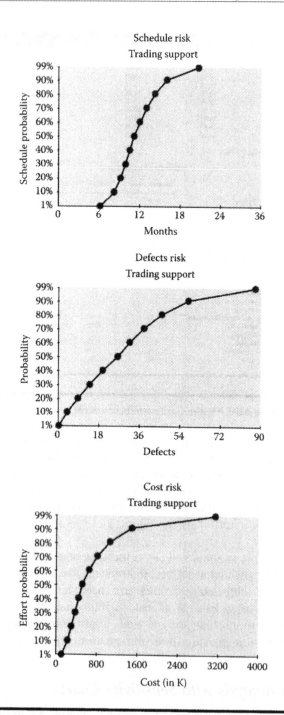

Figure 11.19   Representative SEER-SEM probability estimate.

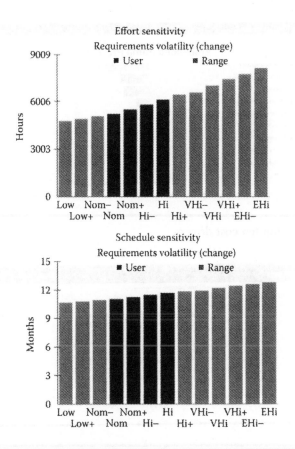

Figure 11.20   Representative SEER-SEM sensitivity charts.

Ranked Risks with Top Ten Cost Drivers Chart

A major part of a project manager's mandate is to identify and mitigate sources of risk. SEER-SEM offers an analogous automated capability through its Top Ten Cost Drivers Chart (Figure 11.21), which rates the extent to which each parameter setting drives estimated cost. Use its ratings as guides to which parameters need a closer look.

Precise Estimate Distributions through Risk Analysis Report

After you have determined the probability level at which to extract estimates, the next step is to use the risk analysis report to view the effort, schedule, etc., at the desired probability. This report (Figure 11.22 is an example) offers precise numbers in an easily viewed format.

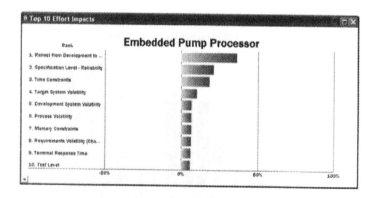

Figure 11.21   Top ten cost drivers.

| Probability | Sched Months | Development | | | | Maintenance | |
		Effort Months	Effort Hours	Cost		Effort Months	Cost
1%	5.56	5.42	823.94	79,684		6	68,706
10%	6.58	8.01	1,216.77	117,675		9	127,785
20%	7.02	9.39	1,426.23	137,931		10	148,167
30%	7.34	10.50	1,596.47	154,395		11	164,546
40%	7.62	11.55	1,756.01	169,824		12	179,680
50%	7.89	12.62	1,917.85	185,476		13	194,941
60%	8.32	14.68	2,231.12	215,773		16	235,339
70%	8.80	17.20	2,613.69	252,771		19	286,287
80%	9.37	20.60	3,131.87	302,865		24	357,786
90%	10.20	26.28	3,995.06	386,364		33	482,612
99%	12.36	45.51	6,916.96	668,942		64	942,193

Figure 11.22   Representative risk analysis report.

Figure 11.23 illustrates the confidence tuners for changing probability and the differences in staff levels, effort, and schedule. In this example it appears that the 80 percent probability increases the minimum time schedule and the effort.

SEER-SEM Estimation Process Step 7: Review, Verify, and Validate Estimate

I once visited a top-level official in the office of the Secretary of Defense who expressed concerns that he had no way to understand whether an estimate he received was valid. I then showed him the SEER-SEM estimate assessment chart. Although he had seen many SEER-SEM estimates, no one had ever shown him the estimate assessment chart. I was surprised because the chart clearly revealed how the current project stacked up

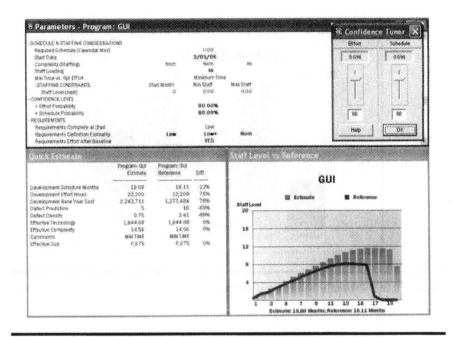

Figure 11.23   SEER staffing levels.

against others and whether the input parameters were reasonable for the system under estimation.[14]

Of the many internal sanity checks that SEER-SEM provides, the easiest to use is the color-coded estimate assessment chart. Green, yellow, and red are used to indicate how closely the estimate compares to the knowledge base ranges. The need for such a tool became apparent when I noticed that one of our new analysts was inappropriately changing technology parameters. When asked if he had looked at the effective technology and effective complexity based on the changes he made, he froze and I then realized I could not depend on analysts to look at the effective technology, effective complexity, and other sanity check numbers in models. The estimate assessment became a simple means of comparison as shown in Figure 11.24.

After an estimate is completed, it is often useful to compare it to industry ranges and/or historical projects to compare with prior systems and see where it falls in comparison to past projects. If results are significantly higher or lower than history, the chart provides some insight and allows the reasons for differences to be reconciled. This is illustrated in Figure 11.25 and Figure 11.26.

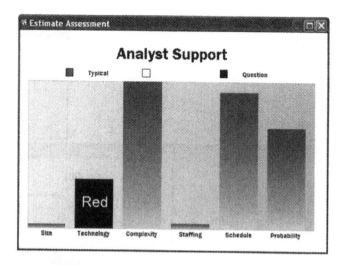

Figure 11.24   Estimate assessment chart.

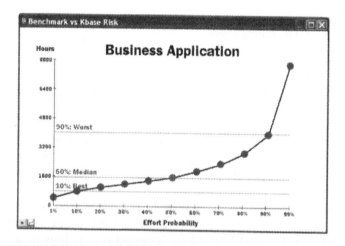

Figure 11.25   Benchmark versus KBase shows how this project compares to others.

SEER-SEM Estimation Process Step 8: Generate Project Plan

See Chapter 12, titled "SEER-SEM Solution for Project Management and Control," for a detailed discussion of how SEER-SEM can be used to achieve this step in the software estimation process.

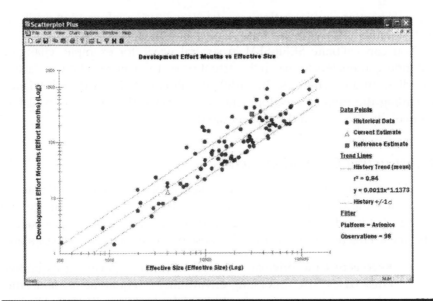

Figure 11.26   Scatterplot of effort versus size.

SEER-SEM Estimation Process Step 9: Document Estimate and Lessons Learned

The SEER-SEM method of software estimation automatically documents the estimate and the lessons learned, including the WBS, project parameters, and any notes created.

Custom Knowledge Bases and Calibration

SEER-SEM provides the option of developing a custom knowledge base to document a project for future reference. You can include such details as calibration numbers from completed projects and parameter ranges for particular development scenarios. Additionally, scenarios capture estimate templates including multiple WBS elements, knowledge base selections, and other information.

Calibration (Part of Lessons Learned)

You can calibrate SEER-SEM to your data or environment if desired by changing individual parameters or using SEER-SEM's calibration factors.

The information in this section was developed using information available in Galorath's *OSD Software Estimation Guidebook.*[13]

You can calibrate SEER-SEM in several ways, for example, changing the input parameters to match the actual project or using calibration factors to adjust future estimates. In order to calibrate SEER-SEM, information regarding the original development of the application must be available, particularly the time and effort required.

Constructing Calibration Factors

A calibration factor — which is an adjustment to a project estimate — constitutes the difference between the default outcome of an estimate and a range that is judged for a particular case in order to be more representative. The most effective ways to find the best possible calibration factors are:

1. Reconstruct the original software project by specifying its knowledge bases, size, operating environment, requirements, and other related parameters. Obtain SEER-SEM schedule and effort estimates for this project.
2. Compare the estimates to the actual schedule and effort data on the project. The proportional difference or variance (actual divided by estimate) is the initial calibration factor. Of course SEER-SEM does the generation automatically.
3. If information on projects completed by the proposed development team is available, generate SEER-SEM estimates for those projects as well. Find the variances for those estimates.
4. You can now obtain a new calibration factor. Compare the variance for the application under consideration with variances found for projects the proposed development team has completed (see Figure 11.27).
5. Enter final calibration factors for effort or schedule (whichever is available) into a class knowledge base.

SEER-SEM Estimation Process Step 10: Track Project

See Chapter 12 for a detailed discussion of the use of SEER-SEM and its Project Manager Edition to track a project throughout its life cycle.

SEER-SEM Internals

The following material covers basic SEER-SEM mathematics as well as definitions.

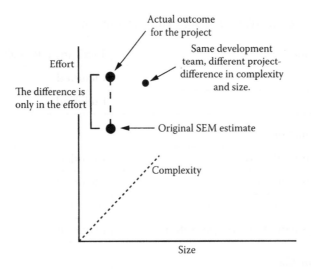

Figure 11.27   Identifying project variances.

SEER-SEM Basic Size Definition

SEER-SEM uses the logical SLOC identified in Chapter 5 and unadjusted function points. However, SEER-SEM can be recalibrated to your unique size definition if desired.

SEER-SEM Staff Hour Definition

Table 11.2 identifies the labor included and excluded in an out-of-the-box SEER-SEM estimate. You can calibrate SEER-SEM and include activities and labor categories that SEER-SEM initially excludes or exclude activities and labor categories that SEER-SEM normally includes.

SEER-SEM Mathematical Model Overview

This section describes significant mathematical relationships in the SEER-SEM parametric software estimating model. The Figure 11.28 flowchart provides a high level view into some of the major components of SEER-SEM computations.

Effective Size Mathematics

Effective Size (S_e) is used by SEER-SEM as a key input to compute effort, schedule, and defects. Effective size is calculated from user inputs. Size

Table 11.2 Basic SEER-SEM Staff Hour Definition

Type of Labor	Totals Include (Full SEER-SEM)
Direct	Included
Indirect	Excluded
Hour Information	
Regular time, salaried	Included
Regular time, hourly	Included
Overtime, salaried, compensated	Included
Overtime, salaried, uncompensated	Included
Employment Class	
Reporting organization, full time	Included
Reporting organization, part time	Included
Temporary contractor	Included if direct labor
Subcontractor working on task, reporting to organization	Included if direct labor
Subcontractor working on subcontracted task	If included in direct labor
Consultants	If included in direct labor
Labor Class	
Software Management	
Level 1	Included
Level 2	Included if direct labor
Level 3	Included if direct labor (rare)
Level 4	Included if direct labor (rare)
Technical Analysts and Designers	
System engineer	Included for software work only
Software engineer/analyst	Included
Programmer	Included
Test personnel	Included

Table 11.2 (continued)   Basic SEER-SEM Staff Hour Definition

Program-to-Program integration	Included
IV&V	Excluded
Test and evaluation group (HW–SW)	Included
Software configuration management	Internal CM included
Programmer librarian	Included
Database administrator	Excluded
Documentation/publications	Excluded
Training personnel	Excluded
Support staff	Excluded
SEER-SEM Activities	Totals Include (Full SEER-SEM)
Primary development activity	Included
Concept demo/prototypes	Included if described by user
Tools development, acquisition, installation, and support	Excluded
Nondelivered software and test driver	Included
Maintenance	
Repair	Included
Enhancements and major updates	Included if user requests
Program-Level Functions (Major Functional Element)	
Software requirements analysis	Included
Preliminary design	Included
Detailed design	Included
Code and development testing	Included
Program integration and testing	Included
IV&V	Excluded
Management	Included
Software quality assurance	Included
Configuration management	Included

Table 11.2 (continued) Basic SEER-SEM Staff Hour Definition

Documentation	Program specifications and data
Rework software requirements	Included
Redesign	Included
Recoding	Included
Retesting	Included
Documentation	Included
Program-to-Program Integration and Checkout	Included
Hardware/software integration and testing	Included
Management	Included
Software quality assurance	Included
Configuration management	Included
Documentation	Included
IV&V	Excluded
System Level Functions (Software Effort Only)	
System requirements and design	Included
Systems requirements analysis	Included
System design	Included
Software requirements analysis	Included
Integration, testing and evaluation	Included
Production and deployment	Excluded
Management	Included
Software quality assurance	Included
Configuration management	Included
Data	Included
Training	
Training of development employees	Excluded
Customer training	Excluded
Support	Excluded

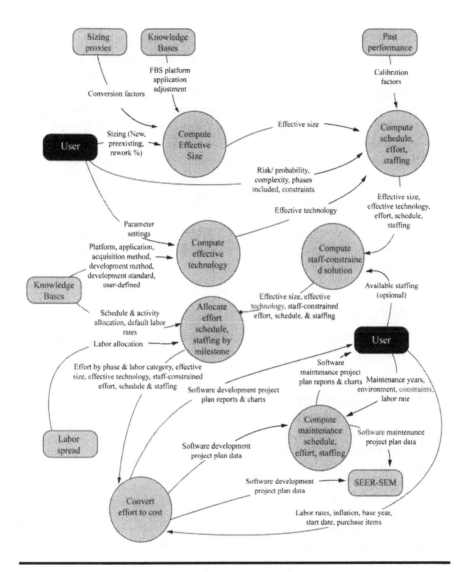

Figure 11.28 Core SEER-SEM mathematics overview.

inputs in SEER-SEM can be entered via a variety of metrics including source lines of code (SLOC) and unadjusted function points (UFP). Definitions of SLOC vary somewhat by language, but essentially SLOC include logical lines of code, excluding comments, blanks, nondelivered utilities and debug codes. Effective size considers new, reworked, and COTS code. Effective size calculations are covered in detail in Chapter 8.

Function-Based Sizing Mathematics

Function-based sizing (FBS) uses functional size measures to scope a software project. SEER-SEM uses definitions of functions consistent with the counting standards of the International Function Point Users Group (IFPUG). Functional inputs may be entered at a very detailed level (input screens, data tables), at a function count level (EI, EO, EQ, ILF, EIF, and IF), or as UFP count. Effective Size (S_e) is based on a given language and expressed in effective effort units. The size can be calculated as:

$$S_e = L_x \times \left(AdjFactor \times UFP \right)^{(Entropy/1.2)}$$

L_x is the language expansion factor. AdjFactor is the product of the complexity, count phase, platform, and application adjustments. Entropy ranges from 1.04 to 1.2.

Parameters

The effort, schedule, staffing, and other calculations in SEER-SEM are driven primarily by size but also by other parameters that characterize:

- Personnel capabilities and experience
- Development support environment
- Product development requirements
- Product reusability requirements
- Development environment complexity
- Target environment
- Schedule and staffing considerations
- Requirements
- System integration
- Economic factors
- Software maintenance

A complete list of SEER-SEM parameters and their definitions is available in the *SEER-SEM User's Manual*.

Knowledge Bases

SEER-SEM incorporates knowledge bases that provide parameter settings typical for a given software development scenario. To date, Galorath has examined well over 8,000 software development projects and continues to gather and analyze data to provide reasonable parameter settings that reflect particular development scenarios. Knowledge bases will populate all parameters, but any parameter setting may be overridden with user settings when the analyst has more specific knowledge. Knowledge bases are segregated into several categories:

A *platform knowledge base* is a collection of input parameter settings that characterize a particular host environment.

An *application knowledge base* is a set of parameter settings that characterizes the primary function or application technology type.

An *acquisition method knowledge base* is a collection of input parameter settings that characterizes the source of the software and associated rework requirements.

A *development method knowledge base* is a collection of input parameter settings that characterize the particular software development life cycle method or paradigm that will be used.

A *development standard knowledge base* is a collection of input parameter settings that characterize a particular software development process standard that will be used.

Effective Technology Calculation

The SEER-SEM parameters (from analyst capabilities to security requirements; see Figure 11.30) are combined in a quantitative measure called effective technology (C_{te}). The effective technology and size parameters are used in effort and schedule calculations. Effective technology measures the potential to be productive on a project. It quantifies the combined impact of the technology and environment parameters. The greater the effective technology, the more productive the development will be. The effective technology has a theoretical range of 0 to 20,000. An intermediate value called basic technology (C_{tb}) is used in the calculation of effective technology.

Basic technology calculation — Inputs going into the basic technology are:

■ Analyst capabilities (ACAP)	■ Analyst's application experience (AEXP)
■ Programmer capabilities (PCAP)	■ Application class complexity (APPL)
■ Automated tool use (TOOL)	■ Log on through hardcopy turnaround (TURN)
■ Modern development practices (MODP)	■ Terminal response time (TERM)

Each parameter has a sensitivity range that translates the low, nominal, and high rating to a quantitative value. AEXPAPPL is the combined impact of analyst application experience and application class complexity. Calculations are as follows:

$$ctbx = ACAP \times AEXPAPPL \times MODP \times PCAP \times TOOL \times TERM$$

$$C_{tb} = 2000 \times \exp\left(\frac{\left(-3.70945 \times \ln\left(\frac{ctbx}{4.11}\right)\right)}{5 \times TURN}\right)$$

Effective technology uses the computed C_{tb} along with the remaining technology and environment parameters. Each parameter has a sensitivity range that translates the low, nominal, high rating to a quantitative value. The related experience and complexity parameters are combined into a single sensitivity used in the calculation of effective technology. The combined parameters include:

Parameter	Parameter	Combined
Language type (complexity) (LANG)	Programmer's language experience (LEXP)	LANGLEXP
Target system complexity (TSYS)	Target system experience (TEXP)	TSYSTEXP
Development system complexity (DSYS)	Development system experience (DEXP)	DSYSDEXP
Process improvement (PSYS)	Practices and methods experience (PEXP)	PSYSPEXP
Software impacted by reuse (SIBR)	Reusability level required (REUS)	SIBRREUS

A single parameter adjustment is calculated using the sensitivity of the remaining parameters along with the combined parameters:

ParmAdjustment = LANGLEXP ×
TSYSTEXP × DSYSDEXP ×
PSYSPEXP × SIBRREUS ×
Multiple site development (MULT) × Resource dedication (RDED) ×
Resource and support location (RLOC) × Development system volatility (DSVL) ×
Process volatility (PSVL) × Requirements volatility (change) (RVOL) ×
Specification level–reliability (SPEC) × Test level (TEST) ×
Quality assurance level (QUAL) × Rehost from development to target (RHST) ×
Special display requirements (DISP) × Memory constraints (MEMC) ×
Time constraints (TIMC) × Real-time code (RTIM) ×
Security requirements (SECR) × Target system volatility (TSVL)

The basic technology is divided by the parameter adjustment to give effective technology:

$$C_{te} = \left. C_{tb} \middle/ ParmAdjustment \right.$$

Effort, Schedule, and Staffing Calculations

Basic Definitions

Key Inputs

S_e Effective size.
C_{te} Effective technology.
D Staffing complexity; quantitative value for the staffing complexity parameter.
Pk Staff loading; place on the staffing curve where staff peaks; quantitative value that relates to the staff loading parameter.
F_s Staff loading scale factor computed from Pk.

Key Outputs

K Life-cycle effort; total area under staffing curve. Development effort is generally the area under the staffing curve up until the effort peaks. Development effort is about 40 percent of the area under the curve. In its raw form, this represents effort in person years. It is later converted to effort months and hours.
t_d Schedule to peak of staffing curve; in raw form it is expressed in calendar years; is later converted to schedule months.

Basic Effort and Schedule Equations

Minimum Time

Effort and schedule calculations are based on key relationships among size, complexity and effective technology:

Software equation: $S_e = C_{te} \sqrt{K} t_d$

Staffing: $M = \dfrac{F_s K}{\left(Pk\%t_d \right)^2}$

$$\text{Complexity:} \qquad D = \frac{K}{t_d^3}$$

The minimum time estimate appears when the complexity equation and software equation intersect. The first step is to take the software equation and solve for *td*:

$$t_d = \frac{S_e}{C_{te}\sqrt{K}}$$

Then plug the *td* value into the complexity equation and solve for *K*:

$$D = \frac{K}{t_d^3} = \frac{K}{\left(\dfrac{S_e}{C_{te}\sqrt{K}}\right)^3} = K^{\frac{5}{2}}\left(\frac{S_e}{C_{te}}\right)^3$$

Solving for *K* gives:

$$K = D^{0.4}\left(\frac{S_e}{C_{te}}\right)^{1.2}$$

Plug *K* back into the software equation to get the schedule:

$$t_d = D^{-0.2}\left(\frac{S_e}{C_{te}}\right)^{0.4}$$

Optimal Effort Calculations

If an optimal effort solution is selected, the calculations are the same as described in the previous section, but the effective complexity relating to the staffing rate is adjusted. The minimum time estimate assumes the software project is staffed as aggressively as possible to achieve the least amount of time. When optimal effort is selected, the staffing rate is slowed sufficiently so that the project takes longer but still maintains a cohesive development team. The effective complexity is computed using the staffing complexity input as follows:

$$EffectiveD = 0.55 \times D^{0.9}$$

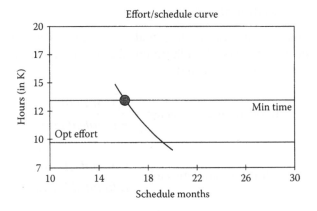

Figure 11.29   Time and effort trade-off.

EffectiveD is then used in the effort and schedule formulas (*K* and t_d) described in the previous section. SEER-SEM illustrates the trade between minimum time and optimal effort (Figure 11.29).

Relaxed Schedule Calculations

For cases where a required schedule input is entered and it is longer than the minimum time schedule, effort that fits the schedule scenario must be computed. This involves adjusting the input schedule so it does not include requirements or integration and test schedule. After this adjustment, the effort relating to that schedule is calculated using the software equation and solving for *K*:

$$t_d = Normalized(InputSchedule)/12$$

$$K = \left[\frac{S_e}{(C_{te} \times t_d)} \right]^2$$

The basic mathematics included here provide the framework of SEER-SEM's hundreds of equations and models.

Calibration Calculations

Calibration mode includes additional parameters that are normally hidden from view. At the top of the list of parameters are entries for actual effort and actual schedule, along with flags for whether the requirements and systems integration and test activities are included. At the bottom of the list, a set of adjustment factors appears.

Computing Adjustment Factors

Calibration mode can use both actual effort and actual schedule to compute effort and schedule adjustment factors. Each adjustment factor is the ratio of actual to estimated.

$$\text{EffortAdjustmentFactor} = \frac{ActualEffort}{EstimatedEffort}$$

$$\text{ScheduleAdjustmentFactor} = \frac{ActualSchedule}{EstimatedSchedule}$$

Calculated results appear in a calibration summary report.

Applying Adjustment Factors

The effort adjustment factor is a multiplicative factor on the uncalibrated effort estimate used to scale it to the specified actual effort. Similarly, the schedule adjustment factor is a multiplicative factor on the uncalibrated schedule estimate used to scale it to the specified actual schedule. SEER-SEM also provides nonlinear technology and complexity calibration factors that may alternately be used. After the adjustment factors have been computed, they may be applied directly to a program or saved in a knowledge base and used for future estimates.

$$\text{CalibratedEffort} = \text{EstimatedEffort} \times \text{EffortAdjustmentFactor}$$

$$\text{CalibratedSchedule} = \text{EstimatedSchedule} \times \text{ScheduleAdjustmentFactor}$$

SEER-SEM Parameter Definitions

The following definitions of SEER-SEM parameters are included with permission from Galorath Incorporated. Parameter definitions are refined occasionally, new ones are added, and occasionally parameters are deleted. These definitions of input parameters are from SEER-SEM Version 7.1. This information is copyrighted and used by permission of Galorath Incorporated.

Contents

SEER-SEM estimates are derived from parameter data. The set of parameters that define a particular work element is largely determined by its

WBS level (program, component, unit, COTS) in relation to the project hierarchy (highest- to lowest-level member in a program group) and by sizing metrics.

Sizing Parameters

The software size parameter categories are lines of code, functions, and proxy sizing. A number of other proven sizing techniques are selectable in proxy sizing. While all sizing parameters are available, they are used for estimations only if you supply data to them. Two parameters closely linked with size estimation also are: the function implementation mechanism (language), and the number of programs included in size.

Parameters for COTS sizing are unique. The quick size, number of features, and COTS object sizing systems apply to COTS components only.

If you are using more than one metric, be careful not to double count. For each selected metric, an associated size category is presented for input, although you can ignore categories or parameters that are not relevant to a given work element.

In most categories, parameters classify software as new or preexisting and further classify preexisting software as designed for reuse or not designed for reuse.

SEER-SEM Size Parameters

Parameter	Definition
LINES (Classic)	
New lines of code	Number of lines that will be completely developed (designed, implemented and tested) from scratch. For an upgrade to an existing system include lines that represent new functionality added to existing code.
Preexists, not designed for reuse AND preexists, designed for reuse	The computed effective size rather than an input.

SEER-SEM Size Parameters

Parameter	Definition
Preexisting lines of code	Reused code is differentiated according to whether it was designed for reuse. SEER-SEM knowledge bases assume that software designed for reuse requires less rework to adapt, modify, or integrate into the current system being developed than software that was not so designed. Calculated values are based on lower-level parameter data and are weighted by the redesign, reimplementation, and retest percentages. The following five parameters (line counts and rework percentages) are included in both categories.
Lines to be deleted in preexisting	Number of lines of code that will be deleted outright from the estimated number of reused lines before any work begins. These have been included in the preexisting lines of code parameter and are simply discarded before any calculations begin. SEER-SEM does not calculate any effort to delete preexisting code. The effort is accounted for on the redesign, reimplementation, and retest of the software left after the deletion.
Redesign required	Percentage of existing software that must be redesigned to make reused software functional. This includes the changes to the overall design or system architecture that will be required to reuse the existing design. Include amounts that must be learned or reverse engineered, redocumented, or revalidated to make the changes as well as the actual amount of redesign work. Designing from scratch requires 100 percent effort. Redesign may be greater than 100 percent if the work involved in designing involves severe reverse engineering. Several methods are available to compute redesign required including knowledge bases, engineering analysis (see Chapter 8), and prior work analysis.
Reimple-mentation required	Percentage of existing software that must be reimplemented (coded and tested at unit level) to make the reused software functional. Include portions that must be learned or reverse engineered to make the changes.
Retest required	Estimate percentage of existing software that requires testing (integration, component, and program testing) to ensure that software functions within performance, reliability, and other criteria after changes.

SEER-SEM Size Parameters

Parameter	Definition
Function implementation mechanism	The programming language or implementation mechanism, such as a code generator or screen generator that will be used to build the current element. This parameter can significantly impact other parameters, depending in part on the sizing metrics, as discussed below.
	For function-based estimates, language particularly impacts the amount of effort required.
	Choice of language affects defect estimates, as some languages are more prone to defects than others.
	Function implementation method is closely related to the language type parameter. If one of these two parameters is changed, the other should be checked to ensure consistency. For example, if function implementation mechanism is changed from SQL to C, language type should also be changed.
Programs included in size	The number of stand-alone computer programs defined within this one. If you are performing early or system-level estimation and know system-level sizing only, enter the estimated number of computer programs (they can be developed by separate teams, with their own schedules, and often require their own documentation).

FUNCTIONS (Classic)

New functions	All new functions that will be implemented from scratch or added as new functionality to preexisting software.

Software phase at estimate

	Phase	Description
	Proposal	Early concept definition. The functionality may not be well understood yet. Function counts are preliminary. Function growth will occur.
	Requirements	The detailed requirements are in the process of being established. More visibility to the software functionality is available.

SEER-SEM Size Parameters

Parameter	Definition	
	Phase	Description
	Design	The design process is underway. Even more visibility into required functionality.
	Code	Implementation is proceeding. Function counts are nearly stable and have been recounted.
	Test	Software is under test. Function counts are stable and accurate and have been recounted.
	Done	Function counts are actuals counted from a completed system.
Preexists, not designed for reuse AND Preexists, designed for reuse	Same as defined above.	
Preexisting functions	The number of unadjusted function points (UFPs) from preexisting functions (functions completed before this development that will be reused). Functions are measured in the total number of IFPUG unadjusted function points (UFPs).	
Functions to be deleted in preexisting	The number of functions that will be deleted outright from the preexisting functions before any work begins.	
Software phase at estimate	The current development phase, as described for new functions.	
Redesign required	Same as defined above.	
Reimplementation required	Same as defined above.	

SEER-SEM Size Parameters

Parameter	Definition
Retest Required	Same as defined above.
Proxy sizing	Proxy sizing allows you to select an existing proxy set for use as a sizing metric. A proxy set can consist of one to ten additional parameters, depending on how the set has been defined. All sizing methods included are supported either directly or as proxies. Use cases, objects, etc., fall into the proxy category.
New	All software that will be developed from scratch.
Parameter	*Definition*
Software phase at estimate	The current development phase, as described for new functions.
Preexists, not designed for reuse AND preexists, designed for reuse	Same as defined above.
Redesign required	Same as defined above.
Reimple-mentation required	Same as defined above.
Retest required	Same as defined above.

Technology and Environment Parameters

Figure 11.30 illustrates the technology and environment input parameters and their relative total impacts on cost and effort. Parameters generally are rated on a scale ranging from very low to extra high. Each rating may be modified by a plus or minus to indicate actual ratings that are slightly higher or lower than what is indicated on the scale. For example, nominal+

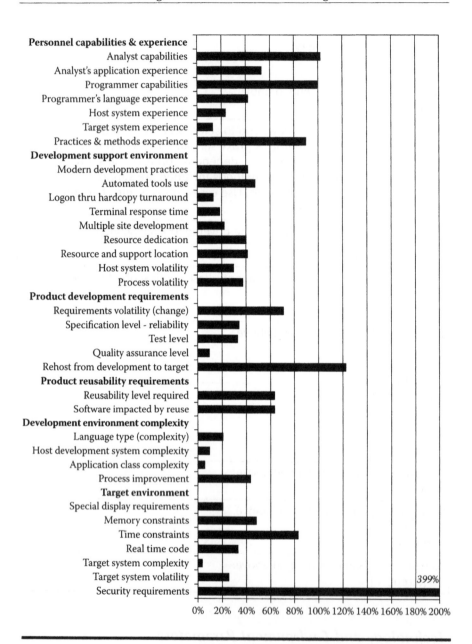

Figure 11.30 Relative impacts of parameters on cost and effort.

would be slightly higher than nominal. Most parameters accept three estimates: least, likely, and most. The probability or confidence levels of the several technology parameter categories used to compute effort or schedule can be independently assigned.

Parameter	Definition	
PERSONNEL CAPABILITIES and EXPERIENCE		
Analyst capabilities	Analysts include personnel developing software requirements and specifications and preparing high-level software design (architecture). A nominal team is quite respectable, performing at an average level. Performance may be impacted by inherent learning abilities, efficiency, motivation, communication abilities, etc. Conflicts within a team and an uncooperative environment can reduce this rating. Because capabilities should not be confused with experience, this parameter rates the inherent potential of individual team members and of the team as a whole, independent of experience. More experienced personnel are not necessarily more capable, and less experienced personnel are also not necessarily less capable.	
	Rating	*Description*
	Very high	Near-perfect functioning (90th percentile)
	High	Extraordinary (75th percentile)
	Nominal	Functional and effective (55th percentile)
	Low	Functional with low effectiveness (35th percentile)
	Very low	Poorly functioning (15th percentile)
	Very low	Nonfunctional (5th percentile)
Analyst application experience	The analyst team's relevant experience in designing similar applications. This rates team experience when design begins. For example, if a new program started with three analysts, two of whom were fresh out of college, and a third with ten years' experience, the average experience would be about three years or a nominal rating on the analyst experience scale. A related parameter is application class complexity. Less experience with more difficult applications causes more difficulty than the same experience with easier applications.	
	Rating	*Description*
	Very high	10+ years or reimplementation by same team
	High	6 years average

Parameter	Definition	
	Rating	Description
	Nominal	3 years average
	Low	1 year average
	Very low	Less than 4 months average
Programmer capabilities	Programmers perform "code to" detailed design (program design languages, flowcharts, etc.), write code, and prepare and run initial unit test cases. Rate the team, not only the individuals. Consider inherent ability, motivation, programming efficiency and thoroughness, program quality, and the ability to communicate within the development team.	
	As with analysts, capabilities should not be confused with experience. This parameter rates the inherent potential of the individual team members and the team as a whole independent of experience.	
	Rating	Description
	Very high	Near-perfect functioning (90th percentile)
	High	Extraordinary (75th percentile)
	Nominal	Functional and effective (55th percentile)
	Low	Functional with low effectiveness (35th percentile)
	Very low	Poorly functioning (15th percentile)
	Very low	Nonfunctional (5th percentile)
Programmer language experience	At the start of development, the programming team's average experience with the programming language or implementation mechanism used. Some experience may be credited for similar languages. For example, a new project begins with seven programmers, a lead programmer with ten years of experience with the language used, three programmers with two years' experience each, and the other three with no applicable experience with this language. The average experience would be about two years or high on the rating scale. A related parameter is language type complexity. Inexperience with simpler languages causes less difficulty than inexperience with more complicated languages.	

Parameter	Definition	
	Rating	*Description*
	Extra high	4+ years average
	Very high	3 years average
	High	2 years average
	Nominal	1 year average
	Low	4 months average
	Very low	Less than 4 months average
Development system experience	At the start of the project, the development team's average years of experience with the development system, the combination of hardware, operating systems, job control languages, and all the things the developers will use to develop the software. Other parameters that can be related to this parameter include development system volatility and development system complexity.	
	Rating	*Description*
	Extra high	4+ years average
	Very high	3 years average
	High	2 years average
	Nominal	1 year average
	Low	4 months average
	Very low	Less than 4 months average
Target system experience	The average years of experience the development team has with the target (final) system on which the software product under estimation will execute, including both the hardware environment and the resident operating system, if any. If the target system hardware and operating systems are under development, target system experience will almost automatically be low because the system did not exist previously. On the other hand, if the target system is a workstation or PC, then target system experience might be the same as development system experience. Other parameters that can be related to this parameter include hardware integration level, target system volatility, and target system complexity.	

Parameter	Definition	
	Rating	Description
	Extra high	4+ years average
	Very high	3 years average
	High	2 years average
	Nominal	1 year average
	Low	4 months average
	Very low	Less than 4 months average
Practices and methods experience	At the beginning of development, the average number of years of experience the team will have with the software practices and methods that will be used. Software practices are processes, methods, and tools that establish the managerial and technical environment in which software products are developed (e.g., design reviews, quality assurance activities, and software engineering methods).	
	Rating	Description
	Extra high	4+ years average
	Very high	3 years average
	High	2 years average
	Nominal	1 year average
	Low	4 months average
	Very low	Less than 4 months average
DEVELOPMENT SUPPORT ENVIRONMENT		
Modern development practices use	The usage of modern software development practices and methods at the time the software design begins, including analysis and design, structured or object-oriented methods, development practices for code implementation, documentation, verification and validation, database maintenance, and product baseline control. Only successful incorporation of practices as standard procedures within the organization and by this team count as full use. Having books, a few experts, or academic courses does not count as experience. This is related to the process improvement parameter that	

Parameter	Definition	
	measures change (improvement) in development practices over the course of the project under estimation.	
	Rating	*Description*
	Very high	Routine use of a complete software development process, SEI level 3 or above
	High	Reasonably experienced in most practices, SEI level 2 or above
	Nominal	Reasonably experienced in some practices
	Low	Beginning experimental use of practices
	Very low	No use of modern development practices
Automated tools use	The degree to which the software development practices have been automated and will be used on this development. Consider tool use across all aspects of the software development process, not only programming tools.	
	Rating	*Description*
	Very high	Advanced fully integrated tool set
	High +	Modern fully automated application development environment, including requirements, design, and test analyzers
	High	Modern visual programming tools, automated CM, test analyzers plus requirements or design tools
	Nominal +	Visual programming, CM tools, and simple test tools
	Nominal	Interactive, programmer work bench
	Low	Base batch tools (compiler, editor)
	Very low	Primitive tools (bit switches, dumps)
Turnaround time	Computer turnaround time experienced by the project team. Time required to access virtual environment, start development environment, checkout source file, submit to compile and link and receive the desired output. This parameter is designed to measure the amount of lost time doing nonproductive tasks associated with the development computer.	

Parameter	Definition	
	Rating	*Description*
	Very high	Turnaround 8 hours
	High	Turnaround 4 hours
	Rating	*Description*
	Nominal	Turnaround 2 hours
	Low	Turnaround 30 minutes
	Very low	Less than 6 minutes
Response time	Average transaction response time from the time a developer presses a key until that key is acknowledged and its action is completed. This parameter measures the efficiency of interactive development operations.	
	Rating	*Description*
	Extra high	>3 seconds
	Very high	2 seconds
	High	1 second
	Nominal	0.5 second
	Low	<0.25 second
Multiple site development	Organizational and site diversity within personnel developing the software based on physical locations, political boundaries, contractual issues, or even security issues. Anything that would isolate one part of the development team from another should be considered for this parameter. A program developed in a mixed-security level environment should be considered as multiple organizations. Collaboration features and networking techniques such as e-mail, WANs, Web meetings, Web based collaboration tools, and teleconferencing can reduce the impacts of physical separation but will not negate it. For example, development at two separate sites, normally would be rated very high. If the two sites were connected by a WAN, the impact might be reduced to high. On the other hand, if the groups were separated by an international boundary, the rating would be increased to extra high.	

Parameter	Definition	
	Rating	*Description*
	Extra high	Multiple sites, located more than two hours' travel from each other, or international participation
	Very high	Multiple sites, same general location, or mixed clearance levels
	High	Single site and multiple organizations
	Nominal	Single site and single organization
Resource dedication	The availability of the development and target resources to the development organization. Physical interference due to site operations (maintenance, testing) or contending project organizations (on a data processing facility operated by a separate organization) can result in reduced access to the system. Limited licenses that can reduce the number of people that are allowed to work in parallel. Also, in secure or classified environments the sharing of scarce hardware resources can lower resource dedication if the developers are locked out.	
	Rating	*Description*
	Nominal	100 percent fully dedicated computing resources
	Low	70 percent access to computing resources
	Very low	40 percent access to computing resources
	Very low	10 percent access to computing resources
Resource and support location	The time required to access needed development resources and support, such as outside system consultants, programming language support, hardware engineering support, and development tool support. Corporate processes or support relationships may contribute to support delays.	
	Rating	*Description*
	Extra high	More than a day
	Very high	5 hours
	High	1.5 hours
	Nominal	Immediate development resources and support

Parameter	Definition	
Development system volatility	The difficulty caused by changes and/or upgrades to the development system. These may be changes or upgrades in program editors, compilers or other tools, changes in the operating system and command languages, or changes in the development hardware. If a development operating system upgrade is released during development, there will be no impact if developers continue to use the old version rather than switch.	
	Rating	*Description*
	Extra high	Major change every 2 weeks, minor 2 times a week
	Very high	Major change every 2 months, minor each week
	High	Major change every 6 months, minor every 2 weeks
	Nominal	Major change every 12 months, minor each month
	Low	No major changes, minor change each year
Process volatility	Process volatility is the frequency of changes to the processes, methods, and tools that establish the managerial and technical environment in which software products are developed (design reviews, quality assurance activities, software engineering methods). This rating depends on the scope or magnitude of the changes and the frequency with which they occur. A minor change would have some impact on the development team but would not require significant adjustments to the way in which they work. For example, filling out an additional form or consulting an additional management source for a design decision approval is a minor change. A major change would require a significant adjustment of the way the development team works, and would have a noticeable impact on the development effort.	
	Rating	*Description*
	Extra high	Major change every 2 weeks, minor 2 times a week
	Very high	Major change every 2 months, minor each week

Parameter	Definition	
	Rating	*Description*
	High	Major change every 6 months, minor every 2 weeks
	Nominal	Major change every 12 months, minor each month
	Low	No major changes, minor change each year
PRODUCT DEVELOPMENT REQUIREMENTS		
Requirements volatility (change)	The anticipated frequency and scope of change in the requirements after they are baselined (after preliminary design starts). Detailed software requirements may change while system-level requirements stay the same. Minor changes may include work such as software subsystem specification clarification of a user interface menu; moderate changes are items such as tighter performance requirements; major changes are items such as rework of major system specifications related to mission changes.	
	Rating	*Description*
	Extra high	Frequent major changes
	Very high	Frequent moderate and occasional major changes
	High +	Evolutionary software development with significant user interface requirements
	High	Occasional moderate redirections, typical for evolutionary software developments
	Nominal	Small noncritical redirections
	Low	Essentially no requirements changes
Specification level–reliability	The level of development specification required; refers primarily to engineering level documentation, not finished end user documentation. The level of documentation is often dictated by the development standard used. Specification level is related to system reliability requirements. More reliable systems must be specified more stringently during development to ensure that they are sufficiently reliable to perform within acceptable limits. This parameter is related to test level and quality assurance level, both of which also are driven by reliability requirements for most developments.	

Parameter	Definition	
	Rating	Description
	Very high	Highest reliability, public safety requirements. Documentation required for all aspects of system development, including architecture, design, programming, testing, and interface specifications. Most documentation will follow rigorous guidelines for content and format. Documentation considered part of software system, and if applicable, delivered to customer.
	High +	Full military specification with IV&V, remote financial transactions.
	High	Major financial loss. Typical military specifications or other standards with full documentation. Documentation usually delivered with software system (e.g., full J Standard 016, full Military Standard 498, full IEEE, full DoD Standard 2167A, critical financial transactions).
	Nominal	Moderate loss, recovery without extreme penalty. Typical military specification or other standard tailored to include complete essential documentation. Documentation usually delivered with software system (e.g., tailored Military Standard 498, tailored J Standard 016, Military Standard 483/490, tailored DoD Standard 2167A, FAA).
	Low	Low, easily recoverable, minimal documentation. Examples include non-mission-critical applications, business systems, and commercial software. May follow informal organizational standards or highly tailored (relaxed) military standards. Typical shrink-wrapped software.

Parameter	Definition	
	Rating	*Description*
	Very low	Slight inconvenience. Documentation not dictated or required. Any specifications created are incidental. Examples include prototypes, personal software, entertainment, internally developed non-mission-critical applications.
Test level	Rigor and formality of software testing. Test level based on potential for loss if software malfunctions during operation. More reliable systems must be tested more stringently during development to ensure sufficient reliability to perform within acceptable limits. This parameter is related to specification level and quality assurance level which normally are driven by reliability requirements.	
	Rating	*Description*
	Very high	Highest reliability, public safety requirements. Rigorous, formal testing following prescribed plans, procedures, and reporting to ensure highest reliability.
	High	Major financial loss, high potential loss. Complete formal testing procedures, reporting and sign-off on test results. Major retest of unchanged functionality.
	Nominal	Moderate loss, recovery without extreme penalty. Formal testing. Key software features may follow specific testing procedures where noncritical features will not have special testing considerations. Regression testing for unchanged functionality (normal military standard testing).
	Low	Low, easily recoverable. Informal testing. Examples include non-mission-critical applications, information systems, and much shrink-wrapped software.

Parameter	Definition	
	Rating	Description
	Very low	Slight inconvenience. Testing minimal; does not follow any prescribed procedures or processes. Examples include prototypes, personal software, entertainment, internally developed non-mission-critical applications.
Quality assurance (QA) level	Evaluation of completeness of QA activities. QA level usually is directly related to the impact that a software failure would have during operational phase. More reliable systems often have more stringent quality assurance to ensure that they are sufficiently reliable to perform within acceptable limits.	
	Rating	Description
	Very high	Highest reliability, public safety requirements. rigorous, formal QA following prescribed plans, procedures, and reporting to ensure highest reliability.
	High	Major financial loss, high potential loss. Formal QA activities, quality engineering, quality management.
	Nominal	Moderate loss, recovery without extreme penalty. Formal (normal military standard) QA.
	Low	Low, easily recoverable. Informal QA. Examples include non-mission-critical applications, information systems, and commercial software.
	Very low	Slight inconvenience. No specific QA activities; QA performed is incidental to development. Examples include prototypes, personal software, internally developed nonmission-critical applications.
Rehost from development to target	Effort to convert the software from the development system (computers, operating systems, etc.) to the target system on which the software will execute. This is related to the difference between the development and target environments, including both hardware and software considerations.	

Parameter	Definition	
	Rating	Description
	Extra high	Major language and system change
	Very high	Major language or system change
	High	Minor language and system change
	Nominal	No rehosting, same language and system

Product Reusability Requirements

Parameter	Definition	
Reusability level required	Requirements for producing software designed to be reusable within other programs.	
	Level of reusability required is determined by how widely the final software will need to be reused and how much the developer is willing to invest. This parameter is used in conjunction with software impacted by reuse, which establishes how much of the total code will be reused on other systems. This parameter rating should be greater than nominal only with a specific requirement for reuse. Incidental reuse should not be included.	
	Note that software can be reused even if it was developed with a nominal rating, but reuse normally is more costly.	
	Rating	Description
	Extra high	Mission software developed with full reusability required. All components of software must be reusable. Reusability is a primary objective of development organization.
	Very high	Software will be reused within a single product line. Reusability may impact multiple development teams.
	High	Software will be reused within a single application area.
	Nominal	No reusability requirement.
Software impacted by reuse	Amount of the software under development that is required to be reusable. This parameter works in conjunction with reusability level required.	

Parameter	Definition	
	Rating	*Description*
	100 percent	100 percent of this component must be reusable
	50 percent	50 percent of this component must be reusable
	25 percent	25 percent of this component must be reusable
	0 percent	0 percent of this component must be reusable
DEVELOPMENT ENVIRONMENT COMPLEXITY		
Language type (complexity)	Difficulty of programming language(s) used in development. The language type (complexity) parameter estimates the difficulty of learning the programming language that will be used during coding of the task. It can be compared to the number of years of actual work experience or study required to master all the features of the language. This parameter is related to the function implementation mechanism. If either of these two parameters is changed, the other should be checked to ensure that they are consistent.	
	Rating	*Description*
	Very high	Full Ada, Pl/I Version F
	High	JOVIAL, CMS-2, mainframe assemblers
	Nominal	C++, C, C#, COBOL, Java, Pascal, FORTRAN, PL/1 Subset G, Visual Basic, PC Basic, micro assemblers, Ada without tasking
	Low	Basic, many 4GLs
Development system complexity	Relative complexity of the development system, compilers, JCL, file interfaces, and support environment. This parameter is linked to development system experience. More experienced personnel are not penalized as heavily for working on a more complex development system.	

Parameter	Definition	
	Rating	*Description*
	High	Distributed network where developers must have cognizance of the distributed functionality
	Nominal	Multiuser systems (Windows server, LINUX)
	Low	Single user machines (Windows, Mac), stand-alone systems, may be networked
Application class complexity	Overall level of application difficulty. This parameter is linked to analyst application experience. Very experienced analysts are not penalized.	
	Rating	*Description*
	High	Networks, operating systems, compilers, fire control systems
	Nominal	Applications with complex systems or complex file or user interfaces, such as client–server systems, command and control, communication networks and systems
	Low	Business data processing applications, interface systems
Process improvement	Impact of improving development technology by comparing current, established development practices with those planned for this development. This is related to modern development practices use (input parameter) and the SEI equivalent rating (output metric).	
	Rating	*Description*
	Extra high	Extreme change; organization improving development technologies (any two-level jump in SEI CMMI rating)
	Very high	Major change; organization improving rating (moving from SEI CMMI level 1 to 2; implementing ISO)
	High	Moderate change; organization improving development technologies (any one-level jump from SEI CMMI level 2 or above)

Parameter	Definition	
	Rating	*Description*
	Nominal	No change in modern development practices or SEI CMMI rating

TARGET ENVIRONMENT		
Special display requirements	The amount of effort required to implement user interface display interaction involved with this computer program. If the program has no user interface, such as when the user interface is performed by another stand-alone program, effort would be rated nominal. For example, a Windows-based application with a simple menu driven interface would be rated high. Even though the application would accept mouse input, the mouse interaction is handled by the operating system and is "free" to the application. However, if the application also includes advanced usage of mouse features directly, special displays should be rated very high.	
	Rating	*Description*
	Extra high	Complex: CAD/CAM, 3D solid modeling
	Very high	Interactive: light pen, mouse, touch screen, Windows, etc., controlled by the software being developed
	High	User-friendly: error recovery and menus, basic Windows GUI not controlled by application
	Nominal	Simple inputs and outputs: batch programs
Memory constraints	Anticipated effort by developers to reduce memory usage. No memory constraint exists, even when the available memory is 99 percent utilized, if no conservation action is required by the development team to conserve memory.	
	Rating	*Description*
	Extra high	Complex memory management and economic measures
	Very high	Extensive overlaying or segmentation

Parameter	Definition	
	Rating	Description
	High	Some overlaying or segmentation
	Nominal	No memory constraints
Time constraints	Percentage of software that must have specific coding effort to enhance timing performance. Rate only the percentage of the code that receives special coding effort to enhance timing performance, not simply a time budget allocation.	
	Rating	Description
	Extra high	75 percent of code is time constrained
	Very high	50 percent of code is time constrained
	High	25 percent of code is time constrained
	Nominal	No time constraints
Real-time code	Amount of software involved in real-time functions that are driven by an external clock, e.g., gathering data from hardware devices or time-sensitive control of such devices where waiting can alter or lose data. Real-time functions must be performed during the actual time that an external process occurs so that the computation results can be used to control, monitor, or respond in a timely manner to the external process. Real-time code manages data exchange across interfaces, but not the less constrained processing of data. For example, telemetry is gathered in real time, but is processed in non-real time. Although real-time code is not directly related to time-constrained code, some code may require timing constraints because of real-time considerations.	
	Rating	Description
	Extra high	100 percent of code with real-time considerations
	Very high	50 percent of code with real-time considerations
	High	25 percent of code with real-time considerations
	Nominal	0 percent of code with real-time considerations

Parameter	Definition	
Target system complexity	Level of complication of target operating systems, compilers, controllers, and other attached processors the developer must understand to perform the development task. This parameter is related to target system experience.	
	Rating	*Description*
	High	Distributed network target; developers must have cognizance of the distributed functionality
	Nominal	Multiuser target systems (Windows Server, LINUX)
	Low	Single user target machines (Windows, Mac), stand-alone systems, may be networked
Target system volatility	Difficulty caused by changes to target system (system on which the software will execute when implemented). These may be changes in compilers, or other tools, changes in command languages, or changes in target hardware. Each change may cause developers to lose time due to learning the system, changing code or procedures, etc. More volatile target hardware will affect software-to-hardware integration adversely.	
	Rating	*Description*
	Extra high	Major change every 2 weeks, minor 2 times a week
	Very high	Major change every 2 months, minor each week
	High	Major change every 6 months, minor every 2 weeks
	Nominal	Major change every 12 months, minor each month
	Low	No major changes, minor change each year
Security requirements	Development impact of security and/or safety requirements for the delivered target system. This parameter captures special work to be performed during this stand-alone program development only. If security requirements will be met by the operating system, by other software, or by a physically secure environment	

Parameter	Definition
	(e.g., behind locked doors), security requirements should be nominal. This parameter can be the single largest driver in a software estimate. Higher security levels can be extremely expensive to implement with software; it usually is more cost effective to meet these requirements with physical security than within your software development.

	Rating	Description
	Extra high +	Class A1: Security formally verified by mathematical proof (very rare). DO178B – Level A: Software whose anomalous behavior, as shown by the system safety assessment process, would cause or contribute to a failure of system function resulting in a catastrophic failure condition for aircraft.
	Extra high	Common Criteria – EAL 7: Formally verified design and testing. The formal model is supplemented by a formal presentation of the functional specification and high level design showing correspondence. Evidence of developer "white box" testing and complete independent confirmation of developer test results are required. Complexity of the design must be minimized.
	Very high +	DO178B – Level B: Software whose anomalous behavior as shown by the system safety assessment process would cause or contribute to a failure of system function resulting in a hazardous or severe major failure condition for aircraft. Common Criteria – EAL 6: Semiformally verified design and testing. Analysis is supported by a modular and layered approach to design and a structured presentation of the implementation. The independent search for vulnerabilities must ensure high resistance to penetration attack. The search for covert channels must be systematic. Development environment and configuration management controls are further strengthened.

Parameter	Definition	
	Rating	Description
	Very high	Class B3: System excludes code not essential to security enforcement. Audit capability is strengthened. System almost completely resistant to penetration. Common Criteria – EAL 5: Semiformally designed and tested. Analysis includes all implementation. Assurance is supplemented by formal model and semiformal presentation of the functional specification and high level design and a semiformal demonstration of correspondence. The search for vulnerabilities must ensure relative resistance to penetration attack. Covert channel analysis and modular design are also required.
	Very high –	DO178B – Level C: Software whose anomalous behavior as shown by the system safety assessment process would cause or contribute to a failure of system function resulting in a major failure condition for aircraft.
	High +	Class B2: System segregated into protection-critical and non-protection-critical elements. Overall system resistant to penetration (critical financial processing). Common Criteria – EAL 4: Methodically designed, tested, and reviewed. Analysis is supported by the low-level design of the modules of the target of evaluation (TOE) and a subset of the implementation. Testing supported by an independent search for obvious vulnerabilities. Development controls supported by a life-cycle model, identification of tools, and automated configuration management.

Parameter	Definition	
	Rating	*Description*
	High	Class B1: In addition to C2, data labeling and mandatory access control present. Flaws identified by testing are removed (classified or financial processing).
		Common Criteria – EAL 3: Methodically tested and checked. Analysis supported by "gray box" testing, selective independent confirmation of the developer's test results, and evidence of a developer search for obvious vulnerabilities. Development environment controls and TOE configuration management also required.
	High –	Class C2: Users individually accountable via log-on operations, auditing of security relevant events, and resource isolation (typical multiuser operating system such as Windows server, Linux).
		DO178B – Level D: Software whose anomalous behavior as shown by the system safety assessment process would cause or contribute to a failure of system function resulting in a minor failure condition for aircraft.
		Common Criteria – EAL 2: Structurally tested. Analysis of security functions using a functional and interface specification and high-level design of the subsystems of the TOE. Independent testing of the security functions, evidence of developer "black box" testing, and evidence of a development search for obvious vulnerabilities.
	Nominal +	Class C1: Access limited. Based on system controls accountable to individual user or groups of users. Simple project-specific password protection.

Parameter	Definition	
	Rating	Description
		Common Criteria – EAL 1: Functionally tested. Provides analysis of the security functions using a functional and interface specification of the TOE to understand security behavior. The analysis is supported by independent testing of the security functions.
	Nominal	Class D: Minimal protection – no security
		DO178B – Level E: Software whose anomalous behavior as shown by the system safety assessment process would cause or contribute to a failure of system function with no effect on aircraft operational capability or pilot workload. After software has been confirmed as Level E by the certification authority, no further guidelines apply.
		Common Criteria – EAL 0: Inadequate assurance

Commercial Off-the-Shelf (COTS) Parameters

Listed below are several parameter categories that apply specifically to COTS elements. For convenience, sizing parameters that apply only to COTS elements are documented.

Parameter	Definition
QUICK SIZE (COTS only)	
Application type	This parameter is used in conjunction with functionality required parameter to develop estimates as part of the quick size feature. Based on practical considerations, application type size estimates are approximate. If better information about the size of an application is available, use either the features or object sizing method rather than the quick size method. The quick size application types include small, medium, and large attributes for many general application types.

Parameter	Definition
Functionality required	Portion of COTS component functionality that the integrating developers are required to learn. This parameter is directly related to the selection in the application type parameter. Choose the percentage of total component functionality that will be used. Developers must have or acquire a working knowledge of this functional portion.

	Rating	Description
	Very high	100 percent of functionality
	High	75 percent of functionality
	Nominal	55 percent of functionality
	Low	25 percent of functionality
	Very low	0 percent of functionality

Parameter	Definition
Number of features used	Category of parameters designed to capture sizing considerations for COTS components. Although parameters are described in terms of functionality typically seen in COTS components, they are translated into IFPUG standard function points.
Unique functions	Number of unique functions that must be understood to integrate the component. Functions may reside in APIs, program libraries, etc. A function may pass data, receive data, or both pass and receive data. Include the number of unique functions that are used or must be understood.
Data tables referenced	Number of unique data tables that are referenced. Unique data tables include configuration files, databases, external data structures, etc. A single database having several closely related tables should be referenced once only, unless the tables are sufficiently different from one another. These are data groupings being referenced only, but not changed.
Data tables configured	Total number of data tables that must be configured, changed or created to integrate the component. Data tables include configuration files, databases, and external data structures. A single database having several closely related tables should be counted once only, unless those tables are sufficiently different from one another. Count

Parameter	Definition
	each table being created or configured. If an existing table is being used only to learn how tables should be created or configured, do not count it.
COTS OBJECT SIZING	
Input services	Number of external Inputs to be found as services in all object classes. Use the standard IFPUG definition for an external input.
Output services	Number of external outputs to be found as services in all object classes. Use the standard IFPUG definition for an external output.
Inquiry services	Number of external inquiries to be found as services in all object classes. Use the standard IFPUG definition for an external inquiry.
External class	Number of object classes to be found outside the application boundary. These will be treated like IFPUG standard external logical files.
Internal class	Number of object classes to be found inside the application boundary. These will be treated like IFPUG standard internal logical files.
OFF-THE-SHELF PRODUCT CHARACTERISTICS	
Component type	General form of the COTS component from the integrator's view. Consider how the component is packaged, the manner in which it is integrated, and the level of code detail that a programmer sees when implementing this component.
Component volatility	Probability of frequent, extensive, or fundamental vendor modifications to a component. More volatility in a product may make it more difficult to use or may force more frequent updates by developers to keep pace with changes.

	Rating	Description
	Very high	The component is not well defined and could undergo revisions that fundamentally alter its use; this is typical of a prototype
	High	The component may undergo significant change; this is typical of a beta release or Version 1.0

Parameter	Definition	
	Rating	*Description*
	Nominal	The component may undergo significant change over time, but moderate changes are much more likely; this is typical of a Version 2.0 or higher
	Low	No new releases over the course of development; a highly stable product having already gone through several full release cycles
Component application complexity	Overall difficulty of the application in terms of study or experience required for an analyst to become proficient (not expert) in its use. Differences between analysts with higher levels of experience are very small.	
	Rating	*Description*
	High	Applications that are quite complex and with complex interfaces, such as within networks or fire control; other complex components intended for a highly complex environment or a component that is tightly integrated with another application
	Nominal	Applications that are fairly complex and which may have more involved or context-dependent files or user interfaces, such as client–server and command–control communication systems or a component subsystem integrated within another application
	Low	Applications that are inherently simple and have discrete, well-isolated interfaces, such as in business and data processing or a simple, integrated component that is easily accessible from within another application
Interface complexity	Complexity of the integration effort, overhead, and thought required to fulfill integration. In some ways this integration effort has dynamics similar to a programming language, in which a programmer must become proficient at nuances and knowledgeable of many extensions. Interface complexities also entail a significant discovery process.	

Parameter	Definition	
	Rating	*Description*
	Very high	Serious complexity, making the integration a considerable customization effort with a serious learning curve; integration with heterogeneous environments. Substantial linkage of complexity issues
	High	Detailed configuration; knowledge of how the component works required. Intimate glue code typically required to make component work correctly
	Nominal	Can be straightforward but easily permits a more sophisticated approach
	Low	Straightforward; complexities hidden to the integrator. Simple table setups, file and string passing. Integrating component requires no knowledge of data types, timing, etc.
Product support	Degree of access (by proximity) to development resources and support, such as system consultants, programming language support, and development tool support.	
	Rating	*Description*
	Extra high	Immediate and comprehensive on-site or phone support
	Very high	Attentive support, good response time to queries made
	High	Response times varying toward next-day support
	Nominal	Spotty and unreliable vendor support
USE		
Component selection completeness	Extent to which COTS component has been identified and evaluated. This parameter will reflect how much work must be dedicated to the selection and evaluation of alternative COTS components. Consider the number and availability of COTS component choices and differences among them.	

Parameter	Definition	
	Rating	*Description*
	High	Off-the-shelf component has been selected. No effort for identification and evaluation of the component will be included in the estimate
	Nominal	Evaluation among a small set of off-the-shelf components is required. Alternative packages have been identified; evaluation of alternatives required
	Low	No evaluation of COTS components done. Alternative components have yet to be identified
Experience with component	Average experience among all programmers and analysts with the component being used and their experience in installing the component. Credit some experience with similar applications. Assess the level of experience before special training is received. Consider also whether each integration of COTS component is a significantly new and complex task or becomes a regular activity.	
	Rating	*Description*
	Extra high	Expert, could almost be the developers of component
	Very high	Able to handle any sophisticated task and push use to edge of envelope
	High	Quite good and getting better at "tricks"
	Nominal	Effective with component
	Low	Still learning
	Very low	Without any real experience
Learning rate	Speed at which people can learn while they are implementing a component. With experience comes efficiency; when working with a component, the learning-while-doing process may have a substantial impact on overall progress. Consider how learnable the activities associated with the component are. With a conventional, difficult programming language, programmers may become efficient over the long term, perhaps a year or more. By comparison, with a straightforward component, learning may be far more efficient.	

Parameter	Definition
	Component complexity is one of several factors that can affect learning rate; this parameter is a people-only measurement.

	Rating	*Description*
	Very high	Implementation involves small tasks with repetition or exceptional learning-while-doing occurs
	High	Good opportunity for learning over the course of installation
	Nominal	Only a few separable tasks and only moderate progress on learning curve
	Low	One massive task or very little or no learning-while-doing; each integration is new territory
Reverse engineering	Percentage of component functionality that must be "taken apart" to understand it well enough to use it. For example, a 100 percent code review may imply a scan across all code, but review really occurs only at the level of function calls; contents of functions are not examined. In this case, the percentage of reverse engineering is really far lower than 100 percent; it may even be 1 percent or less!
	This parameter influences the effective size of the application. This relationship is assumed because a need for reverse engineering effectively increases the amount of the application that a developer must know; hence the application's effective size is greater.

	Rating	*Description*
	Extra high	Complete or nearly complete review — 80 to 100 percent of the functionality reverse engineered
	Very high	Quite thorough — 50 to 75 percent of the functionality must be reviewed.
	High	A high level of reverse engineering — 20 to 50 percent of the functionality — that indicates more than a simple need for understanding. This level of reengineering may be required to certify low-level specs or as preparation for modifications

Parameter	Definition	
	Rating	*Description*
	Nominal	Careful level of reverse engineering — 10 to 20 percent of the functionality. Usually not required except when modifications are considered
	Low	Slight analysis — 5 to 10 percent; access to detailed specifications is necessary
	Very low	Minimal — 0 to 5 percent; neither detailed specifications nor source code available or required
Component integrate and test	Integration effort required for this component. Rank it against what typically is required to integrate an internally developed unit of code into a software program. Include in the rating the amount of testing that must be performed to ensure this component functions within performance, reliability, and other criteria after changes are made.	
	Rating	*Description*
	Very high	Requires more integration than does an "average" unit integration. This implies that above-average, intimate dependencies must be addressed and adjusted
	High	Requires as much integration effort into a program as an "average" unit of internally developed code. It is assumed that good coding practice builds a fair amount of separability at the unit level, but an iterative adjustment may nonetheless be required, typically through tables, scripts, settings, calls, architecture modifications, etc.
	Nominal	Requires somewhat less integration effort than an "average" unit of internal development code. Component peculiarities will require some "getting used to" and specific allowances
	Low	Requires very little effort to be integrated into program. Additional adjustments — even to team members' thinking — must be made to suit the component to various implementation specifics

Parameter	Definition	
	Rating	*Description*
	Very low	Requires virtually no effort to be integrated into program
Test level	Same as defined above.	

COSTS		
Recurring cost	Cost of using the component for a specified number of years. Total nondevelopmental component costs, if they recur, can be represented in this parameter. Outright initial purchases should be categorized as nonrecurring costs.	
Non-recurring cost	This parameter should be used to capture total (one-time) nondevelopmental costs for component that may include purchase and one-time license costs and cost of initial training. Training costs should include staff hours spent in training.	

Other Parameters

The parameters that follow are related neither to size nor to technology and environment.

Parameter	Definition
SCHEDULE AND STAFFING CONSIDERATIONS	
Required schedule (calendar months)	Number of schedule months available for development, including requirements analysis, systems integration, and testing. Use this schedule only if you want the effort computed for a fixed schedule; otherwise SEER-SEM will compute a schedule. This parameter cannot be used to compress a schedule below a minimum time development; it can be used to "relax" a schedule. If you want a schedule shorter than the minimum time, you could (1) reduce the probability of completion, (2) build less software, or (3) improve the development technology. By using smaller development teams and lengthening the total schedule, cost savings can be achieved. The relaxed schedule generally should not be stretched more than 50 percent beyond the minimum time schedule.

Parameter	Definition	
Start date	Date when the development is scheduled to begin. Start date is used when evaluating the overall elapsed schedule for all stand-alone programs in the project. It also is used as an initial point on detailed monthly and annual cost reports.	
Complexity (staffing)	A software system's inherent difficulty in terms of the rate at which staff can be added to a project. Highly complex projects have highly complex interdependencies that constrain the order in which engineering problems can be solved and thus have lower staffing increase rates. Complexity relates to the rate at which personnel can be added to a development program and thus drives both costs and schedule. Schedule constraints can override this parameter setting. In other words, stretching the schedule will cause staff to be added to a project more slowly than what is dictated by this parameter, thus forcing the project to work with smaller, more efficient teams and take longer to complete while saving effort overall.	
	Rating	*Description*
	Extra high	Development primarily using micro code for the application, for example, a signal processing system with extremely complex interfaces and control logic
	Very high +	Top of the scale for 99 percent of all defense software
	Very high	New systems with significant interfacing and requirements for interaction within a larger system structure. Examples include operating systems and real-time applications with significant logical code
	High	Applications with significant logical complexity, perhaps requiring changes to the operating system, minor real-time processing or special displays and hardware
	Nominal +	Typical command–control programs
	Nominal	New stand-alone systems/applications developed on firm operating systems. Minimal interface problems with underlying operating system or other system parts. Complexity characteristics also map into processing as follows:

Parameter	Definition	
	Rating	*Description*
		Control operations: mostly simple nesting, some intermodule control
		Computational operations: standard mathematical and statistical functions
		Device-dependent operations: device selection, status checking
		Error processing data management operations: multifile inputs, single file, simple structural changes.
	Low	Software of low logical complexity using straightforward I/O and primarily internal data storage (typical of component and unit work elements). Additional staff may be added easily to project
	Very low	Extremely simple software with primarily straightforward code, simple I/O, and internal storage arrays (typical of component and unit work elements). Staffing may increase rapidly
Staff loading	Characterizes how a project is to be staffed in terms of adding staff. Development method should be considered when rating staff loading parameter.	
	Rating	*Description*
	Extra high	Staff peaks toward front of project. Typical of prototype and informal developments (prototypes, spiral, evolutionary)
	Very high	Staff for integrated product team development; also typical for object-oriented developments
	High	Staff for incremental development (more people added faster)
	Nominal	Staff for serial development (waterfall process); staff peaks toward end of project

Parameter	Definition		
Minimum time versus optimal effort	Use this parameter to choose between optimizing the schedule or optimizing the effort in the estimate. Optimizing for schedule (minimum time) assumes the development will be finished as quickly as possible. Staff will be added as quickly as possible, but larger teams will reduce efficiency. Although the project will be completed sooner, it will cost more. Optimizing for effort assumes the software will be developed in as economical a fashion as possible, but will take longer to complete. Staffing will be lower and thus smaller; more efficient teams will realize cost savings.		
Staffing constraint	Category is designed to set minimum or maximum staffing levels (or both) for a variable number of time intervals, each represented as a parameter. It can illustrate the effects of flat staffing.		
	Start month	Month in which you want the constraint to start. The first interval starts with Month 1.	
	Min staff	Minimum staff planned. The staff predicted by SEER-SEM will not be less than the minimum staff entered.	
	Max staff	Maximum staff available for this development. The staff predicted by SEER-SEM will not be more than the maximum staff entered.	

CONFIDENCE LEVEL			
Effort probability	Probability for which the effort estimate will be computed.		
	Rating	*Description*	
	90 percent	Sometimes used as a worst-case scenario	
	80 percent	High confidence, potentially used for fixed-price bids	
	50 percent	Most likely outcome	
	20 percent	Low confidence, sometimes used for bidding cost-plus developments (not recommended)	

Parameter	Definition	
Schedule probability	Probability for which the schedule estimate will be computed.	
	Rating	*Description*
	90 percent	Sometimes used as a worst-case scenario
	80 percent	High confidence, potentially used for fixed-price bids
	50 percent	Most likely outcome
	20 percent	Low confidence, sometimes used for bidding cost-plus developments (not recommended)
Size risk	Probability or confidence level of the size estimate used to compute effort or schedule, depending on selected category. Size inputs include all those found within the following categories: lines, functions, others (proxies, user-defined size inputs).	
Confidence level– technology risk	Probability or confidence level of the technology inputs used to compute effort or schedule, depending on selected category.	
Requirements risk	Probability or confidence level of the requirements inputs used to compute effort or schedule, depending on the selected category.	
System integration risk	Probability or confidence level of system integration inputs used to compute effort or schedule, depending on selected category. System integration inputs include programs concurrently integrating, concurrency of I&T schedule, and hardware integration level.	
Maintenance risk	Probability or confidence level of maintenance inputs used to compute maintenance effort.	
Requirements complete at start	Amount of requirements effort that will have been completed prior to the beginning of this project.	
	Rating	*Description*
	High	Software requirements review complete and requirements baselined; no requirements effort before baseline computed

Parameter	Definition	
	Rating	Description
	Nominal	Proposal-level requirements work complete
	Low	No software requirements analysis performed, still in system requirements phase
Requirements definition formality	Detail and formality to which software requirements will be analyzed and specified.	
	Rating	Description
	Extra high	Formal requirements method and tool, plus independent verification and validation of requirements (does not include independent cost of verification and validation)
	Very high	Formal requirements method and tool used
	High	Formal requirements method and tool used, but not required deliverable
	Nominal	Mission-critical and military standard software requirements analysis, no formal requirements tool required
	Low	Informal requirements analysis and specification
	Very low	No requirements analysis included in estimate
Requirements effort after baseline	Option to choose whether software requirements effort should be costed after up-front software requirements activity is complete.	

SYSTEM INTEGRATION COMPLEXITY

Programs concurrently integrating	Number of computer programs that will be integrated with this program. Count only programs with which this program must interface directly. This number will determine how much software-to-software systems integration and testing required. In the rating scale below, the numbers in brackets represent the percentage	

Parameter	Definition
	amounts of effort (preliminary design through program test phases) added to the estimate for software-to-software integration. If the programs included in size parameter is greater than one count an average program.

	Rating	Description
	8	Extra high [24 percent]
	3	Very high [9 percent]
	2	High [6 percent]
	1	Nominal + [3 percent]
	0	Nominal, no software to software integration [0 percent]

Parameter	Definition
Concurrency of I&T schedule	Degree of concurrency or overlap between development activities and the integration and testing activities.

	Rating	Description
	Extra high	All systems integration will occur during development; product will be fully integrated and tested with the system when delivered
	Very high	Most system integration will occur during development before testing is complete
	High	System integration begins during software integration testing
	Nominal	System integration occurs after software WBS elements are completely tested individually

Parameter	Definition
Hardware integration level	Difficulty of integrating software with operational or target hardware. This effort often is driven by concurrent hardware development or the use of custom hardware. The rating will determine how much software-to-hardware systems integration and testing are required. In the rating scale below, the numbers in brackets represent the percentage amounts of effort (preliminary design through program test phases) added to the estimate for hardware integration.

Parameter	Definition	
	Rating	*Description*
	Very high	Significant integration with hardware, concurrent hardware development [32 percent]
	High	Significant integration with hardware, some custom hardware in configuration [28 percent]
	Nominal	Same type hardware, different configuration [22 percent]
	Low	Same system or COTS hardware [16 percent]
	Very low	No hardware integration [0 percent]

ECONOMIC FACTORS

Parameter	Definition
Cost input base year	Base year associated with cost inputs such as labor rates and purchased items. This is used to calculate then-year cost from base-year cost by applying the cost escalation factor. Changing the cost input base year will not impact the base-year cost unless the labor rate is changed accordingly.
Purchased items	Costs of any purchased software or COTS packages that will be added to the final estimate or to any other throughput costs. Purchased items costs are reported separately from base-year costs on the quick estimate and basic estimate reports. Purchased items costs are included in the initial fiscal year of base-year cost and then-year cost reports. Detailed recurring and nonrecurring cost inputs are available for COTS WBS elements.
Average monthly labor rate	This category can be used to itemize labor rates. A composite average rate can be entered directly at the category level to set all itemized rates to the average composite. Direct software management Software system engineering Software design Software programming Software data preparation Software testing Software configuration management Software quality assurance

Parameter	Definition	
SOFTWARE MAINTENANCE		
Years of maintenance	Number of years for which software maintenance costs will be estimated. Maintenance begins when operational test and evaluation are completed.	
Separate sites	Number of separate operational sites where the software will be installed and users will have significant input into system enhancements.	
Maintenance growth over life	Percentage of anticipated size growth from the point immediately after the software is turned over to maintenance to the end of the maintenance cycle. An input of 100 percent means that the software will double in size. Software growth may include additions of new functionality. (Major enhancements should be modeled separately as block changes or incremental builds rather than as maintenance.)	
	Rating	*Description*
	100 percent	Very high, major updates adding many new functions
	35 percent	High, major updates adding some new functions
	20 percent	Nominal, minor updates with enhancements to existing functions
	5 percent	Low, minor enhancements
	0 percent	Very low, sustaining engineering only
Personnel differences	Comparison of capabilities and experience of maintenance and development personnel. If maintenance is estimated as a separate program, this parameter should be set to nominal, and the personnel capabilities and experience parameters should be rated individually.	
	Rating	*Description*
	Very high	Significantly better than development personnel
	High	Slightly better than development personnel
	Nominal	Same as development personnel

Parameter	Definition	
	Rating	*Description*
	Low	Somewhat less than development personnel
	Very low	Significantly lower than development personnel
Development environment differences	Quality of the maintenance environment in comparison to the tools and practices used in the development environment. If maintenance is estimated as a separate program, this parameter should be set to nominal, and the development support environment parameters should be rated individually.	
	Rating	*Description*
	Very high	Significantly better than development environment
	High	Slightly better than development environment
	Nominal	Same as development environment
	Low	Somewhat worse than development environment
	Very low	Significantly worse than development environment
Annual change rate	Average percentage of software impacted by software maintenance and sustaining engineering per year. This could include changes, revalidation, reverse engineering, redocumentation, or minor changes for new hardware or recertification.	
	Rating	*Description*
	35 percent	Very high
	15 percent	High
	11 percent	Nominal
	5 percent	Low
	0 percent	Very low
Maintenance level (rigor)	Thoroughness with which maintenance activities will be performed.	

Parameter	Definition	
	Rating	Description
	Very high	Thorough maintenance for all types of software maintenance activities, including regular documentation updates. Software maintenance is well planned in both the long and short term with frequent reviews of priorities. Dedicated staff assigned. Software will remain useful for users and will not degenerate over time
	High	Complete maintenance including maintenance planning and priority review. Software documentation is updated on a semiregular basis. Software will not degenerate over time
	Nominal	Average maintenance activity. Short-term planning and prioritization of maintenance activity. Documentation is updated less than annually (change pages and addenda). Software will become less useful over time
	Low	Basic maintenance with most activities reactive to emergencies and problems as they arise. No planning of maintenance activity. Documentation is updated only with page and addenda changes. Software will degenerate over time
	Very low	Bare-bones maintenance. Nondedicated team making emergency repairs. Maintenance performed on ad hoc, sporadic basis. Little to no documentation update. Software will degenerate rapidly. Setting may represent sustaining engineering effort of a delivered incremental build by developers during development of subsequent builds
Minimum maintenance staff (optional)	Minimum number of personnel who will be assigned to maintain software. Use this parameter for fixed staffing or level of effort maintenance.	

Parameter	Definition
Maximum maintenance staff (optional)	Maximum number of personnel who will be assigned to maintain software. Use this parameter for fixed staffing or level of effort maintenance.
Maintenance monthly labor rate	Average monthly labor rate for maintenance personnel.
Additional annual maintenance cost	Annual throughput costs for maintenance.
Maintenance start date	Date on which maintenance will begin. If no date is entered, maintenance will begin when operational evaluation and testing are completed.
Percent to be maintained	Percentage of total that will be maintained. For example, if some software is in a read-only memory and cannot be changed, exclude this part of the computer program from software maintenance costs by reducing this percentage.
Maintain total system	Total size (yes) or effective size (no) should be used to estimate maintenance. This parameter normally is set to indicate total size so that maintenance is estimated based on the entire completed program, and not on only changes estimated.
Steady state maintenance	Steady state staffing level estimated for maintenance requirements.

	Rating	Description
	Yes	Estimate maintenance with fixed annual staff level
	No	Estimate maintenance with additional effort in the first years; appropriate for new or immature systems that may have higher levels of undetected defects

Software code metrics	These parameters allow user inputs into various software code metrics used to calculate reliability of the produced code: Halstead Software Science Metrics McCabe Complexity Metrics

Parameter	Definition
Adjustment factors	Function-based sizing (FBS) adjustment factors used internally by function-based sizing to compensate for different application- and platform-specific factors.
FBS application adjustment factor	Captures additional effort based on platform type as part of FBS; set by knowledge bases.
FBS platform adjustment factor	Captures additional effort based on platform type as part of FBS; set by knowledge bases.
Calibration effort adjustment	Calibration adjustment for actual effort.
Calibration schedule adjustment	Calibration adjustment for actual schedule.
Calibration technology adjustment	Calibration adjustment factor for effective technology. The adjusted effective technology rating is used in calculating estimated effort and schedule.
Calibration complexity adjustment	Calibration adjustment factor for effective complexity. The adjusted effective complexity rating is used in calculating estimated effort and schedule.
Calibration size adjustment (COTS only)	This parameter adjusts effective size to represent the effective size of the COTS element being estimated.

Summary

This chapter is intended as an introduction, not a complete SEER-SEM user guide. It provides basic information and definitions for SEER-SEM and illustrates its use as a critical project planning tool. Definitions for most SEER-SEM inputs are provided. Additionally, it contains sufficient mathematical foundations to provide the reader with a flavor of Brooks' law and other key estimation concepts. A few of the input and output reports and charts were included to show how SEER operates as a tool in project planning and control. SEER-SEM Estimation Process Step 10 (Track Project throughout Development) is the focus of the next chapter.

See this book's associated Web page (www.galorath.com/ estimationbook2006) for an electronic SEER-SEM input form, a data collection form, and other useful materials.

Endnotes

1. Brooks, Frederick P. *The Mythical Man-Month: Essays on Software Engineering.* New York: Addison Wesley, 1995.
2. Galorath Incorporated. *SEER-SEM User Manual.* El Segundo: Galorath Incorporated, 2004.
3. Fischman, Lee, Karen McRitchie, and Dan Galorath. "Inside SEER-SEM." *CrossTalk: The Journal of Defense Software Engineering,* 2005.
4. Brooks, Frederick P. *The Mythical Man-Month: Essays on Software Engineering.* New York: Addison Wesley, 1995.
5. Yourdon, E. *Death March,* 2nd ed. Upper Saddle River: Prentice Hall, 2004.
6. Galorath Incorporated. *SEER-SEM User Manual.* El Segundo: Galorath Incorporated, 2004.
7. Fischman, Lee, Karen McRitchie, and Dan Galorath. "Inside SEER-SEM." *CrossTalk: The Journal of Defense Software Engineering,* 2005.
8. Galorath Incorporated. *SEER-SEM User Manual.* El Segundo: Galorath Incorporated, 2004.
9. ACEIT. *ACEIT User Manual.* Santa Barbara: Tecolote Research, Inc., 2004.
10. Frontier Technologies, Inc. *ICE User Manual.* Goleta: Frontier Technologies, Inc., 2004.
11. Engineous Software. *Fiper User Manual.* Cary: Engineous Software, 2004.
12. Covey, Stephen R. *The Seven Habits of Highly Effective People.* New York: Free Press, 1989.
13. Galorath Incorporated. *OSD Software Estimation Guidebook.* El Segundo: Galorath Incorporated, 1997.
14. Galorath, Dan. Personal experience.

Chapter 12

SEER-SEM Solutions for Project Management and Control

What may be done at any time will be done at no time.

Scottish Proverb

Introduction

Simply put, software project management encompasses the work required to plan, organize, manage, direct, and control the activities and resources of a software project. Of course, this work is anything but simple. However, effective tools exist to facilitate these important tasks. For project management and control, this chapter introduces three solution areas: (1) application of basic SEER-SEM,[1] (2) use of SEER-SEM Client For Microsoft Project,[2] which converts a SEER-SEM estimate into a detailed plan (down to root-level tasks) in Microsoft Project, and (3) the power of a SEER-SEM add-on, Parametric Project Monitoring and Control (PPMC),[3] for monitoring and controlling projects. This chapter explains how to apply these tools to increase efficiency and accuracy in managing and controlling a software project.

These SEER tools empower you by providing the essential information required to make decisions that are most appropriate to the specific circumstances of your software project. These functions are important for two steps in software cost and schedule estimation covered in Chapter 4: Step 8, Generate Project Plan, and Step 10, Track Project throughout Development. Much of this material comes from SEER manuals and internal records of Galorath Incorporated. This chapter is intended to summarize and inform regarding the process, not serve as a primary user's manual.

CMMI Process Areas for Project Management

The SEER Software Estimation Suite of tools supports any development process or quality initiative. Galorath internal documents[1] show how this suite provides project management support in three of the Software Engineering Institute's CMMI process areas that relate to software management and measurement.[5]

Each top-level element of the CMMI is called a process area. The SEER suite has been structured to ensure that it provides both the methods and tools to support these three process areas of the CMMI (see Figure 12.1). These processes are crucial to effective and efficient software project management as follows:

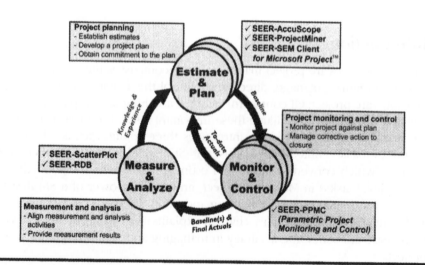

Figure 12.1   SEER and the CMMI Process.

1. Project planning — Establish estimates, develop a project plan, and obtain commitment to the plan. Methods and tools within these process areas include history-based sizing, direct measure sizing, parametric estimation, estimation by data mining, and planning.
2. Project monitoring and control — Monitor project against plan and manage corrective action to closure. Methods and tools within these process areas include performance (earned value) measurement, health and status indication, and performance-based forecasting.
3. Measurement and analysis — Align measurement and analysis activities, and provide measurement results. Methods and tools within these process areas include estimation accuracy assessment and improvement, calibration, knowledge base management, and benchmarking.

Solution 1: Application of Basic SEER-SEM for Project Management and Control

SEER-SEM provides significant project management and control functionality even without the Project Manager Edition. After an initial plan is established, you can employ SEER-SEM's basic functionality to perform trade studies to determine the effects on the project of changes, risks, and opportunities as well as estimates to complete, recommended staffing plans, and estimated defect insertion and removal for measuring progress.

When you update project constraints or parameters as new circumstances are identified, such as changes in staffing level, project risk levels, volatility, etc., SEER-SEM will update the initial estimate and provide an estimate of the resources required to complete the project as shown in Figure 12.2. Its reference function enables you to identify differences between the current estimate and the initial project plan; this information will in turn enable you to refine the estimate, replan the project, redirect effort, and update the completion forecast. SEER-SEM also enables you to enter different levels of risk at different points in the project to provide a range of estimates.

The developer's actual staffing plan and actuals to date can be overlaid on the SEER-SEM estimate as shown in Figure 12.3. This information provides a manager with the necessary data to plan for future staff or make schedule adjustments if required staffing levels cannot be or are not being met. You can also use the actual and planned staff features to determine whether the projected schedule with the current staff meets an acceptable probability as shown in Figure 12.4.

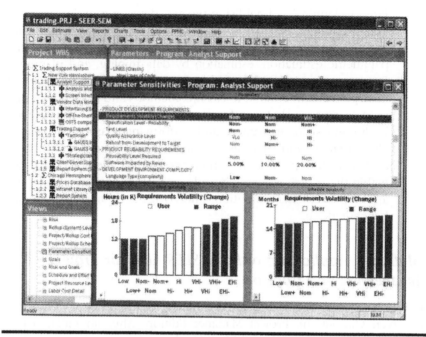

Figure 12.2 SEER-SEM requirements volatility trade-off.

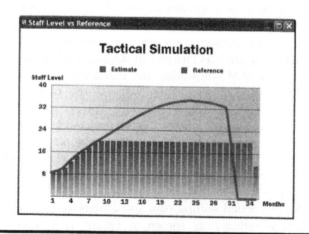

Figure 12.3 Actual/planned staff versus estimated staff.

Figure 12.4 indicates approximately a 28 percent chance of meeting the schedule goal if the staffing continues as planned. This information then can be used to make the decisions necessary to go forward. Perhaps this particular WBS element is not as critical to the entire project as other WBS elements that are consuming the resources needed here. Or the WBS element may be on the critical path and resources will have to be

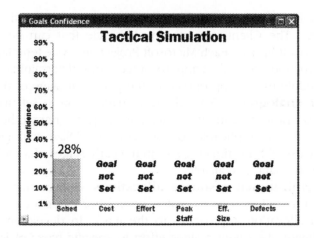

Figure 12.4 Probability of meeting goals.

redirected to decrease the damage that could be caused to the entire project if this WBS element is delivered late.

Solution 2: SEER-SEM Client for Microsoft Project

SEER-SEM Client for Microsoft Project (commonly referred to as "the Client") starts with the initial SEER-SEM estimate and turns it into a detailed, executable, project plan that managers can use to perform detailed planning and control for the project. SEER-SEM is used to estimate a project's schedule and resources and describe required labor categories. The Client uses the SEER-SEM estimation engine and refines the estimate by allocating effort, staff, and schedule to specialized SEER Microsoft Project plan templates including mapping of schedule and staff that serve to describe the software developer's processes.

Life-cycle process templates are provided by the Client or can be created in Microsoft Project. At the appropriate point in the project, you can use these templates to plan the project as it develops and define the tasks and interdependencies as they relate to the project life cycle. The Client can be configured to describe the particular processes and activities your organization uses. For example, you can configure the following elements:

- **Master knowledge base** — Customize the master knowledge base to specify which SEER-SEM knowledge bases can be used with each type of project to help enforce a standard set of assumptions for all users.
- **Life-cycle process** — This element of the Client determines how a project will be divided into tasks. Organization-specific life-cycle

templates enable you to build best practices directly into your plans. The Client can use any life-cycle that can be created in Microsoft Project. Each Microsoft Project life-cycle template includes instructions for allocating resources and determining a realistic schedule that is appropriate to the particular stage of the project.

■ **Size analogies** — This element enables you to set up analogies to size projects using your own past projects or any other historical data that is applicable to your company. Size analogies can be very useful for estimating size in the early stages of a project before specific data is available.

■ **Organizational resource allocations** — You may tailor the resource allocations to match your labor categories, work titles, and allocation approaches to the work. In developing a project estimate, the Client assigns effort to specific types of labor (often called *roles* or *resources*), and you can customize these labor category descriptions to reflect how your organization assigns tasks, either at an individual or departmental level.

■ **Specific SEER-SEM Parameter Settings** — The Client factors tab (Figure 12.5) provides access to the full range of parameters that SEER-SEM uses for refining estimates. You can configure the available factors to include only the parameters that specifically apply to your organization and project type, and you can update them as circumstances change.

The Client can be used alone to develop a plan from scratch or a SEER-SEM estimate can be imported to generate the plan.

Developing plan from scratch — You can enter project specifics, including size, constraints, knowledge bases, etc., using the tab dialogue interface shown in Figure 12.6. When you are ready to generate your project plan, the Client employs SEER-SEM as an estimation engine. Using SEER-SEM, via automation and server remote commands, the Client obtains an estimate for the project described in the Client, then allocates effort resources and schedule. With this approach, the user need not have knowledge of or access to SEER-SEM itself.

Importing existing SEER-SEM project — You can also use SEER-SEM to generate a project estimate and then import it into the Client. The advantage of this method is access to SEER-SEM's entire range of functionality. This access facilitates development of the estimate and different trade-offs.

Using the Client for Detailed Project Planning

The Client is a powerful tool that enables you to generate a detailed project plan that allocates tasking, sequencing, and resources in accordance

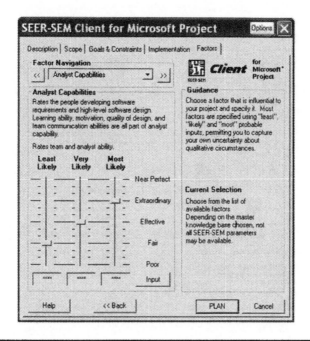

Figure 12.5   Client factors tab.

Figure 12.6   SEER-SEM Client for Microsoft Project description tab.

Figure 12.7 SEER-SEM Client for Microsoft Project goals and constraints tab.

with the organizational standards and process defined in the template. It also enables you to use your own judgment to refine a plan, e.g., reallocate tasks, extend or shorten the duration of tasks, etc. Figure 12.7 illustrates setting risk tolerance. If it becomes necessary to replan the project or make essential trade-offs, the Client enables you to enter new project parameters and constraints to determine the best approach. Figure 12.8 illustrates a partial plan developed for the Rational Unified Process.

The Client also provides access to all the power of Microsoft Project, enabling you to set baselines, reschedule tasks, enter completion percentages, etc., as the project progresses and to forecast the completion date by moving schedule slips to the right.

Solution 3: SEER-PPMC (Parametric Project Monitoring and Control)

Much of this information came from the *Parametric Project Monitoring and Control Users Manual.*[6] SEER-PPMC is a set of add-on features to SEER-SEM that enable you to monitor and control a software project by independently tracking progress, effort, growth, and defects. It also allows you to refine the estimate in response to changing conditions and thus accurately forecast a completion date. SEER-PPMC combines earned value

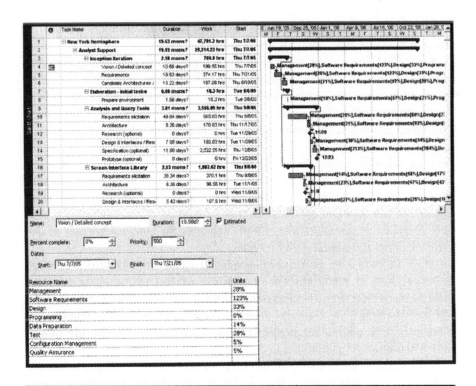

Figure 12.8   Resulting plan generated by SEER-SEM Client.

and performance-based forecasting with parametric analysis. It is intended to complement the earned value management (EVM) process. SEER-PPMC's concepts and terminology use ANSI/EIA Standard 747 as a foundation.

As discussed in Chapter 9, earned value management is considered a best practice for monitoring and controlling the progress of a software project. SEER-PPMC combines accepted algorithms used for cost and schedule estimation during the planning process with accepted equations used for traditional earned value management, and then uses the power of SEER-SEM to provide a parametric project completion forecast. SEER-PPMC goes beyond the earned value management systems used on major programs by allowing you to track progress at the root level when a project is under way.

At the heart of PPMC is the ability to forecast the final outcome of a project based on what has occurred to date, considering the assumptions made for your baseline estimate (plan). Before your project starts, the expected outcome (in terms of cost, effort, and schedule) is based on an estimate. An estimate is, by definition, the best statement you can make about something based on the information that you have. In SEER-SEM, estimates consider your knowledge base selections (platform, application, acquisition method, development method, and development standard) along with your size estimate and parameter settings.

SEER-SEM is an accurate and reliable method for predicting a project outcome. Once a project is started, the information you have becomes more extensive. PPMC allows you to combine your baseline estimate with actual project progress to compute an expected estimate at completion. The basic approach to doing this is to replace part of the estimate with the actual results to date. The estimate at completion would be actual cost (or schedule) plus the estimate of the remaining cost (or schedule).

Because PPMC reforecasts schedule and effort, it considers actual progress toward software development milestones to determine what portion of the baseline estimate has been completed. This actual progress is referred to as *earned value*. PPMC replaces the *earned* portion of the estimate with the actual costs to date.

SEER-PPMC's idea of combining earned value in parametrics goes all the way back to a Department of Defense project in the early 1990s. A group discovered that tracking earned value and combining that with the SEER-SEM parametric estimate allowed them to estimate the actual completion of any contracted project that was underway within one month and $50,000.

The earliest versions of SEER-SEM implemented a relatively simple estimate-to-complete function that used basic earned value concepts whereby actual achieved progress was determined and the schedule was slipped to the right accordingly to determine a new estimated completion date. SEER-PPMC took this approach to the next level, adding a performance-based estimate-to-complete along with the concept of baselines, all based on sophisticated mathematical analysis for a parametric estimate to complete. This is far more sophisticated than the analysis of products such as Microsoft Project which, when used alone, simply shift remaining work to the right.

Figure 12.9 shows a representative SEER-PPMC view that combines some of the available reports and charts. The upper left quadrant shows the original planned schedule and effort and the currently forecasted completion date. The original estimate has been overspent and the schedule has slipped. The upper right quadrant shows performance indices that indicate the project is in trouble, both in terms of schedule and effort (cost and schedule performance indices less than 1).

The bottom left quadrant shows the actual amount spent and the actual forecasted date of September 2005. You can clearly see that the project has slipped by several months. The bottom right quadrant shows the project's health and status. These charts show at a glance that the project is in trouble and will severely overrun its cost and schedule. With this

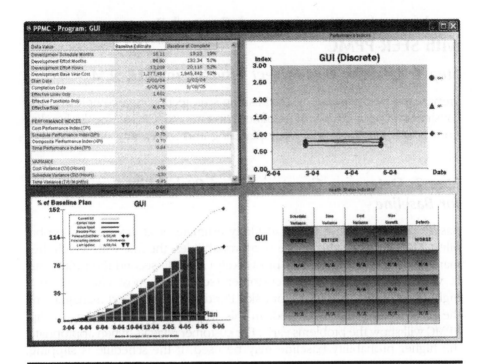

Figure 12.9   SEER-PPMC screen showing project progress versus effort spent.

information in hand, a manager can consider different approaches to remediate a project and understand the new schedule and cost implications. SEER-PPMC employs the following four EVM dimensions:[7]

- Activity completion: tracks actual progress made toward completion of the project. This progress is independent of effort spent and is measured as earned value.
- Expenditures: tracks actual hours spent independently of progress.
- Artifact completion: tracks the completion of the artifacts of the software development activity, i.e., number of requirements completed, number of units completed, number of reviews successfully completed.
- Defect discovery and removal: tracks defects including anticipated defects inserted and removed and actual defects discovered and removed.

The process for using SEER-PPMC may be summarized as five steps described in the next section.

Implementing Planning and Control Process with SEER-PPMC

Step 1: Establish Best Project Estimate in SEER-SEM

Prepare the best estimate by establishing size, technology, complexity, and constraints in your SEER-SEM estimate. This estimate will become the baseline from which PPMC earned value planning and forecasting will be based.

Step 2: Determine Constraints and Probability Required for Baseline

Baselines can be set at the most likely estimate or at any desired probability. Managers can also utilize two probabilities: the first with which they manage the project (generally most likely) and the second the probability at which they promised the customer (sometimes most likely, often a higher probability to account for risk). For day-to-day project management, the most likely estimate is used. In this way if the project begins to slip, PPMC will show the problems early. For customer reviews, when appropriate, the higher probability baseline may be used. If the schedule is slipping, the project manager will know it early using the most likely estimate.

Step 3: Set Baseline

A baseline freezes the current estimate so that actual progress can be reported and compared. The baseline provides the yardstick against which a project is tracked and evaluated. A baseline is different from a current estimate. Managers make changes to a current estimate while preserving a baseline. This allows the ability to perform trade-offs on the current estimates while maintaining the baseline plan. A baseline may also be updated at any time, becoming a replan.

Step 4: Enter Work Complete

Figure 12.10 shows how SEER-PPMC combines earned value and estimation. Work complete is entered in SEER-PPMC as snapshots. Each snapshot includes work complete along with effort required to accomplish the work. Additionally, software size growth and defects are tracked. A snapshot depicts a project metric at any given point in time. Figures 12.11 and 12.12 typify the information captured in a snapshot: The two key components of a snapshot are (1) work complete and (2) actual effort. Snapshots can include organization specific information.

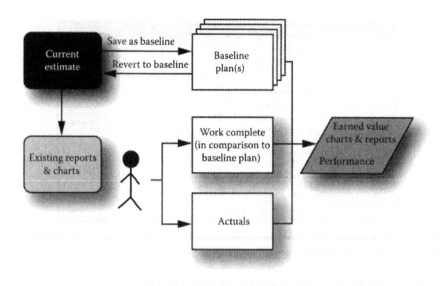

Figure 12.10   SEER-PPMC high level flow chart.

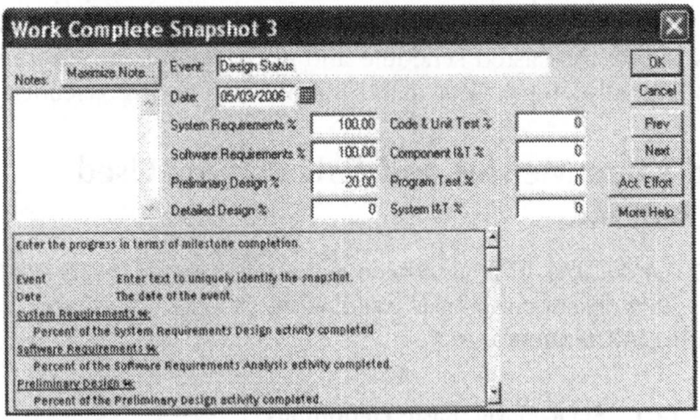

Figure 12.11   SEER-PPMC work complete snapshot.

Work complete is a description of progress in terms of milestone completion. Actual effort covers measurable project metrics: (1) actual hours to date, (2) defects reported and removed to date, and (3) size completed to date.

Snapshots are flexible in terms of interval or frequency. Managers may generate snapshots at regular intervals such as monthly or quarterly or produce them as needed, for example, before a key project review.

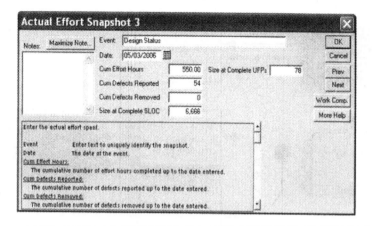

Figure 12.12 SEER-PPMC actual effort snapshot.

Step 5: Evaluate and Replan as Necessary

As discussed in Chapter 8, cost and schedule performance indices identify project trends. One rule of thumb dictates that if a cost performance index is below 0.90, and a project is more than 15 percent complete, the plan cannot be achieved and a replan is necessary.[8] SEER-PPMC automatically provides a new forecasted schedule and effort based on performance to date. Additionally, the project may be replanned and rebaselined.

Earned Value Metrics and Calculations Used in SEER-PPMC

Table 12.1 and Table 12.2 have been extracted from the *SEER-PPMC Users Manual*. They describe the basic calculations of SEER-PPMC and correlates them with EVM terminology.[9]

Table 12.1 SEER-PPMC Basic Definitions

SEER-PPMC Parameter	Earned Value Equivalent	Definition
Development effort hours	Budget at completion (BAC)	Total budget
Baseline plan	Budgeted cost of work scheduled (BCWS)	Baseline plan
Earned value	Budgeted cost of work performed (BCWP)	Accomplished effort
Actual expenditures	Actual cost of work performed (ACWP)	Actual effort spent

Table 12.2   SEER-PPMC Definitions and Formulas

SEER-PPMC Value	*Definition*	*Formulas*
Cost performance index (CPI)	Achieved cost efficiency	CPI = earned value/actual effort CPI = earned value through latest snapshot/hours through latest snapshot CPI = BCWP/ACWP
Schedule performance index (SPI)	Achieved schedule efficiency	SPI = earned value/baseline plan SPI = earned value through latest snapshot/planned hours through latest snapshot SPI = BCWP/BCWS
To-complete performance index (TCPI)	Assumed cost efficiency to complete	TCPI = (development effort hours – earned value through latest snapshot)/(estimate at complete hours – hours through latest snapshot) TCPI = (BAC – BCWP)/(EAC – ACWP) TCPI = CPI × SPI
Time performance index (TPI)	Achieved time (elapsed schedule) efficiency	TPI = (elapsed time between actual start date and baseline date)/(elapsed time between actual start date and snapshot date)
Cost variance (CV)	Difference between earned value and actual effort spent expressed in hours	CV = BCWP – ACWP CV – earned value – actual effort CV – earned value through latest snapshot – hours through latest snapshot
Cost variance percentage (CV%)	Difference between earned value and actual effort spent expressed as a percentage of earned value	CV% = (CV/earned value) × 100 CV% = [CV (hours)/earned value through latest snapshot] × 100

Table 12.2 (continued) SEER-PPMC Definitions and Formulas

SEER-PPMC Value	Definition	Formulas
Schedule variance (SV)	Difference between earned value and baseline plan expressed in hours	SV = earned value – baseline plan SV = earned value through latest snapshot – planned hours through latest snapshot SV = BCWP – BCWS
Schedule variance percentage (SV%)	Difference between earned value and baseline plan expressed as percentage of baseline plan	SV% = (SV/baseline plan) × 100 SV% = (SV) hours/planned hours through latest snapshot) × 100 SV% = (SV/BCWS) × 100
Time variance (TV)	Difference in schedule months between earned value and baseline plan; when roll-up element is selected, TV equals worst TV of its subordinate programs	N/A
Time variance percentage (TV%)	Difference in time between earned value and baseline plan expressed as percentage of baseline plan	TV% = [TV/(planned baseline date – start date)] × 100
Size growth variance (SGV)	Difference between anticipated size at completion and baseline total size expressed as percentage of baseline size	SGV (lines) = [(size at complete SLOC/total lines only) – 1] × 100 SGV (UFPs) = [(size at complete UFPs/total functions only) – 1] × 100 SGV (lines and UFPs) = [(size at complete SLOC/total lines only) – 1] × 100

Table 12.2 (continued)   SEER-PPMC Definitions and Formulas

SEER-PPMC Value	*Definition*	*Formulas*
Baseline at completion (BAC)	Actual effort spent up to latest snapshot plus baseline to complete; or budget at completion divided by cost performance index	BAC = actual effort + total hours – earned value BAC = hours through latest snapshot + development effort hours – earned value through latest snapshot BAC = total hours/CPI BAC = development effort hours/CPI
Estimate at completion (EAC)	Actual effort spent up to latest snapshot plus estimate to complete; or budget at completion divided by cost performance index	EAC = actual effort + total hours – earned value EAC = hours through latest snapshot development effort hours – earned value through latest snapshot EAC = total hours/CPI EAC = development effort hours/CPI
Variance at completion (VAC)	Difference between what total effort is supposed to be and what total job is now expected to be	VAC (effort) = baseline development effort months – baseline at complete development effort months

Figure 12.13 allows a manager to track progress over time. Figure 12.14 illustrates schedule accomplishments and basic earned value concepts.

Looking at Progress Over Time

See how actual and earned effort measure up to the baseline plan

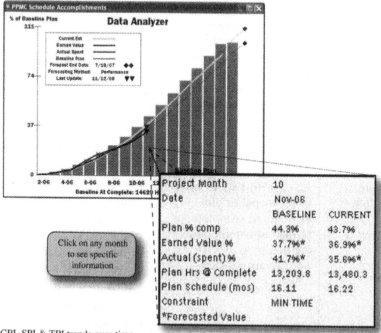

See CPI, SPI & TPI trends over time

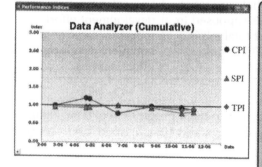

Figure 12.13   Representation of progress over time.

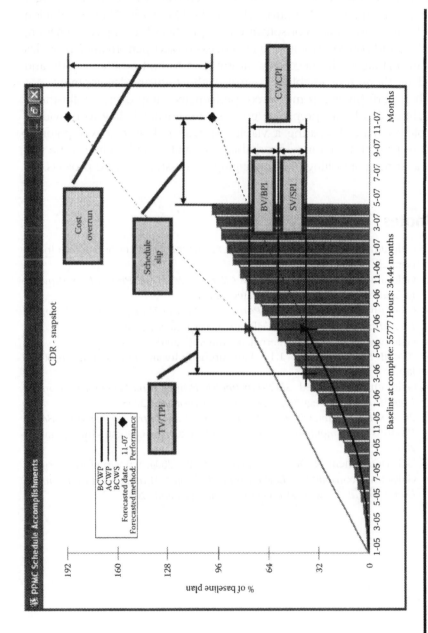

Figure 12.14   Schedule accomplishments with EVM terminology.

Summary

SEER-SEM and the SEER-SEM Client for Microsoft Project provide insight for project planning and control. The SEER-SEM Project Manager Edition provides tools to implement software best practices for project estimation, planning, and control. Monitoring in-process project performance provides software managers the necessary information to find problems early and remediate them, thus enabling control of the software development.

When performance is measured, performance improves. As illustrated throughout this book, preparing good size estimates is key to providing a viable estimate. Preparing a viable estimate is key to a well-planned software project. Preparing a workable plan with a set baseline is the key to measuring, controlling, and managing successful software projects.

Endnotes

1. Galorath Incorporated. *SEER-SEM User Manual.* El Segundo: Galorath Incorporated, 2005.
2. Galorath Incorporated. *SEER-SEM Client for Microsoft Project User Manual.* El Segundo: Galorath Incorporated, 2004.
3. Galorath Incorporated. *SEER-Parametric Project Management and Control User Manual.* El Segundo: Galorath Incorporated, 2005.
4. Galorath Incorporated. Internal documents, 2005.
5. "CMMI SE/SW Version 1.1." Pittsburgh: Software Engineering Institute, January 2002.
6. Galorath Incorporated. *SEER-Parametric Project Management and Control User Manual.* El Segundo: Galorath Incorporated, 2005.
7. Ross, Mike. *Parametric Project Monitoring and Control Performance-Based Progress Assessment and Prediction.* El Segundo: Galorath Incorporated, 2005.
8. U.S. Department of Defense. Survey Results, 2004. www.pmforum.org
9. Galorath Incorporated. *SEER-Parametric Project Management and Control User Manual.* El Segundo: Galorath Incorporated, 2005.

Index

E

T - #0221 - 101024 - C0 - 234/156/31 [33] - CB - 9780849335938 - Gloss Lamination